Financial Management
of
Commercial Banks

JOHN M. MASON (Ph.D., Michigan State University) is Assistant Professor of Finance at The Wharton School, University of Pennsylvania, where he has developed and teaches a course on the financial management of commercial banks for advanced undergraduate and M.B.A. students. Dr. Mason has written many professional articles on commercial banking and financial and housing markets and has consulted with private financial institutions, industry groups, and the federal government. Prior to joining the Wharton faculty he was a Special Assistant to the Secretary of the Department of Housing and Urban Development, Washington, D.C. He has also worked in the Federal Reserve System and for a commercial bank.

Financial Management of Commercial Banks

JOHN M. MASON
The Wharton School
University of Pennsylvania

WARREN, GORHAM & LAMONT
Boston and New York

To the memory of my grandfather,
T. R. Shaffer, a Missouri banker

Preface

Financial management has to do with the three types of decisions that are important in determining the value of the firm: the investment decision, the financing decision, and the dividend decision. Owners and managers desire a combination of investments, financing, and dividend payout that will achieve the greatest long-run value of the firm consistent with existing regulatory and market constraints. Management problems related to reaching this combination in nonfinancial institutions are dealt with extensively in textbooks on corporate finance, which give scant attention to financial institutions. Textbooks on commercial banking tend to be descriptive, treating banking from an external point of view. The reader is told what banks do, how they make loans, what is looked for in bank customers, what kinds of liabilities banks carry on their balance sheets.

This volume brings the theory and techniques of corporate finance and microeconomics to bear on matters of importance to commercial bankers. Its view is internal to the bank; the perspective taken is that of top management. Among the subjects treated are bank portfolio construction, bank capital structure, and short-run cash management. Commercial bank management is analyzed in terms of what bank managers should look for in portfolio management and why, what market conditions they should be aware of, what techniques they can use to meet changing economic and financial conditions. The objective is to develop a way of looking at the problems of commercial bank management that will lead to asking appropriate questions.

Although intended primarily for advanced undergraduate and MBA students, the book is also suitable for others interested in commercial banking. Individuals employed in corporate finance, marketing, accounting, and economics, as well as students of these disciplines, may find the book interesting and useful, either because it helps them relate their own special interests to the banking field or because they deal with bankers and wish to understand why bankers act the way they do. Economists interested in the economics of financial institutions can also benefit from reading many portions of the text.

I have assumed that the reader has had at least an introductory course in business finance; familiarity with the concepts and techniques of corporate financial management would be helpful. Some knowledge of the economic theory of the firm and a course in money and banking or macroeconomics is desirable. Mathematics is minimal in the main text; calculus is confined to appendixes.

Those who use this book as a textbook will find several features that aid understanding of the concepts of commercial bank management. First, a consistent theoretical development of the banking firm allows the reader to continually relate management decisions and market relationships to a unified framework. This allows the material in the book to be supplemented with examples from current events and recently published articles and with cases if desired. Second, the model developed graphically and verbally in the main text is presented mathematically in appendixes so that instructors and students who are mathematically inclined can go more deeply into the mathematical models if they wish. Finally, questions at the end of each chapter facilitate class discussion and problem solving. Many of the questions have no "correct" answer. As indicated throughout the book, answers to management problems often depend on what attributes the owners and managers wish their bank to have and what market conditions the bank must face. Guidelines for discussing the questions are provided in a separate instructor's manual.

This book is an outgrowth of a course on the financial management of commercial banks developed at the Wharton School. In developing the course I have found the sequence followed here to be the most satisfactory. If desired, the material on commercial lending (Chapters 8 through 11) can be presented before capital structure (Chapters 5 through 7). Other changes should be minimal. The crucial thing for students of banking to understand is that the lending function is the primary concern of the bank. If they understand this, they will find the other subjects of the book falling into place.

Many people have contributed to the writing of this book by way of encouragement and information, making it better than it otherwise would have been, and I am thankful to them all. At the University of Pennsylvania, my colleagues Jack Guttentag, Mark Flannery, Jim Walter, Anthony Santomero, and Paul Smith helped provide an environment conducive to the intellectual pursuit of bank management in theory and practice. Many people in the banking community helped me to understand modern banking practice. In New York, they include Fred Deming and Tom Dwyer at Chemical Bank, Guy Noyes and William Reifler at Morgan Guaranty, Edward Palmer at Citibank, and Peers Brewer at Manufacturers Hanover. In Philadelphia, I was aided by A. Gilbert Hebner, Tom Lippert, and Chip Moffit of Philadelphia National Bank, Steve Garfinkle of First Pennsylvania, and Alan Gart, formerly with the Girard Bank of Philadelphia and now with the Insurance Company of North America.

I also thank Dwight B. Crane of Harvard University, Harry Blythe of Ohio State University, and G. K. Rakes of the University of Virginia, who read drafts of the manuscript and made many helpful and clarifying comments. They cannot, however, be held responsible in any way for the final content, and may not be assumed to agree with all my interpretations and conclusions.

Finally, I would like to thank my two associates at Warren, Gorham & Lamont. Eugene Simonoff brought the book to fruition with true insight and professionalism; it has been a pleasure and an education to work with him. My editor, Jo Satloff, cajoled and prodded in an attempt to meet deadlines; her patience was tested many times before the book was in print.

JOHN M. MASON

Contents

THE NATURE
OF BANKING

1

The Environment
of Commercial Banking

Commercial banks are business organizations that are similar in many respects to firms that produce or market automobiles and television sets. Consequently, many bank activities are like those of any business enterprise: Banks must define their market areas and customer base, price their product correctly, determine their capital structure, and provide a reasonable return to their owners.

However, unlike nonfinancial organizations, commercial banks do not produce or market physical goods; they produce loans. Bank loans are inputs into other productive operations, which spur industrial growth, home ownership, and government services. To ensure a sufficient flow of loans to meet society's needs, commercial banks must collect various inputs of labor and capital and also attract deposits and obtain other funds.

In conducting their operations, banks must define their customer base—whom they will deal with, both as a borrower and as a lender. Decisions relating to type of product, relative pricing schedules, advertising, convenience factors such as retail outlets (branches), and personnel problems are all part of bank operations. Questions concerning capital structure and dividend policy are also important because banks are owned by wealthholders who must obtain a sufficient return for a given risk to justify their investment.

Banks deal in financial assets denominated in nominal values—paper claims. They must be arbitragers of markets, buying funds in one market and selling them in another, living off interest rate spreads that result from market imperfections, the diversity of risk characteristics, and specialization. Banks mediate between the ultimate savers and ultimate investors in society. They form the foundation for the payments mechanism by which money exchanges are made.

Their position within the framework of the economy has created wide public interest in both individual banks and the industry as a whole. Banks represent great concentrations of wealth, both locally and in the aggregate. This concentration of wealth and the great economic power it implies have made the banking industry the subject of much suspicion and fear throughout America's history. To guard against the misuse of its power, and because the industry plays a central role in the payments mechanism, banking is highly regulated.

This chapter presents an overview of the nature of commercial banking in the United States. The following section discusses how analysts have approached the commercial banking firm in the past and how it will be treated in this book. This is followed by an examination of the structure of a bank's balance sheet and income statement; the makeup of the balance sheet and its potential impact on income are primary factors in all management decisions, as will become apparent in the chapters that follow.

After a discussion of economies of scale within the banking industry and the objectives of bank management, some thought is given to the extent to which discussions of bank regulation will enter into the book and affect the applications of its principles. The chapter concludes with a short description of the remainder of the book.

THE BANKING FIRM

Only recently has the commercial banking firm been completely and rigorously treated in terms of economic theory. There appear to be two reasons for this. First, whereas theories of the firm are developed in terms of explicit inputs (labor, capital, and raw materials) and explicit outputs (cars and television sets, for example), many economists think of banks as having explicit inputs of labor and capital but no explicit output. Some economists consider money and debt a veil covering the real activity of the producer and therefore believe that financial transactions have no place in the theory of the firm. It is difficult to examine an institution that does not have all the necessary classifications inherent in the theory. This problem is heightened because of the multiproduct, multi-input nature of banks. It is difficult to conceptualize how to treat an organization that has no distinct output let alone one whose outputs cannot be differentiated clearly.

Secondly, many analysts feel that individual markets and bank characteristics dominate the economic characteristics of banks in any general discussion of banking, because commercial banks are heavily regulated and of limited geographical scope. Although there are a few sound banking principles that apply to all banks, it has been deemed impossible to generalize the theory of the banking firm. Thus, books on the commercial banking industry have been almost entirely descriptive, illustrating the industry but providing few theoretical generalizations about its operating principles.

The failure to develop a complete theory of the banking firm has resulted in several deficiencies in our understanding of the individual commercial bank and the banking industry. For example, analysts have been unable to present clearly the true nature of asset/liability management. Other problem areas that have not been developed adequately include transfer pricing, the customer relationship between a bank and a borrower, compensating balances, and loan pricing. However, with an acceptable framework, managers and analysts will be able to generalize banking activity and make use of recent advances in the theory of financial management of the nonfinancial firm.

HISTORICAL DEVELOPMENT OF BANKING THEORY

The first breakthrough to a general theory of financial management came with the development of portfolio theory in the late 1950s.[1] Portfolio theory provided wealthholders, including financial institutions,[2] a consistent method of managing their balance sheets using market information on the various risk-return tradeoffs available to the portfolio manager. Over the next decade, analysts refined portfolio models and extended their applications. Linear programming and dynamic programming models of bank behavior were developed. They proved to be interesting, but, from the point of view of bank management, not very useful.[3]

[1] Harry M. Markowitz, *Portfolio Selection* (New York: John Wiley and Sons, 1959). James Tobin, "Liquidity Preference as Behavior Towards Risk," *Review of Economic Studies*, XXV (February 1958), pp. 65–86.

[2] Richard C. Porter, "A Model of Bank Portfolio Selection," *Yale Economic Essays*, 1, no. 2 (Fall 1961), pp. 323–59. Reprinted in Donald D. Hester and James Tobin, eds., *Financial Markets and Economic Activity* (New York: John Wiley and Sons, 1967), pp. 12–54.

[3] William F. Beazer, *Optimization of Bank Portfolios* (Lexington, Mass.: Lexington Books,

The models have been helpful in managing institutions or individual portfolios where the assets (often the liability side of the balance sheet is completely ignored) are obtained in secondary markets that are broad and deep enough that an individual market participant does not influence the price at which the assets are trading. However, they were not directly applicable to banking.

First, banks do not usually operate in this type of market. Most of a commercial bank's assets and liabilities are obtained in primary markets, where imperfections are the rule rather than the exception. Thus, what the bank charges on loans or pays on deposits will affect the quantity of loans and deposits it is able to obtain. Second, assets and liabilities are often tied together, so that movements in an asset category cannot be treated as independent of movements in liabilities. For example, compensating balances (the deposit balances a borrower is required to keep at the bank) are often based on the amount of the borrower's loan. Therefore, if a borrower borrows more, the deposit balances kept at the bank will have to increase. Finally, institutional relationships, such as the customer relationship (the close tie between a bank and its "good" customers) cannot be adequately handled within the context of portfolio theory. Thus, further advances had to be made before a general theory of the banking firm could be achieved.

In recent years, these advances have taken place, although they have not previously been brought together in a unified description of bank behavior. A few pages will therefore be devoted to the major advances in the theory of the banking firm that led to the developments presented in this book.

The first major contribution to the theory of the banking firm was published in 1963 by Bernard Shull.[4] Shull was the first to discuss bank output so that it could be treated within the framework of the neoclassical theory of the firm. As mentioned earlier, the intangibility of bank output had been a major stumbling block in the development of banking theory. In a more elegant presentation, Michael Klein[5] provided a comprehensive and consistent definition of the inputs and outputs of the bank so that general portfolio decisions and wealth maximization could be han-

---

1975). Joel Fried, "Bank Portfolio Selection," *The Journal of Financial and Quantitative Analysis* 5, no. 2 (June 1970). K. J. Cohen and F. S. Hammer, "Linear Programming Models for Optimal Bank Dynamic Balance Sheet Management," in G. P. Szego and Karl Shell, eds., *Mathematical Methods in Investment and Finance* (Amsterdam: North-Holland, 1972).

[4] Bernard Shull, "Commercial Banks as Multi-Product, Price Discriminating Firms," in Deane Carson, ed., *Banking and Monetary Studies* (Homewood, Ill.: Richard D. Irwin, 1963).

[5] Michael Klein, "A Theory of the Banking Firm," *The Journal of Money, Credit and Banking* (May 1971).

dled within the limitations of imperfect asset and liability markets. Following Klein, John Wood was able to show how the customer relationship might enter into bank portfolio decisions and how this relationship would affect pricing decisions and the cyclical behavior of banks.[6] Wood's results are extended in the present volume to examine the phenomenon of credit rationing and the use of nonprice terms in loan contracts.[7]

The theory of decision making under uncertainty, which has been well developed by others for the nonfinancial firm, has been extended here to a number of areas of commercial bank management: asset/liability management, compensating balance requirements, the customer relationship, and loan pricing.[8]

The theory of the banking firm has advanced considerably over the past fifteen years. The more sophisticated analytical tools have made it easier to examine and analyze the various aspects of the financial management of commercial banks. There is no doubt that the coming decade will see further advances, leading to greater understanding of the management problems peculiar to the industry and the use of better management techniques within the individual banking organizations.

THE BANK'S BALANCE SHEET

The bank's balance sheet is composed primarily of financial claims, either the bank's claims on other organizations or individuals or claims these organizations or individuals have on bank assets. One of the main tasks of this book is to explain the composition and interrelationships of these financial assets and liabilities. Physical assets account for a very small proportion of the balance sheet. As can be seen from Table 1-1, building and equipment form only about 1.6 percent of the banking industry's total assets. Therefore, in subsequent discussions physical assets will be omitted from the balance sheet.[9]

Tables 1-1 and 1-2 are presented to show how bank balance sheets can be grouped into many classes of assets and liabilities. Whereas Table 1-1 is more detailed than Table 1-2, it is composed of aggregate data collected from many banks by a federal agency and cannot be taken to pertain to any

[6] John Wood, "A Model of Commercial Bank Loan and Investment Behavior," in H. G. Johnson and A. R. Nobay, eds., *Issues in Monetary Economics* (Oxford University Press, 1974).

[7] See Chapter 3 and its appendix.

[8] See Chapter 2 and its appendix.

[9] Physical assets pertaining to the retail side of banking and bank branching systems will be treated in Chapter 4.

TABLE 1-1   Aggregate Balance Sheet for Insured U.S. Commercial Banks,
December 31, 1976ᵃ (In millions of dollars)

ASSETS

Cash and Due from Banks, Total	129,578
Cash items in process of collection	48,260
Demand balances with banks in the United States	32,964
Other balances with banks in the United States	5,763
Including interest-bearing balances	5,463
Balances with banks in foreign countries	4,509
Including interest-bearing balances	4,124
Currency and coin	12,115
Reserve with Federal Reserve Bank	25,968
Securities, Total	248,980
Investment securities, total	239,557
U.S. Treasury securities	96,449
Maturity, 1 year and less	37,010
Over 1 through 5 years	50,132
Over 5 through 10 years	8,582
Over 10 years	724
Obligations of other U.S. government agencies and corporations	34,279
Maturity, 1 year and less	10,695
Over 1 through 5 years	15,748
Over 5 through 10 years	3,634
Over 10 years	4,201
Obligations of states and political subdivisions	103,049
Maturity, 1 year and less	16,627
Over 1 through 5 years	29,532
Over 5 through 10 years	30,817
Over 10 years	26,073
Other bonds, notes, and debentures	5,780
Maturity, 1 year and less	1,242
Over 1 through 5 years	2,221
Over 5 through 10 years	1,119
Over 10 years	1,199
Corporate stock	1,541
Trading account securities	7,882
Loans, Net	514,303
Plus: Reserve for possible loan losses	6,116
Loans, total	520,419
Plus: Unearned income on loans	12,526
Loans, gross	532,945
Real estate loans, total	149,280
Construction and land development	16,638
Secured by farmland	6,710
Secured by 1-4 family residential properties:	
Insured by FHA and guaranteed by VA	7,919
Conventional	72,346

(continued)

TABLE 1-1 (Continued)

Real estate loans (cont.)
  Secured by multifamily (5 or more) residential properties:
    Insured by FHA 406
    Conventional 4,132
  Secured by nonfarm nonresidential properties: 41,129
Loans to financial institutions, total 35,738
  To real estate investment trusts and mortgage companies 9,855
  To domestic commercial banks 2,774
  To banks in foreign countries 6,617
  To other depository institutions 1,341
  To other financial institutions 15,151
Loans for purchasing or carrying securities, total 15,089
  To brokers and dealers in securities 11,075
  Other loans for purchasing or carrying securities 4,015
Loans to farmers.. 23,259
Commercial and industrial loans 177,142
Loans to individuals, total 118,033
  To purchase private passenger automobiles on installment basis 39,577
  Credit cards and related plans:
    Retail (charge account) credit card plans 11,317
    Check credit and revolving credit plans 3,036
  To purchase other retail consumer goods on installment basis:
    Mobile homes (excludes travel trailers) 8,742
    Other retail consumer goods 7,189
  Installment loans to repair and modernize residential property 6,522
  Other installment loans for household, family, and other
      personal expenditures... 17,358
  Single-payment loans for household, family, and other
      personal expenditures 24,293
All other loans.. 14,405
    Total Loans and Securities 763,283

Federal Funds Sold and Securities Purchased under Agreements to Resell, Total 45,767
With domestic commercial banks.. 37,876
With brokers and dealers in securities and funds 5,693
With others 2,198

Direct Lease Financing 5,111

Bank Premises, Furniture and Fixtures, and Other Assets
    Representing Bank Premises....................................... 16,597

Real Estate Owned Other Than Bank Premises 2,850

Investments in Unconsolidated Subsidiaries and
    Associated Companies 2,303

Customers' Liability on Acceptances Outstanding 9,147

Other Assets 29,384

    Total Assets 1,004,020

(*continued*)

TABLE 1-1   (Continued)

LIABILITIES AND EQUITY CAPITAL

Business and Personal Deposits, Total	690,919
Individuals, partnerships, and corporations, demand	254,221
Individuals, partnerships, and corporations, savings	196,555
Individuals and nonprofit organizations, savings	187,922
Corporations and other profit organizations, savings	8,633
Individuals, partnerships, and corporations, time	228,522
Deposits accumulated for payment of personal loans, time	146
Certified and officers' checks, travelers' checks,	
letters of credit, demand	11,475
Government Deposits, Total	71,330
United States Government	
Demand	3,020
Savings	56
Time	675
States and political subdivisions	
Demand	17,648
Savings	6,044
Time	43,885
Domestic Interbank Deposits, Total	44,348
Commercial banks in the United States	
Demand	35,926
Savings	10
Time	6,709
Mutual savings banks in the United States	
Demand	1,385
Savings	1
Time	317
Foreign Government and Bank Deposits, Total	18,405
Foreign governments, central banks	
Demand	1,846
Savings	103
Time	8,481
Banks in foreign countries	
Demand	6,761
Savings	—
Time	1,213
Total Deposits	825,002
Demand	332,283
Savings	202,770
Time	289,949

(*continued*)

TABLE 1-1   (Continued)

Miscellaneous Liabilities, Total	101,850
Federal funds purchased and securities sold under agreements	
to repurchase, total	70,188
With domestic and commercial banks	40,613
With brokers and dealers in securities and funds	5,577
With others	23,998
Other liabilities for borrowed money	5,120
Mortgage indebtedness	774
Acceptances outstanding	9,755
Other liabilities	16,013
Total Liabilities (excluding subordinated notes and debentures)	926,852
Subordinated Notes and Debentures	5,098
Equity Capital, Total	72,070
Preferred stock, par value	67
Shares outstanding (in thousands)	6
Common stock, par value	16,143
Shares authorized (in thousands)	1,999
Shares outstanding (in thousands)	1,691
Surplus	28,791
Undivided profits	25,266
Reserve for contingencies and other capital reserves	1,803
Total Liabilities and Equity Capital	1,004,020

Source: Federal Deposit Insurance Corporation, *Annual Bank Statistics,* 1977.

[a] Errors in totals are due to rounding.

one bank. Although the groupings shown in Table 1-1 for the banking system are richer in detail than those in a bank's individual balance sheet in Table 1-2, the reader is likely to have available only data like those of Table 1-2.

It is often possible to subdivide banking data even further as in Table 1-3, where commercial and industrial loans are subclassified into industry groupings. If the internal balance sheet of a bank were available for examination, it would be found that loans and investments could be grouped into even finer categories according to the credit rating or geographic location of the borrower. The same is true of liabilities, although not to the same extent. Thus, it can be concluded that it is possible for banks to classify their depositors and borrowers into many classes and subclasses according to such characteristics as type of industry, credit rating, maturity, and geographic location.

TABLE 1-2   Consolidated Balance Sheet for a Large Commercial Bank[a]
             (In thousands of dollars)

	12/31/77	12/31/76
ASSETS		
Cash and due from banks	$ 4,470,563	$ 3,630,353
Interest-bearing deposits at banks	5,735,457	5,500,455
U.S. Treasury securities	876,040	1,723,041
Obligations of U.S. government agencies	165,495	191,928
Obligations of states and political subdivisions	1,387,507	1,109,077
Other investment securities	556,997	499,904
Trading account securities, net	48,183	331,032
Federal funds sold and securities purchased under agreements to resell	386,739	283,482
Loans and lease financing	15,713,243	13,641,481
Less: allowance for possible credit losses	148,424	147,573
Net loans and lease financing	15,564,819	13,493,908
Customers' acceptance liability	972,909	801,635
Premises and equipment, net of accumulated depreciation of $87,401,000 in 1977 and $77,204,000 in 1976	124,547	123,038
Other real estate	33,430	74,287
Other assets	774,995	591,268
TOTAL ASSETS	$31,097,681	$28,353,408
LIABILITIES AND STOCKHOLDER'S EQUITY		
Demand deposits	$ 7,595,684	$ 6,766,641
Time deposits	4,053,699	3,014,193
Deposits in foreign offices	12,191,189	12,035,009
Total deposits	23,840,572	21,815,843
Federal funds purchased and securities sold under agreements to repurchase	2,648,185	2,586,060
Commercial paper of a subsidiary	111,015	92,484
Other liabilities for borrowed money	778,447	674,535
Accrued taxes and expenses	470,551	398,042
Liability on acceptances	978,224	806,688
Dividend payable	27,000	25,000
Convertible debentures of a subsidiary (4¼%, due 1987)	50,000	50,000
Capital notes (6⅛%, due 1978)	100,000	100,000
Capital notes (5%, due 1992)	77,344	80,718
Other long-term debt	31,350	14,590
Other liabilities	437,973	271,438
Total Liabilities	29,550,661	26,915,398
Capital stock, $25 par value (authorized and outstanding: 10,000,000 shares)	250,000	250,000
Surplus	518,385	518,385
Undivided profits	778,635	669,625
Total Stockholder's Equity	1,547,020	1,438,010
TOTAL LIABILITIES AND STOCKHOLDER'S EQUITY	$31,097,681	$28,353,408

Source: Consolidated statement of condition, Morgan Guaranty Trust Company of New York, 1977 Annual Report, J. P. Morgan & Co. Incorporated.

TABLE 1-3 Commercial and Industrial Loans of Large Weekly Reporting Commercial Banks (In millions of dollars)

Industry Group	Total Loans[a]	Term Loans[b]
Durable goods manufacturing:		
Primary metals	2,391	1,449
Machinery	4,588	2,587
Transportation equipment	2,208	1,365
Other fabricated metal products	1,697	767
Other durable goods	3,116	1,549
Nondurable goods manufacturing:		
Food, liquor, and tobacco	3,400	1,449
Textiles, apparel, and leather	3,121	1,033
Petroleum refining	2,645	1,925
Chemicals and rubber	2,549	1,456
Other nondurable goods	1,908	975
Mining, including crude petroleum and natural gas	7,444	5,793
Trade:		
Commodity dealers	1,925	227
Other wholesale	6,211	1,483
Retail	6,120	2,085
Transportation	5,043	3,720
Communication	1,409	810
Other public utilities	5,595	3,762
Construction	3,874	1,638
Services	10,789	5,212
All other domestic loans	7,533	2,383
Bankers acceptances	5,101	—
Foreign commercial and industrial loans	5,988	3,623
Total	94,655[c]	45,291

Source: *Federal Reserve Bulletin,* Board of Governors of the Federal Reserve System, February, 1977.

[a] Includes term loans.

[b] Outstanding loans with an original maturity of more than 1 year and all outstanding loans granted under a formal agreement—revolving credit or standby—on which the original maturity of the commitment was in excess of 1 year.

[c] Includes $361 million in commercial paper.

Legal definitions may also play a part in the division of the balance sheet and may account for changes that take place in balance sheets over time. For example, until 1976, reserves against loan losses were included in a bank's capital accounts. Since then, loan-loss reserves have been carried on the asset side of the balance sheet in the aggregate loan account. Other examples of legal constraints could also be cited.

Conceptual Development of the Bank's Balance Sheet

It is desirable, in developing a complete theory of commercial bank management, to conceptualize actual bank practice.[10] In order to treat the commercial bank's balance sheet in a more general framework, it will be necessary to abstract from the individual markets and discuss the general characteristics of loans that apply to all loan markets. Thus, the bank will be assumed to have m different loan and investment markets, where m is any number needed to exhaust the bank's asset categories. Also, it will be assumed that there are n different markets in which the bank sells its liabilities, where n is the number needed to exhaust the bank's categories of liabilities. These m and n markets will at times be given names coinciding with the classifications on the balance sheets presented in Tables 1-1, 1-2, and 1-3 when a point is to be made. The generalization achieved in going to an abstract balance sheet allows the analysis to break away from what any one particular bank does.

As just discussed, commercial banks distinguish among different asset and liability categories by the characteristics of the particular industries or firms within them. The bank makes these distinctions by a process of credit, industry, and market analysis through which it attempts to divide customers into finer and finer subdivisions not only so it may serve its customers better but also so that it may be able to price its services better and improve its earnings. Throughout this book, therefore, assets and liabilities will usually be discussed in terms of these distinguishing characteristics rather than in terms of individual cases or situations. The balance sheet relationships for the individual bank can be represented in general form as

$$\sum_{i=1}^{m} L_i = \sum_{j=1}^{n} D_j + K \qquad (1\text{-}1)$$

where L_i is the ith asset class, D_j is the jth liability class, and K is the sum of all the capital accounts of the bank. L_6, for instance, might be short-term

---

[10] In general, in this volume, mathematics will be confined to appendixes. However, where it will simplify the presentation, mathematical notation will be introduced into the text.

U.S. Treasury bills, and D_1 might be IPC demand deposits (the demand deposits of individuals, partnerships, and corporations). Equation (1-1) is simply a restatement of the basic accounting identity: Assets are equal to Liabilities plus Owners' Equity.

THE INCOME STATEMENT

Interest Revenues and Costs

Most revenues and expenses of a commercial bank come from interest received on loans and investments and paid on liabilities. This can be seen from the income statements for the industry as a whole and for an individual bank, presented in Tables 1-4 and 1-5, respectively.

Several changes have taken place in the bank income statement over the past ten years, and care must be exercised in comparing statements over time. Many of the changes will be noted in the sections of text where they are particularly relevant. For the present, however, the reader need have only a general idea of the major sources of bank revenues and expenses. These categories will be fleshed out within the course of the book.

Whereas the data presented to the public are consolidated figures of all interest income, fees, and expenses, internally each bank has available records showing the interest income and fees from each asset, the interest paid on each account, and the expenses that relate to all functions of the bank. In examining the individual bank, therefore, it will be assumed that the bank's internal income statement is disaggregated according to the asset and liability categories on its balance sheet. Interest income for each class is computed by multiplying the average interest rate (captured by a percentage figure r_i or r_j) applicable to a particular class of assets or liabilities by the amount (L_i or D_j) in that class to obtain the corresponding total income, $r_i L_i$, or expense, $r_j D_j$.

Noninterest Revenues and Expenses

Allocating fee income or service changes is a minor problem, because the fees or charges will be related to specific assets or liabilities. It can be assumed that a percentage charge, f, can be computed and that total revenues can be obtained by multiplying this charge by the relevant asset or liability amounts; for example, total fee revenues for asset class i would be $f_i L_i$.

TABLE 1-4   Income of Insured Commercial Banks for Twelve Months
            Ending December 31, 1976
            (In thousands of dollars)

Operating Income

Interest and fees on loans	51,645,260	
Interest on balances with banks	4,486,655	
Income on federal funds sold and securities purchased under agreements to resell in domestic offices	1,984,757	
Interest on U.S. Treasury securities	5,976,210	
Interest on obligations of other U.S. government agencies and corporations	2,415,164	
Interest on obligations of states and political subdivisions of the U.S.	5,134,676	
Interest on other bonds, notes, and debentures	751,007	
Dividends on stock	105,046	
Income from direct lease financing	534,254	
Income from fiduciary activities	1,794,732	
Service charges on deposit accounts in domestic offices	1,635,463	
Other service charges, commissions, and fees	2,182,927	
Other income	2,017,702	
Total Operating Income		80,663,853

Operating Expenses

Salaries and employee benefits	14,752,297	
Interest on time certificates of deposit of $100,000 or more issued by domestic offices	7,111,054	
Interest on deposits in foreign offices	8,749,673	
Interest on other deposits	19,143,238	
Expense of federal funds purchased and securities sold under agreements to repurchase in domestic offices	3,311,741	
Interest on other borrowed money	667,197	
Interest on subordinated notes and debentures	344,952	
Occupancy expense of bank premises, gross	3,262,005	
Less: Rental income	497,201	
Occupancy expense of bank premises, net	2,764,804	
Furniture and equipment expense	1,721,382	
Provision for possible loan losses	3,691,378	
Other expenses	8,492,452	
Total Operating Expenses		70,750,168
Income before Income Taxes and Securities Gains or Losses		9,913,685
Applicable Income Taxes		2,290,772
Income Before Securities Gains or Losses		7,622,913

(continued)

TABLE 1-4   (Continued)

Income Before Securities Gains or Losses		7,622,913
Securities Gains (Losses), Gross	312,267	
Applicable Income Taxes	118,233	
Securities Gains (Losses), Net		194,034
Income Before Extraordinary Items		7,816,947
Extraordinary Items, Gross	28,104	
Applicable income taxes	1,774	
Extraordinary Items, Net		26,330
Net Income		7,843,277

Source: Federal Deposit Insurance Corporation, *Annual Bank Statistics,* 1977.

There are problems relating to other items, however. Theoretically, salaries, office expenses, and so forth should be computed and allocated to the appropriate asset or liability category. That is, banks should be able to cost out each expense and charge it to the activity that generated it. This cost could be summarized in a charge, b, expressed as a percentage figure, that would be allocated to a given classification to determine total expenses for the classification, say $b_i L_i$ for asset class i.

In practice, banks do not often have this cost information available. Although the Federal Reserve has made an effort in recent years to generate such information,[11] only small and medium-sized banks have made use of the opportunity provided by the Federal Reserve for collecting cost data. Most large banks have attempted to improve their internal accounting, but success in achieving highly efficient cost accounting systems has not been overwhelming.

A commercial bank, then, will generally have available only aggregate expense data on its assets and liabilities and will not be capable of reaching decisions exactly as proposed in this volume. However, it will be assumed throughout the book that such data are available. The only sensible way to approach the construction of bank portfolios is with the as-

---

[11] W. O. Pearce, "Functional Cost Analysis: A Tool of Bank Management," *Monthly Review*, Federal Reserve Bank of Richmond, 1967, reprinted in Paul F. Jessup, ed., *Innovations in Bank Management* (New York: Holt, Rinehart and Winston, 1969).

TABLE 1-5   Consolidated Statement of Income
(In thousands, except per share)

	1977	1976
Interest Income From:		
Loans	$1,031,514	$ 989,775
Federal funds sold and securities purchased under		
agreements to resell	18,113	10,014
U.S. Treasury securities	112,732	116,519
Obligations of states and political subdivisions	81,605	60,616
Other investment securities	58,181	50,108
Trading account securities		
Obligations of states and political subdivisions	4,072	3,154
Other securities	18,260	31,814
Other sources, mainly interest-bearing deposits at banks .	338,379	297,681
Total interest income	1,662,856	1,559,681
Interest Expense Due To:		
Deposits..	892,128	816,018
Federal funds purchased and securities sold under		
agreements to repurchase	172,025	151,551
Other borrowed money	43,375	46,354
Notes and debentures	34,368	29,205
Total interest expense	1,141,896	1,043,128
Interest income net of interest expense	520,960	516,553
Provision for possible credit losses	47,573	68,208
Interest income net of interest expense and provision		
for possible credit losses	473,387	448,345
Noninterest Operating Income		
Trading account profits (losses) and commissions.........	$ (3,453)	$ 29,437
Corporate trust, other trust, and agency income	107,816	101,480
Foreign exchange trading income	40,322	33,844
Other operating income, mainly fees and commissions ...	89,032	87,682
Total noninterest operating income.....................	233,717	252,443

(continued)

sumption that costs can be identified and allocated.[12] Furthermore, it seems reasonable to expect that banks will have better accounting systems in the future and thus will be able to acquire more accurate approximations of the necessary data.

[12] The assumption that a bank does not identify costs and allocate them correctly implies that each bank must be considered individually and that generalizations about pricing and portfolio composition are inapplicable.

TABLE 1-5   (Continued)

	1977	1976
Total operating income net of interest expense and provision for possible credit losses	707,104	700,788
Other Noninterest Operating Expenses		
Salaries..	146,592	142,043
Deferred profit sharing	15,139	14,185
Additional compensation	6,081	5,170
Other employee benefits	48,326	42,686
Net occupancy expense	41,433	37,591
Equipment rentals, depreciation, and maintenance	18,380	16,071
Other operating expenses	71,145	67,115
Total other noninterest operating expenses	347,096	324,861
Income before income taxes and securities gains (losses) ..	360,008	375,927
Applicable income taxes	141,695	173,169
Income before Securities Gains (Losses)	$ 218,313	$ 202,758
Per share	$5.36	$5.04
Net securities losses	(6,193)	(2,955)
Income tax benefit....................................	4,227	2,880
Net Income	$ 216,347	$ 202,683
Per share	$5.32	$5.04
Dividends declared per common share	2.05	1.85

Source: J. P. Morgan & Co. Incorporated.

The treatment of taxes is also an important part of the income state-ment. Problems arise in applying taxes directly to income sources, how-ever, because of bank use of tax shelters such as the investment tax credit, the foreign tax credit, tax-free bonds, and loan-loss provisions. Chapter 6 deals in greater detail with the tax-planning aspects of commercial bank-ing. For the present, to avoid difficulties that arise from the differential application of taxes to bank income, taxes and tax rates will be assumed to be outside the discretion of the bank.

Capital gains and losses and extraordinary items must be included on the income statement. In the balance sheet, these are added to or sub-tracted from income in the appropriate place. Theoretically, these amounts represent changes in the valuation of balance sheet items. That is, banks will start out a period with, say, $100,000 in U.S. government securities. If, because of declining interest rates, the value of these securities rises to $120,000 and the bank realizes the capital gain, it must adjust the average interest return on the securities to reflect the realized holding period yield—that is, adjust r—or adjust the quantity on its balance sheet to the realized quantity of the asset, L. If this is done, the capital gain will be entered correctly in the generalized income statement represented by equation (1-2). This presents another situation in which the average tax rate may have to be adjusted. If capital gains are taxed at a different rate than regular income, the average tax rate will have to be adjusted as income comes from different sources. This point is discussed more fully in Chapter 6.

Summarizing the income statement of the commercial bank, total after-tax income, π, can be described as

$$\pi = (1 - t) \left[\sum_{i=1}^{m} (r_i + f_i - b_i)L_i - \sum_{j=1}^{n} (r_j - f_j + b_j)D_j \right] \qquad (1\text{-}2)$$

where t is the average tax rate of the bank; r_i and r_j are the interest rates charged the ith asset class and paid on the jth liability category, respectively; f_i and f_j are the fee and service charge levied against the ith asset class and the jth liability class, respectively; and b_i and b_j are the bank's administrative cost of servicing the ith asset and jth liability category, respectively.

ECONOMIES OF SCALE

The possible existence of economies of scale in commercial banking is a topic of some importance both to the theory of the banking firm and to the practice of commercial bank management. This is a hazardous topic, fraught with many traps, but it is worthwhile to the study of bank management to briefly present the issues and some of the problems of determining whether or not economies of scale exist in banking.

First it is necessary to define the output of a commercial bank. As mentioned earlier, this has caused some difficulties in the past. For the purposes of this book, output is simply taken to be loans to private individuals, businesses, or governments. This still leaves the problem of determining whether the most relevant measure of output is the number of loans or their dollar amount. Inputs consist of either the dollar amount or number of deposits and other liabilities.

Second, costs must be defined and allocated. How are different portfolios of assets and liabilities weighted so that comparisons can be made? It is generally assumed that each asset or liability category is homogeneous as to quality or type of borrower or lender. Therefore, the interest expense or revenue paid or received by the bank should be the same within each classification of assets or liabilities. Rates may change with the size of the loan, the type of customer and the nature of the customer–bank relationship, the maturity of the loan, the collateral, the total demand or supply of the particular asset or liability, and so on. However, there is sufficient distinction among asset and liability classifications that only relatively homogeneous economic units and loan or deposit terms fit into each class. The division of customers into loan classes is a matter of information. Since information and its interpretation are costly, the number of asset/liability categories used by any bank is limited.

Fees and other charges will vary according to the different characteristics of the asset/liability classes but will be constant within any given class. Administrative and operating costs will also be assigned to their appropriate asset/liability classes. It is not altogether settled, however, that these costs will be constant over all levels of activity.

Administrative and operating costs are influenced by (1) the technology available to the bank, (2) the bank's ability to divide its physical assets into small units, (3) the quality of management, and (4) local resources. In most studies of economies of scale, items 3 and 4, although they will significantly affect the profitability of the individual bank, are generally found to be random occurrences when the banking system as a whole is studied.[13] Technology and divisibility are the main items contributing to any observed economies of scale. Technology is defined as the state of the art in collecting inputs (assets and liabilities) and producing output (loans). Divisibility, the ability to divide physical assets into smaller usable units, affects the economies of scale because the size of a bank may prohibit the use or purchase of certain physical assets or prevent the efficient use of either human resources or machines.

If a bank's physical assets could be divided in half and output was only one-half of what the whole bank could produce, then divisibility would not be a problem. However, if output declined by more than half

---

[13] See William F. Ford, "Profitability: Why Do Some Banks Perform Better Than Average? An In-Depth Analysis," *Banking* (October 1974), p. 31.

when physical assets were halved, the reason might be that some assets cannot be used efficiently at the smaller size. Computers are an example. Small banks do not find it economically feasible to own a computer, because they do not generate enough work for a computer sophisticated enough to meet their needs. A larger bank may be able to justify a computer economically. In this sense the computer is indivisible, because the bank must reach a certain size before the purchase of a computer is a financially sound decision.

Diseconomies may arise when a bank reaches the maximum efficiency of its physical assets (and their embodied technology) or the greatest possible division of labor or specialization for the equipment available to it. A shortage of qualified management resources may also limit the efficient size of the bank.

Administrative and operating costs are captured in the variables b_i and b_j in equation (1-2), which reflect individual economies of scale for each asset/liability class. However, the specification presented so far does not pick up interactions between the various overhead costs or the influence of the size of the bank on scale economies. With respect to interactions, it can be argued, for example, that increases in the size of the time deposit component of liabilities may lead to a decline in the administrative and operating costs of handling time deposits, but the costs of handling demand deposits may also decline, because the resources needed to handle both types of deposits are very similar and if one is affected the other will probably be affected as well.

Bank size may also be important because an increase in the asset size of the bank may lead to a decline in the administrative and operating costs applied to each asset/liability category regardless of the size of the category.

The empirical work pertaining to economies of scale in banking up to 1967 was summarized and appraised that year by Guttentag and Herman.[14] After discussing all the problems associated with defining bank output and input, they stated that "all studies show that $10 million banks have lower expense ratios—in many cases substantially lower—than $1–$2 million banks."[15] In the intermediate range, between $10 to $50 million and $100 to $500 million, the evidence was less clear, although the studies they examined reported some slight decline in costs. If scale economies did exist in this range, Guttentag and Herman felt they were not very pro-

---

[14] Jack M. Guttentag and Edward S. Herman, "Banking Structure and Performance," *Bulletin*, New York University (February, 1967).

[15] Ibid., p. 116.

nounced. As for large banks, they concluded that nothing definite could be said.

Thus, Guttentag and Herman noted that although substantial economies of scale may be evident in going from a $1 million bank to a $10 million bank, it is not altogether clear that they are present in larger banks. Since the studies they referred to were completed over ten years ago, it is necessary to alter the size ranges to reflect the inflation that has taken place since then. Some experts say that because of inflation, scale economies may exist for banks with assets up to $25 to $30 million. There is no current empirical support for this figure, and until further studies are completed in this area, the precise figure can be accepted only provisionally.

In a more recent review, George Benston[16] reported and commented on the results of two studies of his own, one of them concerned with savings and loan associations, and a study done by Bell and Murphy.[17] The reason for lumping all three studies together is the similarity of the results, which indicated an estimated elasticity of cost with respect to assets of about 0.93. That is, a 1 percent increase in the asset size (of an average bank) brought about a 0.93 percent increase in costs. According to these results, economies of scale exist throughout the full range of bank sizes.[18] However, Benston draws the following conclusion: "Economies of scale are not so great that medium sized banks would necessarily be 'squeezed out' if entry, growth and mergers were not regulated. . . . However, very small banks probably cannot effectively compete with larger banks, with respect to operating costs."[19]

This conclusion is not substantially different from that reached by Guttentag and Herman. It is hard to distinguish a cost curve with an elasticity of approximately 0.93 from one that exhibits constant costs after $25 million in asset size. Furthermore, one could argue that because of errors in the measurement of variables and the difficulty in defining homogeneous outputs, the estimation of declining costs for larger banks is probably not statistically significant. This cannot be said for the smaller banks. Thus, it is concluded from these studies that smaller banks do exhibit a

[16] George J. Benston, "Economies of Scale of Financial Institutions," *The Journal of Money, Credit and Banking*, IV (May 1972), pp. 312–41.

[17] F. W. Bell and N. B. Murphy, *Costs in Commercial Banking: A Quantitative Analysis of Bank Behavior and its Relation to Bank Regulation*, Research Report No. 41. (Boston: Federal Reserve Bank of Boston, 1968).

[18] A result consistent with this was found to exist for credit unions. See Mark J. Flannery, "Credit Unions as Consumer Lenders in the United States," *New England Economic Review*, Federal Reserve Bank of Boston (July/August 1974), pp. 3–12.

[19] Benston, "Economies of Scale, . . .," p. 336.

tendency toward large reductions in average costs of operations as asset size increases, but the assumption of constant costs is not unreasonable for banks with assets of $25 to $30 million or more.

Constant costs will be assumed in this book, because (1) the assumption simplifies the analysis in most cases and allows major points to be brought out more clearly and (2) the banks that are most interesting are large enough for the assumption to be realistic. Thus, neither the total size of the bank nor the quantity of a particular asset or liability will affect the average administrative and operating costs applied to individual asset or liability classes. In addition, the average costs applied to each category will be assumed to be independent of the average costs associated with other categories. That is, changes in quantity or technology applied to one class will not affect average costs in another.

Despite this general assumption, the effects that economies of scale have or might have on portfolio decisions are discussed, either in the text or in footnotes, whenever they are relevant.[20]

OBJECTIVES OF THE COMMERCIAL BANK

The major objective of the banking firm should be no different from that of any other profit-making institution. Management should attempt to maximize the value of the firm to its owners, an attempt that is generally translated into an effort to maximize the price of the bank's common stock, which represents owners' wealthholdings. However, it is clear that wealth maximization may not be the only goal of the banking firm.[21]

The possibility of the firm having multiple goals or objectives results from imperfections in the capital markets, the product markets, or the factor markets. Since banks work predominantly in imperfect markets, discussion of alternative goals is particularly pertinent. For example, it has been pointed out that large firms face a separation of ownership and management and sufficient transactions costs in transferring ownership to allow goals other than wealth maximization to be present in an organization's utility function.[22] Thus, although the firm may be maximizing the

---

[20] Particularly in Chapter 6, on internal sources of funds.

[21] Some other goals that may be chosen by the management or the owners of a bank are presented in C. M. White, "Multiple Goals in the Theory of the Firm," in K. E. Boulding and W. A. Spivey, eds., *Linear Programming and the Theory of the Firm* (New York: The Macmillan Company, 1960). For a discussion specifically concerned with the goals of financial institutions, see D. D. Hester and J. L. Pierce, *Bank Management and Portfolio Behavior* (New Haven, Conn.: Yale University Press, 1975).

[22] This was first pointed out by O. E. Williamson, "A Rational Managerial Behavior," in

utility function of those in control, there may be a "social loss" because the bank may hire more labor than it needs for efficient operations and provide management with such perquisites as lavish executive suites and thus report lower profits than would otherwise be possible. The firm would be producing maximum output for its choice of inputs but would not be producing the output possible if these extra considerations were not present in the utility function.[23]

Another factor that might cause suboptimal behavior is the degree of imperfection in the loan market. For example, the greater the degree of imperfection within the market, the less efficient the bank will be with respect to operating costs, because it can be inefficient and still earn a "satisfactory" return.[24] In addition, in an imperfect market, its managers will be more willing to trade off a lower return for a lower level of risk.[25]

It is very likely that the utility function of the bank owners or managers will contain something other than shareholder wealth to be maximized, such as asset growth or bank size, since banks operate in highly imperfect markets. However, wealth maximization will still be assumed to be the major goal in most discussions in this book. The reasons are as follows.

1. In dealing with the financial management of commercial banks, it must be assumed that banks operate in the most efficient manner. That is, they use the most efficient production function available to the banking industry, so operating costs are at their lowest levels for a given level of output.

2. Many of the other goals or objectives of the firm mentioned in the studies cited earlier are not quantifiable. Some factors, such as image or power, while related to wealth, are themselves not subject to measurement. Furthermore, maximization of profits assures the firm's survival, which is another potential objective of the bank.

3. The degree of risk aversion varies among banks but is assumed to be constant for any particular bank.

R. M. Cyert and J. G. March, eds., *A Behavioral Theory of the Firm* (Englewood Cliffs, N.J.: Prentice-Hall, 1964). It has been confirmed for the banking industry by F. R. Edwards, "Managerial Objectives in Regulated Industries: Expense-Preference Behavior in Banking," *The Journal of Political Economy*, 85 (February 1977), pp. 147–62.

[23] R. Rees, "A Reconsideration of the Expense Preference Theory of the Firm," *Economica*, 41 (August 1974), 295–307.

[24] Edwards, "Managerial Objectives." Also, see the discussion on expenses in Chapter 6.

[25] F. R. Edwards and A. A. Heggestad, "Uncertainty, Market Structure, and Performance: The Galbraith-Caves Hypothesis and Managerial Motives in Banking," *The Quarterly Journal of Economics* (August 1973), 455–73.

BANK REGULATION

No effort is made in this volume to examine the specific rules and regulations with respect to branching, holding company formation, and so on, or the regulatory bodies that administer the plethora of laws and rules governing the banking system.[26] Although regulation plays a major role in bank operations, it is best to begin by treating management decisions as unconstrained so that the economics of the problem can be fully presented. Regulation just puts limits, maxima or minima, on what the bank can do, forcing the bank into a suboptimal position. Thus, for most problems treated here, it will first be assumed that management is unconstrained in its decision-making process. Then, if necessary, appropriate regulatory constraints will be introduced and the decision will be reexamined.

One of the best known constraints is the limitation on the number or geographical extent of branches.[27] In some states, primarily in the Midwest, banks are limited to their main office. In others, banks may branch into "contiguous counties," whereas in yet others they may branch statewide. At the time of writing, banks are prohibited from branching across state lines.

The numerous branching laws present a good example of how regulations can impede generalization. Since there are several types of branching restrictions, it would be impossible to develop a general model of the banking firm that takes branching into account. Therefore, it will be assumed initially that no restrictions exist. Then, in applying the techniques presented here to a specific bank, the state laws governing that bank can be introduced as constraints on the model. For example, a bank in a unit banking state obviously cannot consider an aggressive branching program to enlarge its customer base, although such a program is considered a major alternative in the discussions of Chapter 4.

On the other hand, several constraints will be incorporated into the general development.

1. Reserve requirements on various types of deposits will be assumed to be binding. This is not really important in long-run planning, but in short-run reserve management, reserve requirements become the "cutting edge" against which banks must work.

---

[26] For background material the interested reader can refer to Chapter 2 in Howard D. Crosse and George H. Hempel, *Management Policies for Commercial Banks* (Englewood Cliffs, N.J.: Prentice-Hall, 1973) or Chapter 2 in E. W. Reed, R. V. Cotter, E. K. Gill, and R. K. Smith, *Commercial Banking* (Englewood Cliffs, N.J.: Prentice-Hall, 1976).

[27] The more modern version of this problem is "What constitutes a branch?"

2. It is assumed that there is some effective constraint on entry into the banking industry. This means that the number of banks in the system will be less than optimal and that some market imperfections will continue *ad infinitum*. Because of this assumption, bank markets can be assumed to contain some imperfections; other banks cannot enter the market and eliminate existing imperfections.

3. Although capital requirements are not assumed to be binding, the influence of regulatory practice must be discussed. Many banks assume that the guidelines of the regulatory authorities represent "good banking practice." Consequently, these banks, particularly small ones, adopt the methods of analysis used by the regulators as their standard procedure for determining capital structure.

Is There a Need for Bank Regulation?

Before leaving the subject of bank regulation, it may be useful to question the reasons for its existence. If one examines the history of banking in the United States, there seem to be two main reasons for public control of the industry.

1. To limit the concentration of wealth.   Throughout U.S. history, Americans have been wary of concentrations of wealth, and commercial banks, whose individual holdings are usually measured in millions of dollars, have therefore been subject to distrust. Thus, there have been recurrent attempts to weaken the control banks exercise over these vast wealthholdings by limiting their prerogatives, particularly with respect to expansion into other fields of operation. In the late 1970s, this concern with bank power has centered on their trust business and their voting rights in major corporations. Many concerned people feel that banks should not be allowed to vote trust-held stock because the size of their holdings would allow them to dominate corporate decisions.

2. To decrease the chance of multibank failures.   Since commercial banks play such a large role in the payments mechanism, there has been increasing interest in the potential for breakdowns in this mechanism. Because of the homogeneity of the banking system, its interlocking nature, via correspondent relationships and participations, and its overall susceptibility to the credit cycle, there is always the possibility that if one bank fails, others will also fail. The concern felt by both the public and the policy makers over this possibility has led to federal and state legislation and a number of government efforts to analyze and preserve the safety of the banking system.

The thrust in either area has not been even. One reason is that different standards have been applied to the banking industry during different historical periods. However, another reason is that confidence in the government's ability to maintain the country's economic stability ebbs and flows, and most periods of economic collapse have been associated with instability in the banking system. The financial panic of 1907 caused enough stir to result in the creation of the Federal Reserve System in 1914. The Great Depression resulted in many new banking laws aimed at eliminating the excesses or bad management techniques of the previous period.[28] The recession of 1974, the worst since World War II, saw the banking system in its most precarious position since the 1930s.

These ups and downs in legislation and in the administration of regulations seem to be caused by the variability in the perceptions and conduct of all those connected with banking: the bankers themselves, the regulators, the customers, and, more recently, the stockholders and stock analysts. Following a financial collapse, everyone is quite conservative concerning capital structure, the credit rating of borrowers, and liquidity management. Not only are laws made more constraining, but rules and regulations are more strictly administered.

As time passes and people who experienced the crises retire from authority, there remain fewer and fewer management personnel who remember the troubled times. Banks become more leveraged, more aggressive loan policies are followed, and practices that were frowned upon earlier are reinstated. The regulators and the stockholders offer no objection, for they too see no problem, given the economic stability that has been achieved and the increased earnings these practices bring. There is no doubt that movement in this direction over time makes the banking system more fragile, more easily buffeted by some shock such as inappropriate monetary policy or a surge in private-sector demand resulting from crop failure or other weather-induced disasters.[29]

It could be argued that regulators, if they are going to regulate, should be the most conservative at times when the banks want to be the most liberal and the most liberal when the banks want to be the most conservative. However, this seems to contradict human nature, so the banking system will tend to have varying standards over time and must be willing and able to change as the competitive and economic climate changes.

---

[28] For descriptions of this see J. K. Galbraith, *The Great Crash, 1929* (Boston: Houghton Mifflin, 1954) and M. Friedman and A. J. Schwartz, *A Monetary History of the United States: 1867–1960* (Princeton: Princeton University Press, 1963).

[29] H. P. Minsky, *John Maynard Keynes* (New York: Columbia University Press, 1975), Chapter 6.

PLAN OF THE BOOK

This book is divided into three parts. Chapters 2 and 3 conclude Part I with a more specific discussion of the nature of banking. Because it deals with the general principles common to all banks, the discussion is relatively abstract. The results derived in these two chapters are referred to throughout the book.

Parts II and III deal with subjects related to particular time horizons. Long-term concerns of the commercial bank are treated in Part II (Chapters 4 through 11). Before bank managers can concern themselves with short-term problems, they must make a number of decisions on such long-term matters as customer base, capital structure, organizational form, and general managerial philosophy. These decisions heavily influence the ultimate success or failure of the bank and cannot be altered over a short period of time.

In Chapter 4, the long-term planning function is examined. The appropriate time horizon for the strategic plans of the bank is discussed along with the objectives and problems of long-range planning. Specific attention is given to how decisions should be made with a view toward maximizing the value of the banking firm.

Chapters 5, 6, and 7 examine the bank's capital structure. In Chapter 5 the reader is introduced to the unconstrained determination of a bank's optimal amount of capital. The appendix to Chapter 5 contains the mathematical derivation of the results given in the chapter. Chapter 6 discusses the internal sources of bank capital, reviewing profit, dividend strategy, and tax planning in some detail. In Chapter 7, the external sources of bank capital are discussed. This chapter examines the cost of capital and the ability of the market to evaluate the riskiness of a bank.

In Chapters 8 through 11, the loan portfolio and its composition are reviewed. Chapter 8 contains a discussion of the annual budgeting process that leads to the long-run plan for construction of the loan portfolio. Types of loans and the terms of the loan contract available to the bank are then examined. Chapter 9 reviews the essentials of credit and market analysis of potential borrowers, and Chapter 10 develops loan pricing schemes. Chapter 11 then looks at the means by which a commercial bank can evaluate the customer once the loan has been made. This process is often called customer profitability analysis.

Part III (Chapters 12 through 14) examines problems of the intermediate and short term. In these chapters, it is assumed that the bank has already made its long-run decisions and thus is ready to make decisions related to reserve settlement periods and credit cycles. Chapter 12 discusses the money markets and the instruments and institutions that are particularly important for bank operations within the intermediate and short term.

Short-run reserve management is treated in Chapter 13. Management decisions relating to the credit cycle are called asset/liability decisions and are the subject matter of Chapter 14. The relevant time horizon in asset/liability management is limited by the shortness of the maturities in which the bank deals in any quantity and the extent to which there exist broad and deep markets in which funds can be bought and sold.

The volume as a whole is designed to present a complete and consistent format for the study of the financial management of commercial banks. Several areas of practical interest or of a mathematical nature do not fit easily into the flow of development of the subject. Because these are important to the student of banking, they are included as appendixes to appropriate chapters. Thus the reader can either follow the main argument of the book by reading the chapters straight through, skipping the appendixes and then returning to them, or read the appendixes in sequence as an extension of the chapter materials.

The appendix to Chapter 1 lists the major sources of current articles relevant to banking. The appendixes to Chapters 2, 3, and 5 give the mathematical derivations of the models presented in those chapters. Chapter 4 has an appendix on correspondent banking, and Chapter 7 is followed by an appendix on how to analyze a bank. The appendix to Chapter 8 discusses how a bank can forecast interest rates and reserve availability, and the appendixes to Chapters 9 and 10 discuss leasing and alternative loan-pricing schemes, respectively. Finally, the bank's investment portfolio is the subject of the appendix to Chapter 14.

SUMMARY

The assets and liabilities of a bank's balance sheet can be grouped into many different classes according to risk, type of loan or deposit, maturity, collateral, and market characteristics. The objective of bank management is to maximize the economic value of the bank, which is to maximize the price of the bank's common stock. To do this, the bank's portfolio of assets and liabilities must be chosen to obtain the greatest return possible for the accepted level of risk. This book develops an integrated framework within which the financial management of the bank can be discussed and presents a unified approach to bank portfolio construction.

The following assumptions, which were introduced in Chapter 1, underlie most of the discussions in later chapters:

- Commercial banks operate, by and large, in imperfectly competitive markets.
- Most banks with which this book is concerned can be assumed to operate under constant costs.
- Rules and regulations in many cases do not allow for a general exposition of banking, and therefore it will be assumed that bank decisions are unconstrained except in those cases in which the rules and regulations are generally binding to all banks.

SELECTED REFERENCES

Baltenspeuger, E. "Economies of Scale, Firm Size and Concentration in Banking." *The Journal of Money, Credit and Banking* (August 1972), pp. 467–88.

———. "Costs of Banking Activities—Interactions Between Risks and Operating Costs." *The Journal of Money, Credit and Banking* (August 1972), pp. 595–612.

Beazer, W. F. *Optimization of Bank Portfolios.* Lexington, Mass.: Lexington Books, 1975.

Bell, F. W., and Murphy, N. B. *Costs in Commercial Banking: A Quantitative Analysis of Bank Behavior and Its Relation to Bank Regulation.* Research Report No. 41, Boston: Federal Reserve Bank of Boston, 1968.

Benston, G. J. "Economies of Scale of Financial Institutions." *The Journal of Money, Credit and Banking* (May 1972), pp. 312–41.

———. "The Optimal Banking Structure: Theory and Evidence." *The Journal of Bank Research* (Winter 1973), pp. 220–37.

Cohen, K. J. and Hammer, F. S. "Linear Programming Models for Optimal Bank Dynamic Balance Sheet Management." In G. P. Szego and K. Shell, eds., *Mathematical Methods in Investment and Finance.* Amsterdam: North-Holland, 1972.

Crosse, H. D., and Hempel, G. H. *Management Policies for Commercial Banks.* Englewood Cliffs, N.J.: Prentice-Hall, 1973.

Edwards, F. R. "Managerial Objectives in Regulated Industries: Expense-Preference Behavior in Banking." *The Journal of Political Economy* (February 1977), pp. 147–62.

———, and Heggestad, A. A. "Uncertainty, Market Structure, and Performance: The Galbraith-Caves Hypothesis and Managerial Motives in Banking." *The Quarterly Journal of Economics* (August 1973), pp. 455–73.

Flannery, M. J. "Credit Unions as Consumer Lenders in the United States." *New England Economic Review*, Federal Reserve Bank of Boston (July/August 1974), pp. 3–12.

Ford, W. F. "Profitability: Why Do Some Banks Perform Better Than Average? An In-Depth Analysis." *Banking* (October 1974).

Fried, J. "Bank Portfolio Selection." *The Journal of Financial and Quantitative Analysis* (June 1970).

Gramley, L. E. *A Study of Scale Economics in Banking.* Kansas City: Federal Reserve Bank of Kansas City, 1962.

Guttentag, J. M., and Herman, E. S. "Banking Structure and Performance." *The Bulletin*, New York University (February 1967).

Hester, D. D., and Pierce, J. L. *Bank Management and Portfolio Behavior.* New Haven: Yale University Press, 1975.

Klein, M. "A Theory of the Banking Firm." *The Journal of Money, Credit and Banking* (May 1971).

Markowitz, H. M. *Portfolio Selection.* New York: John Wiley and Sons, 1959.

Mason, J. M. "Market Discrimination, Credit Rationing and the Customer Relationship at Commercial Banks." Working Paper 2-77, Rodney L. White Center for Financial Research, The University of Pennsylvania, 1977.

———. "Theory of the Banking Firm with Uncertain Demand and Supply of Funds." Finance Department Working Paper, The University of Pennsylvania, 1978.

———. "An Ordered Choice Approach to a Bank's Capital Structure." Finance Department Working Paper, The University of Pennsylvania, 1978.

Minsky, H. P. *John Maynard Keynes.* New York: Columbia University Press, 1975.

Pearce, W. O. "Functional Cost Analysis: A Tool of Bank Management." *Monthly Review*, Federal Reserve Bank of Richmond, 1967. Reprinted in Paul F. Jessup, ed., *Innovations in Bank Management.* New York: Holt, Rinehart and Winston, 1969.

Porter, R. C. "A Model of Bank Portfolio Selection." *Yale Economic Essays* (Fall 1961), pp. 323–59. Reprinted in D. D. Hester and J. Tobin, eds., *Financial Markets and Economic Activity.* New York: John Wiley and Sons, 1967.

Reed, E. W., Cotter, R. V., Gill, E. K., and Smith, R. K. *Commercial Banking.* Englewood Cliffs, N.J.: Prentice-Hall, 1976.

Rees, R. "A Reconsideration of the Expense Preference Theory of the Firm." *Economica* (August 1974), pp. 295–307.

Shull, B. "Commercial Banks as Multi-Product, Price Discriminating Firms." In D. Carson, ed., *Banking and Monetary Studies.* Homewood, Ill.: Richard D. Irwin, 1963.

Tobin, J. "Liquidity Preference as Behavior Towards Risk." *Review of Economic Studies* (February 1958), pp. 65–86.

White, C. M. "Multiple Goals in the Theory of the Firm." In K. E. Boulding and W. A. Spivey, eds., *Linear Programming and the Theory of the Firm.* New York: The Macmillan Co., 1960.

Williamson, O. E. "A Rational Managerial Behavior." In R. M. Cyert and J. G. March, *A Behavioral Theory of the Firm.* Englewood Cliffs, N.J.: Prentice-Hall, 1963.

———. *The Economics of Discretionary Behavior: Managerial Objectives in A Theory of the Firm.* Englewood Cliffs, N.J.: Prentice-Hall, 1964.

Wood, J. H. "A Model of Commercial Bank Loan and Investment Behavior." In H. G. Johnson and A. R. Nobay, eds., *Issues in Monetary Economics.* Oxford University Press, 1974.

REVIEW QUESTIONS

1. In what ways are commercial banks comparable to nonfinancial firms? In what ways are they not?
2. One reason for the heavy regulation of the banking industry is the regulators' belief that banks have been subject to decreasing costs. Do you think their reaction is justified? In what ways might either such a cost structure or the regulators' actions explain the imperfections that exist in banking markets?
3. Bankers have been accused of being very "clubby." They seem to dislike anything or anyone who disturbs the status quo. Is this a sign that the industry is noncompetitive?
4. Is the fear that banks control too much wealth realistic or well-founded? Explain.
5. Money is a very homogeneous product. Therefore, does it make any sense for banks to divide their borrowers into so many classes?

APPENDIX
Sources of Banking Information

There are many sources of current information on banking and topics related to banking. Below are listed some of the publications that regularly have articles or present data about banking and areas related to banking. Since the subject matter of this book is domestic commercial banking, no reference is made to publications having to do with the international aspects of banking.

Daily:
> The American Banker
> The Wall Street Journal
> The New York Times

Weekly:
> Business Week
> The Money Manager
> Barron's

Biweekly:
> Fortune
> Forbes

Monthly:
> Banking
> Bankers Monthly
> The Independent Banker
> Journal of Commercial Bank Lending
> Journal of Bank Administration
> Federal Reserve Bulletin, Board of Governors of the Federal Reserve System
> Monthly Reviews of the District Federal Reserve Banks

Bimonthly:
> The Bankers Magazine

Quarterly:
> Journal of Finance
> Journal of Money, Credit and Banking
> Journal of Bank Research
> Journal of Financial and Quantitative Analysis

Journal of Banking and Finance
Journal of Accounting, Auditing, and Finance
Annual:
Bankers Desk Reference (published 1978, with annual supplements)
Publications in related areas:
Federal Home Loan Bank Board Journal (monthly)
The Mortgage Banker (monthly)
Journal of the Savings and Loan League (monthly)
Mutual Savings Banks Journal (monthly)
Real Estate Review (quarterly)

The Commercial Bank Under Conditions of Certainty and Uncertainty

The banking firm arbitrages between financial markets; it takes advantage of spreads between interest rates in different markets that arise either from conditions peculiar to the markets or from market imperfections. It also uses its ability to pool resources to diversify against the risk inherent in any one customer or market. Chapters 2 and 3 develop the theory of the banking firm and build a general framework that can be used to discuss actual banking practice.

First, a model of the firm is developed from a few simple behavioral assumptions and the firm's objective of maximizing the value of the bank. Next the problem of uncertainty is introduced. (Uncertainty will be defined in the context of the chapter.) Following this, asset markets, liability markets, and their interaction are discussed. Then the portfolio solution for the bank that operates under conditions of certainty is treated, followed by the solution for the bank operating under uncertainty. The chapter closes with a discussion of the recent controversy over asset/liability management and the implications of the model developed in this chapter.

THE BANK

The bank's balance sheet equation, which was presented in its most general form as equation (1-1), is reproduced here:

$$\sum_{i=1}^{m} L_m = \sum_{j=1}^{n} D_j + K \tag{2-1}$$

Two adjustments are made to allow for cash holdings. First, it is assumed that reserves held to satisfy the reserve requirements of either the central bank or another regulatory agency, such as a state banking agency, are netted out against the liabilities they serve. Thus, reserves required against demand deposits are subtracted from the total of demand deposits available on the liability side of the balance sheet.[1]

Second, bankers may wish to hold cash in excess of that required by the regulatory agencies. At present no mechanism will be developed to explain their desire to hold these excess reserves, but there is assumed to be some desired ratio between liabilities and excess reserves.[2] It is then possible to handle these reserves exactly as required reserves were handled, netting them out against the liability to which they apply.[3]

The income statement expressed mathematically in terms of after-tax income, π, is then

$$\pi = (1 - t) \left[\sum_{i=1}^{m} (r_i + f_i - b_i)L_i - \sum_{j=1}^{n} (r_j - f_j + b_j)D_j \right] \tag{2-2}$$

Finally, as mentioned in Chapter 1, it is assumed that the objective of a bank's owners is to maximize the value of their wealthholdings. This means that they want to maximize the net worth of the bank or, in other words, to maximize the price of the bank's stock. Thus, if the riskless rate

[1] If r_d is the reserve requirement on demand deposits and D is the level of demand deposits, then $r_d D$ is the level of required reserves held by the bank. Netting these out against the liability side of the balance sheet leaves the amount $(1 - r_d)D$ as the relevant quantity on the right-hand side of (2-1). This has the effect, as will be shown later, of increasing the effective cost of the liability in question, something that is intended by the regulatory authorities.

[2] This behavior could be explained in terms of an "asset allocation" approach to balance sheet planning. This type of asset management is discussed in Chapter 14.

[3] Thus x_d, the excess reserve ratio, is the amount of excess reserves the bank wishes to hold divided by demand deposits, D, so that excess reserves are $x_d D$. The entry on the liability side of the balance sheet is therefore $(1 - x_d)D$.

of return, ρ, is used to discount future cash flows, then the value of the firm, V, in a situation where returns are certain and cash flows in all future periods are constant and equal to π, is

$$V = \frac{\pi}{\rho} \qquad (2\text{-}3)$$

This formulation can be used if it is assumed that the cash flow in one period is independent of all other cash flows. In the next chapter, when customer relationships are examined, the model will have to be modified in order to account fully for an intertemporal customer–bank association. Thus, maximizing profits in each period maximizes profits in all periods and hence maximizes the value of the firm.

In the case where the bank is uncertain of the demand for and the supply of funds, the valuation formula of (2-3) must be modified. As a first approximation to determining the value of the banking firm under uncertainty,[4] the owners wish to maximize V, which in this case is a risk-adjusted value defined as

$$V = \frac{1}{\rho} [E(\pi) - R\sigma_{\pi m}] \qquad (2\text{-}4)$$

Here, E is the expectations operator, so that $E(\pi)$ is expected profits. The variable R is the market value of a unit of risk. This is defined as $R = [E(R_m) - \rho]/\sigma_m^2$, where R_m is the rate of return to the market portfolio and σ_m^2 is the variance of market returns. The variable $\sigma_{\pi m}$ is the covariance of bank profits with the market. Since the demand for loans and the supply of funds in one period are assumed to be independent of those in other periods, it follows that if the bank maximizes profits in one period, it will maximize them over all periods. Thus, π does not have to relate to any given time period.

Time Horizon of the Model

Before going further, a word should be said about the time horizon of the model. It is convenient to use a one-period model to study bank behavior. Yet in applying the model to real bank problems, the length of the time period chosen can be crucial. The relevant time period in this chapter is

[4] John M. Mason, "Theory of the Banking Firm with Uncertain Demand and Supply of Funds," Finance Department Working Paper, The University of Pennsylvania, 1978.

what is referred to later as the "intermediate time horizon" or the time horizon for asset/liability management. As will be explained more fully in Chapter 12, this time period is, on average, sufficient for the bank's portfolio of assets and liabilities to "turn over" but not long enough for the bank to alter either its customer base or its capital position. Therefore, it is assumed that the bank mades no effort, through its pricing structure, advertising, branch strategy, or other means, to alter its relative market share. It is also assumed that its capital accounts remain constant.[5] Given these constraints, it is estimated that for the model under discussion, the time period may be as short as one month or as long as nine months, depending on the bank, its management philosophy, and its market characteristics.

Certainty and Uncertainty

The characteristics of asset demand and liability supply will initially be discussed with the assumption that the bank knows with certainty the riskiness of each class of assets and liabilities and the market conditions of demand and supply. Knowing these, the bank can adjust returns for risk and base all decisions on risk-adjusted returns. Differences in yields on loans or costs of liabilities would be expressed primarily in terms of the market imperfections that exist for each class.

This case cannot be the only one treated, since bankers do not know exactly what their loan-loss experience will be or what actual demand and supply conditions will be. Moreover, they do not know with any degree of certainty the extent to which market imperfections exist within the different classes of assets and liabilities. Therefore, two types of uncertainty will be introduced into the model:

1. The bank will not know with certainty the exact amounts of demand and supply that will be forthcoming for given interest rates in a market.

2. The bank will not know with certainty the elasticities of the demand and supply curves that exist in the markets in which it operates.

Uncertainty, in portfolio or financial models, has generally been introduced in the sense of not knowing the rate of return that will be earned on the various assets or liabilities held by the firm. This approach is not misleading if the demands and supplies of the assets and liabilities are

---

[5] The model is expanded to discuss capital questions in Chapter 5.

perfectly elastic: Quantity constraints are then unimportant, and any variation in profit is caused by variation in loan yields.[6]

However, in the world of banking, imperfect markets are the general rule rather than the exception. Because of this, the balance sheet constraint (that is, the requirement that assets be equal to liabilities plus net worth) becomes crucial, and uncertainty about quantities rather than about prices takes on added importance. The important implication of this for bank behavior is that liquidity becomes the most significant aspect of certain asset markets or liability markets, and in some cases the ability to obtain funds becomes more important to the bank than the cost of the funds.

ASSET/LIABILITY CLASSIFICATIONS

Liability classifications are easily defined. They are determined by the legal definition of the type of account (such as demand deposits or savings deposits); by type of instrument (certificates of deposit as opposed to Eurodollars); and by maturity. Since these market segments are fairly well determined, commercial banks need spend very little time or money to separate them further, although when the need for funds becomes great they will make an effort to redefine markets or instruments in an attempt to obtain more funds. This often leads to a period of financial innovation, such as the development of the negotiable certificate of deposit in the early 1960s, the Eurodollar in the later 1960s, and the variable rate note in the early 1970s.

Some differentiation of asset classifications is easily achieved. For example, loans can be classified according to type of borrower (individual, firm, or government), type of loan (secured or unsecured), and maturity.

The commercial bank usually goes a bit further in its loan classification scheme, grouping customers on the basis of risk and market position.[7] Credit analysis, market analysis, and industry analysis are means by which the bank can separate its customers into a larger number of loan classifications. These are information-seeking efforts, and information is costly. Therefore, although the bank desires more and more information, it is willing to obtain additional information only if doing so adds more to profits, by affording either a better evaluation of risk or a better evaluation of the market position of the borrower, than it adds to costs. This limits the

[6] John M. Mason, "The Difference Between a Mutual Fund and a Commercial Bank," Finance Department Working Paper, The University of Pennsylvania, 1978.

[7] The reasons for this process of differentiation and separation are presented more fully in the next section of this chapter.

amount of information a bank will seek on customers; the number of loan classes will be less than the total number of borrowers.

In addition, since there is uncertainty as to whether the credit analysis can accurately measure a given company's riskiness and its market position, the bank will generally have fewer loan classifications based on risk than it would if those classifications represented exact information. In fact, the number of risk classes may be limited to four or five, with two or three more distinctions made on the basis of market characteristics, and the resulting categories may be further subdivided, as mentioned earlier, according to type of borrower, industry, type of collateral, and loan maturity.

ASSET MARKETS

Asset markets are initially divided into two segments, investments and loans. This division makes sense in that loans are generally made directly to the borrowers, whereas investments are purchased in secondary markets. It is to be expected that the credit analysis and market analysis that go into each will be somewhat different.

Bank Investments

General Considerations   A bank's investments consist of U.S. government securities, government agency securities, state and local government issues, and other types of instruments the bank can legally purchase. The credit analysis for the first two of these is minimal. The extent of the analysis needed for the others varies with the bank and its management philosophy. Banks often rely on rating services to do the credit analysis for them. The types of securities held will depend on the bank's size and management policy.

Government securities require very little market analysis. In general, the markets they are traded in are broad enough and deep enough that no one bank would be able to affect the price at which an issue was traded, regardless of the amount the bank wanted to buy or sell. The supply of these instruments (or, to look at it another way, the demand for bank funds from market participants) is assumed to be perfectly elastic, as shown in Figure 2-1A; banks can obtain all the government securities they want at the going market interest rate, r_G.[8]

---

[8] This assumes that even the bigger banks will not purchase securities or dump them

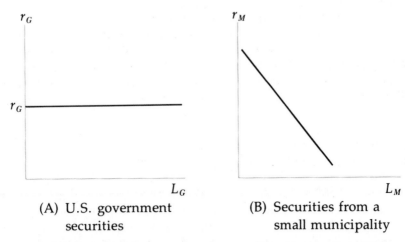

(A) U.S. government
securities

(B) Securities from a
small municipality

FIGURE 2-1   Typical Supply Curves of Investment Securities

Some other securities a bank might invest in are not traded on markets that meet the qualifications set out above for the government securities markets. This is because the issues of some borrowers may not be very large or their credit rating may not be as good. As a consequence, the supply curve of these securities (to the bank) slopes downward, as shown in Figure 2-1B. If the bank wishes to hold more of these securities, it will be able to do so only by receiving a lower yield on its investment.

Costs of buying and selling, say b_G for government securities, will lower the effective yield received on these instruments. These costs may vary for different banks; a money-center bank would probably find b_G lower than would a small rural bank. However, correspondent relationships may keep costs of buying and selling low for the smaller bank. If there are no economies or diseconomies of transacting—that is, if costs do not become greater or smaller with the amount of securities held or traded—these costs should only shift the perfectly elastic curve shown in Figure 2-1A downward by the amount b_G to a parallel position.

In the case of imperfectly supplied securities (Figure 2-1B), the curve would also shift downward by the amount b_M at every quantity of the security supplied. (M is used here to stand for "municipal issue.")

---

within a day or two. The time chosen for the single period of the model is, at a minimum, one month. If any bank spaces its purchases or sales over this time horizon, they will have little effect on market prices.

Uncertainty Uncertainty will affect only the market of inelastically supplied securities, since the bank is more concerned about quantity uncertainty than rate uncertainty. A security that is elastically supplied, such as U.S. government securities in Figure 2-1A, has no quantity uncertainty.

The interest rates on elastically supplied investments may vary, but that has little to do with managing the balance sheet. Thus, no alteration need be made to the supply curve of government securities.[9] This will not be the case for securities supplied inelastically to the bank. Since these instruments are purchased on secondary markets, there is no uncertainty about overall demand for funds from their suppliers; there are fixed quantities of the securities traded on the secondary market. The only source of uncertainty, therefore, is the risk of default. Thus, when it purchases some of these securities, the bank must be concerned with the possibility that at some time the issuer may fail and the bank will lose or find worthless its holdings of L_M and be unable to meet its balance sheet constraint. Uncertainty will therefore cause the supply curve of L_M, as perceived by the bank and as represented in Figure 2-1B, to shift downward and to the left.

In general, both curves will shift with changes in other market interest rates, which may be caused by economic activity and the monetary or fiscal policy of the federal government, or with changes in the supplies of the securities entering or leaving the secondary market arising from new primary financings or the paying off of existing issues. The extent to which the supply curve for each instrument responds depends on how close a substitute or complement it is to other market instruments.

Bank Loans

General Considerations The situation for bank loans is somewhat different. Here the bank must put considerable effort into credit analysis and market analysis. Whereas some information can be obtained from credit collecting and rating services, the bulk of the collection and review is done within the bank itself. Thus, administrative costs will play a bigger role in loan portfolio decisions than they do in determining the securities portion of the portfolio. The bank must be even more careful because no secondary market exists for most of the kinds of loans with which it deals.

It is easy to see why previous experience with the customer is such an important factor in bank decisions. Previous experience means knowledge

[9] The proof of this is derived in Mason, "The Difference Between a Mutual Fund and a Commercial Bank."

of the borrower's operations over many years, knowledge of the people who run the organization, and knowledge of the customer's repayment practices. All these things give the bank more information at a lower cost than would be the case with a new customer. Therefore, differences in administrative cost may lead to preferential pricing for those borrowers who have established a long and satisfactory history of dealing with the bank, because the bank can determine the riskiness of such a customer at lower cost, or for the same cost can better identify the true riskiness of the borrower.

Another major difference between bank loan and securities markets is that the bank loan market is predominantly an imperfectly competitive market (that is, the bank faces downward sloping demand curves), whereas many of the securities the bank trades in are characterized by perfect elasticity.

This must be qualified by saying that the lender faces many different degrees of imperfection, which depend on the bank and its markets. For example, large banks that deal with national and multinational firms generally find that they face relatively (if not completely) elastic demand curves in the prime loan market. Thus, even the largest bank will contend that it simply "follows the market" when dealing with prime customers. The demand curves of the other customers of the bank, however, will exhibit some degree of inelasticity. On the other hand, a smaller bank that is relatively isolated geographically will find the demand for loans fairly inelastic, even for its best customers.

These market imperfections should not necessarily be considered to be independent of the riskiness associated with the given loan class. A borrower that is riskier than others will not only find the cost of funds higher but may also have fewer alternative sources of funds than a less risky borrower; hence such a borrower will be associated with a less elastic demand curve. A riskier borrower may also find that although the same number of lenders are willing to supply funds, the amount available from each is reduced because of the higher risk.

The general situation, then, is one where the bank has a number of different loan customers that may be separated into several different loan classes, according to type of borrower, type of loan, collateral, risk, alternative sources of funds, loan maturity, and past borrowing experience at the bank. Because of the limitations imposed on the bank by the cost of information, each class is considered homogeneous with respect to these factors. Each has its own demand characteristics. Each is responsive, in some degree, to the rates charged on its borrowings from the bank and on alternative sources of funds (if any); to national, local, and industry economic factors; and to the relationship it has built up with individual banks.

Uncertainty Uncertainty is a more important factor for bank loans than for investments, for three reasons:

1. In general, the risk of default is greater for bank loans than for most of the securities held by a bank.

2. The demand curves for loans tend to be less elastic than those the bank faces in the open markets for securities. Thus, the variability of loan demand becomes more important for most banks than the variability of the supply of securities. This factor may cause some cyclical problems, particularly for larger banks, as well as secular problems, as a bank may experience either extremely heavy loan demands when the economy booms or extremely light loan demands during periods of recession. This is, of course, another reason why the good, steady loan customer is so valuable to the bank.[10]

3. Knowledge of the elasticity of demand of a loan class is vital if the bank is to price the class correctly. Uncertainty about elasticities makes pricing extremely difficult. It will be shown in Chapter 3 that, in the absence of knowledge about these elasticities, banks have developed rules of thumb for determining relative loan rates.

THE MULTIPRODUCT FIRM—
THE DISCRIMINATING MONOPOLIST

The theory of the discriminating monopolist has often been applied to the commercial banking firm. This theory may not at first seem applicable to banking because, except for a few geographically isolated cases, commercial banks are not monopolists. However, current organizational theory gives an explanation of why a number of firms, without engaging in collusive action, may act like a single monopoly firm. Paul Joskow explains how this type of behavior can exist in terms of what he calls the "proximity" of firms; firms in close proximity to one another "produce the same product, use similar technologies, or are in contact with one another via market exchanges of products."[11] Banks certainly can be thought of as "close" to

---

[10] A smaller bank may not experience such wide cyclical swings in loan demand because of its limited geographical exposure or because most of its borrowers are good, steady customers.

[11] Paul L. Joskow, "Firm Decision Making Processes and Oligopoly Theory," *The American Economic Review* (May 1975), pp. 276–77.

one another in this sense. It can be assumed, then, that although many commercial banks may compete within a given market, they may act as a monopoly in terms of loan classifications and pricing schemes.

The discriminating monopolist is a firm that can effectively separate its customers into different market segments and price each market segment differently. The most important factor in the division of customers is the elasticity of demand forthcoming from each market segment. The theory is well developed in the economic literature[12] and already has found significant application in banking literature.[13]

Essentially, what a bank or group of banks can accomplish in its credit and market analysis is the separation of customers into homogeneous loan classifications. These are homogeneous in the sense that the bank and all other banks will tend to put similar firms in similar loan classes. This allows the bank, or group of banks, to price each class differently. As is shown in the economic literature, differential pricing affords higher profits than the firm would obtain if it made no distinction among customers. If a bank or group of banks cannot classify borrowers in a meaningful and sustainable way, it will not be able to maintain the differential pricing scheme. This factor highlights the "proximity" question, because the assumption of proximity requires that other banks also maintain similar loan classifications. If the industry were not able to sustain the different loan classes, then the banks as an industry would not be able to maintain differential pricing.

It is assumed, therefore, that commercial banks operate as discriminating monopolists, separating customers into different loan classes so as to price differentially and raise bank profits.[14] They will collect information in an effort to aid classification up to the point where the added cost of obtaining more information is just equal to the added profits that can be achieved by the added differentiation.

CREDIT AND MARKET ANALYSIS

Commercial banks have spent most of their time and resources on determining the default risk associated with an individual firm, and very little

---

[12] James M. Henderson and Richard E. Quardt, *Microeconomic Theory*, 2nd ed. (New York: McGraw-Hill Book Company, 1971), pp. 215–18.

[13] Bernard Shull, "Commercial Banks as Multi-Product, Price-Discriminating Firms," in Deane Carson, ed., *Banking and Monetary Studies* (Homewood, Ill.: Richard D. Irwin, 1963).

[14] Banks, in the real world, may price different classes slightly differently because of differences in costs. However, competition will be sufficient to force higher-cost banks to

time and effort on studying the elasticity of demand in their loan markets. It could be argued that a bank could obtain greater profits by devoting more resources to studying elasticity characteristics and pricing more efficiently. However, bankers have less information on the elasticity of demand of various customers or customer classes than they have on the riskiness of the borrower or borrowers. Thus, whereas this chapter and the next place a great deal of emphasis on knowing the elasticity of demand, it is not at all unlikely that bankers have acted wisely in allocating more time and money to analyzing credit risks than to analyzing demand conditions. This does not mean that banks should not try to obtain more information in this area, only that the rewards per dollar spent may not be as great.

LIABILITY MARKETS

General Characteristics

The commercial bank benefits from being able to separate the suppliers of liabilities into different markets, just as it benefits from being able to classify its borrowers. Differentiating its liability markets allows the bank to reduce its average cost per dollar of funds.

As was mentioned earlier, liability markets are generally easier to distinguish than asset markets because they are often separated according to instrument and maturity. The instruments themselves are usually suited to the demand characteristics associated with them. However, uncertainty also plays a role.

For example, demand deposits are generally wanted for transactions purposes, and hence the demanders of these are not extremely sensitive to the interest rates paid either on the demand deposits themselves or on other short-term instruments. Consumer-type time accounts, such as passbook savings accounts, serve as a "temporary abode of purchasing power" or as a means of holding precautionary balances. Whereas some interest return may be desired on these instruments, they are not very interest sensitive unless the rates paid on them depart very much from open-market rates, such as yields on U.S. Treasury bills.[15]

---

adjust their technology to reduce costs or else be less profitable than lower-cost banks. Real world differentials exist, then, because the banks are in transitional states or because the markets are so imperfect as to allow these differentials to exist.

[15] The new EFTS technology has caused and will continue to cause a blurring of the distinctions drawn here.

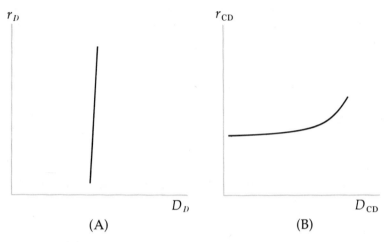

FIGURE 2-2   Typical Supply-of-Funds Curves

Longer-term time certificates are important in the portfolio decisions of individuals, and negotiable certificates of deposit are excellent for corporations wishing to place surplus funds for short periods of time. One characteristic that differentiates the supply of these instruments from that of demand deposits or passbook savings accounts is their interest elasticity. Differentiation of price in liability markets is based on this market characteristic, just as it is in the banks' asset markets. Two types of liability markets are shown in Figure 2-2.

Figure 2-2A shows the supply of funds available to a bank through demand deposits. Although one may talk about the demand for demand deposits on the part of wealthholders, it is more meaningful in the present context to treat it as a supply of funds to the commercial bank. Note that the supply curve is completely inelastic, because explicit interest payments to holders of demand deposits are legally forbidden. Depositors may receive implicit interest payments, by receiving more services on their demand accounts than they pay for in service charges, but only explicit interest payments are reflected in these charts. Implicit payments will be treated later.

The supply of funds through consumer-type time accounts is quite inelastic, although it would not be completely inelastic as in the case of demand deposits. In contrast, the supply curve of funds from negotiable certificates of deposit is seen to be quite elastic (Figure 2-2B), at least over a large volume of CDs. These funds are extremely sensitive to movements in interest rates, and it is to be expected that one bank, at least over much of the supply curve and in "normal" times,[16] will not be able to affect the interest rate paid on these instruments by varying the quantity taken from the market.

Administrative Costs

Differential costs play a big role in these markets. Administrative costs, as can be seen in equation (2-2), are additive in the case of liabilities and so push up any given supply curve. Costs can have a significant effect on the different interest rates the bank pays on its liabilities, as can be seen by comparing the costs of time and passbook savings accounts against the costs of negotiable CDs. Consumer-type time accounts are more expensive to administer than negotiable CDs. The supply curve of these consumer-type time accounts will therefore be shifted up further, for a given quantity, than the supply curve of CDs. Obviously, this will affect portfolio choices.

As mentioned earlier, the provision of services without offsetting charges can result in implicit interest payments on an account even though payment of explicit interest is forbidden. In the case of demand deposits, even though $r_D = 0$ by law, $r_D - f_D + b_D$ can be greater than zero, because f_D (fees charged) may be less than the actual expense of administering the accounts. Thus, the model may show a positive cost of all liability accounts. This condition should be remembered when the model result is compared with actual practice.

Uncertainty—Demand Deposits and Consumer Savings Accounts

Uncertainty plays its role in these markets. It is perhaps most evident in the variability of demand deposit accounts. Funds in these accounts are payable on demand and represent, in many banks, the most variable component of bank liabilities. Historically, movements in these accounts have been a major factor in forcing some commercial banks into positions in which they have had to convert assets at unfavorable prices. Although the assurance given depositors by the Federal Deposit Insurance Corporation has reduced the variability of demand deposits, these accounts have still caused some banks, particularly troubled ones, a great deal of difficulty.

[16] By "normal" times is meant times when neither excessive tightness nor excessive looseness exists in the money markets due to the Federal Reserve policy or to other causes.

Consumer savings accounts are also subject to some uncertainty in terms of the quantities left on deposit. However, variation in these accounts has been forced on the banking system at particular times in the credit cycle by the Federal Reserve's administration of its Regulation Q ceiling. Regulation Q gives the Federal Reserve System authority to set maximum rates on time and savings accounts at member commercial banks. The ceiling set by the Federal Reserve, when effective, can cause wide spreads to develop between rates paid on consumer time accounts and open-market yields, such as those that can be earned on U.S. Treasury bills. This can cause a greater loss of funds from these accounts than would have occurred in the absence of the restrictive Regulation Q ceiling.

Bankers do not have to be too concerned, however, about information on the elasticity of supply of time and savings accounts. All the evidence available suggests that the supply curves of these funds are quite inelastic. A bank will not lose much money if it does not know the exact elasticity of these curves, because interest rates on these accounts will generally be low and the suppliers will not be very responsive to the rates paid on alternative investments. Furthermore, the bank may be able to underprice consumer savings accounts and still retain most of the accounts because these depositors may also have demand deposit accounts at the bank. This means that a covariance between demand deposits and consumer savings accounts may take on some importance in determining interest costs.

Uncertainty—Corporate Accounts

The situation may be somewhat different for corporate accounts, because the elasticity of supply for these accounts may be much greater than for other accounts. When funds are supplied elastically, variations in quantity are not crucial, because the markets are perfectly liquid for the bank, which allows it to engage in liability management. If the bank can purchase all the liabilities it wants at the going market rate of interest, then it can meet its balance sheet constraints without suboptimizing.

If the bank cannot obtain funds elastically in these markets, then the markets cannot be considered perfectly liquid, and the bank cannot be a liability manager. Thus, knowledge of the elasticity of supply becomes extremely important for a bank that wants to rely on selling liabilities for its liquidity. If it cannot obtain funds without affecting the price it pays for the funds, then it cannot be a liability management bank. If the supply of funds is not perfectly elastic, then these accounts must be treated in a way similar to those discussed in the previous section.

Another situation could occur. Banks may assume that they can buy funds elastically in these markets at all times. However, this may not be true in times of tight money. For example, many regional banks could buy funds elastically in times of easy money, but in times of tight credit, such as the 1974–1975 period, they found their supply of funds curve less than perfectly elastic. They were obviously forced into a suboptimal position.

The practical application of liability management must also take into consideration the term structure of interest rates pertaining to these instruments.[17] Recall that the time horizon being discussed in this model is approximately one to nine months. The bank can obtain funds through very short-term borrowing in the federal funds market or, for longer periods of time, in the market for negotiable certificates of deposit. Interest rate spreads between federal funds and negotiable CDs may be very important. If, in the absence of any expectation of a rise in interest rates, the bank can continually turn over federal funds borrowings at cheaper rates than it must pay to borrow on negotiable CDs, then there is a great incentive for it to do so (other than to obtain greater flexibility). This would be the case if a "liquidity premium" existed in the short-term market.

To avoid such problems at this time, it will be assumed that interest rates are expected to remain constant and that the market does not require a "liquidity premium" in this range of the term structure. Thus, the federal funds rate, net of administrative costs, will be assumed to be equal to the rate paid on negotiable certificates of deposit. Differences in portfolio composition will then result from differences in the perceived elasticity of the supply of each asset or liability.

OPTIMAL PORTFOLIO COMPOSITION— THE CERTAINTY CASE

All the strands of the discussion can now be brought together to determine the optimal asset/liability portfolio of the bank.

For simplicity, only two assets and two liabilities will be used at first. The two assets are an elastically supplied investment vehicle, such as U.S. government securities, and loans that are supplied inelastically, but not completely inelastically. These curves are shown in Figure 2-3A. The curve L_G, representing the supply of government securities, is horizontal at the going market interest rate, r_G^0. The curve labeled L_l is the supply of loans to the bank, or conversely, the demand for borrowings from the bank. This

---

[17] For a discussion of the term structure of interest rates, see Chapter 12, on asset and liability markets.

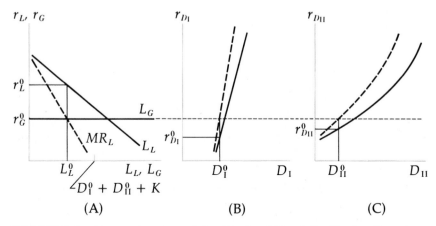

FIGURE 2-3   Determination of the Optimal Portfolio Under Certainty

curve slopes downward, showing that the bank can lend more only if it lowers its interest rate on loans.

The dotted line labeled MR_l is the revenue curve that is marginal to the demand for loans curve and is quite important in determining the optimal asset portfolio of the bank. It represents, for each quantity of loans the bank makes, the added revenue that accrues to the bank from the last dollar increment of loans.

The supply curve for government securities does not have a separate marginal revenue curve, because the supply of government securities to the bank is perfectly elastic. The marginal revenue of government securities is the interest rate paid on these issues for every quantity the bank can obtain. Therefore, the marginal revenue curve coincides with the supply curve.

The government securities rate must be interpreted in a slightly different way, however, to understand the operations of portfolio choice in this model. Rather than being the marginal revenue of investing in government securities, it must be regarded as the *marginal opportunity cost* of not investing in loans. Since the bank can invest in only two assets (loans and government securities), it can choose to invest in loans or not to. If it invests in loans, it receives the marginal revenue of the additional loans, but in doing so it gives up the marginal revenue that it could have earned by investing in government securities. Thus, the latter marginal revenue is the opportunity cost of choosing loans over government investments.

The optimal portfolio, therefore, will be at the loan quantity where the marginal revenue of loans is exactly equal to the marginal opportunity cost of investing in government securities. This is denoted by the intersection of MR_L and r_G^0 in Figure 2-3A. Here the optimal amount of loans the bank will carry is L_L^0.

To show that this is the optimal amount, consider what would happen to revenue if some other loan quantity were chosen. Look at Figure 2-4, which is just a reproduction of Figure 2-3A, and assume that the bank reduces its loans from L_L^0 to $L_L^0 - \$1$. In doing so, it would give up an amount of revenue somewhat greater than r_G^0, say $r_G^0 + X$, as shown in the figure. However, investing the additional dollar in government securities would increase revenues by r_G^0. Hence, profits would go down, because the net loss per dollar of assets would be $r_G^0 + X - r_G^0 = X$.

The same would be true of an increase in loans from L_L^0 to $L_L^0 + \$1$. Again refer to Figure 2-4. Here the increase in revenues by the addition of a dollar in loans would be somewhat less than r_G^0, say $r_G^0 - Y$. The revenue lost due to a $1 reduction in investments would be r_G^0. Profits would again decline, because the net loss in revenue would be $r_G^0 - (r_G^0 - Y) = Y$. Hence, L_L^0 is the optimal loan quantity for this bank under the conditions postulated.

The determination of the quantity of U.S. government securities the bank will hold must wait until the liability side is discussed. As shown in

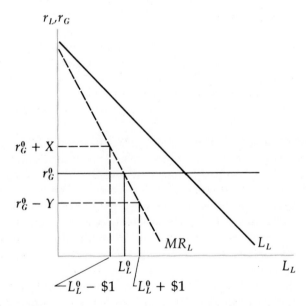

FIGURE 2-4   Determination of Optimal Quantity of Loans

Figure 2-3, only two types of liabilities are offered to the public by this bank. Type I deposits, D_I, can be considered to be a combination of demand deposits and time and passbook savings accounts. An explicit interest rate is allowed, possibly a weighted average rate, and the supply of funds is assumed to be quite interest inelastic (as shown in Figure 2-3B). Type II deposits can be thought of as consisting of different types of certificates of deposit or other liabilities that are quite responsive to interest rates and therefore have a relatively elastic supply curve (Figure 2-3C).

The dashed lines above the supply curves of the two types of liabilities in parts B and C of the figure are the marginal cost curves pertaining to the respective supply curves.[18] These curves will obviously play a crucial role in the optimal amounts of liabilities of each type to be held by the bank. In fact, the optimal amounts of each liability will be the quantity at which the marginal revenue of government securities is equal to the marginal cost of the liability under examination. This occurs at the quantity D_I^0 for Type I liabilities and at the quantity D_{II}^0 for Type II liabilities.

These amounts of liabilities are optimal because movements away from the amounts D_I^0 and D_{II}^0 will reduce the bank's profitability. For example, reducing deposits of Type I from D_I^0 to $D_I^0 - \$1$ will reduce costs by $r_G^0 - Z$, but the resulting \$1 reduction in investment in government securities will reduce revenues by r_G^0. Profits will decrease by $r_G^0 - (r_G^0 - Z) = Z$. Increasing deposits of Type I by \$1, from D_I^0 to $D_I^0 + \$1$, will increase costs by $r_G^0 + W$ and will increase revenues by r_G^0. Again, profits will decline, this time by the amount $r_G^0 + W - r_G^0 = W$. The situation for deposits of Type II can be treated in a similar fashion.

Knowing the equilibrium marginal revenue for the bank, r_G^0, makes it possible to determine the optimal amount of deposits of Type I and Type II. When the amount of these funds and of the bank's capital funds, K (which are assumed to be constant over the time horizon being discussed), are known, the total sources of funds available for investment in loans and securities can be obtained. The optimal amount of government securities in the bank's portfolio can now be determined. Subtracting the optimal quantity of loans, L_L^0, from total liabilities and net worth, $D_I^0 + D_{II}^0 + K$, leaves the amount of funds to be invested in these securities. The amount can be determined in Figure 2-3A by plotting $D_I^0 + D_{II}^0 + K$ on the L_L, L_G axis. One note of clarification about this optimal portfolio is in order: The supply curves of Type I and Type II deposits are net of cash holdings the bank desires or is forced to hold relative to the respective deposit amounts.

---

[18] For a proof that the marginal cost curves lie above the supply curves, see the appendix to this chapter.

Now it can be seen that the interest rate on loans is higher than the interest rate received on government securities. Furthermore, the interest rates paid on Type I and Type II liabilities are below the rate on government securities, and the less interest-elastic liability, Type I deposits, will bear a lower interest rate than the more elastic Type II deposits.

The average spread can be computed either as the spread between the loan rate, r_L^0, and the weighted average cost of liabilities, $(r_{D_I}^0 D_I^0 + r_{D_{II}}^0 D_{II}^0)/(D_I^0 + D_{II}^0)$, or as the spread between the weighted average return on assets,

$$\frac{r_L^0 L_L^0 + r_G^0 (D_I^0 + D_{II}^0 + K - L_L^0)}{L_L^0 + (D_I^0 + D_{II}^0 + K - L_L^0)}$$

and the weighted average cost of liabilities.

More Assets and Liabilities

The last thing to be considered in this section is the expansion of the asset and liability menus to include m asset and n liability classes. This is done by considering a demand curve for loans in each asset class and a supply curve of funds in each liability class. There will be $m - 1$ charts for assets and n charts for liabilities. The number of asset charts is $m - 1$ because it is assumed that the government market is the sole market, for the time being, in which securities are supplied elastically or funds are supplied elastically. Each class will have its own demand or supply characteristics as represented by the elasticity of demand or supply. The optimal size of the bank will be determined by the condition that the interest rate on government securities, r_G^0 (i.e., the marginal revenue of investments), is equal to the marginal cost of each liability of the bank. The optimal asset portfolio is determined by equating the government rate with the marginal revenue in each asset class. The amount of government securities held will then be the residual $D_I^0 + D_{II}^0 + \cdots + D_n^0 - L_1^0 - L_2^0 - \cdots - L_{m-1}^0$. Average spreads can be computed as shown in the preceding paragraph.

OPTIMAL PORTFOLIO COMPOSITION—
THE UNCERTAINTY CASE

Introducing uncertainty into the picture changes things slightly. In all cases, the perceived demand or supply curve, that is, the actual demand curve and supply curve the bank will ultimately face, may differ from the expected curves the bank uses to make up its portfolio of assets and

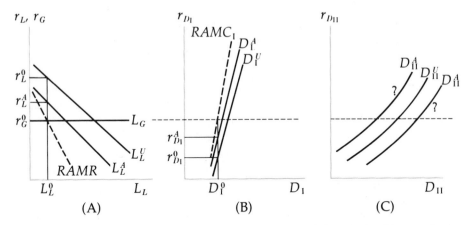

FIGURE 2-5   Determination of the Optimal Portfolio Under Uncertainty

liabilities. In the model presented in this book, there are several reasons why actual behavior may be different from expected behavior.

The bank has two concerns about the quantity of loans it will have on its books at the end of the period, or on which it will receive interest and principal payments. First, the loan demand that the bank actually encounters could be greater or smaller than expected. Second, defaults too could be more or less than the amount planned on. The bank works with an expected loan demand curve. The net effect of taking into account the default risk of a loan class and the potential variance of demand with changes in market conditions is that loan demand, at each market rate, must be adjusted by the bank for the risk that demand may be other than expected.

This can be seen in Figure 2-5A, where curve L_L^U is the loan demand curve unadjusted for the uncertainty of default and possible covariance with the market. This was the curve used for decisions under certainty. In choosing its optimal portfolio when the uncertainties mentioned above are present, the bank uses the curve L_L^A.

The government securities curve is not affected, because there is no quantity uncertainty with respect to the supply of these securities. There may be rate uncertainty, but this is a minimal problem for the bank, because the liquidity of the market is more important to the bank than the actual return on the funds. Thus, the bank will use the expected government rate, r_G^0, to determine its *ex ante* portfolio, and the potential variation in the rate will play no role at all.[19]

[19] The proof of this is in the appendix.

The optimal level of loans will be less under uncertainty than when demand is certain. The relevant marginal revenue curve is the one related to L_L^A. The risk-adjusted marginal revenue of loans, RAMR, is set equal to the expected marginal opportunity cost of funds, r_G^0, to determine the *ex ante* optimal quantity of loans, L_L^0. The rate that will be charged on these loans is r_L^0, because this is the expected market curve, higher than in the certainty case, and the expected return on these loans is r_L^A. The latter rate is the appropriate one to use in determining the profit of the firm, because it takes into account the cost to the bank of subjecting itself to the uncertainty of this market. Over time, if loan demand performs in a truly random fashion, this amount will be used to offset loan demand that is higher than expected or lower than expected. That is, the difference is a payment to the bank for accepting this uncertainty.

With respect to deposits, the only risk is that supply may differ from the expected amount. For some types of deposits the results seem unambiguous; for others the effects are not so clear.

The supply of Type I deposits, which is highly interest inelastic, seems to affect the bank in the way shown in Figure 2-5B. Because of the high variability of these deposits, banks adjust their expectations, under uncertainty, to the supply curve D_I^A, rather than use the market curve D_I^V. Optimal quantity is again determined at the point where the marginal revenue of government securities, r_G^0, is equal to the risk-adjusted marginal cost of Type I deposits. This will result in a lower interest rate on demand deposits in the uncertainty case than in the certainty case. The risk-adjusted cost, $r_{D_I}^A$, will be higher than the certainty cost.

Figure 2-5C presents an entirely different picture. The adjusted supply curve in this case may shift upward to the left or downward to the right. The result is an empirical one relevant to the individual bank and cannot be judged *a priori*. The trouble here is that the correlation between different liabilities and the market may be positive or negative and may cause the supply curves to shift upward or downward depending on the relationship.[20] There is no empirical evidence to show which result can be expected.

If the curve shifts upward to the left, the conclusion will be the same as in the case of Type I deposits. If it shifts downward and to the right, the following results are obtained: First, the rate paid by the bank will be higher in the uncertainty case than in the certainty case. In fact, the rate on these liabilities could exceed the interest rate on government securities. This might explain why some banks (primarily large regional banks and

---

[20] This is fully explained in the appendix to this chapter.

some medium-sized banks) pay higher rates on these purchased funds than the very largest banks, which pay rates very close to the government rate. Second, the risk-adjusted cost of these funds may be higher or lower than the cost of the funds under certainty. The result is ambiguous. Third, if the supply curve shifts downward to the right, the optimal quantity of Type II deposits will be greater than either the certainty case or the case of the supply curve shifting upward and to the left.

In general, although the bank will still be maximizing the value of the owners' wealth, the value of the bank under uncertainty will be smaller than it would in a world of certainty. The reasons are obvious. The bank will in general be smaller: It will allocate more funds to "liquid" assets, in the present case U.S. government securities, that earn a lower return; expected earnings from loans will be smaller due to defaults and due to the uncertainty of demand; and finally, the expected costs of deposits will be higher. These are not unexpected results.

ASSET/LIABILITY MANAGEMENT—
THE CONTROVERSY

In recent years there has been considerable discussion about the viability of a bank using liability markets as a permanent source of liquidity. The above model can be extended to throw some light on the controversy surrounding this subject. The situation presented in Figure 2-3 shows an asset-management situation. The marginal revenue earned from holding U.S. government securities determines the optimal liability structure of the bank. The only problem the bank has to solve is the allocation of this quantity of funds plus capital between loans and investments or, in the multicustomer case, among various asset classes. The bank does not engage in liability management, because it is unprofitable to do so; it is obtaining more than enough funds to satisfy the "legitimate" loan demands it faces.

In Figure 2-3, it is obvious that the optimal amount of loans on the bank's books is less than the sum of the liabilities and capital of the bank. Suppose the bank's market is such that, through expansion into national or international markets, loan demand expands so as to shift the demand curve for loans to a position where the optimal quantity of loans exceeds this amount. A situation like this is described in Figure 2-6A, where the supply curves for Type I and Type II deposits are the same as in Figure 2-3.

The question is, What will the bank do? The bank will not hold any

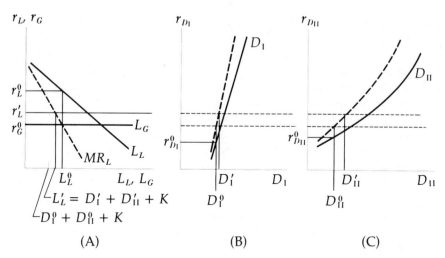

FIGURE 2-6   Optimal Portfolio Conditions for a Liability Management
             Bank Under Certainty Without an Elastic Supply
             of Type II Deposits

government securities, and hence r_G^0 ceases to be the basis of the bank's decisions about its optimal portfolio. The decision will still be made by equating marginal revenues and marginal costs, but now only loans and the two types of liabilities are considered. The optimal size of the bank is $D_I' + D_{II}' + K$, and the optimal amount of loans held is $L_L' = D_I' + D_{II}' + K$.

This situation, however, does not possess all the characteristics of modern liability management. For example, if risk is introduced with respect to the variability of loan demand and deposit supply, the bank could easily find itself forced, from time to time, into a suboptimal position. This is because an unexpectedly large loan demand or an unexpectedly small deposit supply could force the bank to pay nonoptimal rates in order to meet its balance sheet requirements. If the supply curves of liabilities are quite inelastic, rates might be astronomical or funds might not be available at any price. This would not be a very comfortable world for the banker, and hence something must be added to this scenario in order to yield a more accurate portrayal of the complete modern liability-management world.

What needs to be added is a financial innovation. A market is needed with enough participants and enough money to have interest rates in it unaffected by the activity of any one bank. That is, a market is needed where funds will be supplied elastically to banks. This is shown by chang-

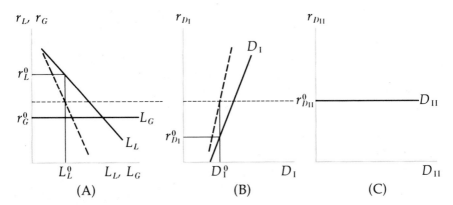

FIGURE 2-7   Optimal Portfolio Conditions for a Liability Management
Bank Under Certainty

ing the supply conditions underlying the supply curve of Type II deposits
in Figure 2-6C to that in Figure 2-7C.[21]

A market like this is necessary for true liability management, and the
development of the federal funds market in the late 1950s and the negotiable certificates of deposit market in the early 1960s provided the means for
banks to engage fully in liability management. It was the large New York
City banks that pioneered in national and international markets and
created a situation where their demand for loans exceeded their ability to
obtain funds from markets that supplied funds inelastically. Therefore, it
was necessary to find or create markets that allowed them to satisfy this
demand.

The optimal conditions are the same as before, except that now a
"true" marginal cost of funds exists. The amount of Type II liabilities
purchased will now be the balance sheet residual when optimal loan quantities and inelastically supplied funds are taken into account. That is, the
bank will buy an amount $L_L^0 - D_I^0 - K$ of Type II deposits.

As shown in Figure 2-7, the asset portfolio of the bank will be entirely
in loans.[22] If a multiasset bank is considered, only loans that were not

---

[21] This supply curve is drawn slightly above the government rate because it represents the
cost of money in the market for negotiable CDs, and these costs have historically been higher
than the government rate. At a lower limit, it is not expected that the latter rates will be less
than government rates, so that in the limit the supply curve would be at the same level as r_G^0.
No government securities will be held, and the CD rate will become the marginal cost because
CD funds are needed by the bank to satisfy the balance sheet requirement.

[22] In a more realistic sense, U.S. government securities may be held, but they would be
held only to meet the pledging requirements of having U.S. Treasury deposits or deposits of
state and local governments.

demanded elastically would be held, and the allocation of the loan portfolio would be on a basis similar to that described above.

An uncertain supply of Type II funds plays no role: The governing factor is that the supply curve of Type II liabilities is completely elastic. Thus, bankers who engage in liability management say they do not care, in the short run, what they pay for these funds, as long as funds are available. This really means that interest rate uncertainty is not important; only the elasticity of the supply curve matters. As long as the supply curve is perfectly elastic, the bank knows it can meet its balance sheet requirements.

This is why uncertainty relating to the elasticity of supply is the important consideration of liability managers. If it is possible that the supply curve of Type II liabilities may become less than perfectly elastic at some time, then the possibility exists that the bank's entire structure of liability management might collapse. Thus, bankers who are not sure of their current position in the market or what their position will be at a given time in the future need to rely less on obtaining their liquidity from the market than on obtaining liquidity from their own balance sheet.

Many analysts have observed that, since the supply of funds is not unlimited, then at times when all banks are relying heavily on purchased funds, particularly when the central bank may be trying to reduce the aggregate supply of funds available, some banks will have to come up short of money. This is an aggregate explanation of why the supply curves of individual banks may become less than perfectly elastic at some time.

As mentioned above, bankers must be fully cognizant of their position or potential position in the market. Organizations that are not capable of sustaining their position in the liability markets must make provisions for other sources of liquidity as times change. In times of relatively easy money, the supplies of these liabilities may be perfectly elastic. However, as money tightens, this favorable situation may cease to exist, as many of the large regional banks in the United States found during the tight money period of 1974.

LIABILITY MANAGEMENT AND PROFIT MARGINS

Another question pertains to spread management and what liability management does to profit margins. Some bankers and analysts have argued against the use of liability management because of the consequent reductions in spreads and profit margins that occur in switching from asset management to liability management. It is true that spreads and profit margins will decline if this switch takes place, but banks will earn greater profits under liability management if the necessary conditions for liability management exist than if they tried to operate solely under the rule of asset management. This leads to the conclusion that liability management is neither bad nor good, intrinsically, but is a condition of the historical factors affecting bank markets. Once banks fully understand their position within the historical context of the situation, they will be asset managers at certain times and liability managers at other times. Only in this way will they be consistent with the objective function of the firm, to maximize the wealth of the owners.

The explanation of this will take the form of an example. Suppose, first of all, that loan demand is not large enough to exhaust funds that are supplied inelastically. The demand for loans and the supply of Type I deposits are assumed to be as follows:

$$r_L = 0.11 - 0.000375L$$

$$r_{D_1} = -0.03 + 0.000421D_1$$

Now, assume that government securities are supplied elastically at $r_G = 0.05$ (i.e., 5 percent), and reserve requirements on D_1 deposits are 10 percent. If the capital–deposit ratio is 10.0 percent, then the following optimal solutions are obtained.[23]

$$L = \$80$$

$$D_1 = \$95$$

$$K = \$9.50$$

$$\text{Required reserves} = \$9.50$$

$$\text{Government securities} = \$15$$

Given these factors, the average return on earning assets is found to be 7.5

---

[23] To obtain this solution, first find the marginal revenue curve of loans and the marginal cost curve of Type I deposits. Total revenue is obtained by multiplying r_L by L, or Total revenue $= 0.11L - 0.000375L^2$. Marginal revenue is found by taking the derivative of total revenue with respect to loan quantity, L, setting the result equal to 0.05, the marginal (opportunity) cost of government securities, and solving for L. The amount of Type I deposits is found in a similar way by first obtaining total costs and then marginal costs. The average return on assets is

$$\frac{[0.11 - 0.000375(80)]80 + 0.05(15)}{95} \cong .075$$

percent and the average cost of deposit funds 1 percent. The bank is earning a spread of 6.5 percentage points.

Now, introduce greater loan demand achieved by, say, the bank lending in a national market. Assume further that there also exist Type II
deposits that are supplied elastically to the bank at a rate near the government rate, or at 5 percent. Deposits of Type II will carry a reserve requirement of 5 percent of balances. The new demand for loans curve is

$$r_L = 0.11 - 0.000250L$$

These new assumptions imply that the optimal loan portfolio of the bank
will be $120, with the following optimal values:

$$D_I = \$95$$

$$D_{II} = \$26.30$$

$$\text{Required reserves} = \$10.80$$

$$\text{Government securities} = 0$$

Capital is assumed to remain at $9.50, but liabilities now total $121.30, so
the capital–deposit ratio falls to 7.3 percent. The rate of return on assets is
now 8 percent, and the average cost of deposits is 1.9 percent; this reduces
the average spread earned by the bank to 6.1 percentage points.[24]

The bank is still maximizing profits, since profits before the movement
into Type II deposits were $6.20 and profits after the use of Type II deposits
are $7.33. Any other level of loans and deposits in the two cases would
result in smaller profit levels. The only thing not considered in this example is the effect of risk. If there is some uncertainty about the elasticity of
supply of Type II deposits, the situation might be considered less desirable. Otherwise, the bank is obviously doing the best it can by taking on
the added loans and financing them with the more expensive funds.

---

[24] The average return on assets is just $r_L = 0.11 - 0.000250(120) = 0.08$. The average
cost of deposits is

$$\frac{[-0.03 + 0.000421(95)]95 + 0.05(26.30)}{121.30} \cong 0.019$$

SELECTED REFERENCES

Gable, L. R. "Liability Management: An Indictment." *The Journal of Commercial Bank Lending* (August 1974), pp. 2–10.

———. "Asset and Liability Management: A Supervisor's View." *The Journal of Commercial Bank Lending* (August 1975), pp. 23–40.

Joskow, P. L. "Firm Decision Making Processes and Oligopoly Theory." *The American Economic Review* (May 1975), pp. 276–77.

Klein, M. "A Theory of the Banking Firm." *The Journal of Money, Credit and Banking* (May 1971).

Mason, J. M. "Theory of the Banking Firm with Uncertain Demand and Supply of Funds." Finance Department Working Paper, The University of Pennsylvania, 1978.

———. "The Difference Between a Mutual Fund and a Commercial Bank." Finance Department Working Paper, The University of Pennsylvania, 1978.

Schweitzer, S. A. "Bank Liability Management: For Better or For Worse?" *Business Review,* Federal Reserve Bank of Philadelphia (December 1974), pp. 3–12.

———. "Liability Management: Guilty as Charged?" *The Journal of Commercial Bank Lending* (May 1975), pp. 30–36.

Shull, B. "Commercial Banks as Multi-Product, Price-Discriminating Firms." In D. Carson, ed., *Banking and Monetary Studies.* Homewood, Ill.: Richard D. Irwin, 1963.

REVIEW QUESTIONS

1. What are some of the costs associated with dividing borrowers into many different classes?
2. Many theorists have treated the individual bank as a discriminating monopolist. What other models might be used to describe individual behavior? What are some of the strengths and weaknesses of these models?
3. Give some explicit examples of bank behavior that would lead an analyst to claim that banks are in close "proximity." In what other industries do such close ties exist?
4. What is the difference between uncertain return on an asset and uncertain demand? Why is it necessary to know what markets an industry faces to fully understand its behavior?
5. In the asset-management case, why is the interest rate on U.S. government securities an opportunity cost? Is the marginal opportunity cost the same as a true marginal cost?

6. How meaningful is the spread (average or otherwise) the bank earns on its operations? What, if anything, is the significance of a rising or falling spread?

7. Is it conceivable that some bank liabilities may be negatively correlated with market returns? Explain what this means in terms of market behavior.

8. Why do some bankers and analysts consider liability management riskier than asset management?

9. It has been claimed that liability management has made it more difficult for the Federal Reserve to conduct monetary policy, particularly to tighten credit. Considering the model of the individual bank presented in this chapter, would you agree with this conclusion? Explain your answer.

10. Discuss how a bank's dealings in asset/liability markets are affected by its choice of time horizon.

APPENDIX

Mathematical Formulation of Models
Presented in Chapter 2

THE MODEL

The balance sheet of the banking firm, which was presented within the body of Chapter 2, is reproduced here:

$$\sum_{i=1}^{m} L_i = \sum_{h=1}^{n} D_h + K \tag{2A-1}$$

The income statement considers the revenues, fees, charges, and costs associated with each asset or liability category, reproduced from equation (2-2) but ignoring taxes.

$$\pi = \sum_{i=1}^{m} (r_i^a + f_i - b_i)L_i - \sum_{h=1}^{n} (r_h^d - f_h + b_h)D_h \tag{2A-2}$$

The variable π refers to profits before taxes. The loan demands of the firm are

$$L_i = f_i(r_i^a, u_i); \quad E[L_i] = L_i^*; \quad E[(L_i - L_i^*)^2] = \sigma_{L_i}^2$$
$$\text{for all } i = 1, 2, \ldots, m \tag{2A-3}$$

where E is the expectations operator.

Funds are supplied to the bank in the form of deposits and other liabilities,

$$D_h = g(r_h^d, V_h); \quad E[D_h] = D_h^*; \quad E[(D_h - D_h^*)^2] = \sigma_{D_h}^2$$
$$\text{for all } h = 1, 2, \ldots, n \tag{2A-4}$$

The relevant covariances are

$$E[(L_i - L_i^*)(L_j - L_j^*)] = \sigma_{ij} \quad \text{for } i > j \tag{2A-5}$$

$$E[(D_h - D_h^*)(D_k - D_k^*)] = \sigma_{hk} \quad \text{for } h > k \tag{2A-6}$$

67

$$E[(L_i - L_i^*)(D_h - D_h^*)] = \sigma_{ih} \qquad (2A\text{-}7)$$

The variance of profits can then be derived.

$$\sigma_\pi^2 = \sum_{i=1}^{m} (r_i^a + f_i - b_i)^2 \sigma_{L_i}^2 + \sum_{h=1}^{n} (r_h^d - f_h + b_h)^2 \sigma_{D_h}^2$$
$$+ 2 \sum_{i>j} (r_i^a + f_i - b_i)(r_j^a + f_j - b_j)\sigma_{ij}$$
$$+ 2 \sum_{h>k} (r_h^d - f_h + b_h)(r_k^d - f_k + b_k)\sigma_{hk}$$
$$- 2 \sum_i \sum_h (r_i^a + f_i - b_i)(r_h^d - f_h + b_h)\sigma_{ih} \qquad (2A\text{-}8)$$

The value of the firm will be assumed, as a first approximation, to be determined by the capital asset pricing model developed by Sharpe, Lintner, and Mossin. In this work the equilibrium value of the firm, V, is

$$V = \frac{1}{1 + \rho} [E(\pi) - R\sigma_{\pi m}] \qquad (2A\text{-}9)$$

where ρ is the riskless rate, R is the market value of a unit of risk, and $\sigma_{\pi m}$ is the covariance between the profits of the bank and the market. $R = [E(R_m) - \rho]/\sigma_m^2$, where R_m is the return on the market portfolio and σ_m^2 is the variance of market returns.

In a world in which asset demands and liability supplies are known with certainty, all the variances and covariances are zero. Hence, $\sigma_{L_i}^2 = \sigma_{D_h}^2 = \sigma_{ij} = \sigma_{hk} = \sigma_{ih} = \sigma_{\pi m} = 0$. Therefore, under certainty, equation (2A-9) reduces to

$$V' = \frac{\pi}{1 + \rho} \qquad (2A\text{-}10)$$

since $E[\pi] = \pi$.

THE CERTAINTY CASE

The problem now is to maximize V', subject to the balance sheet constraint (2A-1). For simplicity, it is assumed that f, the fees and charges, and b, the administration and overhead costs, are constant. The maximization proceeds as follows for the certainty case:

$$\underset{r_i^a, r_h^d, \lambda}{\text{Maximize}} \; \Phi = V' + \lambda \left[\sum_{i=1}^{m} L_i - \sum_{h=1}^{n} D_h - K \right] \qquad (2A\text{-}11)$$

This is done by taking the derivatives of (2A-11) with respect to the decision variables and setting the results equal to zero. It is assumed that the second-order conditions for a maximum are satisfied.

$$\frac{\partial \Phi'}{\partial r_i^a} = \frac{1}{1 + \rho} \left[(r_i^a + f_i - b_i) \frac{\partial L_i}{\partial r_i^a} + L_i \right] + \lambda \frac{\partial L_i}{\partial r_i^a} = 0 \qquad (2A\text{-}12a)$$

$$\frac{\partial \Phi'}{\partial r_h^d} = \frac{1}{1 + \rho} \left[-(r_h^d - f_h + b_h) \frac{\partial D_h}{\partial r_h^d} - D_h \right] + \lambda \frac{\partial D_h}{\partial r_h^d} = 0 \qquad (2A\text{-}12b)$$

$$\frac{\partial \Phi'}{\partial \lambda} = \sum_{i=1}^{m} L_i - \sum_{h=1}^{n} D_h - K = 0 \qquad (2A\text{-}12c)$$

Equation (2A-12c) is just the balance sheet constraint. Equations (2A-12a) and (2A-12b) are now solved for $-(1 + \rho)\lambda$ and the results are set equal to one another to derive the equilibrium pricing relationship. This is

$$r_i^a \left(1 + \frac{1}{e_i^a} \right) + f_i - b_i = r_h^d \left(1 + \frac{1}{e_h^d} \right) - f_h + b_h \qquad (2A\text{-}13)$$

where e stands for the elasticity of assets or liabilities with respect to the rate charged or paid on the assets or liabilities. That is,

$$e_i^a = (r_i^a / L_i)(\partial L_i / \partial r_i^a) \quad \text{and} \quad e_h^d = (r_h^d / D_h)(\partial D_h / \partial r_h^d)$$

If there are markets, such as the markets for Treasury bills or negotiable certificates of deposit (CDs), in which funds are demanded or supplied elastically, then the elasticity, e, in these markets approaches infinity. If there are no fees in these markets and administrative and overhead costs are negligible, then

$$r_G = r_i^a \left(1 + \frac{1}{e_i^a} \right) + f_i - b_i = r_h^d \left(1 + \frac{1}{e_h^d} \right) - f_h + b_h = r_{CD} \qquad (2A\text{-}14)$$

where the subscript G is used for Treasury bills and CD for negotiable CDs.

This is the solution to the certainty case described in Chapter 2 and pictured in Figure 2-3.

THE UNCERTAINTY CASE

The uncertainty case is a little more complex. In this case, $\sigma^2_{L_i} = \sigma^2_{D_h} \neq \sigma_{ij} \neq \sigma_{hk} \neq \sigma_{ih} \neq \sigma_{\pi m} \neq 0$, so that the second term in brackets in the valuation formula (2A-9) does not drop out. Maximization proceeds as before, using V instead of V'.

$$\underset{r^a_i, r^d_h, \lambda}{\text{Maximize}} \ \Phi = V + \lambda \left[\sum_{i=1}^{m} L_i - \sum_{h=1}^{n} D_h - K \right] \qquad (2A\text{-}15)$$

Again, differentiating with respect to the decision variables and setting the results equal to zero yield the following equations:

$$\frac{\partial \Phi}{\partial r^a_i} = \frac{1}{1+\rho} \left[(r^a_i + f_i - b_i) \frac{\partial L_i}{\partial r^a_i} + L_i - R \frac{\partial \sigma_{\pi m}}{\partial r^a_i} \right] + \lambda \frac{\partial L_i}{\partial r^a_i} = 0 \qquad (2A\text{-}16)$$

$$\frac{\partial \Phi}{\partial r^d_h} = \frac{1}{1+\rho} \left[-(r^d_h - f_h + b_h) \frac{\partial D_h}{\partial r^d_h} + D_h - R \frac{\partial \sigma_{\pi m}}{\partial r^d_h} \right] + \lambda \frac{\partial D_h}{\partial r^d_h} = 0$$

$$\frac{\partial \Phi}{\partial \lambda} = \sum_{i=1}^{m} L_i - \sum_{h=1}^{n} D_h - K = 0$$

Once again, solving for $-(1 + \rho)\lambda$ and setting the results equal to one another yield

$$r^a_i \left(1 + \frac{1}{e^a_i} \right) + f_i - b_i - \frac{R \partial \sigma_{\pi m}}{(\partial L_i / \partial r^a_i) \partial r^a_i}$$

$$= r^d_h \left(1 + \frac{1}{e^d_h} \right) - f_h + b_h \frac{R \, \partial \sigma_{\pi m}}{(\partial D_h / \partial r^d_h) \partial r^d_h} \qquad (2A\text{-}17)$$

Note that the ∂r^a_i on the left-hand side of the equation and the ∂r^d_h on the right-hand side of the equation do not cancel out. This is because the $\sigma_{\pi m}$ is composed of σ_π, which, as can be seen in equation (2A-8), contains r^a_i and r^d_h but does not contain L_i or D_h. Thus, $\partial \sigma_{\pi m} / \partial L_i$ and $\partial \sigma_{\pi m} / \partial D_h$ are meaningless: The ∂r^a_i's and the ∂r^d_h's must be kept in the equation.

This is a key result because of the implication it carries for the risk to the bank of operating in the Treasury bill market or the CD market. The reason for this is obvious. The bank is worried about quantity variation. In the Treasury bill and CD markets, if funds are demanded or supplied perfectly elastically, there is no quantity uncertainty. Thus, these markets provide liquidity to the bank, i.e., they become the "residual" markets in which banks can make portfolio adjustments when the demand for funds or the supply of funds is something other than what is expected. Mathematically, this is shown by the elasticities of these markets going to infinity, in which case $\partial L_i / \partial r_i^q$ and $\partial D_h / \partial r_h^d$ also go to infinity. Then, in the absence of fees or administrative costs,

$$r_G = r_{CD} = r_i^q \left(1 + \frac{1}{e_i^q}\right) + f_i - b_i - \frac{R\partial\sigma_{\pi m}}{(\partial L_i/\partial r_i^q)\partial r_i^q} \qquad (2A\text{-}18)$$

$$= r_h^d \left(1 + \frac{1}{e_h^d}\right) - f_h + b_h - \frac{R\partial\sigma_{\pi m}}{(\partial D_h/\partial r_h^d)\partial r_h^d}$$

How uncertainty affects the demand or supply curve depends on the sign of $\partial\sigma_{\pi m}/\partial r_i^q$ or $\partial\sigma_{\pi m}/\partial r_h^d$. To see what is important here, the mathematics must be carried one step further. By definition, $\sigma_{\pi m} = \rho_{\pi m}\sigma_\pi\sigma_m$, where $\rho_{\pi m}$ is the correlation coefficient between the market return and the return to the bank. Thus, concentrating solely on ∂r_h^d,

$$\frac{\partial\sigma_{\pi m}}{\partial r_h^d} = \frac{\partial(\rho_{\pi m}\sigma_\pi\sigma_m)}{\partial r_h^d} = \sigma_m \left[\sigma_\pi \frac{\partial\rho_{\pi m}}{\partial r_h^d} + \rho_{\pi m} \frac{\partial\sigma_\pi}{\partial r_h^d}\right] \qquad (2A\text{-}19)$$

First of all, σ_m is assumed to be constant. No matter what the firm does it cannot affect the return to the market. Second, $\rho_{\pi m} \gtrless 0$, so that nothing can be said, *a priori*, about the sign of these two items. Finally,

$$\frac{\partial\sigma_\pi}{\partial r_h^d} = \frac{1}{\sigma_\pi} \left[(r_h^q - f_h + b_h)\sigma_{D_h}^2 \right.$$
$$\left. + \sum_{h>k} (R_k^d - f_k + b_k)\sigma_{hk} - \sum_i (R_i^q + f_i - b_i)\sigma_{hi}\right] \qquad (2A\text{-}20)$$

which is also $\gtrless 0$, in general, because if the bank is adequately diversified the covariances dominate the variances. Since there is no *a priori* reason to expect covariances to be positive or negative, there is no reason to believe $\partial\sigma_\pi/\partial r_h^d$ to be positive or negative.

Thus, the sign of $\partial\sigma_{\pi m}/\partial r_h^d$, as well as that of $\partial\sigma_{\pi m}/\partial r_i^q$, will be indeterminate and must be estimated for each bank. In general, however, for loans it appears that $\partial\sigma_{\pi m}/\partial r_i^q$ is positive, so that the risk-adjusted demand curve drops downward and to the left as was assumed in Part A of Figure 2-4. For deposits supplied inelastically, such as demand deposits and passbook time and savings accounts, $\partial\sigma_{\pi m}/\partial r_h^d$ is also positive. This causes the risk-adjusted supply curve to shift upward to the left as was assumed in Part B of Figure 2-5.

In the case of other liabilities the result is unclear. The $\partial \sigma_{\pi m} / \partial r_h^d$ for some liabilities may be negative. A question mark was used in Figure 2-5C because the direction of the shift in the supply curve is uncertain.

In terms of liability management it is obvious that there must be a liability market in which the quantity of funds is not an uncertainty for "true" liability management to exist. Other than this, the firm must have asset demands that exceed the funds supplied by all other inelastically supplied liabilities; otherwise, CDs will not be issued. As is shown in (2A-14), the bank will not issue CDs to invest in government securities because $r_G = r_{CD}$.

APPENDIX REFERENCES

Klein, M. "A Theory of the Banking Firm." *The Journal of Money, Credit and Banking* (May 1971).

Lintner, J. "The Valuation of Risk Assets and the Selection of Risky Investments in Stock Portfolios and Capital Budgets." *Review of Economics and Statistics* (February 1965).

Mason, J. M. "Theory of the Banking Firm with Uncertain Demand and Supply of Funds." Finance Department Working Paper, The University of Pennsylvania, 1978.

————. "The Difference Between a Mutual Fund and a Commercial Bank." Finance Department Working Paper, The University of Pennsylvania, 1978.

Mossin, J. "Equilibrium in a Capital Asset Market." *Econometrica* (October 1966).

Sharpe, W. F. "Capital Asset Prices: A Theory of Equilibrium Under Conditions of Risk." *Journal of Finance* (September 1964).

3

Generalized Loan Pricing, Portfolio Administration, and Nonprice Terms

The model developed in Chapter 2 is now refined to take into account special topics having to do with loan pricing and the use of nonprice terms. This lays the groundwork for the more institutionally oriented chapters concerning the lending and borrowing process. Thus, the loan-pricing decision will be discussed along with the assessment of any fees the borrower has to pay. Next, the use of nonprice terms is presented. The customer relationship, the long-term association that may exist between a borrower and its bank, is then specified. This concept must be understood because of the central role it plays in actual banking practice. How these factors affect portfolio management, either through customer or risk considerations or both, is examined. The two closing sections of the chapter discuss the pricing of demand deposits and transfer pricing—the pricing of funds transferred within the bank itself.

GENERALIZED LOAN PRICING

Three payments must be incorporated into any interest rate charged by the bank: the payment for the pure use of money, the payment for the risk

associated with the borrower, and the incremental charges arising from
any imperfections in the loan market. Maturity, collateral, and other terms
of the loan are ignored for the present.

The risk-free rate is assumed to be the interest rate on U.S. government securities. As explained earlier, this rate will be also be approximately equal to the rate paid on liabilities that are supplied elastically. All
other loan rates will be calculated relative to these rates, since they represent the marginal (opportunity) cost of funds to the bank.

The analysis of an individual loan applicant, therefore, includes an
examination of the riskiness of the potential borrower and its industry or
occupation, and a review of the borrower's other sources of funds. However, in general practice, more effort goes into analyzing individual credit
risk than into examining how well the applicant, or those in the applicant's
loan class, can obtain funds from other institutions or markets.

The general reason for this is that there is usually more information
available on the customer than on the elasticity of demand for funds from
commercial banks. Whereas the bank can obtain historical balance sheet
and income statement data as well as pro forma statements that allow for a
more refined analysis, it estimates the borrower's alternative sources of
funds intuitively. Obviously, the bank should rely more on specific
information.

However, this does not mean that the data on individual borrower
risk are so reliable that banks are satisfied with their ability to discriminate
among different classes of risk. In fact, it appears that banks cannot finely
divide customers according to their risk class at any one time, nor can they
make subtle alterations as credit conditions change. Thus, banks *in general*
have only a small number of risk classes, other than for loan maturity,
collateral, or loan type, and make only marginal alterations in customer
ratings as economic conditions change.

It has become a practice in some banks in recent years to separate
borrowers along product and industry lines rather than geographic lines.
Not only does this allow the number of loan classes to be increased considerably, but, with increased specialization of loan officers, the bank can
obtain additional knowledge of firms and the industries in which they
operate and develop a better feel for industry borrowing capabilities, i.e.,
market imperfections. This is also true of classification on the basis of
specialized lending arrangements, such as mortgages, inventory financings, and accounts receivable financings.

It can safely be assumed, therefore, that commercial bankers have
incomplete information concerning the borrower's riskiness and its position in the credit markets. They also have incomplete information about

how the financial condition of the firm changes over the credit cycle. This is not an unusual situation in an oligopolistic industry, but it does lead to problems in setting prices. Oligopolists, in general, have responded to this lack of information by using rules of thumb to set prices or relative prices.[1] One of the most common rules of thumb is a markup scheme in which the price quoted or charged on products is a fixed markup over average cost of production. This would be a logical response for banks to pursue except that they have not been able, historically, to compute their relevant costs adequately.

First of all, banks until recently have been asset managers. Thus, they would have had to mark up their loans over the implicit interest paid on demand deposits or the explicit interest paid on passbook savings accounts. Both of these rates, as was shown in Chapter 2, lie far below the marginal opportunity cost of funds.

Second, if a bank is a liability manager, it faces the problem that liability management depends not only on the existence of a market in which funds are supplied elastically but also on its loan demand being in excess of funds that are supplied inelastically. If loan demand is not always sufficient to exhaust these sources of funds, the bank will not always be engaged in liability management. If it is not demanding funds from its liability market, its pricing scheme will not reflect true cost conditions. Its pricing scheme would, therefore, have to change over time.

As an alternative, bankers could tie all loan rates to open-market rates. The problem with this is that the bank loan is not a pure loan in the sense that most open-market loan contracts are; there is the customer relationship to be considered. The customer relationship is discussed more fully later, but it can be said at this point that it implies steady borrowing on the part of the bank customer and the future availability of bank funds to meet the customer's needs. Thus, the relationship between interest rates charged on bank loans and those charged in the open market will change as the relationship alters between present and future costs and benefits of the borrower–lender association.

As a result of these factors, bankers have developed a pricing scheme in which the interest rates on most loans are quoted as some markup over the prime rate, which is the interest rate charged the biggest and most creditworthy customers of the bank. There are two reasons for this. First,

---

[1] For nonbanking references see A. Kaplan, J. Dirlam, and R. Lanzillotti, *Pricing in Big Business* (Washington, D.C., 1958), or F. Schaver, *Industrial Market Structure and Economic Performance* (Chicago, 1970), or P. L. Joskow, "Firm Decision Making Processes and Oligopoly Theory," *American Economic Review* (May 1975), pp. 270–79.

prime rate customers have the most alternative sources of funds of any of the bank's borrowers. Since they deal in national and international markets, with other banks and also with other institutions, and in the open market, they can shift their borrowing from one source to another in response to small differentials in the interest rates offered by various institutions and markets. Thus, commercial bankers know the elasticity of demand of these borrowers better than that of anyone else who borrows directly from the bank. Demand is extremely elastic to the individual bank.

The second reason for using the prime rate as the base rate is that prime customers do not need to formalize the customer relationship with the bank. Since they have many alternative sources of funds, they can get funds just about any time they need them. Banks give them the privileges of the customer relationship because they extend those privileges to customers in a weaker borrowing position. Prime customers do not seek a customer relationship, so a loan to a prime borrower is more of a pure loan of money than a loan to a borrower who does not have as many alternative sources of funds. Therefore, banks make every effort to price these customers "right" relative to the market.

It should be noted that the pricing of prime loans relative to the market will change over time. Thus, the setting of prime rates with the use of a formula must not be so rigid that this changing relationship cannot be handled easily over the credit cycle.[2]

Commercial banks will, therefore, determine the rate they want to charge prime customers and then use this rate as the markup base for loan rates to all other borrowers. The markups will include two components: one to cover the increased riskiness of moving from the prime risk class to a higher-risk class, and one that takes into account the imperfections of the credit market with respect to the ability of the bank's customers to borrow

---

[2] A "formula" prime rate is an interest rate set in relationship to an open-market interest rate or a weighted average of open-market interest rates. These "formula" rates were first initiated in 1971 during the Nixon wage-price freeze. Commercial banks had been toying with the idea of "formula" rates for some time previous to this because of the greater fluctuations taking place in interest rates in the late 1960s. The potentiality of a freeze on interest rates, which was within the authority of the Committee on Interest and Dividends, made it politically desirable to institute such rates in the latter half of 1971.

First National City Bank (Citicorp) is the only bank that, at the time of this writing, still uses a "strict" formula. It bases its prime rate on the three-week moving average of the interest rate on four- to six-month commercial paper as reported by the Federal Reserve System. Historically, the relationship between the prime rate and this base rate, i.e., the formula, has changed as credit conditions have changed.

from other sources. Expressed mathematically, the contract rate charged a borrower in the ith loan class is

$$r_i = r_p + x_i \qquad\qquad (3\text{-}1)$$

where r_p is the prime rate of interest and x_i is the markup over prime charged the ith loan class.

A corollary to the preceding analysis is that prime customers will never be rationed; that is, they will never be supplied less than would be demanded at the quoted prime rate of interest. This is easily explained. The demand curve for loans to prime customers is the only one for which the bank has some knowledge of its elasticity: The bank must price this market correctly or, due to the competitiveness of the prime loan market, it will lose its good, most creditworthy customers.

Changes in the Pricing Scheme

An important consideration in the pricing of different loan classes has to do with how the pricing scheme should change as demand and supply conditions vary over the economic or credit cycle. To understand the response of banks to these changes, it is important to understand the difficulty of operating in a world of uncertainty.

First, bankers must discriminate between permanent and temporary changes in the demand for funds or the supply of funds. A fundamental change in one of these factors is likely to last for a while. If the change is not a fundamental one, then it will probably soon reverse itself. For example, if bankers observe an increase in loan demand, they must decide whether or not there have been fundamental changes in the economy, or in the industry, or in particular firms.

To obtain some understanding of how business organizations respond to this type of situation, the reader must go to the literature on industrial organization. Analysts of industrial behavior have observed that firms will not be interested in or capable of continuous global optimization in a changing environment. That is, they will maintain their pricing rules of thumb, thereby letting quantities find their own level, or constrain both price and quantity, thus placing the organization off the demand curves they face and creating a situation known as rationing. Writers on industrial organization refer to this type of response as "bounded rationality."[3] In a bank, this type of behavior results in "credit rationing."

[3] For a more complete discussion of bounded rationality, see Joskow, "Firm Decision Making Processes."

A second reason for banks acting as they do is that they lack information. If bankers do not know the elasticity of demand for loans of a given loan class in a period when economic conditions are relatively stable, they will certainly have no idea of how this elasticity will change as economic conditions change. Thus, they cannot know what the new markup should be to incorporate actual alterations of the economic environment.

There is another reason why markups, in general, do not change over the economic or credit cycle. Borrowers, as well as the banks themselves, interpret the markup solely in terms of risk classification. Therefore, banks can move marginal borrowers from one class to another without much difficulty as the risk characteristics of their individual firms change. However, unless the firms in a given risk class have a very poor bargaining position in the market, or few other terms associated with their borrowing,[4] changing markups for any class is strongly resisted because of the implication that the riskiness of the entire loan class has changed. There will be market opposition to such a move, however rational it may seem. Movements in nonprice terms are a much more acceptable way to alter the yield of a loan, since changes in these items do not carry the same implication.

All banks seem to operate together in this respect. The major explanation for this is the close "proximity" of commercial banks, which leads the banking industry to act as a single monopoly and thus avoid distributional problems that might come about with fixed pricing schemes. As was mentioned in Chapter 2, the term *proximity* does not refer to just geographical configuration; it is defined by organizational economists in terms of firms that "produce the same product, use similar technologies, or are in contact with one another via market exchanges of products."[5] Commercial banks are "close" to one another through their dealings in the federal funds market, correspondent relationships, and loan participations. Therefore, it is to be expected that banks will exhibit a fairly uniform response to changing loan demands and market conditions.

CREDIT RATIONING AND THE CUSTOMER RELATIONSHIP

Credit rationing occurs when banks offer terms that take them off the demand curves of the borrowers. In other words, borrowers cannot obtain all the funds they desire at the interest rate posted by the lender, the

[4] Real estate builders borrowing funds for construction, for instance.
[5] See Joskow, "Firm Decision Making Processes," pp. 276–77.

commercial bank. As described earlier, this type of behavior is called *bounded rationality*, and it occurs when organizations maintain their rules of thumb in spite of changing conditions. In this case, the credit terms leading to rationing come about from a combination of price constraints *and* quantity constraints in the face of rising interest rates. The price constraint is a result of the pricing mechanism just discussed, and the quantity constraint is due to the fact that the bank is still trying to optimize its portfolio relative to the market.

It can easily be imagined that once the bank institutes a rigid, rule-of-thumb pricing scheme, such as the markup-over-prime method, a monkey wrench is thrown into the operations of the market. However, it can be shown that this *alone* will not bring about credit rationing. This is because when interest rates rise, the prime rate, and hence all loan rates, if determined by market forces, will always be lower than would be achieved under the markup scheme. Rationing will take place only if loan rates determined by market forces would be higher than those achieved by the markup formula.[6]

The additional factor needed to cause credit rationing seems to be the phenomenon called the *customer relationship*. The customer relationship develops between the bank and those good borrowers who borrow regularly. Therefore, a borrower that becomes a steady customer will bring more loan demand to the bank in the future than it had in the past. As interest rates rise, future loan demand and the steady loan demand of good customers become more important to the bank. That is, bankers see that future cash flows arising from the future demand for funds can become more important than current cash flows; as a result, they will reduce the spread between loan rates to good customers and open-market interest rates.

The loan class of interest here is, of course, the market for prime loans. Since the bank perceives the future loan demand of those borrowers as particularly important to its future success, it wishes to price these customers in a way that encourages that future demand.

The evidence on this very definitely indicates that the spread between the prime rate and, say, the interest rate on commercial paper with four- to six-month maturity narrows as interest rates in general rise, and widens as interest rates fall. This behavior is charted in Figure 3-1.

What this means for the discussion of credit rationing is that since the increase in the prime rate is proportionately less than that in open-market interest rates, the whole structure of bank loan rates will rise less than in

---

[6] This is shown mathematically in the appendix to this chapter.

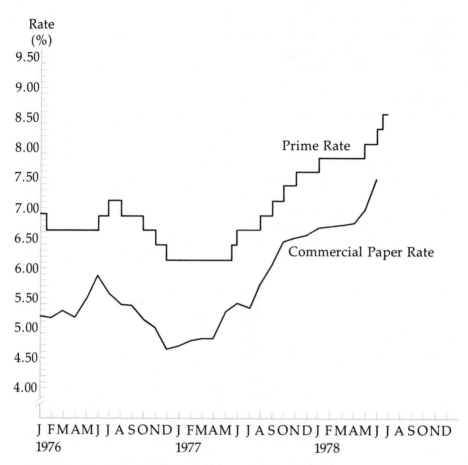

FIGURE 3-1   Relationship between the Prime Rate and the 4- to 6-Month
             Commercial Paper Rate (Source: Federal Reserve System.)

proportion to open-market rates. In some cases, the interest rate for a
given class of loans (prime plus markup) will be lower than the rate that
would be determined by market forces, that is, lower than the loan rates
that would exist if the marginal (opportunity) cost of funds were equal to
the marginal revenue of each loan class. In that event, credit rationing
can develop.

   Another constraint touched upon earlier is the quantity constraint.
The bank, in trying to achieve some kind of optimum risk-return portfolio,
will try to maintain optimum quantities even though it may not be able to

set optimum prices.[7] Thus, in loan classes for which the interest rate is less than would be charged if market forces ruled, the quantity of loans the bank is willing to "book" is less than the borrowers in the class want at the posted interest rate.

Perhaps the most important factor in determining whether or not a loan class will be rationed is the strength of the customer relationship in that loan class. That is, loan classes that exhibit strong customer ties with the bank will find that the interest rate charged their class will respond to rising interest rates to the same degree as the prime market responds to rising interest rates; that is, as interest rates rise, market-determined loan rates will not rise in proportion to market rates. Thus, the good, steady borrowers will probably find that the rate they are charged by the bank will be greater than what they would have been charged if market conditions had ruled. They will, therefore, face no quantity constraint. They will perhaps borrow less than they would have if the bank used a more flexible pricing scheme,[8] but they are more likely to be on their demand curve. Good customers are less likely to be rationed than borrowers who are not good, steady customers of the bank.

Either all members of a loan class will be rationed or none will.[9] However, it is not the case that all classes that are rationed in one period of rising interest rates will be rationed in another period. Rationing depends on how severely interest rates rise, how economic conditions have affected individual borrowing classes, and what supplies of funds are available to the bank. Thus, whereas some borrowers, such as the construction industry, may be rationed every time monetary conditions tighten up, other classes may experience rationing at one time but not at another.

As interest rates fall, the spread between the prime rate and open-market rates increases. Thus, the structure of bank loan rates falls less than proportionately with market rates. This will have the opposite effect to that described above, in that borrowers in loan classes likely to be rationed will find funds more readily available or, if they were not rationed before, available in greater quantities than they desire at the interest cost and

---

[7] Quantities are of crucial importance to the bank because of balance sheet considerations. Banks seem, at least in the short run, to try to move toward optimal balance sheet even though they will not be optimizing profits because of their inability to price each customer correctly.

[8] This may not be true if the bank were to adjust nonprice terms, as will be described in the next section.

[9] Dwight Jaffee and Franco Modigliani argue that only some may be rationed within a loan class. See D. M. Jaffee and F. Modigliani, "A Theory and Test of Credit Rationing," *American Economic Review* (December 1969). See also D. M. Jaffee, *Credit Rationing and the Commercial Loan Market* (New York: John Wiley and Sons, 1971).

nonprice terms offered. This occurs because these classifications will find that actual "posted" loan rates are falling less rapidly than market rates, making the borrowers in this loan class a much more attractive prospect for lenders.

NONPRICE TERMS

The nonprice terms of a loan include such things as its maturity, the collateral backing the loan, compensating balance requirements, and down payment. In all the cases mentioned so far, it has been assumed that these nonprice terms have remained constant or have not existed. This resulted in the possibility that in some loan markets the bank would be quoting an interest rate and "booking" a quantity of loans that would not be "on" that market's demand curve. This situation is an undesirable, short-run phenomenon.

It is undesirable because borrowers are unhappy at being unable to obtain all the funds desired at the quoted loan rate. This unhappiness is translated into general frustration and uneasiness, because, if all lenders are acting in the same way, borrowers cannot relieve their frustrations by moving to other markets or other lenders. It is a short-run situation, because banks will maintain a disequilibrium only if they believe there is a good chance that economic or credit conditions will be reversed and they will have to alter their terms once again, bringing them back to the previous combination of prices and terms. This is not a costless adjustment for the bank. Banks do not like a disequilibrium situation any more than borrowers do; hence, they will alter nonprice terms in an effort to get themselves back on market demand curves. But they must be sure that fundamental market conditions have changed and that the change is great enough to warrant a movement of nonprice terms. Changes in nonprice terms are made in lumpy, discrete amounts. Compensating balances will not be moved from 15 percent to 16 percent; they will be moved from 15 to 20 percent. Loan maturities will be changed from one year to two years, not from one year to one year and two months. Thus, market conditions must change substantially for the bank to want to change terms.

In all cases, if terms become more restrictive (i.e., if banks shorten loan maturities or require higher down payments, larger compensating balances, or more collateral), the effective cost of the loan to the borrower rises. Therefore, changes in nonprice terms have the effect of shifting the demand curve for loans in a given market for a given loan rate.

This can be seen in Figure 3-2. The first demand curve, L_1, is drawn

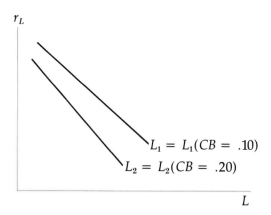

r_L

$L_1 = L_1(CB = .10)$
$L_2 = L_2(CB = .20)$

L

FIGURE 3-2   How the Demand for Loans Shifts in Response to a Change in
Compensating Balance Requirements

with a compensating balance requirement of 10 percent ($CB = 0.10$). The second demand curve, L_2, is drawn with the compensating balance requirement at 20 percent ($CB = 0.20$). This means that the firm that had to borrow approximately $111 to obtain $100 over its required compensating balance would now have to borrow $125. That is, if interest rates are held constant, it would have to pay interest on the larger amount of money to get the same net funds as before; the effective cost of the $100 has risen. It will therefore borrow less at every interest rate than it would have before the change.

Since these nonprice terms are changed in discrete amounts, a persistent change in the credit markets will be needed before commercial banks will ultimately move their nonprice terms to eliminate market disequilibrium conditions. Empirical evidence supports the bank behavior just described.[10] First, interest rates on loans rise or fall with general movements in open-market rates. However, they do not move sufficiently to clear markets. Second, the nonprice terms of loans move in the same direction as interest rates, i.e., toward tighter or easier terms, and therefore reinforce the movement in interest rates while maintaining the pricing structure based on markups over prime. Figure 3-3 shows how various loan terms have moved in concert with one another over time.

The use of nonprice terms to clear markets is sometimes referred to as

[10] See the two articles by D. G. Harris, "Some Evidence of Differential Lending Practices at Commercial Banks," *Journal of Finance* (December 1973), and "Credit Rationing at Commercial Banks: Some Empirical Evidence," *The Journal of Money, Credit and Banking* (May 1974).

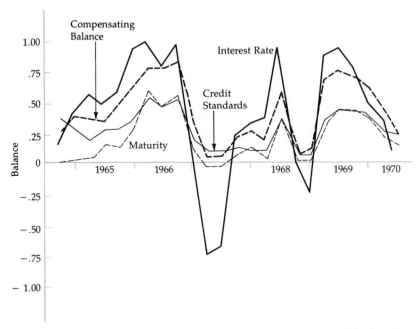

FIGURE 3-3   Changes in Loan Terms over a Five-Year Period [After Duane
              G. Harris, *Journal of Money, Credit and Banking* (May 1974).]

nonprice credit rationing. The reader should be careful to distinguish it
from the "pure" credit rationing discussed earlier, in which the terms of
the loan were not represented by a point on the demand curve for loans of
a given class. Nonprice credit rationing is an attempt to keep the terms of
the loan on the demand curve by altering the nonprice factors in a loan
arrangement to limit borrowers to fewer funds, at the going interest rate,
than they would have had if nonprice terms had not changed.

     Not all loan classes are treated in this way. Some borrowers may have
very little bargaining power in the credit market because they have so few
alternative sources of funds, but may also be subject to few nonprice terms
in a loan agreement. Construction borrowers are a case in point. In dealing
with these borrowers, banks cannot move nonprice terms to reduce the
demand for loans at given loan rates. As a consequence, they will change
the markup over prime for these borrowers, moving from, say, one percentage point over prime in good times to three percentage points over
prime in times when funds are not readily available. In most cases, however, the increased markup will not be sufficient to clear the market, and

the borrowers affected may be "permanently" rationed. That is, as long as funds are relatively scarce, the banks either will not loan as much to these customers as they would be willing to take at going rates or will ration them out of the market entirely, lending them nothing.

Only as market rates and the prime rate drop will funds once more become available to these borrowers. First, rationing will cease at the larger spread, and then the spread will be lowered as the passage of time, under favorable monetary conditions, eventually leads to a decline in spreads once again. These borrowers, even though some may be excellent customers of the bank, are continually faced with a feast-or-famine availability of credit, mainly because of their weak position in the credit markets due to a lack of alternative sources of funds.

RISK MANAGEMENT

Even though the discussion so far has been relatively abstract, something can be said about how commercial banks go about controlling the riskiness of their loan portfolios. Again, this is a dynamic problem in that it concerns the way in which the riskiness of a portfolio changes over a credit cycle. If credit conditions that affect the riskiness of the bank itself did not change, then the bank would be able to aim for just one given level of risk for its total loan portfolio and, since the choice of assets determines the risk class of the bank, the riskiness of the bank would then be determined. However, as monetary conditions become tighter, the liquidity of the bank's portfolio is reduced and its ability to purchase funds from the market (liquidity in the liability-management sense) is also reduced. Hence, the need arises to reduce the risk of its loan portfolio, because it is not as capable of bearing potential loan losses as it was before the change in credit conditions. The reverse would, of course, be true in the case of an easing in monetary conditions.

In discussing problems of risk management with loan officers, one is often struck by the emphasis the bankers place on lending to customers, those good borrowers deemed to have a customer relationship with the bank. For example, the following scenario is not uncommon:

> Question: To whom do you lend when money gets tight?
> Loan officer: We lend to customers.
> Question: How do you manage the riskiness of your loan portfolio during times of changing credit conditions?
> Loan officer: We lend to customers.

Although this is highly simplified, it carries an important message about risk management. First, the borrowers that are considered to be customers of the banks are usually their biggest, most creditworthy borrowers. This is because the bigger the borrower, the stronger it is financially and, in all likelihood, the greater its access to other sources of credit. Second, because the "customer" is usually large, it will tend to have more consistent needs for funds than the average borrower and hence will tend to be a steadier borrower and more valuable to the bank. "Customers," therefore, tend to provide greater revenues, as well as steadier revenues, to the bank.

When these factors are put into the context of the discussion of credit rationing, it can be seen that "customers" in the sense defined here are the least likely borrowers to be rationed (with the exception of some like those in the construction industry). They are also the least risky to the bank with respect to both the probability of default and the uncertainty of demand.

Thus, the description of who is rationed conforms to the stylized answers to the questions presented above. As monetary conditions tighten and interest rates rise, each bank will tend to ration those borrowers whose position in the credit market is weakest and also those whose position at that bank is weakest. These borrowers, as it happens, are the riskiest borrowers. After a time, once the change in monetary conditions has been accepted as permanent, the bank will alter nonprice terms to the less creditworthy borrowers so that portfolio composition will be achieved by the price and nonprice terms of the loan rather than by the mechanism of rationing.

Thus, in periods of tight credit, risk is controlled by continued lending to steady customers of the bank. As monetary conditions ease, less rationing takes place, nonprice terms are eased, and the borrower not considered to be a "good" customer is once again accepted. Thus, the riskiness of the loan portfolio increases as the bank is able to bear the additional risk, that is, as the market and the bank become more "liquid."

LINES OF CREDIT AND COMMITMENT FEES

As mentioned above, prime borrowers and many customers with extremely good credit standing will never be rationed at the commercial banks. However, some potential borrowers who need funds on a regular basis, either because of the cyclical needs of their business or for seasonal reasons, are weak enough credit risks or hold weak enough market positions that their chances of being rationed out of the market at some time take on a probability high enough to be bothersome to them. They would like some protection against the possibility that should the need arise to borrow funds, they would be unable to obtain the amounts needed. In their eyes, the availability of funds is a form of insurance against an illiquid situation.

Commercial banks are willing to promise this future availability of funds, because the promise to lend implies some potential future loan demand, the use of some of the loan availability. This is in essence the rationale for what is known as the *line of credit:* a bank's promise to a customer that the customer can come in at any time and borrow funds up to a certain limit, at a prearranged price (which may be a variable rate) and with prearranged nonprice terms (such as a given compensating balance requirement). This arrangement, however, is not costless to the bank, and thus a price must be paid for it somewhere or at some time. The price is determined in the following way.

The bank obtains from such a relationship an expected amount of future loan demand from the ith class, say $E(L_i)$, where E is the expectations operator and L_i is the potential loan amount of the ith loan class. The expected return to the bank of this relationship would be the expected revenues derived from the expected loan amounts discounted back to the current period. This will give the present value of the line of credit.

The bank will also incur a cost of funds to support the loan. This is simply the cost of money used to fund the loan multiplied by the expected loan amount discounted back to the current time period.

If the bank knew with certainty the amount and the time of the borrowing, then its asset portfolio could be structured so that the correct amount of funds would be available when needed. However, since neither the amount nor the timing of the loan is known with certainty, the bank must be liquid enough, either in its own assets or in its ability to purchase funds, to supply funds to the customer if and when they are needed.

In the case of keeping a liquid asset portfolio that can be drawn upon to support such a loan, a bank suffers a lower return on assets than it would otherwise. If it purchases funds in its liability markets, it may buy funds at a higher rate than it is lending at in order to have money available when needed. In other cases it may need to remain in some markets, such as the Eurodollar market, at all times to ensure the lowest interest rates on purchased funds when it needs them. In any case, the bank would suffer lower net earnings on its assets because of its need to maintain liquidity to support potential borrowings.

The potential borrower, on the other hand, must estimate its expected need for funds and weigh this against the potential cost of not having the funds available when needed. In this way the potential borrower can determine what it is willing to pay for various amounts of availability.

Thus, a demand and supply situation exists for lines of credit and the fee that will compensate the lender for making a commitment to the line. The quantity of lines of credit available and the price of these lines will then be determined by market forces and the changing expectations that impinge on both the potential borrower and the lender.

The prime customers or other borrowers who believe the probability is very small that they will be rationed will not demand these arrangements, which is another way of saying that the price they would offer for a line of credit would be zero. These borrowers, however, are the bank's most desirable customers, in terms of credit risk and size and steadiness of borrowing. Banks have, therefore, cemented their relationship with these firms by extending lines of credit to them at no cost. If they did not do this to recognize a situation that in fact existed and to make loan arrangements consistent throughout the better portion of their customer portfolio, they did it to compete by offering additional services to their customers. Although nothing is gained by a bank offering its excellent borrowers lines of credit, if one bank does it, other banks generally do it also. They do not wish to appear to be offering less than a full range of services.

Payment for Lines of Credit

There are three ways the bank can charge for lines of credit: by charging an explicit commitment fee,[11] by including an implicit fee in the loan rate, and by requiring compensating balances.

As described previously, a commitment fee would be determined by the demand for and supply of lines of credit.[12] It would be accounted for separately, as payment for an explicit service provided by the bank, and would not be combined with fees or terms that covered other services or usages provided for in the customer's loan arrangement. This commitment fee should rise or fall with the conditions borrowers and lenders expect to occur in the financial markets over time. If businesses become more concerned about the availability of funds in the future, with no change in

---

[11] This could be called an insurance premium because the potential borrower is not actually engaging in a futures contract except for the expected amount it will be using for normal operations. What it is actually buying is insurance that the bank will not close its loan window and will finance its requirements. Since average usage in "normal" times is about 25 to 30 percent of the lines available, it would seem that the lines are more for insurance needs than anything else.

[12] How this is actually paid in practice, i.e., a front-end or facility fee or a usage fee assessed after the fact, will be discussed in Chapter 10. In the present analysis it makes no difference to the development of the argument.

expectations of the bank's availability of funds, then the fee should be bid up. If bankers feel money will be more readily available in the future, given no change in borrowers' expectations, then the fee should be bid down. This would help borrowers and lenders to efficiently position themselves and their balance sheets relative to the future and is consistent with the arguments for "unbundling" bank services developed recently by many analysts.[13]

Another way to charge for providing a line of credit is to embed a commitment fee into the loan rate. To do this, banks would have to estimate the average potential usage of the line of credit for each loan class and include a charge for this expected usage in the loan rates for each class. If expected average usage increased, then the charge for this facility would also rise. If expected usage declined, then the charge would decline.

This, of course, has been the common technique used in the past in charging for the availability of funds. The problem here, however, is that the users, the good and steady borrowers from the bank, actually subsidize the nonborrowers or those economic units that borrow only when there is extreme pressure in the financial markets. Consider two borrowers that are exactly alike, each with a $1 million line of credit with a bank. The only difference between the two is that customer A uses, on average, 60 percent of its line while customer B uses only 20 percent of its line. The total loan rate will be divided into two parts, r_L and r_c, where r_L is the "pure" loan rate and r_c is the average implicit commitment fee for the loan class *added into the interest rate for this loan class.* The loan rate r charged on the loan is the sum of the two components, that is, $r = r_L + r_c$. Compensating balance requirements and other terms of the loan are not included in this example. Also, the borrowing is for the unit of time on which the interest rate is based.

Customer A is charged $r \times \$600,000$ for its loan, or $r_L \times \$600,000$ for the "pure" loan and $r_c \times \$600,000$ for the insurance of having another $400,000 available to it if it needs the funds. The effective commitment fee, if only one period is considered (to place interest rates on a common basis), is $r_c \times \$600,000/\$400,000$ or $1.5r_c$.

Customer B is charged $r \times \$200,000$ for its loan, or $r_L \times \$200,000$ for the "pure" loan and $r_c \times \$200,000$ for the insurance of having another $800,000 available to it if it needs the funds. The effective commitment fee for customer B is $r_c \times \$200,000/\$800,000$, which is $0.25r_c$, or considerably less than the effective commitment fee for customer A.

---

[13] See, for example, L. L. Bryan, "Put a Price on Credit Lines," *The Bankers Magazine* (Summer 1974), pp. 47–48.

The point of this is that since the price of the line of credit is "bundled" with the "pure" price of borrowing, the borrowers to whom the bank has a smaller future commitment of funds carry the expense of the infrequent borrowers, who expose the bank to a greater risk in terms of a potential future demand for funds.[14]

The experience of the late 1960s and 1970s highlights the problems that can result from unbundled pricing arrangements. Many potential borrowers established "insurance" lines of credit at that time to ensure their liquidity during periods of tight money. Usage rates or fees were quite low, so that the cost of obtaining the availability was close to zero.[15] However, as banks learned to their distress in the 1973 period of monetary restraint, the variance of demand on the part of these borrowers was extremely high. That is, the commitments the banks took on in the late 1960s and early 1970s caused the banks to assume more risk than they charged for, because the pricing mechanism they used did not compensate them for the potentially large loan demands they might have to face and in fact did face as events unfolded.

In addition, it can be argued that banks' better customers actually borrowed less than they otherwise would have at that time because, in subsidizing the firms that had lines but did not use them, they paid higher loan rates on the money they borrowed relative to other sources of funds than if they had not subsidized the nonusers. These conditions led to the more explicit pricing of credit line arrangements in the mid-1970s.

The final way the bank can charge for lines of credit is by collecting compensating balances as the "fee" for the future availability of funds.[16] If the compensating balance is required explicitly as an insurance fee, then it certainly can be used for this purpose, with the only concern being that perhaps it would be more efficient to charge an explicit fee. This is even more true if the fee is to be set by market forces, because it is much easier to adjust an explicit interest fee, usually in terms of an eighth of a percentage point, than to adjust compensating balance requirements, which, as mentioned previously, banks have been reluctant to change in small amounts.

---

[14] Since the line relationship should be based on expected values, the distribution of borrowings may affect the answer. That is, the potential exposure is based not only on the expected amounts of borrowing but also on the expected variance of these borrowings. In this case it is assumed that the customer who has a smaller mean usage may well have a larger variance.

[15] No facility fees or usage fees were charged at this time, and compensating balances, if they were required at all, were often computed on the outstanding loan amount. Hence, firms paid little in terms of fees or balances to obtain access to funds.

[16] For an exposition of this point, see J. M. Guttentag and R. G. Davis, "Compensating Balances," *Essays in Money and Credit*, Federal Reserve Bank of New York, 1964.

The biggest problem seems to be, however, that compensating balances are double counted. They serve not only as a fee for the future availability of funds, but also as a means of increasing the effective cost of the loan in the face of rigid explicit pricing schemes. If banks account for these two different reasons for having compensating balances, then there is still the problem of "bundled" services and prices. Furthermore, if compensating balances are used for other reasons, such as to ensure a more stable supply of funds to the bank, then they serve as a risk-reducing element that should be compensated for by reducing other charges. Thus, the use of balances as a "payment" for the future availability of funds is at best a confusing means of accomplishing something that could be done much more easily in other ways.

In conclusion, then, banks perform a useful economic service in providing customers with lines of credit. To many customers, a line of credit is a valuable economic commodity for which they are willing to pay. Because the lines expose banks to additional liquidity problems, it is desirable to levy a fee to cover the cost of this exposure. The proper fee can be determined, therefore, by the supply and demand conditions in the market for these services. Commercial banks, however, have moved slowly, as economic conditions have changed, to explicit pricing of lines of credit.

PRICING DEMAND DEPOSITS

Commercial banks have been prohibited by law from paying explicit interest rates on demand deposits since the 1930s, although they have, in fact, paid implicit interest on these deposits. It has been argued that paying explicit interest on demand deposits would raise expenses of the banks and thus force them into riskier assets in an effort to achieve higher returns to cover the greater expenses. Those who have argued that banks do, in effect, pay interest have pointed out that the gross costs of administering and operating a demand deposit function exceed the remuneration obtained in fees and charges from the holders of these accounts.

Abstracting from equation (1-2), net expenses for demand deposits, NE_D, can be expressed as

$$r_D - f_D + b_D = NE_D \tag{3-1}$$

where r_D is the interest rate paid on demand deposits, b_D is the allocated operating expense per dollar of demand deposits, and f_D represents the fees and charges per dollar of demand deposits collected from holders of those accounts.

First of all, if r_D is institutionally set equal to zero, then NE_D is just the difference between costs per dollar of demand deposits and fees and charges per dollar of demand deposits. If costs exceed remuneration, then the net expense per dollar of demand deposits is positive, and hence it appears to be true that banks have paid implicit interest on these accounts.

Second, under equilibrium conditions, marginal cost is equal to marginal revenue. Thus when $r_D = 0$, the marginal cost of demand deposits, which would be nothing more than the marginal cost of servicing deposits, MC_{b_D}, less the marginal revenue from fees and charges, MR_{f_D}, will be set equal to the marginal revenue of assets, MR_L:

$$MR_L = MC_{b_D} - MR_{f_D} \tag{3-2}$$

Finally, it has been argued that banks will be forced into riskier assets if they are allowed to pay interest on demand deposits. However, unless there is a change in MR_L, which is assumed to be either the U.S. Treasury bill rate or the short-run CD rate, if the bank operates in a liability-management world, it will not be adversely affected by the change in regulation. Its profits may be lower; its size may be smaller, because of the increased cost of demand deposits; it may hold fewer U.S. government securities or issue more CDs; but it will not alter its loan portfolio if it still wants to maximize its profits, for a given level of risk. The only alternative would be for the bank to change its risk class in order to achieve the former rate of return. Whether a bank did this or not would depend on the risk-return frontier available to investors and on the willingness of investors to trade off risk for return.

In terms of marginal conditions, the schedule for fees and charges will in all likelihood be changed, i.e., the marginal cost to the depositor, which is the marginal revenue MR_{f_D} to the bank, would have to rise. This can be seen from the equation

$$MR_L = MC_{r_D} + MC_{b_D} - MR_{f_D} \tag{3-3}$$

where for constant MR_L, if MC_{r_D} increases while MC_{b_D} remains constant, MR_{f_D} must rise. However, the optimal conditions for the loan portfolio would not change, because the loan demand schedules and MR_L have not changed. Moreover, the average level of fees and charges would rise, as can be seen from equation (3-1).

Thus, payment of an explicit interest rate on demand deposits would not force banks to hold riskier assets and thus would not change the risk class of the bank. It would simply begin to unbundle costs; in the limit, if the market rate on demand deposits were achieved, then MC_{b_D} should be equal to MR_{f_D} and depositors would get *explicitly* what they were paying for.

A NOTE ON TRANSFER PRICING

It has been assumed, until now, that the bank consists of one administrative unit or profit center that takes in deposits, raises capital, and makes loans. In many banks, however, this is not the situation. These banks are composed of many profit centers, some of which may only collect deposits and some only grant loans, while others are actually net suppliers or net users, both obtaining and using funds. Very seldom does a profit center in a bank actually achieve a balance between what it takes in and what it gives out.

In seeking an overall balance, a bank faces the problem of resource allocation: how to achieve the "best" allocation of surplus funds throughout the bank, the allocation that will provide it with the most profit for a given amount of risk. As in most problems of allocation, the question centers on the appropriate pricing mechanism to be used. Since the main concern is with the transfer of funds within the bank, the cost of moving these funds is generally referred to as the *transfer price*.

The transfer price can be computed in different ways, two of which will be discussed here. In the first method, the bank uses the marginal cost or marginal opportunity cost of funds as the price of transferring funds within the bank; in the second, the bank "pools" its liabilities, computes their weighted average cost, and then charges this "pool" rate on all internal transfers.

To compare these methods of transfer pricing, two cases must be considered: the case of asset management and the case of liability management. First, the situation as it occurs in an asset-management world will be explained, with reference to the example presented in Figure 2-5 (page 57).

Asset Management Transfer Pricing

The marginal (opportunity) cost of funds in this example is the rate that can be earned on U.S. government securities. The pool of funds consists of the equilibrium quantities of Type I and Type II deposits, D_I^0 and D_{II}^0.[17] The pool rate is $(r_{D_I}^0 D_I^0 + r_{D_{II}}^0 D_{II}^0)/(D_I^0 + D_{II}^0)$. Since $r_{D_I}^0$ and $r_{D_{II}}^0$ are less

---

[17] Capital, at present, is assumed to be allocated at a fixed rate to all loans. This is discussed more fully in Chapter 11.

than the government rate of interest, the pool rate will be less than the marginal opportunity cost. Since the positions of the curves will always be as depicted in Figure 2-5, this conclusion can be generalized to say that, except in transitional states, the marginal opportunity cost of funds will always be greater than the pool rate of interest.

Since the two rates will not be the same, the question is, which rate is the correct one to use? The answer can be seen by considering that there are three profit centers in the bank: The first collects Type I and Type II deposits, the second makes nongovernment loans, and the third buys and sells government securities. The deposit center can transfer funds to either the loan department or the government securities department. The loan department can obtain funds from either the deposit center or the government securities department.

If the pool rate is used, then it becomes the internal "marginal" cost of funds to the bank. Since the pool rate is below the government rate, there would always seem to be opportunity to increase profits by raising more funds, by increasing deposit rates, and by investing in government securities. However, more funds will not be put into the loan department because the marginal return on loans would thus drop below the marginal return on government securities; it is profitable, in this sense, to allocate funds to government securities and not to loans.

If the pool rate is used, the bank will be larger than if it used the marginal rate, it will place a higher proportion of its funds in government securities, and, as is known from the results in Chapter 2, its profits will be lower. With regard to judging the profitability of each profit center, there will be a definite bias toward making the loan center and the government securities center appear to be more profitable relative to the deposit center than in the case of marginal cost transfer pricing. In fact, in this example, the deposit center would show a zero profit. This center would be more profitable if its manager took some of the department's funds and invested them directly in the government securities market rather than give them up to either internal department.

This seems to be the true test of the adequacy of the internal pricing mechanism in an asset-management world. Is it more profitable for all managers of profit centers with a surplus of funds to place these funds outside the bank than to put them to use in other departments within the bank? The government rate, which in this case is the marginal opportunity cost of funds, represents the alternative opportunity to the surplus departments and thus should be the true transfer price within the bank.

Liability Management Transfer Pricing

In the case of liability management, the situation is somewhat similar, except that the bank does not deal with the question of where it should place its given quantity of funds but is concerned instead with whether or not it should buy more funds. The marginal cost in this case is a true cost, because it is the rate of interest paid to obtain funds in the market of elastically supplied liabilities. In Figure 2-6 (page 60), the marginal cost of funds is $r^0_{D_{II}}$. The pool rate is the same as in the previous example, $(r^0_{D_I}D^0_I + r^0_{D_{II}}D^0_{II})/(D^0_I + D^0_{II})$, and again it is easy to see that the marginal cost of funds exceeds the pool rate. Furthermore, it is easy to see that if the bank wants to lend more, the deposit center would obtain deposits of Type II as opposed to raising any more funds from the Type I market, because the marginal expense would rise in the latter instance but stay constant in the former.

The question is, Why would the manager of the deposit center want to raise more funds to support loans, since he would be obtaining the additional funds at $r^0_{D_{II}}$ but would only be getting credit at the pool rate for the funds raised and transferred to the loan department?

In judging the profitability of centers within the bank, the bias would again be against the deposit center and in favor of the loan center. The deposit center would be faced with zero profits, since it would just be getting back its average cost of funds. In fact, the deposit center would be better off, as was seen above, if it took some of its funds and invested them in government securities than if it placed them internally in the bank. The loan department, appearing to be more profitable than it would be under a marginal cost transfer price, would try to increase the size of its portfolio. Since the marginal cost of loans would drop as the size of the loan portfolio increased, it would seem desirable to get back into government securities. Again, using pool rate pricing, the bank would be larger than it would be under the other pricing scheme, it would have a larger portfolio of U.S. government securities, and it would be less profitable. Hence, it is shown again that the bank would not be allocating funds as efficiently using pool rate transfer pricing as it would be using marginal cost transfer pricing.

Transfer Pricing and Traditional Changes in Interest Rates

Analysts have argued against the use of a marginal rate as a bank's transfer price, because in periods when interest rates are changing, the marginal rate, being quite sensitive to movements in open-market rates, will vary a great deal more than an average, or pool, cost of funds. The pool rate obviously will vary less than a marginal rate, because the pool rate is made up of different maturities of liabilities and hence will include interest rates that are fixed for the time period under review. Given, then, a fixed cost to a portion of the portfolio, the average rate must vary less than a marginal rate on an instrument whose maturity is within the bank's operating horizon. In practice, therefore, the marginal rate will often be chosen to be the rate on 90-day negotiable certificates of deposit.[18] The average maturity of the pool will, in all likelihood, be longer than 90 days. Thus, the pool is made up of liabilities that have fixed rates, as far as this time period is concerned, and the pool rate will tend to lag movements in market rates because of the unchanging nature of a portion of the liability portfolio. When interest rates are rising, the marginal cost of funds will be even further above the pool rate than at times when interest rates are not changing. When rates fall, the spread between the marginal rate and the pool rate will fall and may even become negative.[19]

Therefore, bankers have argued that marginal rates are not usable, because (1) they are too variable and (2) they understate or overstate the actual cost of funds being used to support the loan portfolio. These arguments are not valid, however.

One reason why these arguments are invalid is that liabilities obtained at interest rates that are considered fixed for the time period under consideration represent a fixed cost to the bank; that is, they are considered a "sunk" cost much as the fixed costs of physical assets are considered a sunk cost in determining the optimal operating size of the manufacturing firm. Sunk costs do not enter into current decisions, because they have to be paid whether or not the firm produces anything. The only costs that matter are those of items over which the firm has control in this time period. In the case of the bank, these are the new liabilities purchased and the new loans being placed on the books.

The second reason why the arguments are invalid has to do with movements in the term structure of interest rates.[20] New loans are made at terms consistent with expected future movements of interest rates. Thus, pricing spreads and maturities should change as the marginal cost of funds

[18] The choice of this instrument and maturity will be discussed more thoroughly below in Chapter 12.

[19] R. E. Knight, "Customer Profitability Analysis—Part II: Analysis Methods at Major Banks," *Monthly Review*, Federal Reserve Bank of Kansas City (September-October 1975), pp. 17–18.

[20] For a brief discussion of the term structure of interest rates, see Chapter 12.

changes and expectations of its future movements also change. Therefore, bankers should respond to movements in the marginal cost of funds by using the information contained within the movements in interest rates for the booking of new loans. They may use a moving average of this rate, such as an average of the rates posted in the previous three weeks, to eliminate random fluctuations in the rate, but they should use the marginal rate as the transfer price even in periods of transition.

SELECTED REFERENCES

Bryan, L. L. "Put a Price on Credit Lines." *The Bankers Magazine* (Summer 1974).

Campbell, T. S. "A Model of the Market for Lines of Credit." *The Journal of Finance* (September 1977).

Guttentag, J. M., and Davis, R. G. "Compensating Balances." *Essays in Money and Credit,* Federal Reserve Bank of New York (1964).

Harris, D. G. "Some Evidence of Differential Lending Practices at Commercial Banks." *The Journal of Finance* (December 1973).

———. "Credit Rationing at Commercial Banks: Some Empirical Evidence." *The Journal of Money, Credit and Banking* (May 1974).

Jaffee, D. M. *Credit Rationing and the Commercial Loan Market.* New York: John Wiley and Sons, 1971.

———, and Modigliani, F. "A Theory and Test of Credit Rationing." *The American Economic Review* (December 1969).

Mason, J. M. "Market Discrimination, Credit Rationing and the Customer Relationship at Commercial Banks." Working Paper 2-77, Rodney L. White Center for Financial Research, The University of Pennsylvania, 1977.

———. "Loan Commitments and Borrowing at Commercial Banks." Finance Department Working Paper, The University of Pennsylvania, 1978.

REVIEW QUESTIONS

1. Why have bank loan rates been marked up over prime rates? Why not over the cost of funds?
2. Why do markups not change when financial market conditions change?
3. What is the economic rationale for the customer relationship between a bank and some of its borrowers? Do banks ration "good" customers?
4. Why would a bank ration credit rather than change loan terms?
5. Changes in nonprice terms are said to cause loan demand to shift. What does this mean, and why does it happen?
6. Discuss the economics of the bank line of credit. What is the rationale for a positive price on bank lines of credit?
7. Why do prime customers not need a line of credit? If they do not need a line of credit, what should the price of a line of credit be to prime customers?
8. Explain the difference between marginal cost transfer pricing and "pool rate" transfer pricing. Why does one provide a better guide for allocating bank funds than the other?
9. It has been stated that some borrowers subsidize others by paying a higher interest rate on loans, including a cost for the "insurance contract" implied by bank lines of credit. Why don't these borrowers demand lower rates?
10. Analysts have concluded that an electronic funds transfer system (EFTS) will cause people to be more aware of the time value of money. What might happen to "rule-of-thumb" pricing schemes in such a world?

APPENDIX

Mathematical Formulation of Models
Presented in Chapter 3

CUSTOMER RELATIONSHIP

Two attributes were given the "good" customer in the body of Chapter 3. First, the good customer is a steady borrower; second, on becoming a customer, the borrower will provide more loan demand to the bank in the future than it would otherwise. These two attributes are now introduced into the model developed in the Appendix to Chapter 2.

The effects of steadier loan demand can be easily shown. Take the equilibrium pricing relationship of the bank under conditions of uncertainty (given in equation (2A-14) in the Appendix to Chapter 2) and look just at the asset side:

$$r_{MC} = r_i^a \left(1 + \frac{1}{e_a^i} \right) + f_i - b_i - \frac{R \partial \sigma_{\pi m}}{(\partial L_i / \partial r_i) \partial r_i} = \widehat{MR}_{L_i} \qquad (3A\text{-}1)$$

where r_{MC} is the marginal cost of funds, r_{CD}, or the marginal opportunity cost of funds, r_G; and $\widehat{MR}_{L_i}$ is the risk-adjusted marginal revenue of the ith loan class. The result being sought is $\partial \widehat{MR}_{L_i} / \partial \sigma_{L_i} = 0 = \partial r_{MC} / \partial \sigma_{L_i}$. That is, what change in $\partial \sigma_{\pi m} / \partial r_i$ will result from a change in σ_{r_i}, and how will the interest rate on this loan class change in order to keep $\partial \widehat{MR}_{L_i} / \partial \sigma_{L_i} = 0$?

It is known from (2A-15) that

$$\frac{\partial \sigma_{\pi m}}{\partial r_i^a} = \sigma_m \left[\sigma_\pi \frac{\partial \rho_{\pi m}}{\partial r_i^a} + \rho_{\pi m} \frac{\partial \sigma_\pi}{\partial r_i^a} \right] \qquad (3A\text{-}2)$$

and from (2A-16) that

$$\frac{\partial \sigma_\pi}{\partial r_i^a} = \frac{1}{\sigma_\pi} \left[(r_i^a + f_i - b_i) \sigma_{L_i}^2 \right.$$
$$\left. + \sum_{i>j} (r_j^a + f_j - b_j) \sigma_{ij} - \sum_h (r_h^d - f_h + b_h) \sigma_{hi} \right] \qquad (3A\text{-}3)$$

Thus,

$$
\frac{\partial^2 \sigma_\pi}{\partial r_i^a \partial \sigma_L} = \frac{1}{\sigma_\pi} \left[2(r_i^a + f_i - b_i)\sigma_{L_i} \right.
$$
$$
\left. + \sum_{i>j} (r_i^a + f_j - b_j)\rho_{ij}\sigma_{Lj} - \sum_h (r_h^d - f_h + b_h)\rho_{hi}\sigma_{D_h} \right] \quad (3A\text{-}4)
$$

where ρ_{ij} and ρ_{hi} are the correlation coefficients between the ith asset class and the jth asset class and between the ith asset class and the hth liability class, respectively.

Since $\partial \sigma_\pi / \partial r_i^a$ was assumed to be negative, it must be true that $\partial^2 \sigma_\pi / \partial r_i^a \partial \sigma_{L_i}$ is negative. If the latter term is negative, then the rate of interest charged on the ith loan class must rise if $\partial \widehat{MR}_{L_i} / \partial \sigma_{L_i} = 0$, and $\partial \sigma_{L_i} > 0$, i.e., if the variance of loan demand increases. Conversely, if the variance of loan demand decreases, then the interest rate must fall to maintain equilibrium. Hence, it can be said that a steadier loan demand is valuable to the bank and that the bank is willing to cut rates to obtain more loans from classes that have a steadier loan demand.

To examine how future loan demand enters into the picture, the model must be modified slightly. Only the certainty case will be treated here, to reduce confusion. Next, the customers' demand for loans must be modified. The current demand for loans will be a function not only of the current interest rate charged on the loan but also of interest rates on funds actually borrowed in the past. In other words, the more a customer borrows today, the more the customer is likely to borrow in the future.

$$
L_{i_t} = f_i(r_{i_t}^a, L_{i_{t-1}}) \quad (3A\text{-}5)
$$

where the subscript t refers to the current period, and $\partial L_{i_t} / \partial L_{i_{t-1}} > 0$. The model can be extended to an infinite number of periods, but to bring out clearly the implications of the model, only two periods will be considered here. These will be period 1, the current period, and period 2, the next period.

As in equation (2A-10), the certainty case, the value of the firm is determined by discounting the profits of the two periods. Thus,

$$
V' = \sum_{i=1}^{m} r_{i1}^a L_{i1} - \sum_{h=1}^{n} r_{h1}^d D_{h1} + \left(\frac{1}{1 + \rho} \right) \left(\sum_{i=1}^{m} r_{i2}^a L_{i2} - \sum_{h=1}^{n} r_{h2}^d D_{h2} \right) \quad (3A\text{-}6)
$$

If V' is maximized subject to each period's balance sheet and the equation is rearranged and solved for the marginal revenue of loans and the marginal cost, r_{MC}, the following result is obtained for loan pricing. [It is assumed that (1) the marginal cost of funds is the same in both periods and (2) the elasticity of the demand curves for a given interest rate is the same in both periods.]

$$r_{MC} = r_{i1}^a \left(1 + \frac{1}{e_i^a}\right) + \left(\frac{1}{1+\rho}\right) r_{i2}^a \frac{\partial L_{i2}}{\partial L_{i1}} \tag{3A-7}$$

$$r_{MC} = r_{i2}^a \left(1 + \frac{1}{e_i^a}\right)$$

The term $\partial L_{i2}/\partial L_{i1}$ is the "customer relationship" term. It shows how much next period's demand will shift as a result of satisfying the customer this period. Since this term is positive, for a given marginal cost of funds, r_{MC}, the interest rate on a given class of loans will be lower as the customer relationship term gets bigger. This implies that the future loan demand is valuable to the bank and the bank is willing to reduce its price in order to achieve the increased future loan demand.

It should be noted that if the demand curves are perfectly elastic, next period's demand curve cannot shift outward, so that $\partial L_{i2}/\partial L_{i1} = 0$ for that loan class.

THE PRICING SCHEME

As described in the text of Chapter 3, commercial banks often build up their relative pricing scheme on the basis of a markup system in which loan rates are set relative to the prime rate. Thus, the interest rate on the ith loan class is set either as

$$\bar{r}_i^a = r_p + x_i \tag{3A-8}$$

or as

$$\hat{r}_i^a = r_p(1 + \hat{x}_i) \tag{3A-9}$$

where r_p is the prime rate, x_i is the average markup over the prime rate, and $\hat{x}_i$ is the percentage markup over the prime rate.

CREDIT RATIONING

It is logical that a pricing scheme such as the one described in the previous section could affect the market-clearing choices of the commercial bank. In an effort to determine whether this kind of situation could occur, the pricing system of (2A-8) is compared with the equilibrium prices determined in (2A-14). If the analysis is begun assuming an equilibrium situation, then

$$r_{MC} = r_p^a \left(1 + \frac{1}{e_{L_p}}\right) = r_i^a \left(1 + \frac{1}{e_{L_i}}\right) \tag{3A-10}$$

where the subscript p stands for prime loans and the subscript i represents the ith loan class.

The loan rate on the ith loan class is then

$$r_i^a = r_{MC} \left(\frac{e_{L_i}}{1 + e_{L_i}}\right) = r_p + x_i \tag{3A-11}$$

and there will be no credit rationing.

Now, let the marginal rate of interest change. It is seen that

$$\frac{dr_p}{dr_{MC}} = \frac{e_{L_p}}{1 + e_{L_p}} \tag{3A-12}$$

and

$$\frac{dr_i^a}{dr_{MC}} = \frac{e_{L_i}}{1 + e_{L_i}} \tag{3A-13}$$

However,

$$\frac{d\bar{r}_i^a}{dr_{MC}} = \frac{dr_p}{dr_{MC}} = \frac{e_{L_p}}{1 + e_{L_p}} \tag{3A-14}$$

and whether $d\bar{r}_i^a/dr_{MC}$ is equal to, greater than, or smaller than dr_i^a/dr_{MC} depends upon what relationship $e_{L_p}/(1 + e_{L_p})$ bears to $e_{L_i}/(1 + e_{L_i})$. Since $e_{L_p} > e_{L_i}$, then $e_{L_p}/(1 + e_{L_p}) > e_{L_i}/(1 + e_{L_i})$ and $d\bar{r}_i^a/dr_{MC} > dr_i^a/dr_{MC}$. No rationing will occur under these conditions, because the rate charged on the ith loan class is greater than the rate that would be determined in the market. However, banks would like a greater quantity of loans from the ith loan class than they are actually receiving. The portfolio will be more risky than would be desired, given market conditions, but the condition is one in which lending more rather than less is in the bank's interest.

The situation changes if the customer relationship is introduced. Again assuming a starting position of equilibrium, the ith loan class has the following price (taken from equation (3A-6)):

$$\bar{r}_i^a = r_p + x_i$$

and
$$= r_{MC} \left(\frac{e_{L_p}}{1 + e_{L_p}} \right) - \left(\frac{r_{p2}}{1 + \rho} \right) \left(\frac{e_{L_p}}{1 + e_{L_p}} \right) \frac{\partial L_{p2}}{\partial L_{p1}} \qquad (3A\text{-}15)$$

$$r_i^a = r_{MC} \left(\frac{e_{L_i}}{1 + e_{L_i}} \right) - \left(\frac{r_{i2}}{1 + \rho} \right) \left(\frac{e_{L_i}}{1 + e_{L_i}} \right) \frac{\partial L_{i2}}{\partial L_{i1}} \qquad (3A\text{-}16)$$

Now,

$$\frac{dr_i^a}{dr_{MC}} = \frac{e_{L_i}}{1 + e_{L_i}} - \left(\frac{1}{1 + \rho} \right) \left(\frac{e_{L_i}}{1 + e_{L_i}} \right) \frac{\partial L_{i2}}{\partial L_{i1}} \frac{\partial r_{i2}}{\partial r_{MC}} \qquad (3A\text{-}17)$$

so that

$$\frac{d\bar{r}_i^a}{dr_{MC}} \gtreqless \frac{dr_i^a}{dr_{MC}} \qquad (3A\text{-}18)$$

depends not only on relative elasticities as before, but also on how strong the customer relationships are. It is now possible that some loan classes will find their markup moving up *less* than if the market had not been interfered with, i.e., $d\bar{r}_i^a/dr_{MC} < dr_i^a/dr_{MC}$ for some i. Note that not all loan classes will be in this situation. Some will find $d\bar{r}_i^a/dr_{MC} > dr_i^a/dr_{MC}$.

In the case where $d\bar{r}_i^a/dr_{MC} < dr_i^a/dr_{MC}$, the bank would desire fewer loans from this loan class than it is actually receiving. In this case, the incentive is to cut back on loans, to ration, in order to try to balance the loan portfolio under existing market conditions. Thus, the pricing scheme in this case does cause credit rationing.

The argument can be taken somewhat further. *Those borrowers with a weaker customer relationship or a highly inelastic loan demand will be the ones most frequently in a situation to be rationed.* If one considers the borrowers who do get rationed, such as the construction firm, this result is consistent with practice.

NONPRICE TERMS

Nonprice terms of the loan are included in the demand function as NP and are negatively related to the quantity of loans demanded in a given loan class. Thus,

$$L_i = f_i(r_i^q, NP_i) \qquad (3A\text{-}19)$$

When the problem is set up as before to maximize V' subject to the balance sheet constraint, the result is

$$r_{MC} = r_i^q \left(1 + \frac{1}{e_{L_i}}\right) + \frac{1}{\partial L_i / \partial NP_i} \qquad (3A\text{-}20)$$

Note that since $(\partial L_i / \partial NP_i) < 0$, the loan rate will be higher than it would be if nonprice terms did not exist. This is because a higher level of nonprice terms will shift the demand curve downward to the left, which has the effect of making the price higher, given that imperfections exist in the loan market.

Now, if r_{MC} changes,

$$dr_{MC} = dr_i^q \left(1 + \frac{1}{e_{L_i}}\right) + \frac{dNP_i}{\partial L_i / \partial NP_i} \qquad (3A\text{-}21)$$

it is easily seen that r_i^q will not have to rise or fall as much as the change in r_{MC} if nonprice terms are moved in the same direction. That is, if interest rates are rising, nonprice terms become more restrictive, and vice versa.

Thus, if a situation of credit rationing is created, as described in the previous section, the problem is one in which the marked-up interest rates do not rise sufficiently to reduce demand as far as the bank would desire under existing market conditions. It is easy to see, now, that nonprice terms can be used to achieve the equilibrium just as well as if prices rose to fully choke off the demand.

Appendix References

Mason, J. M. "Market Discrimination, Credit Rationing and the Customer Relationship at Commercial Banks." Working Paper No. 2-77, Rodney L. White Center for Financial Research, University of Pennsylvania, 1977.

———. "Theory of the Banking Firm with Uncertain Demand and Supply of Funds." Finance Department Working Paper, University of Pennsylvania, 1978.

II

LONG-TERM MANAGEMENT

4

Strategic Planning
in Commercial Banks

In the past, bank managers often spent most of their time dealing with short-run problems, such as the liquidity of the investment portfolio and the seasonal movement of deposits and loans. The only matter of a longer-run nature that top management worried about on any recurring basis was that of maintaining adequate capital, but this required attention to the internal generation of funds rather than to raising the funds externally.

In the static banking world of the past, banks did not have much incentive to look beyond the annual budget or profit plan. Banking markets were fairly well defined, subsidiary activities were restricted, and growth was generally constrained by the health of the local or regional economy. Looking any distance into the future was not worth the effort in most cases.

For many banks this static environment no longer exists. If the only factors impinging on the banking industry were technological ones, bank managers would still have their hands full with planning and interpreting how they were to direct the bank. But the problem is much more complex than this.

It is true that the technology of the banking system is changing, but this represents just a small portion of what is happening in the banking area. Legislation and regulation have been in a constant state of flux in recent years and are not expected to stabilize in the foreseeable future. This means that the activities in which a bank can engage are uncertain. Even what the legal definition of a bank branch will be is, at the present time, uncertain.

Another important area of uncertainty is competition. Not only do banks face greater competition within their own industry because of the national activities of their domestic competitors, but the impact of foreign-headquartered banks cannot be ascertained at this stage of the development of the industry. Furthermore, with the breakdown of barriers between commercial banks and the thrift institutions, more and more competition will be coming from this source. Now that some thrift institutions have third-party payment privileges and some consumer credit abilities and expect more in the future, the marketplace looks even more crowded.

Other areas can be cited that give evidence of change. Banking is a dynamic industry, and bank managers cannot sit back and let the future happen to them as they have in the past. The assumption that the future will be like the past no longer holds, with the exception that, like the present, the future will experience change.

The objective of bank managers must be to implement a program that will help them confidently move into the future while incorporating short-term operating decisions into the long-run program. This must be an effort of top management, because top management must define what the bank is and whom the bank is going to serve.

Thus, in this chapter the process of long-run bank planning, or strategic planning, is examined, and several areas that can be of crucial importance to the overall development of the bank are discussed. Specifically, the idea of strategic planning is discussed along with problems of implementing such a program in a commercial bank. After this, several distinct decision areas that affect the long-run outcome of the bank are investigated to see what general analytical principles can be applied to each.

STRATEGIC PLANNING

Strategic planning implies looking into the future as far as is necessary and reasonable in order to accomplish two things for the organization: first, to determine what the organization wants to be—that is, what markets it wants to serve—and second, to maximize the value of the firm to its owners. Opinions vary as to how far into the future is necessary and reasonable for a bank's strategic planning effort. However, to accomplish their purpose, strategic planners must depend on estimates of the future development of markets, which depends on demographic shifts or movements, market participants, and customer recognition; technological changes of whose final outcome banks are unsure; and legislation, which will ultimately have to be tested and clarified in practice.

Three years seems too short a period for many of these "long-run" factors to work themselves out clearly. On the other hand, ten years seems beyond the realm of practical predictability. Some time horizon between these two extremes would seem to be most practical; five to seven years should be sufficient to handle most of a bank's longer-range problems. However, the individual bank may choose a longer or shorter period of time, depending on its needs and capabilities. Certainly, no specific time horizon is written in stone; the suggestions made here are meant to be helpful to those trying to understand strategic planning and to those trying to implement a strategic planning process.

Philosophy of Planning

After deciding on the appropriate time horizon for strategic planning, it is necessary to choose the particular philosophy the bank will follow to conduct its planning operations. There are two philosophies of planning that have received most of the attention of planners. The first is strictly a forecasting type of effort, in which the bank finds out what it can do (that is, what it is allowed to do by its environment) and then attempts to do it as well as this environment allows. According to the second philosophy, bank management should determine what type of bank it wants to develop (that is, whether it wants to be a wholesale bank or a retail one, or whether or not it wants to go into consumer installment loans) and what it would like to be achieving at the end of the time period considered; then it should check the environment to determine the best way it can go about achieving the desired result.

FORECASTING AND PLANNING

If a bank employs the first technique, it must put a great deal of effort into determining what is attainable. That is, the bank wants to find out where it will be in the fifth or seventh year of its planning horizon. In Figure 4-1,

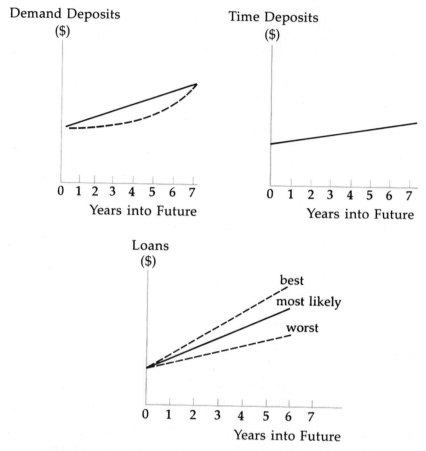

FIGURE 4-1   Forecasting the Bank's Assets and Liabilities

the trend lines for demand deposits, time deposits, and loans are projected into the seventh year of the hypothetical bank under consideration.
Strategic planners care only about the trend, which indicates where the
bank can expect to be at the end of the planning horizon. They are not
concerned with the intermediate points along the path. Five years is time
enough to include a complete business or credit cycle, so that fluctuations
around this trend should not be of concern to the bank. The only exception
would be if bank management expected either an extended boom or a
depression in which demand deposits followed, say, the dashed line in
Figure 4-1A. In that case, deviations from the trend would not cancel out

as in the case of the cyclical path, and the bank would have to take the intermediate-term path into consideration. Unless there is some expectation that the bank will face such a development, the trend is sufficient for the long-run analysis.

Another important consideration to the bank is the uncertainty that pertains to any forecast. Many banks attempt to obtain information on the "best" possible outcome and the "worst" possible outcome as well as the most likely outcome. The potential behavior of loans is shown in this way in Figure 4-1C. The particular distribution of the expected results at the end of the time horizon is of special interest, because it gives some idea of the degree of uncertainty anticipated by the bank. A wider dispersion of results implies a need for caution, because the most likely outcome is less certain than if the final results were more closely distributed.

It is to be expected that in planning, banks will create a contingency plan or plans. A great deal of uncertainty with respect to its potential position should force the bank into more careful consideration of alternative actions and flexibility in building up a balance sheet that will enable it to respond to the evolving market situation as rapidly as possible. Less uncertainty, of course, implies that contingency planning and flexibility, although important, need not be emphasized as much.

Nothing has yet been said about alternatives. In advance planning, the consideration of alternative paths comes after building up the forecast of the potential position of the firm. Basically, in forecasting items like demand deposits, time deposits, or loans, the bank is building up its balance sheet for the end of the planning horizon. Many short-run problems, such as meeting reserve requirements or handling seasonal liquidity needs (which are covered more intensively later), are not important in the long run. Banks do have to consider certain bank liquidity requirements that are permanent in the sense that they should be financed out of "permanent" rather than temporary sources. However, specific liquidity needs are not important within the framework of strategic planning.

Strategic planning is a process of determining the bank's future customer base and risk class. The customer base comprises firms and individuals to whom the bank lends and from whom it borrows. The bank's risk class is defined by the quantity of loans taken from each customer class.[1]

---

[1] In efficient capital markets, the choice of investments determines the risk class of the firm. See E. Fama and M. Miller, *The Theory of Finance* (New York: Holt, Rinehart and Winston, 1972), Chapter 7. There is the possibility that capital structure will also determine the risk class of the firm if the firm's securities are not traded in an efficient capital market. This possibility for the commercial bank is examined in Chapter 5. The capital structure of the bank, although a long-run problem, is not treated in depth in this chapter.

The first attempt to forecast assumes that the bank keeps its current customer base and risk class and, given the changing environment, projects what its position will be in seven years.

Then, using assumptions as to its "permanent" liquidity requirements and the retained earnings it expects to have over the time period, the bank attempts to construct its balance sheet. In all likelihood the items determined in this manner will not balance and the bank management will not be pleased with the results. Bank profitability will also be forecast on the basis of the constructed balance sheet and projected interest rate spreads. Thus, additional efforts must be made to restructure the bank to meet its environment and to do better than the "do nothing" forecast.

The particular direction the next stage of the exercise takes depends on the bank and its planning operations. Perhaps the next stage should be to list the major factors influencing the bank's markets and the shortfalls or excesses that have come out of the first attempt to structure the balance sheet. That is, the legislation, competitive aspects, and technological advances that are built into the forecast should be examined. This study should include such factors as demographic shifts, the movement of thrift institutions into the consumer finance area, the use of automated teller machines, and expected changes in state branching regulations.

Other questions must also be answered. Is the bank expected to face such a growth in loan demand relative to deposit growth that the left side of the balance sheet far outstrips the right side and additional sources of funds must be sought? If so, it may need to consider becoming a liability-management bank, whereas in the past it had been an asset-management bank. But this raises the question of whether or not the bank can operate in liability markets. Is the expansion of bank capital sufficient to meet projected capital requirements? The bank may need to change its dividend policy or seek external sources of capital.

The response to the original forecast should be to ask what the bank can do or what it needs to do to improve its performance. For example, the bank can change relative prices within its existing customer base, which can increase the funds it receives or enable it to make more loans. Alternatively, it can adjust the combination of loans on its books.

If it is in a growth situation, the bank can also attempt to increase the number of markets within which it operates. For example, it can consider issuing negotiable certificates of deposit or buying Eurodollars. These markets, however, require fairly regular activity if the bank is to come to rely on them. Thus, to cultivate this type of market requires a long-run commitment.

The bank may want to increase its customer base by expanding its branching system and drawing in more demand deposits or consumer time and passbook savings accounts. In order to do this, it must enter into a building program or a leasing program that would require a substantial outlay of current resources or a long-term lease commitment that would affect the financial resources of the bank for many years.

The bank could also adjust its plan on the asset side. It might want to expand more into retail business and become a "family service" bank. In that case it not only would want to increase the proportion of deposits it receives from private individuals but would expect to handle more consumer installment loans, automobile loans, and mortgages. Any thrust in this direction may be accompanied by an advertising campaign. If, in this longer run, the bank wishes to change its image, then it must make a concerted effort, over time, to convey its new image to the public. Thus, an overall strategy must be devised to achieve the greatest impact possible. Again, this must be done with care, because the results will be with the bank for many years to come.

These possibilities are only a few of the alternatives the bank can actually consider. However, the second part of the question posed above concerned what the bank needs to do. That is, the bank may be constrained in what it can actually achieve and may have to adjust its efforts to accommodate its constraints. It may not be large enough or active enough to be able to issue negotiable certificates of deposit or to buy Eurodollars. The growth and composition of the area's population may be such that there is not much room for expansion of either consumer deposits or consumer loans. In other words, from the standpoint of the individual bank, the growth of loans may be unsupportable. After all alternative means of supporting loan growth have been discussed, the bank may have to face the fact that in the longer run it may not be able to grow as rapidly as it would like.

Another possibility is that loan demand may not be growing sufficiently (because the economy is not growing as rapidly as forecast) to justify the quantity of funds the bank planned on needing. A bank may have to get out of some liability markets. For example, a bank that was a liability manager in the late 1960s and early 1970s may not be able to justify the quantity of funds the bank planned on needing. A bank may growth of loan demand does not exceed the growth of inelastically supplied funds. The bank must be realistic about what it can achieve. It may investigate ways to increase its loans more rapidly, but if this can be achieved only by taking on riskier loans, the bank must consider whether the increased loan growth is worth the cost of changing its risk class.

These changes must be run through the forecasting process to see if new results come closer to the balance sheet and profit figures desired by bank management. A second and third try may bring the results closer to the desired goal, but the process may have to be repeated again and again until management is able to live with both the "plan" and the customer base the plan implies.

STRUCTURING AND PLANNING

In the second approach to strategic planning, the first step is for top management to declare where they would like the bank to be at the end of the planning horizon; then an effort is made to determine how the bank can achieve these results. In terms of graphs, management lays out the endpoints that describe the deposit and loan levels desired at the end of seven years. These are represented by the x's in Figure 4-2, where the current position of the bank is denoted by the dots on the vertical axes. Again, since the bank is interested only in the longer run, in each part of the figure the two points are connected by a straight line; cycles are unimportant if the expansions and contractions are expected more or less to cancel each other out.

These endpoints imply a balance sheet in balance, because management has chosen the final result. Management also will impose desired spreads on the results, which will mean that the desired income statement and profitability are part of this projection.

It should be pointed out that these figures are not always quantitatively set by top management. Some goals are articulated qualitatively, and it then becomes the responsibility of the planning department to translate into numbers the vague policy statements made by the people deciding on the direction of the bank. Of course, these numbers must be checked with top management to make sure the figures used in the plan are consistent with their policy directives.

Regardless of how policy directives are formulated, in order for the plan to be a working document, some numbers have to be generated that represent the desired position of the bank. The next step is to determine whether this final position and the desired profit figures are attainable, that is, whether the environment will allow such a development. If so, what must the bank do to achieve the result? And if not, how must it revise its desires to profit best from what is attainable?

The forecasting process then works much as before. First, the planning department would put together a forecast assuming that the bank changed nothing but just passively responded to the expected economic

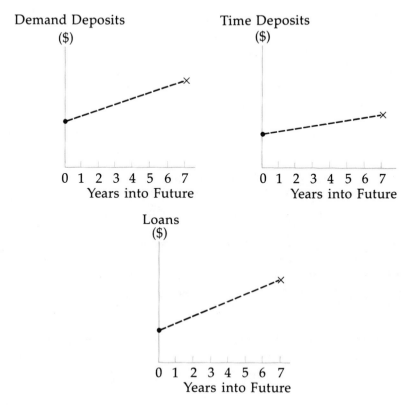

FIGURE 4-2   Structural Determination of the Bank's Assets and Liabilities

development. The effort in this case would be to discern how much the forecasted results differed from the desired plan.

If, as is likely, the proposed plan is different from the "no change" forecast, then the planning department must go back to the drawing board, much as in the forecasting approach described earlier, and determine what changes must be made to achieve the desired position. In many cases, the original policy directives may indicate the alterations desired by the bank management. The directives may be couched in terms of the bank becoming more retail oriented or moving more directly into international lending. If so, then the planning group must incorporate these factors into its forecast.

The effort, therefore, must be one of gradually approaching a given solution, the proposed final position of the bank, whereas the first technique discussed implied a rearranging to arrive at the bank's potential.[2] It cannot be overemphasized that the planning department must be aware of all the relevant costs as well as benefits in developing a plan in accord with the directive. The alternatives must be fully analyzed to make sure that in drawing up a plan that will achieve the desired final results the bank does not change its risk class or alter its original customer base.

For example, in the late 1960s and early 1970s, some large regional banks wanted to be more like the large money-center banks; they wanted to become liability managers or move into international financial circles. Thus, the directive given by top management was to achieve a position that would be consistent with these desires. However, these goals were not commensurate with what the banks could achieve. As was shown in Chapter 2, two things are necessary to become a liability-management bank: (1) "Good" liability markets must be available to the bank, and (2) the bank must have a loan demand that exceeds its inelastically supplied deposits. These large regional banks found that only the first of these two conditions was met. In order to achieve sufficient loan demand, they had to be willing to accept much riskier borrowers.[3] As a result they ultimately paid for becoming liability-management banks by having to write off larger amounts of loans than in previous years.

Those that expanded into international operations experienced similar difficulties. These banks did not have the customers to follow into international markets, and so they had to generate new customers. Since

---

[2] In a certain world, with complete and costless information, and where management's only concern is to maximize the value of the bank's stock, both techniques would result in exactly the same plan. However, in a world of uncertainty where information is not complete or costless and where management goals include factors other than the maximization of bank stock, it is to be expected that the different techniques will result in different plans. Although rather obvious, some of the reasons for this will be given in the next section, on the pros and cons of the two methods.

[3] There is a problem of interpretation here. One criticism of liability management is that the banks that engage in it are forced into riskier assets in order to maintain profit margins. In the argument presented in Chapter 2, it was clearly stated that *both* conditions mentioned here had to be present for liability management to occur and not change the riskiness of the firm. It was said in Chapter 2 that if the liability markets are not available or funds cannot be supplied elastically to the bank at all times, then the bank may be riskier than before it got into liability management. In the example given here, the other condition has been violated. That is, the bank *had* to change the riskiness of its portfolio in order to generate sufficient loan demand to become a liability manager. In the latter case, a liability-management bank that does this is riskier than the asset-management bank that existed before. However, this argument does not change the original statement about the riskiness of liability management if both conditions of liability management are satisfied.

the most creditworthy borrowers had already been serviced internation-
ally by their major lenders, the only credits available to the new entrants
were less creditworthy, less well known, and certainly not local borrowers. Hence, the risk exposure of these banks increased considerably.

The point to be made here is that planners who use this second
technique must be cognizant of the cost of what they are doing so that
some high-priority goals do not conflict with other goals such as maintaining the bank's risk class. If the goals chosen are not consistent with one
another, then the bank using this technique is bound to suffer. There must
be a realistic connection between what is desired and what is feasible, and
these two must be made to coincide through the efforts of the planning
department.

PROS AND CONS OF THE TWO TECHNIQUES

Space is not available to go deeply into the strengths and weaknesses of
the two planning systems. However, several points need to be made before the requirements of a planning system are presented.

The forecasting technique usually suffers from conservatism and a
failure to examine all alternatives. This is because the technique em-
phasizes forecasting from the existing position of the bank. The analyst
starts out assuming that everything will remain as it now is and then
checks where the bank comes up short or long. The bank then makes
adjustments to eliminate this discrepancy.

The problem with this is that the adjustments are usually marginal;
the bank responds to the market rather than leading it. All the alternatives
may not be investigated if the original results appear to be "satisfactory"
to management. Thus, if some institution is planning a substantial change
or if the economic environment is expected to change drastically, the bank
that follows this planning technique will usually be a follower and respond slowly to innovations.

However, the bank plan may be more "realistic" and less subject to
substantial errors than one devised by the second technique. That is, in its
conservatism, it will not be as subject to one particular outcome as are
other plans based on final projections. Thus, variations of results can be
built into the plan, and the bank can easily prepare contingency plans to
handle evolving circumstances.

Planning in this way does not allow banks to "determine" what they
want to be. They respond. To many people who run commercial banks
this is not entirely desirable. They want to have some say in what the bank

is going to be. Thus, a strong manager or management team may first formulate the final goals of the bank only in terms of desirable rates of return, or in terms of certain markets. There may be a tendency for the forecasting technique to break down and become more like the structural approach. This is a problem because if the planning program is set up on the basis of the first technique, it may be weak precisely where the second technique provides strength.

The major problem with the structural technique is that it may produce plans that are unrealistic, and unrealistic plans create frustration and even contempt for the whole planning process. The problem may evolve in the following manner: Top management sets goals or targets for the bank that are grossly out of line with what is feasible, subordinates do not challenge them, and the planning process is not set up to show that they cannot be reached. Thus, the unrealistic figures become incorporated into "the plan," with everyone but top management realizing that the plan cannot possibly be carried out. The planning process becomes a farce, but one in which everyone must play a part in order to remain with the bank. It is not hard to see why people become disillusioned when something like this occurs.

Another problem with the structural technique is that contingency plans are harder to formulate from "desired" results than from forecasts. Desired results are usually point estimates of where management wants the bank to be. Contingency plans must be set up to achieve these results regardless of how economic events unfold. How the bank may best go about this is debatable. Perhaps a more desirable alternative would be to state directives in terms of a most desired result and a minimum acceptable result. Contingency plans could then be based on the alternatives.

The method is very good for those who want to be leaders. Since the bank, in a sense, chooses what it wants to be, it can leap into the future and set the pace for other banks. This method also exposes the bank to greater risks, because its prognosis of the future could be wrong.

CRITERIA FOR A GOOD PLANNING OPERATION

Regardless of the specific approach taken, a planning operation must be composed of three distinct components if it is to be successful:

1. The planning operation must be organized into a system capable of performing its task. Random, haphazard planning with few or no consistent responsibilities or reporting channels can achieve little in the way of a systematic, well-thought-out plan. Some time, therefore, must be spent at

the outset in designing how the system is to be set up and how it is to work.

2. The planning process should be in the hands of creative, productive, and farsighted people who are appropriately rewarded for their role in furthering the bank's development. Many banks will not be able to exist with do-nothing, well-it's-always-worked-that-way type of people in the planning function. Some degree of skepticism is not unwelcome in the planning effort. However, if planning is dominated by the skeptics, it might as well not take place. Skeptics will stifle the planning process and, in all likelihood, keep the benefits of planning below the annual cost of "running through the planning process" again.

3. The bank must have an adequate information system that produces timely information for constructing and monitoring its plans. Although the planning process itself is primarily concerned with the alternatives that have to be decided upon, the latest and most appropriate data must be available to the process so that relevant alternatives can be developed and assumptions checked and rechecked.

Given these broad needs, the planning system must also meet the following criteria.

Management Participation

It is essential that top management actively support and participate in the planning process. Those who are shaping the plan must be confident that their inputs will be heard and will be used by the bank and that they are receiving adequate guidance from top management; otherwise, they will feel either that their work is useless or that they lack the information necessary to contribute effectively to the process. Either they will complete the requirements of the planning process with only minimal effort and thought, or they will be frustrated because they do not know what direction they should be taking.

Top management must be the initiator of the process, laying out in general terms the goals and directions it sees as consistent with both the bank's environment and its image. These directives should be general, because top management's concern is with the overall direction and style of the business, with the kind of institution the bank is going to be. Top management determines the lines of business and the risk class of the bank. It is the job of the lower levels of management to translate these overall goals into more specific component goals, to estimate costs and returns for the various alternatives, and to feed back information about the potential feasibility of some items. Without being given these general directives and without a feeling that top management is interested in the details of the planner's efforts, a planning system will flounder.

Departmental Interface

A good planning system should foster interaction between areas in the bank that would not interact otherwise. The bank must function as a whole. Without some incentive, some departments may never get together. In the planning process the pieces must be made to fit. Therefore, management must create the incentives for people to coordinate their activities.

One of the basic dangers of having no plan at all or an ill-coordinated planning process is that different parts of the system will try to optimize their own operations without thought for the system as a whole. By aiming for consistency, planners attempt to counter these tendencies toward suboptimization by requiring individuals and individual units to be concerned about their relationship to the whole.

Provision for Change

The planning process should compel people to consider alternative courses of action and alternative methods. One of the major criticisms of bankers has always been that they are "stodgy" and "afraid to try something new." Commercial banks are finding that the competitive environment and the changing nature of technology are forcing them to break out of this mold. Of course, this does not mean that bankers should discard proven practices and give in to the new in an indiscriminate fashion. However, as the banking industry moves into the twenty-first century, it must plan change and do so in a way that will preserve its concern for customer interests.

Bankers must consider new directions or new ways to carry out old functions. If they want to encourage bright, responsible young people to join their organization and develop management skills, then planning is one area where the talents of these people can be applied to the benefit of both themselves and the bank. If the bank fosters an atmosphere in which the newcomers feel they can contribute to its growth and development, then they will be much happier and the bank will be able to move profitably into new areas without forsaking its previous responsibilities.

Thus, a good planning system should encourage people to participate in the development of the bank and should set up a means of rewarding those who make bona fide contributions. A system that stifles initiative is hurting the bank in two ways. It is not only ignoring profitable opportunities; perhaps more important, it is also creating an environment that discourages the ambitious, intelligent personnel who are necessary to the bank if it is to thrive in the long run.

Consistency with Objectives

To be consistent with the environment the bank is considering, the planning process must be geared to the appropriate time horizon and also be concerned with the relevant issues within that time horizon. As described earlier in this chapter, the long-run planning horizon is one of several years. The questions that pertain to this time horizon concern the bank's customer base, its capital position, the legislative and technological environment in which it will be working, and its competition. Thus, whether a bank wants to commit itself to regular activity in the Eurodollar market is an appropriate question for strategic planning, whereas the absolute level of Eurodollar borrowings needed for the next year is not.

In most cases this forces the people involved in the planning process to think about some things, such as cooperation with another department, or some time horizon that they usually do not think about. However, this is part of the potential value of making plans. The developers of the planning process must make sure that people understand what types of proposals and information the planners are looking for and the specific time period to which they are to apply. Working with a particular time horizon also forces people to describe clearly the environment they expect to exist over this time period. Are state and federal legislators moving to encourage or discourage bank expansion? Are foreign banks going to be restricted more, or less, than they have been? What about the competition from thrift institutions? Will third-party payment accounts at thrift institutions be a nationwide phenomenon in five years? Will thrift institutions be allowed to offer consumer loans and overdraft privileges? What about the possibilities for nationwide banking? People in different areas of the bank must consider these matters and contribute to the growth and development of the organization.

Feedback

A good planning system must also contain a mechanism for tracking the performance of the bank relative to the plan. Many planning systems stop with the creation of the plan and only pick up again the next time the plan must be put together. Good planning systems are continuous processes. Data must be constantly monitored to update information, to flag deviations from the plan, and to make adjustments to correct the deviations. There are two major ideas here that must be treated.

1. Control is vital to any planning process. Unless there are feedback mechanisms that can provide information on how the plan is working, the bank will begin each new planning cycle as if it were the first because it will not know what went wrong with earlier plans. A plan cannot be made independently of others. Thus, deviations from a plan should be identified as quickly as possible and their causes ascertained. Deviations often result from incorrect assumptions. Information on the correctness of assumptions must be filtered into the new plan so that it will not be incorrect and out of date before the bank tries to implement it. Deviations from plans are an early warning of a changing environment and enable the bank to adjust quickly to evolving events.

2. The bank must create contingency plans in its original planning process. Although it cannot take every possible occurrence into account, it should allow for the possibility that actual performance will turn out better or worse than expected. This means that the bank must be flexible enough to alter its operations to correct for undesirable developments. The people involved with the planning process should devote as much time to discerning their alternatives as they do to setting up the main thrust of operations. Planning must not put a harness on an organization; it must leave room for adaptation.

These two points highlight a basic principle underlying competitive economic systems. An organization is always under pressure to operate as efficiently and as economically as possible, given the information available to it. Planning implies that information will be collected, disseminated, and analyzed, with an eye to enabling the bank to maximize returns to its stockholders over the long run.

Assumptions about the environment, however, are not always correct. The first banks to realize that their original assumptions are incorrect and adjust to this knowledge are going to put together the best performance record over time, because being slow off the mark is very costly in a competitive environment. A planning system with an efficient control and feedback mechanism that enables the bank to modify its direction rapidly will help it move ahead of its competition and reap those transitional profits that help make performance better than average.

It should be noted that a planning system that leads to better than average profits will tend to be emulated by others. Thus, over time, competition will bring about better and better planning systems: ones that collect more relevant data more rapidly than other systems, use the information more efficiently, and help banks adjust more rapidly to changing economic conditions. This type of behavior is, of course, necessary to the existence of efficient markets. Perhaps it has not developed as rapidly in the banking industry as in other industries because of the large spreads and insulated markets that were common in banking. These conditions will probably not be as prevalent in the future as in the past, and there will be a greater incentive to develop more and better planning systems.

Evaluation of System and Objectives

Planning must not only be a continuous operation; it must also be a growing and evolving process that is constantly evaluating itself to determine what it can do better, what else it needs, and what it should not be doing. To be able to produce good, efficient, and timely plans, the process must continually adapt to its environment.

Management goals must also be under constant scrutiny; their objectivity and feasibility must be tested in the light of new information. Often the goals set up by management are "pet projects" of some executive or owner that may bear no relationship to reality or may potentially cost the bank too much in terms of achievement. A good planning system should be able to evaluate these objectives carefully and contribute to the formation of realistic and attainable goals.

Conclusion

A planning system represents a large commitment of human and financial resources on the part of the bank. Thus, a bank implementing such a process must be sure that it is willing to make the commitment and stick with it long enough to see that it works.

It is apparent that more and more banks, primarily large ones, are building planning systems. Narrower interest rate spreads and greater competitive pressures are forcing the situation. Because such incentives will probably grow in the future, banks must be prepared at least to consider some type of formal planning process. The degree of planning and the sophistication of the process will vary, but if bank managers wish to be able to respond rapidly to changing market conditions, they must give some thought to strategic planning.

PLANNING AND CAPITAL BUDGETING

Capital budgeting is a tool that must be used in the planning process. This is because capital budgeting allows the bank to analyze whether an opportunity will be worthwhile from the standpoint of the owners—that is, whether it will raise the economic value of the bank—and if so, whether it is a better project to undertake than another. In this book, the capital budgeting process is not examined in any great depth, and it is assumed that the reader has some familiarity with the subject as developed in the corporate finance literature.[4]

There are four major types of decisions that must be made with respect to long-lived assets:

1. Replacements.
2. Expansion to add capacity in existing product lines.
3. Expansion to add a new product line.
4. Other—caused by regulation or legislation.

These decisions fall into the planning function because the bank is looking five to seven years into the future and asking where it will be, or where it should be, or where it will have to be at the end of that time. Very rarely will the answers to these questions lead to the conclusion that the existing asset base will be sufficient for the future. Even the smallest bank will usually find that some decisions relative to its asset makeup require a capital budgeting analysis.

In the first case, machines and office buildings wear out, become obsolete, and must be replaced. In a small bank, in a relatively stagnant market, replacement decisions may be the only kind of capital budgeting decision necessary. But if even a small bank is to maximize its economic value, optimal replacement decisions must be made.

---

[4] Two good textbooks on the subject are J. F. Weston and E. F. Brigham, *Managerial Finance,* 6th ed. (Hinsdale, Ill.: The Dryden Press, 1978) and J. C. Van Horne, *Financial Management and Policy,* 4th ed. (Englewood Cliffs, N.J.: Prentice-Hall, 1977).

To many larger, growing banks, replacement decisions merge with the second type of decision, the decision to expand in existing product lines. In this case, when a machine or a building wears out, the replacement may also include an expansion of facilities. As information systems wear out, other, larger systems, such as computer systems, either leased, joint ventured, or purchased, may be considered. As bank head offices become old or too small, newer, larger facilities are considered.

Obviously, expansion is not always undertaken for replacement reasons. Proper planning may show that larger, improved physical facilities are necessary for efficient operations or that more comprehensive information systems are required to handle the projected growth in accounts. If the new direction chosen for the bank is to expand existing lines—say, if it is decided that it is to become a more aggressive retail bank—then more branches may be needed, more advertising may be required to alter the bank's public image, and more machines may be needed to process more checks. To determine the feasibility of these plans, as well as the appropriate alternatives, requires a capital budgeting decision.

Expansion into new product lines is also an area in which the bank can use capital budgeting techniques. Decisions as to whether the bank should deal with installment loans, or auto loans, or install an electronic funds transfer system all lend themselves to this type of analysis. Its managers may want the bank to be something different from what it has been, but wise management also wants changes to contribute to the economic value of the firm.

Projects that are considered just because another bank is entering a similar field or because they are the pet idea of the chairman should be discouraged if they would lower the value of the firm. An appropriate capital budgeting system can, and should, point out any problems and show what would be necessary for a project to be worthwhile. Thus, even a pet project may be modified or discarded if the chairman is aware of its development cost. Even if the chairman's mind is not changed, the consequences to be expected from putting the idea into practice have been expressed and the difficulties that may have to be explained at some time in the future have been fully presented.

Finally, banks are sometimes forced into capital budgeting projects by regulators or legislators who are concerned with the structure of banking or the safety of the banking industry. A case in point could be the imposition of an electronic funds transfer system on the banking system by a central bank or a federal legislative body that was attempting to "help" the industry. Banks would then have to invest in the physical facilities necessary to operate within the EFT system. The addition of this equipment could result in a decline in the economic value of some banks. If they had the freedom to choose, they would not purchase the equipment. However, given the necessity of the purchase, they may still minimize the reduction in their economic value by their choice of equipment. This is where capital budgeting techniques may be helpful. By examining the alternative methods of complying with the rules or regulations, the bank can choose the method that minimizes its loss of economic value. In this way the bank is fulfilling its obligation but still operating under the principle of maximizing shareholder wealth.

Another decision that falls into this category is whether or not the bank should belong to the Federal Reserve System. Membership in the Federal Reserve System entails investing in some assets, cash or reserves, in which the bank might not otherwise invest. Management must consider whether investment in these assets makes shareholder wealth higher, lower, or the same as it would be if the bank did not belong to the Federal Reserve System and did not have to hold the greater amounts of non-interest-earning assets.[5]

If the Federal Reserve is allowed to pay interest on bank deposits held at Federal Reserve banks, this will not alter the capital budgeting calculation; it will just change the explicit returns of belonging to the Federal Reserve System. If the interest paid on these deposits is a constant, or if the rate is changed only infrequently, then, given changes in costs and benefits, the number of banks in the Federal Reserve System and out of the system will change over time in response to many of the same stimuli that cause banks to leave or stay in the system now.

Thus, since all these decisions relate to items whose effects on the firm extend over at least several time periods, capital budgeting techniques are an appropriate means for reaching conclusions about whether the bank should or should not take a certain action. In order to bring out the applicability of this technique to the banking industry, this chapter concludes with four examples of decision problems that capital budgeting can handle. Specifically, these examples pertain to (1) expansion along existing product lines—adding a new branch; (2) replacement—adapting strategy from a "brick-and-mortar" branch system to one consistent with an elementary EFT system; (3) expansion into a new product line—going into consumer installment loans; and (4) diversification—the choice of moving into a bank holding company or remaining under an existing structure.

---

[5] Of course, all implicit, as well as explicit, costs and benefits of Federal Reserve membership must be considered.

FOUR EXAMPLES

Expansion in Existing Product Lines:
Adding a Retail Branch

The alternatives in this case are relatively simple. For one, the bank has a commitment to branching, so that the question of whether or not to enter an entire program is not under discussion. Here the bank must decide whether or not to establish a branch or, if capital rationing exists, which of several alternative locations should be picked and which should not be chosen. The case to be considered concerns the building of a branch or the purchase of an existing structure.[6]

In capital budgeting projects the basic decision rule for the acceptance of a project is that NPV_j, the net present value of project j, must be nonnegative. If this holds, then acceptance of the project will increase the economic value of the firm. If NPV_j is negative, then the project should be rejected.[7]

The net present value of a project is defined as the difference between the discounted present value of the project and its cost. In this example, the certainty-equivalent discounted present value is the appropriate measure that is consistent with the models developed in Chapters 2 and 3. This is defined as the risk-adjusted value of project j, i.e., V_j^0, where the superscript refers to the time of valuation, the zero meaning the current period, and is measured as

$$V_j^0 = \frac{E(X_j^0) - \lambda \, \text{Cov}(X_j^0, k_m)}{R_f} \qquad (4\text{-}1)$$

The other variables are defined as follows:

E = expectations operator
X_j = the (constant) cash flow from project j
λ = the market price of risk = $(E(k_m) - R_f)/\sigma_M$

----

[6] A building or area could be leased, or a sale-leaseback arrangement could be used as a financing scheme. The basic economics differ little from the case considered in the text. Hence, these alternatives will not be considered. However, there may be important tax or balance sheet considerations that must be taken into account in reality, and thus the actual examination of such a project should include these options as possibilities.

[7] It is assumed that the reader is familiar with the concept of net present value and the assumptions that go into the development of models of capital budgeting under uncertainty. See Weston and Brigham, *Managerial Finance,* Chapters 10 and 11.

R_f = the risk-free rate of interest
k_m = the rate of return on the market portfolio
σ_m = the standard deviation on the market portfolio
$\text{Cov}(X_j^0, k_m)$ = the covariance between the cash flows of project j and the market rate of return

V_j^0 is a risk-adjusted value because the unadjusted value is just $E(X_j^0)/R_f$.

The value $\text{Cov}(X_j^0, k_m)$ therefore represents the contribution of project j to the riskiness of the firm. The net present value of the project is then

$$\text{NPV}_j^0 = V_j^0 - \text{Cost}_j^0 \qquad (4\text{-}2)$$

In deciding whether or not to establish a branch or in picking the best branch locations, the bank should choose those projects whose net present value is nonnegative or take projects with the greatest NPVs until its capital budget is exhausted. Note that other factors that need to be considered, such as the bank's image or overall penetration into an area, should be filtered into the cash flow and cost of the project. This helps to define mutually exclusive or independent projects. For example, if an individual branch is included in a plan to move into a developing region or a new geographic area for the bank, then treating the branch as an individual project may define the project too narrowly. The total effort of penetration into a market area must be included, because the separate projects are not independent of one another.

The major elements in the decision are the factors that affect the net cash flows. In a branch the major things affecting cash flow are (1) the deposits that can be attracted into the branch and (2) the personnel costs of operating the branch. The collection of retail deposits is the main reason for the existence of a branch. A branch adds very little in the way of revenue to the bank through the loans it makes or the fees it collects. Although these loans and services are profitable, in most cases they serve mainly to keep customers in the bank by offering them convenience and "one-stop" banking services, thus enabling the branch to maintain its deposit base.

The revenue the branch generates generally comes from the internal selling of funds to "deficit" departments, i.e., areas within the bank that lend out more money than they accumulate in deposits and open-market purchases. The rate that the branch earns on these internal transfers of funds is the *transfer rate*.[8] Hence, the branch creates a net amount of funds

[8] The definition of this rate and its appropriate determination was presented in Chapter 3.

that will be transferred to other areas within the bank, and the revenues it generates, over and above the interest return and fees on its own loans and services, are determined by the net funds transferred times the transfer rate.

Thus, on the revenue side of the cash flow equation, the bank must estimate the level of deposits the branch will attract, the net amount of funds it will be able to transfer to other profit centers, the transfer rate applicable, and the other fees and revenues the branch will generate. The most difficult task is to estimate the level of deposits the branch will attract. The other items are not so hard to forecast or so important. The net amount transferred will be easy to figure, because most of the funds accumulated will be transferred. The other fees and revenues collected by the branch will generally constitute only a small proportion of total revenues, and hence, great accuracy in forecasting these items will not be necessary. The transfer rate applies to the whole bank and therefore should be readily available. However, determining the potential level of deposits the branch can expect is a different story, and in many banks a great deal of time and effort is spent on studying a particular situation. It seems that the most important items in examining the potential of a particular branch site are some or all of the following:

1. What is happening to the size and makeup of population in the area? That is, what are the age distribution, the paying habits, and the saving habits of the potential customers? Is the population growing? Is it declining? How do most people receive their income? By check? By cash?

2. What are the site characteristics? Is it in a shopping center? Will there be easy access to the branch? Is it near the businesses the bank wants to serve? How do people in this area get to the people and businesses with whom they want to deal?

3. What businesses are located in the area? Is the area growing economically? What types of business operate in the region? Is any major business planning to move into the area?

4. What is the competition like? Are there other banks or branches in the area? What about savings and loan institutions, mutual savings banks, or credit unions? What share of the market can the bank hope to achieve?

5. Are there special factors to be considered? For example, are state or local government units located nearby?

6. Is the quality of branch management adequate?

Some banks have attempted to estimate these factors using statistical techniques. However, most banks still use a rather primitive method to estimate potential deposit levels. One of the major problems connected with any effort to systematize the approach to the location of a branch is the availability of adequate data; they are usually scarce. It may be the case, therefore, that the small amount of information available for branch decisions may make this process more of an art than a science. Effort must continually be made to improve data sources and methods of analysis so that better decisions can be made.

Still, the cash flow equation requires a reasonable estimate of the costs of operation. As mentioned earlier, its primary component will be the cost of the personnel needed to operate the branch. The variable cost of branch banking is highly labor intensive. Thus, on the basis of the levels of deposits, transactions, loans, and other services the bank expects the branch to handle, a forecast of personnel needs can be drawn up and combined with estimated salary schedules to determine labor costs. These can then be added to the other incidental costs of the branch to derive total costs. Subtracting these total costs from the relevant cash flows provides an estimate of the net cash flows (X_j) for the branch.[9]

The next thing that must be done is to examine the riskiness of the branch, i.e., the value to be placed on $Cov(X_j^0, k_m)$. In the case of the branch, the greatest possible variation in net cash flows will result from changes in deposit levels and in the transfer rate. If the transfer rate is the

---

[9] Note that because net cash flows can be variable over time they must be converted in a present value sense into a constant infinite flow for use in equation (4-1). The assumption of an infinite life is not crucial, because the durable capital good considered here, such as a building, will generally have a very long life. To make the conversion, compute the discounted present value of the variable stream, using the risk-free rate as the discount factor, and then compute the constant stream of net cash flows by multiplying the computed discounted present value by the risk-free rate. The stream of net cash flows thus obtained can then be discounted at the risk-free rate to give a discounted present value that is exactly the same as that achieved by discounting the variable stream by the risk-free rate. This constant stream $\overline{X}_j$ can then be substituted for X_j and equation (4-1) can be modified in the following way:

$$V_j^0 = \frac{\overline{X}_j - \lambda\ Cov(X_j^0, k_m)}{R_f}$$

Instead of making the two calculations described above, equation (4-1) can be modified in the following way:

$$V_j^0 = DPV_j - \frac{\lambda}{R_f}\ [Cov(X_j, k_m)]$$

where DPV_j is the discounted present value of the variable stream of net cash flows and $Cov(X_j, k_m)$ is the covariance of the variable stream with the market return. For a further examination of this process, see Weston and Brigham, *Managerial Finance*, pp. 311–13.

risk-free rate[10] and if the time period used for computing the covariance in the analysis is the time horizon of the bank,[11] then the variance of the transfer rate can be ignored, because this rate can be considered riskless from the standpoint of the bank and the branch. Thus, the only variation to be concerned with is that arising from changes in the level of deposits.

The branch may be in an area where income (wealth) varies very little as economic activity varies, because of the makeup and habits of the area's population and business. In this case $Cov(X_j^0, k_m)$ will be very small. However, in areas where a large part of the population is subject to cyclical layoffs or is employed in unsteady or insecure jobs, the covariance may be quite large. Hence, the latter branch may be considered riskier than the former one.

Again because data are extremely poor and techniques for analysis are still crude in the banking industry, this type of computation may be difficult to achieve. This does not mean that attempts should not be made to discover how risky, in the sense defined above, a branch would be. Without this information the analysis is really incomplete.

The risk-adjusted value of the branch can now be determined from the data gathered and then compared with the initial outlay needed to purchase or to build the branch. As indicated earlier, the appropriate criterion for accepting a particular location is that the risk-adjusted value of the branch should be at least equal to the initial outlay.

The reader should be aware that the appropriate transfer rate must be used in determining the revenue to be earned by the branch. Using a "pool rate" as the transfer rate, as so many banks have done,[12] underestimates the value of a branch and has contributed a great deal to the recent disenchantment with "retail" banking. This just points up the importance of using economically correct variables in allocation problems. Using incorrect variables can lead to false conclusions and wrong decisions.

Replacement: Moving from "Brick-and-Mortar" Branches to an EFT System

The decision whether to install an electronic funds transfer system is considered a replacement decision, because it is assumed that the bank is

---

[10] See Chapter 3.

[11] See Chapters 2 and 14 for descriptions of the choice and meaning of the time horizon.

[12] A definition of the pool rate and a discussion of the problems of using it are found in Chapter 3.

not changing its product line but is merely considering a change in how it meets its market. Thus, the question is, Does the bank continue to service its customers by means of the present branching system or does it replace the present system with one that may be entirely new or may be a combination of the new and the old?

In this type of analysis, the two systems must be considered in opposition to each other, because the decision will be to reject one of the alternatives; both cannot be chosen. The old system serves as the "base" for the computations, and hence the analyst must consider the net cash flow from the investment in the new system to be the difference between the cash flow of the new system and the cash flow of the old system, i.e., the X_j in equation (4-1). The initial cost used to determine the net present value of the new project is just the initial cost of the new system less the revenues received by selling some of the existing branches and equipment.[13]

One thing that must be considered in this analysis is that if the old system is kept, additional "brick-and-mortar" branches may be required over the time period considered. This may be a very relevant consideration in the analysis, because new branches have a minimum initial cost of about $250,000, whereas a free-standing automatic teller machine (ATM) may cost as little as $25,000 to $35,000 depending on the types of transactions it can handle. Moving to an EFTS may not be the only alternative that involves a capital outlay.

Thus, the new system will be accepted if the net present value is positive or zero; the bank, for the present at least, will stay with the old system if the net present value is negative. Risk can be accounted for in the way described in the previous section. One has to be careful here, because it could be assumed that because one system is replacing another the variance of the two is the same. However, before this assumption is accepted, the researcher must ask several important questions. For example, will the change in technology affect how the level of deposits varies with economic and market conditions? Will the relative difference in technology of the bank in comparison with other banks affect the covariance of net cash flows with the market? If these questions, and others like them, are answered in the negative, then the decision can be based on the net present value of the analysis unadjusted for changes in risk. That is, if the riskiness of the bank does not change with the addition of the new system, then the decision to replace the old system can be based on net present values alone.

---

[13] A fuller description of this process can be found in Weston and Brigham, *Managerial Finance*, pp. 303–8.

It should be noted that the bank may want to consider several strategies for the new system, or at least consider some alternatives before the ultimate new system is chosen. One reason for this is that some systems may find greater public acceptance than others.

A second reason is that several alternatives do exist and one of these systems may be better (i.e., more profitable) than another, or the bank may find that some combination of alternatives may be the best approach. For example, point-of-sale (POS) terminals in a grocery store chain may be a better approach for a bank to take, at least initially, than free-standing ATMs. POS terminals allow bank customers to draw directly on their deposits at the checkout counters of grocery stores in order to pay for groceries or obtain cash. Funds are immediately transferred from the account of the person who writes the check to the store's account. Telephonic transfers (which allow a bank customer to transfer funds between the customer's own accounts or to pay certain bills by simply calling a certain number) may work in some areas; however, a geographic region that does not contain many Touch-Tone telephones may find that such a system is not an effective approach to introducing an EFTS.

Furthermore, a bank may find that several or all approaches are needed to develop an area effectively. Some banks feel that free-standing ATMs will work in an area where the bank has a "core" office of brick and mortar run by "real people." This core office would be strategically located at some convenient spot in the bank's market area and would handle such transactions as opening and closing accounts, safe deposit boxes, and personal loans, deal with problems, and handle the multitude of other items that make personal banking and personal contact such an important part of the business. Banking is still an industry where customers need to identify with a building or a person if they are to give their loyalty to that organization.

These banks would also develop a network of conveniently located ATMs or POS terminals to handle routine transactions and thus save the customer the time and annoyance of having to go to a branch office. Besides, the bank would usually have much less invested or committed in terms of original outlays or lease obligations with this type of system than with one that included several branches or minibranches within the same area.

In planning such an operation, the bank must be aware of the legal aspects of a new system and the assumptions it makes about its competitors. Of course, the legal questions pertaining to present and future EFT operations are numerous, and the answers are uncertain. However, the bank must be aware of what the potentialities are for the system it adopts. For example, antitrust regulation may eventually require that ATMs and POS terminals be shared. Although the bank would probably receive some remuneration for the use of its terminals, the system would probably require modifications, and the bank might not achieve its projected share of the market. Thus, expected cash flows may not be as great as originally forecast if these possibilities are not taken into account.

On the other hand, the bank should be wary of making assumptions that facilities will be shared, that once the ATMs and POS terminals are installed other financial institutions will join it in a joint venture or on a fee basis. A large California savings and loan association established a relatively extensive POS system in grocery stores with the expectation that several other savings and loan associations and commercial banks would be induced to join it within a short period of time. However, no one else joined, transactions never reached the breakeven point, and the system eventually had to be scrapped.

The point of much of this discussion is that a thorough analysis of alternatives and potentialities must be considered by a bank in determining the net cash flows to use in evaluating the implementation of an EFTS. This, of course, makes the effort quite complex and time consuming. To make the best decisions possible, particularly in a case where the ultimate outcomes can have such a substantial effect on its profitability, the bank's analysis must be as complete and as precise as possible. However, the framework for analysis is still the capital budgeting model.

Adding a New Product Line: Consumer Installment Loans

Many banks have never gone into consumer credit except to grant some personal loans with a fixed maturity to good customers. Consumer credit can be defined broadly to include personal loans, home improvement loans, automobile loans (including mobile home loans), furniture and appliance loans, boat loans, and credit card privileges. In this section only home improvement loans, auto loans, and furniture and appliance loans are considered, because they are the ones that are secured by some form of collateral (this is not precisely true of the home improvement loan) and lend themselves to installment contracts. Credit cards and bank affiliation with one of the credit card associations are an entirely different alternative that must be considered separately from consumer installment credit.

It should be stated at the outset that the decision to go into consumer installment loans may represent a complete change of image for the bank. Many banks, for example, have had a history as wholesale banks, seeking out the business of profit-making organizations and only reluctantly accepting the accounts and loans of individuals. Now, because of competition or some other development, management may wish to broaden the bank's operations and seek not only more consumer deposits but also more consumer loans. The analysis, then, should reveal the potential contribution to be made to the economic value of the bank by such a decision.

The analysis proceeds much as before: The bank will decide to move into consumer installment loans if the net present value of such a decision appears, on the basis of the information available at the time of the decision, to be positive. Thus, in the data collection and analysis of the consumer installment loan alternative, the bank must assemble all the costs and revenues associated with the institution of such a program.

The degree of penetration a bank achieves in entering the consumer installment field will vary with circumstances. First, the bank may limit itself to providing this type of loan and advertising for it. Loans are made only by approved loan officers. In this case volume is not the objective, and earnings and creditworthiness would count highly in those loans granted. This would not represent much of an effort on the part of the bank. The bank might have to allocate several loan officers to handle applications and add a few credit analysts; perhaps it would subscribe to a credit agency that accumulates credit information on residents of its geographic region.

How great an advertising budget would be allowed is another question. Certainly, a larger budget would bring in more individual borrowers. However, the bank must assess the relative benefits of the alternatives to see which level of effort would be the best. Obviously, there will be a tradeoff between the amount of installment loans brought in and the advertising outlay. A particular level of expenditures should maximize the profits of the bank for the proposed scale of operations.

On the other hand, the bank may develop a whole line of contacts with dealers—auto dealers, appliance dealers, furniture dealers, and others—who can "create" loans for the bank. This will certainly raise the volume of consumer installment loans. It will also raise the cost, in terms of both administrative and overhead costs and loan losses. Another tradeoff situation may develop out of this, because the bank may want to hire one or more collection agencies to keep down loan losses. The tradeoff is that collection agencies get a percentage of the collections and, if their collection techniques turn out to be obnoxious, some future loan demand may be lost.

One thing that must not be forgotten in making the analysis is the other business that may be brought to the bank. The difficulty of obtaining information should not deter the bank from making some type of estimate as to the additional deposits the new customers will bring in or the other types of fee or interest income business. One reason for offering consumer installment loans is to become more of a full-service bank, either to attract more deposits and loans or to keep the bank's present customers from going over to its competitors. Thus, the bank may also include in the cash flow estimate the business it would have lost by not offering consumer installment loans. That is, the bank reduces a potential loss with the implementation of such a program. A double negative makes, for the analysis, a positive amount.

One of the most important considerations in moving into consumer installment loans is their riskiness. Thus, to be thorough, bank analysts must consider the possible covariance of the returns on these loans with the market. They may find that consumer installment loans add some diversification to their portfolios, however. For example, as interest rates go up and the demand for new mortgages goes down and the demand for construction loans drops off, the bank may find the demand for home improvement loans and mobile home loans going up as people substitute home additions or improvements or cheaper housing units (mobile homes) for new or larger homes. The outcome is an empirical matter, and the bank must attempt to estimate the reaction in both markets.

After the information is assembled, the bank proceeds to estimate the risk-adjusted net present value of going into consumer installment loans. A decision is reached on the criteria mentioned above.

Diversification: Bank Holding Company

An individual bank may consider that its opportunities for growth and risk reduction are limited by the constraint of being just a bank. Limitations on geographical diversification or industry diversification may mean that the bank will either have to be content with a stagnant situation or seek to change its organizational structure so as to be able to take advantage of opportunities that are open to holding companies in other areas or in other industries.

Opportunities available to banks in other industries are regulated quite severely by the Board of Governors of the Federal Reserve System. The Federal Reserve System has regulatory authority over all bank holding companies and the types of businesses in which they may engage. Since the Federal Reserve's "laundry list" of approved areas of expansion for bank holding companies is generally limited to banks and bank-related industries, the bank's ability to use the holding company to diversify risk by moving into industries that have a different economic cycle is limited. However, some diversification can be achieved; the bank holding company can certainly diversify geographically, buying a mortgage company here and a consumer finance company there.

Other than diversification to reduce industry or geographic risk, there are several other reasons why banks desire to move into the holding company format. First, holding companies can provide double leverage; the holding company can lever itself financially and the bank can also. Thus, the original owners may be able to pyramid a small amount of equity into substantial holdings of assets. Second, a bank holding company may be able to issue commercial paper or debt where the individual bank could not. For example, in times of tight credit when Regulation Q ceilings are effective, the holding company may be able to tap the money markets by issuing its own commercial paper and then deposit the funds at one of its banks, or purchase loans from the banks, when the banks could not raise funds at all. Also, a holding company may be able to issue a large amount of debt, whereas individual banks within it may have been too small to issue that amount.

The ability to grow may be enhanced by the formation of a holding company. In the first place, a bank's growth prospects may be limited because of geographic restrictions. Organizations limited to one region are dependent on that region for the underlying economic conditions of growth and stability. Regions with only one industry or with mature, relatively stagnant industrial bases are not as conducive to expansion as are areas that have highly diversified, aggressive, and prosperous industry. A bank holding company may be able to overcome this problem by allowing the bank or its owners to move into other banks as well as other institutions in other parts of the state or country that are more prosperous or that are growing more rapidly.

This ability to grow and diversify is also beneficial in other respects. A stagnant bank or one that is growing very slowly and has no other component businesses cannot offer as great a challenge and as much opportunity to talented younger employees as the bank holding company. A slowly growing, undiversified bank usually has only a limited number of challenging jobs that offer an opportunity for moving up to the top. Moreover, promotion will be slow, because these jobs will generally be filled by people who have been with the bank for a substantial period. Consequently, promising younger employees of the bank may become discouraged and leave because they see only a log jam above them in the organization.

An active bank holding company will have management slots to fill and can move people around to give them broad experience with financial operations. There is a synergistic effect of combining organizations because of the more effective use of talented managers.

There are several other financial benefits of a holding company. For example, the bank may be able to expand more easily by acquisition than otherwise. Expanding externally, as opposed to expanding internally, may be more desirable because an acquisition can be financed by an exchange of stock, which reduces cash requirements. To expand internally by *de nova* development, the bank must have more cash available or must go to the market to raise the funds externally—to meet capital adequacy requirements, for example—and the bank may restrict expansion in order to keep its ability to tap the capital maket available for these occasions. Of course, these two alternatives for expansion must be weighed by each management team to determine their real contribution to the bank.

Another factor is that larger economic units generally have a higher capitalization rate than small units. This may be due simply to the recognition factor of larger units or to the synergistic effects of combined organizations. Whatever the reason for it, it tends to make acquisition more feasible for the larger unit.

In acquisitions that involve an exchange of stock, the constraints limiting the negotiating bounds of the buying and selling organization[14] are determined by the price–earnings ratios of the two organizations. That is, the boundaries are determined by the price at which the acquiring bank can sell earnings and the price at which the prospective bank can sell earnings. Thus, a higher price–earnings ratio relative to other organizations puts a bank that is on a path of acquisition in a better position to acquire than if the price–earnings ratio were lower.

Therefore, one of the most important results of holding company formation is the effect such a combination may have on capitalization rates. Many studies have been done on financial and nonfinancial firms to find the effects of an acquisition on capitalization rates. However, this is slightly different from the point just made in that the foregoing discussion was in terms of absolutes; the present discussion is in terms of marginal changes.

---

[14] For a discussion of the boundaries of negotiation, see Van Horne, *Financial Management*, pp. 640–43, or K. D. Larson and N. J. Gonedes, "Business Combinations: An Exchange-Ratio Determination Model," *Accounting Review* 44 (October 1969), pp. 720–28.

The general result of the studies for nonfinancial firms is positive. When a holding company purchases another company, the major effects are that (1) the earnings of the combined units are greater than the earnings of the two individual units, and (2) the diversification achieved because of the dissimilarity of the two organizations tends to reduce the business risk of the holding company below that of the individual organizations. Both work in the direction of raising the price the market is willing to pay for earnings.

For the commercial bank the results are mixed. Whereas the earnings effect is sometimes present, although not as much as in nonfinancial firms, the diversification benefits, as mentioned earlier, are almost nonexistent. In fact, there is evidence that the market interprets an acquisition, at least initially, as having a negative effect on risk. That is, when a bank holding company purchases another bank or company included in the Federal Reserve's list of potential acquisitions, this acquisition is seen as a potential drain on the resources of the lead bank in the holding company and the other financial resources of the holding company. The market in the short run marks down the price of the holding company's stock to reflect its increased risk.[15]

A bank must consider, then, the potential effects of holding company formation and acquisitions on its expected earnings and the riskiness of the holding company as opposed to the individual bank's organization. This, again, can be determined on the basis of the certainty-equivalent method developed earlier in the chapter. Here, however, the bank is considering the total effect that such a move will have on the value of the owners' wealth holdings, because the project concerns the whole firm and not just a component as in the case of analyzing a new branch, or analyzing a replacement for something already there, or adding a new product. The principles are the same but the scope is different.

As mentioned earlier, these types of decisions are crucial for the strategic planning process of a bank. The error in the past has been in thinking that banks should do anything to obtain deposits. Thus, branches and other types of services could be written off as the loss leaders needed to obtain funds for making loans and investments. The motto was, loans and investments cannot be made without funds, so get all the funds you can.

Modern bankers assert that obtaining deposits and providing services

---

[15] A very thorough study of this phenomenon is found in M. A. Jessee, *An Analysis of Risk-Taking Behavior in Bank Holding Companies* (Ph.D. thesis, The University of Pennsylvania, 1976).

and company organization require capital decisions and thus lend themselves to capital budgeting techniques. What banks should do, or what industries they are limited to, should be subject only to the legal constraints placed on the banking industry, the business the owners decide the bank should be in (i.e., the owners' utility function), the extent of the markets, and management capability, the latter two defining the contribution various opportunities make to the risk-adjusted valuation of the organization. Strategic planning should attempt to move the bank into the position where, given these limitations, it accepts all those independent alternatives that show a positive net present value.

REVIEW QUESTIONS

1. The management of a bank must decide, first of all, what kind of bank they wish to have, that is, what customers the bank will serve. Does this mean that the bank should exclude from its customer base profitable opportunities that do not fit management's specifications? What economic justification can you give for your answer?
2. What is the economic justification for efficient planning and control of bank operations? Are their benefits to a bank permanent, or are they like those of advertising, which tend to disappear because once a firm advertises, all its competitors do also?
3. How far into the future can planners adequately forecast bank operations? What limits or constraints are they faced with? In the face of so many unknowns, is forecasting or planning any better than a "no change" assumption?
4. What is the relationship, if any, between long-run strategic planning and capital budgeting?
5. What areas other than those presented in the text lend themselves to capital budgeting techniques within the framework of strategic planning? Discuss some special problems and approaches that apply to each.
6. Should banks be conservative in their approach to planning? That is, should they move with the market rather than try to project the image of what they would like to be?

7. Just how important is it to get people from different divisions to talk to one another? Has doing this always been a problem? Is it a problem in banks of all sizes?

8. How extensive can the planning operation be in small and medium-sized banks? What are the constraints on planning or the need for planning in these banks?

APPENDIX
Correspondent Banking

In addition to commercial enterprises and consumers, the customers of a commercial bank can include other commercial banks. Some banks, in fact, are specialists in dealing with other banks, their correspondents, just as they may be specialists in dealing with any other industry.

The basis for correspondent banking appears to lie in economies of scale, either in terms of the bank as a whole or in terms of individual services or products. If a bank is too small for efficient handling of such things as check clearing or if it engages in only a few transactions per year in, say, foreign exchange, it may "buy" these services from another bank. The problem may be one not just of quantity of transactions, but also of a special expertise needed to carry out a transaction that the bank, because of its small size, cannot provide.

If a bank is asked for such services, in small amounts but several times a year and often at irregular intervals, it may set up a correspondent relationship with a larger bank that provides these services. If it actively seeks this business, the larger bank (1) can reach a scale of operations that allows it to conduct operations in these services efficiently and also (2) can "diversify" over enough customers that the services will be used on a more regular basis.

What does a bank receive for being a correspondent bank? Primarily it receives deposit balances for the services it provides. Although banks have moved somewhat toward charging fees for some services, the predominant means of payment still consists in keeping funds on deposit with the correspondent. To some extent, this increases the amount of deposits the correspondent has available, which means that the correspondent can invest the net funds (deposits net of reserve requirements) at its marginal revenue.

The general argument for requiring balances rather than charging fees is that the package of services the bank provides to the respondent is so diverse, and many of the items are used so infrequently, that it is hard to price *both* the usage of services and the commitment of the bank to have available these services if the respondent should want them. Having these services available is almost like having an insurance policy. Some charge, it is argued, must be assessed on the availability of these items. Therefore, correspondent balances cover a multitude of costs and fees.

What services do the smaller banks receive? Below is a list of some of the services that are more frequently a part of a correspondent relationship, although some banks have offered as many as one hundred.[1]

1. Check clearing.   This is the main service that is provided by correspondent banks. Even if a respondent bank is a member of the Federal Reserve System, it may have its checks cleared through its correspondent. One reason is that many banks get immediate credit from their correspondents, whereas the Federal Reserve gives credit according to a schedule, so that funds may not be made available for one or two days. Moreover, the bank may be able to lend excess balances directly to the correspondent for one or two days, eliminating the search costs of lending the excess balances at the Federal Reserve, and they may be able to deal in much smaller denominations.[2]

2. Loan requests in excess of legal limit.   The smaller bank may not be able to handle certain loan requests because they exceed the legal limit of 10 percent of paid-in capital and surplus. In such cases the correspondent bank may share the loan. The correspondent may also advise its respondents on the technical aspects of some types of loans with which they are unfamiliar, such as term loans.

3. Participation in loans.   In some cases the larger bank may be almost "loaned up." In such cases it may share loans or sell them outright from its portfolio to smaller banks. The helps the smaller bank to diversify somewhat geographically and perhaps earn a better return than it could by investing in government securities. A recent development is the "loan pool," which is composed primarily of short-term prime credits.[3] Participations in the pool are sold to respondents. These participations are redeemable at any time, so that small banks can consider them a part of secondary reserves. The rates earned on these participations are based on demand loan rates, such as on loans to securities brokers to carry inventories of securities.

4. Securities and investments.   A correspondent bank may act as an advisor, transactor, and depository agent for its respondents.

5. Correspondent banks often act as advisors on installation of new machines and equipment or on new methods of operating.

---

[1] R. E. Knight, "Account Analysis in Correspondent Banking," *Monthly Review*, Federal Reserve Bank of Kansas City (March 1976), p. 13.

[2] For more on this aspect of the federal funds market, see the section on federal funds in Chapter 12.

[3] See D. A. Hayes, *Bank Lending Policies*, 2nd ed., Division of Research, Graduate School of Business Administration, The University of Michigan, Ann Arbor, Michigan, 1977, p. 104, for a fuller description of this practice.

6. Foreign services.   The major service provided here is the handling of foreign exchange transactions. However, anything that has to do with a foreign activity that can be done domestically at either bank would fit into this category.

7. Coin and currency.   The correspondent may deliver coin and currency to its respondent as needed or may collect excess cash. This is another service that is provided by the Federal Reserve System to member banks.

8. Credit information.   Smaller banks may not be able to collect and store enough credit information for efficient operations. Correspondents sometimes share credit information facilities with their respondents.

9. Federal funds.   Smaller banks can sell excess funds to their correspondent banks. Also, these smaller banks can borrow from their larger correspondent. Often the larger bank will offer its respondents a "line of credit" that they can use to meet seasonal swings in deposits and loans. In this way, a correspondent serves as a discount window for smaller, non-member banks in the banking system.

10. Legal reserves.   In many states correspondent balances can serve as legal reserve requirements. Thus, these deposits serve a dual purpose. They pay for services obtained from correspondents and also serve to honor legal obligations to the state.

11. International services.   Smaller banks whose customers engage in international transactions can arrange for specific trade services through their correspondent bank. This differs from point 6 because the transactions included here may be carried out in another country, whereas other foreign exchange transactions can be carried out within the United States.

12. Personnel and other services.   A small bank seeking a new president or senior officer from outside the firm can often find qualified applicants through its correspondent bank.

13. Other services.   A correspondent bank can provide a multitude of other services. For example, it may help the bank price a local bond issue and provide economic information to a bank that cannot afford its own economist. The list of services is limited only by the needs and creativity of those involved in correspondent relationships.

The analysis of the correspondent accounts presents some difficulty in measurement. This is because it is difficult for the correspondent bank to compose a balance sheet statement for its customer banks and to price or cost all the services included in the banking relationship.

The customer bank provides deposit balances that can appear on the right-hand side of a balance sheet. However, there is nothing to go on the left-hand side except, perhaps, the reserves the bank must hold behind the deposits and the securities in which the bank invests the net free funds. Theoretically, there should be another liability: the discounted value of the potential services offered the respondent. The offsetting item would be the proportion of assets the larger bank must maintain in order to supply these services. Capital, too, can be allocated to the balance sheet. Thus, the balance sheet that the correspondent bank would construct for its customer banks would be:

Assets	*Liabilities*
Reserves	Deposits
Investments	Potential liability of
Physical assets allocated	services available
	Net Worth
	Capital

Costs and revenues can be derived from this balance sheet, and an income statement and rate of return calculations can be made.

In practice,[4] only the deposit balances and the transfer price or earnings credit applied to these balances are considered. Thus, revenues to the bank are taken to be the deposit balances times the earnings credit, plus any fees that may have been charged for data processing services or other items for which the bank levies specific charges. This earnings credit may be set at the marginal cost of funds or may be adjusted downward to allow for the fact that some reserves must be held. The calculated revenue is then compared with estimated costs to arrive at the profitability of the account.[5]

Since many items are not explicitly costed, and others, such as the potential liability of services available or the potential federal funds borrowing, are not considered in the analysis, profit is generally overstated. However, if the account shows a profit, the bank will generally ignore any pricing problems related to the account.

---

[4] R. E. Knight, "Account Analysis."

[5] Knight ("Account Analysis," p. 19) concluded in his study that "competing banks often do not know their costs and tend to establish unrealistically low charges."

5

Capital Structure—
Unconstrained
Optimization

Up to this point the amount of capital maintained by the bank has been assumed to be held constant, which simplified discussions of loan and deposit pricing and the borrower–depositor customer base. Since many of the institutional factors that affect capital decisions are different from those that affect pricing and the borrower–depositor base, they could be put aside temporarily. It is easy to understand, however, that important decisions on bank capital must be made simultaneously with decisions on the customer base. Without the appropriate capital structure, a bank cannot expand sufficiently to support prospective growth of loans and deposits. This may be true in a market sense as well as in a regulatory sense.

Regulatory authorities can, and do, place limits on the growth of bank assets if "sufficient" capital is not available to support growth. The inability of a bank to obtain the required capital may destroy, or at least modify, the best made plans for the expansion of the customer base. Hence, planning for expansion must include consideration of the bank's capital structure.

The market itself may provide an adequate constraint on bank growth if the acquisition of capital lags behind asset accumulation. If organizations that supply funds to a bank feel, for whatever reason, that the bank is becoming "riskier" in any sense, they will take their money elsewhere. One result would be higher interest costs on liabilities. This would be particularly true in markets, such as the federal funds market or the negotiable CD market, whose participants are fairly sophisticated and highly responsive to changes in a bank's capital position. A second result would be a loss of customers, for borrowers would not want a line of credit if they felt that there was some chance that the bank would not be able to supply funds when they were needed.

Finally, bank capital itself would become dearer, since the loss of borrowers and higher interest costs would reduce profits, and the changes brought about in the customer base would probably result in a further change in the bank's risk class. Thus, like the regulators, the market can impose constraints on expansion by raising the cost or even limiting the availability of equity capital or subordinated debt if it feels that the bank does not have a "sufficient" base of capital.

In this chapter, the capital decision is introduced within the framework of the borrower–depositor customer base, and a simultaneous solution is sought to the overall composition of the bank's balance sheet. More specifically, the need for bank capital is examined a little more deeply, and an analysis of the unconstrained determination of the bank's optimal capital structure, if such an optimum exists, is presented.

Chapter 6 contains a discussion of the internal sources of capital and examines how tax planning can be used to achieve higher after-tax earnings. Chapter 7 discusses external sources of capital, market regulation, and supervisory regulation. Also included there is an examination of some techniques for determining the optimal amounts of capital for the bank.

WHY DOES A BANK NEED CAPITAL?

Risk and Leverage

The capital needs of a bank should be viewed in the same light as the capital needs of any business organization: as a problem concerning the costs and benefits of financial leverage, the percentage of bank funds supplied by fixed-obligation debt. These costs and benefits are associated with factors such as the financial risk incurred by financial leverage, i.e., the risk that profits will not be sufficient to pay off the firm's fixed obligations. Of course, the higher the financial leverage a bank employs, the greater its obligation to make fixed interest and principal payments. The higher the financial leverage, however, the greater the potential for variations in profits. Since some variations in profits may make profits small enough that fixed obligations will not be covered, the firm may have to draw on accumulated retained earnings to pay current debts. If this continues, of course, the firm not only may be unable to make current interest payments but also may be unable to repay the borrowed principal.

The bank is no different in this respect from any other business. The more it obligates itself to contractual payments of interest and fixed-value claims relative to its capital base, the greater the possibility that circumstances may make it unable to fulfill its obligations.

Risk of Asset Conversion

In addition to this problem, the bank is faced with a situation unique to banking. In the first place, many bank liabilities are "demand" liabilities; that is, they are subject to instant repayment. Second, a large proportion of deposits, although not payable on demand, are subject to rapid withdrawal (time and savings deposits may require a 30-day waiting period before they can be withdrawn from the bank, although banks rarely invoke this legality), so that a bank can face massive movements at any one time in certain liability classes.

In the first case, history has many examples of periods when depositors removed their funds in large amounts from a commercial bank, or from the commercial banking industry, and shifted into cash balances. On the other hand, time accounts and negotiable certificates of deposit have, in the past, faced interest rate ceilings markedly out of line with returns that could be earned in the open market. Banks have lost huge amounts of funds in such situations, all from one or two types of liability classes.

On the other side of the balance sheet, the bank is faced with similar problems; circumstances may affect various asset groups in the same way at the same time. For example, the bank may have concentrated unduly on lending to one industry, which is then affected by unusual economic conditions. Whether the effect is bad or good, the bank may be faced with a very difficult problem. If many firms in the affected industry are forced to default on their loans, then the bank will be faced with a collapse of the asset side of its balance sheet that would technically make it insolvent. On the other hand, if the industry meets with a sudden improvement in market conditions, the bank may experience a much greater loan demand than expected as a number of firms decide to draw on their lines of credit. The bank may feel obligated to serve them rather than face an outright loss

of customers and gain a reputation for not honoring contracts, even informal ones. The latter alternative, if taken, would be devastating to the organization. Even if the loan demand comes from firms not considered to be
"good" customers, bank management must weigh the possibility that if
they are given the loans they want now they might become good customers in the future.

If the bank services the unexpectedly great demand for loans, regardless of where it comes from, it must do so out of assets, if it is an asset-
management bank, or purchase liabilities, if it is a liability-management
bank.[1] The difficulty of financing unanticipated loan demand highlights a
fundamental problem of the banking industry. This is the problem that
assets will have to be sold at values substantially less than those reported
on the balance sheet or that liabilities will have to be sold at higher than
expected interest rates, either action causing profits to be lower than the
optimum, at least in the short run.

It is obvious that defaults will result in reduced asset values. However, if deposit losses or loan demands are greater than expected and the
bank is an asset-management bank, then assets must be converted, often
at a capital loss,[2] which means that the bank will realize a reduction in
asset values. That is, it is not the deposit loss or loan demand *per se* that is
the difficulty, but the fact that these occurrences *force* conversion of assets
at a loss.

In the case of a liability-management bank, the problems are perhaps
not so serious. One way to cover the loss of deposits or the unexpected loan
demand is by "filling in" the liability side of the balance sheet. That is, if
the bank finds that asset amounts exceed the amount of funds supplied it,
then it can simply buy more liabilities to take the place of those it lost or
add to those it has to support the additional assets. However, the cost of
liabilities may rise as the bank does this, and this may put the bank in a
less than optimal position, resulting in lower profits.

The point in this analysis is that commercial banks, as individual
economic units, must deal with the fact that several undesirable events
may happen at the same time, owing to the homogeneity of the markets
and customers they serve. There is, however, another factor inherent in

---

[1] The bank could sell participations in loans to other banks and alleviate some of the
problem. However, if money is tight, this may not be a viable alternative.

[2] This capital loss comes from two sources. First, there is the problem of liquidity. If the
assets have to be sold quickly, the bank may have to take some loss due to the imperfect
liquidity of the asset. Second, these conditions often arrive after interest rates have, in general, risen. Thus, the bank may have to realize a market loss that existed but was not reported
due to the fact that the bank recorded the asset at purchase price on the balance sheet and not
at market value.

banking that is more problematic to the banking industry than it is to nonbanking organizations. This is the risk associated with the possibility of multibank failure.

Risk of Multibank Failure

Multibank failure is made possible by the homogeneity of banks in general and the interlocking nature of their operations. It should be remembered that one argument given for using the model of the discriminating monopolist to represent a commercial bank and the commercial banking industry was the similarity of banks and their "proximity" to one another. This closeness, however, makes them susceptible to many of the same stresses, such as general economic conditions, monetary policy, and problem areas in different industries. Thus, for example, as monetary policy becomes more restrictive, all banks feel the same pressure, more or less, and face dwindling reserves, rising interest rates, and loss of deposits together. The possibility of a break in one link of the chain presents the specter that a weakness may exist in other parts of the industry as well.

Not only may several banks fail at the same time because the same conditions affect many members of the industry in the same way, but a failure of one bank may be transmitted to others because of their interdependent business relationships. Correspondent banks, with their compensating balances and loans, federal funds transactions, and syndication or participation in loans to large customers, may bring disaster to one another.

Thus, although the capital needs of the bank and the nonbank organization may be similar, the results of failure may be somewhat more severe in banking because of the implications bank failure has for the functioning of society. Since the failure of one bank may cause the failure of others, it is even possible that, in the extreme, the viability of the "payments mechanism" of the society could be destroyed or at least severely hampered. This societal impact is not implied in the failure of one firm in any other industry.

THE BANK'S CAPITAL STRUCTURE

The Function of Capital

If the bank needs capital to protect itself from the problems of suboptimality caused by demands or supplies being higher or lower than expected, then the theoretical problem of capital adequacy is easily stated. Robinson and Pettway, for example, claim:

> The function of bank capital is that of absorbing short and intermediate term losses resulting from events that managerial foresight cannot be reasonably expected to anticipate; a margin of safety that, preferably, would allow a bank to continue operations without loss of momentum and, at least, would buy time in which a bank could reestablish its operational momentum.[3]

What is the correct amount of capital? The level of capital that minimizes the bank's cost of capital for a given level of assets. To quote Robinson and Pettway again:

> A bank should shape its financial policy so as to minimize its cost of capital and cost of funds. An approximate test of minimization of funds cost is whether a bank is failing to secure deposits or paying a higher price for deposits than it would have to pay with more capital.[4]

These statements make two important points. First, although a bank may be optimizing or attempting to optimize its position on the basis of all other current information available to it, it may not achieve this optimization because of "events that managerial foresight cannot be reasonably expected to anticipate." Therefore, it must have sufficient earnings and capital to absorb temporary suboptimal operation.

It should be noted, too, that banks that accept the temporary suboptimal position and realize their losses in order to take advantage of current market conditions seem to fare better than those that do nothing and hope for things to reverse themselves so that they can buy their way out with little or no loss. The difficulty lies in determining when a position has "permanently" changed so that realizing a short-run suboptimal position may help the bank to attain long-run optimization. If the change is not "permanent," then taking the short-run loss may not lead to longer-run optimization. Examples of this type of behavior arise when actual loan losses are greater than expected, when interest rates move up when they were expected to move down, and when there are unanticipated changes in Federal Reserve policy.

---

[3] R. I. Robinson and Richard A. Pettway, "Policies for Optimum Bank Capital: A Summary," *Policies for Optimum Bank Capital*, Association of Reserve City Bankers, Chicago (February 1967). Reprinted in P. Jessup, ed., *Innovations in Bank Management: Selected Readings* (New York: Holt, Rinehart and Winston, 1969), p. 183.

[4] Ibid., p. 185.

Risk and Economic Profit

Some economists, however, believe that the major reason for a firm's economic profits is the risk the firm takes on with regard to factors that cannot be perfectly anticipated. If everything in society moved along smoothly, then all that would be necessary for the running of a society would be engineers, and businesses would just receive average returns on their investments. Frank Knight felt that true business profit was earned by risk-takers, people who take positions in the market, who base their decisions on the best information available, but who do not know or cannot know everything that could happen to affect the outcome of their decisions.[5]

Robinson and Pettway suggest that the reason a bank needs capital is to protect itself against factors that cannot be completely planned for and to enable it to come back another day and try to even things out. Thus, by the very nature of the enterprise, the commercial bank is exposed to events it cannot be expected to anticipate. Bank capital allows it to keep its doors open to recoup the loss.

Capital Structure and the Cost of Capital

The second factor mentioned by Robinson and Pettway is that there exists a minimum cost of capital for a bank, and it occurs at the "optimal" level of capital. Graphically, this situation is shown in Figure 5-1.

The solid line in this figure depicts the cost of capital to the bank for each possible capital structure, depicted here in terms of the capital–asset ratio, K/A. The minimum cost of capital is shown to be r_k^0, which occurs at the bank's optimal capital structure, $(K/A)_0$.

It is assumed here that the market determines this optimal level of capital. If the capital–asset ratio is to the right of $(K/A)_0$, it is assumed that the bank is not leveraged sufficiently for its mixture of assets and liabilities and its profit is too low for its leverage factor. Thus, the cost of capital will be higher than if the bank is at $(K/A)_0$.

If the capital–asset ratio is to the left of $(K/A)_0$, then the financial leverage will be considered to be too great, deposits and other sources of funds will be more costly, and profits will decline and be too small for the

---

[5] For the classic presentation of these ideas, see Frank Knight, *Risk, Uncertainty and Profit* (Chicago: The University of Chicago Press, 1971). This book was originally published in 1921.

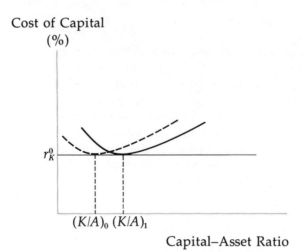

FIGURE 5-1   Determination of the Optimal Capital Structure

level of the capital structure. Thus, the cost of capital will again be higher than r_K^0.

Capital Structure and Bank Regulation

Two arguments that will be discussed again in a later chapter can be made here in support of bank regulation. First, there is the question of whether or not the market can determine this optimum and whether the optimum considers only the individual bank risk or also considers the possibility of multibank risk. The market may have enough information to analyze the individual bank risk, but it may not be able to judge the risk of multibank failure. In such a case, the "optimal" might in fact be to the right of $(K/A)_0$, say at $(K/A)_1$.

Second, to have the market "regulate" banks, it must be assumed that the market for bank liabilities and equity is efficient enough to be able to evaluate the optimal bank capital structure correctly. It may be the case that the largest banks in the country, those whose stock is listed on major exchanges and whose liabilities are sufficiently sought, qualify to have the market regulate them. However, it is indeed another question whether or not the market can regulate small banks whose stocks are traded on local or regional exchanges or in the bank president's top desk drawer. But this point will be examined more completely in Chapters 6 and 7.

THE PSYCHOLOGICAL NEED FOR BANK CAPITAL

Another reason often given for bank capital is that confidence in the banking system is important to the economy. A bank with adequate capital is more assured that depositors will leave their money in their accounts and that borrowers will continue to borrow, even though it may be having some difficulty. Crosse and Hempel state,

> It is probably more meaningful to look on the primary function of bank capital funds not as a cushion of excess assets that enables a bank to absorb losses and still remain solvent but rather as a factor, perhaps the most important factor, in maintaining the confidence a bank must enjoy to continue business and prosper. The primary function of bank capital is to keep the bank open and operating so that time and earnings can absorb losses—in other words, to inspire sufficient confidence in the bank on the part of depositors and the supervisor so that it will not be forced into costly liquidation.[6]

In a sense, all psychological reasons must be considered short run in nature. If a bank is fundamentally sound or if its problems can be solved by "time and earnings," all that is needed is the breathing space necessary to show evidence of soundness. According to this argument, sufficient bank capital gives depositors, borrowers, and supervisors that confidence, so that they will not be in a hurry to "pull the plug" on the bank.

An Example

A current example of the role that psychological factors can play in banking operations is that of the Beverly Hills National Bank, a subsidiary of Beverly Hills Bancorp, a holding company. The holding company apparently had difficulty in 1974 in meeting its commercial paper obligations. Due to the closeness of the two names, the public seemingly confused the lead bank with the holding company, and it withdrew about $20 million from the bank. This represented a net decline of about 45 percent of total deposits. The holding company eventually had to sell the bank to meet its obligations—and, because of its financial condition, at a much lower price than it could have received before the loss of deposits.

---

[6] H. D. Crosse and George H. Hempel, *Management Policies for Commercial Banks* (Englewood Cliffs, N.J.: Prentice-Hall, 1973), p. 70.

Deposit Insurance and Customer Psychology

This points up another problem. Deposit insurance, created during the 1930s, was supposed to have put a stop to runs on banks as a source of bank failure. However, most evidence seems to indicate that every bank that has failed or that has found itself in serious trouble has lost deposits, either on an absolute basis or in comparison to the growth rates experienced by other banks of similar characteristics or in the same geographic area. Deposit insurance may play a role in moderating deposit losses, but it does not seem to eliminate them.

For one thing, some deposits are not insured fully because they exceed the maximum amounts set by the authorities. This pertains to business accounts in particular. It is argued that since these large accounts belong to generally more knowledgeable and sophisticated organizations than the typical depositor, they will usually be withdrawn more rapidly than the others, and, because of their large size, their withdrawal will have a greater impact on total deposit levels. However, it seems that small, protected depositors also leave the bank. Thus, it appears that depositors perceive the cost of a bank failure to be something greater than zero even though deposit insurance exists and the safety of deposits is well publicized.

Psychological Need as a Short-Run Problem

It is to be expected, then, that when a bank is perceived to be in some difficulty, psychological factors will lead to customer behavior that may force a conversion of assets at perhaps a capital loss or even make a bad situation worse to the point of forcing the closing of a bank.

The problem with this argument is that failed banks never seem to have enough capital.[7] The Beverly Hills National Bank, for example, was considered to be a "well run, adequately capitalized" bank, but this did not keep the bank from failing. If depositors and borrowers realize that the total amount of capital a bank has will not keep it from failing, then it would seem that the bank would have to keep some large capital–asset ratio in order to generate sufficient confidence to be able to keep the bank open so that "time and earnings" can overcome the psychological problem.

[7] J. J. Pringle, "The Capital Decision in Commercial Banks," *The Journal of Finance* (June 1974), p. 779.

Thus, one might question the efficiency of capital in protecting a bank from adverse psychological factors. If a bank is sound but subject to temporary setbacks due to factors "that managerial foresight cannot reasonably be expected to anticipate," then it must be liquid enough to withstand the pressure of deposit outflows or lower borrowing until it can show its soundness or improve earnings so as to overcome the temporary reversal. Capital can help to absorb the losses generated in this environment so that technically the bank can honor its obligations. However, it is not a substitute for sufficient liquidity to protect the bank from forced conversions of assets at a capital loss.

LIQUIDITY IN CAPITAL MANAGEMENT

Market Liquidity

As is well known, there are two sources of liquidity. Either it is provided by the economic unit itself in the form of balance sheet management, or it is provided in the market by those lenders that are willing to provide funds rapidly to the economic unit. What really seems needed, therefore, with respect to capital, is sufficient liquidity for the bank to ride over the short-run psychology associated with a given situation, so that capital can serve its usual function, that is, so it can act as a buffer to absorb temporary setbacks.

The bank could have sufficient liquid assets on hand to meet shortfalls in deposits or in loans. However, there are problems here. If the bank is completely liquid, it will not lend beyond its capital accounts. This would not be very rational, nor very good business. The more it reduces its liquidity, the greater the chance that it might at some time have to take a capital loss on some of its assets. Of course, if the bank is completely loaned up, it has very little liquidity and there is a large chance that it will be forced to convert some of its assets.

The problem with asset liquidity is that there are limits to its availability. And, unless the bank were so conservative as not to lend in excess of its capital accounts, it would face the possibility of meeting the limit imposed by its assets at some time. Something more must be available to the bank, then, than just asset liquidity.

Liability liquidity can serve the bank in much the same way as asset liquidity, but only under one condition. Funds obtained through the liability markets must be supplied elastically; otherwise, the bank could be forced into a suboptimal position. This is because funds will be purchased at a marginal cost that exceeds the marginal revenue the bank receives from using the funds. If funds are not supplied elastically or if there is some probability that they will not be supplied elastically at some time in the future, then the bank must resort to asset liquidity to protect itself against short-run problems.

Liquid funds can be available to the bank in two ways. Either the market can provide the funds in efficient markets where the supply curve, to the bank, is perfectly elastic, or the government or central banking agency can supply the funds. It appears that many large banks have found that they can always obtain funds elastically in different markets, and over a relevant time period they can purchase all the funds they need at the market rate of interest. This, as will be shown below, takes the pressure off capital and allows the bank to absorb temporary setbacks efficiently. However, this resource is not available to all banks at all times.

Liquidity Provided by a Central Bank

As an alternative, there could be a central banking agency that provides loans to banks so as to supply this liquidity to the banking system. In many respects, if the Federal Reserve is to serve as a lender of last resort, then this is how it should operate its discount window: It should provide funds elastically to the banking system through its discounts and advances so that the banks have all the short-run liquidity they need to make adjustments in their portfolios. The Federal Reserve should then administer the discount rate to keep it closer to open-market rates, or even make the rate a "penalty" rate so that this availability of funds is not abused. However, this is not precisely what it does. First of all, the Federal Reserve generally lends to banks during transitional periods when monetary policy is tightening. This allows banks more time to adjust from one level or growth rate of bank reserves to another; but since borrowing is a "privilege and not a right," the loans are not available for extended periods of time and the banks eventually have to convert assets and accept losses. Second, the Federal Reserve lends to "troubled" banks. These borrowings can be for extended periods of time, but they still require that the loans be secured, as others are, by U.S. government securities or some other approved paper. Thus, these funds can be received only if a bank is truly troubled and has acceptable assets to secure the borrowings.[8]

Hence, the conclusions can be drawn that discount borrowings from the Federal Reserve are not unlimited and that banks face costs, implicit as

[8] For more on this collateral requirement, see Chapter 12.

well as explicit, in addition to interest costs. The discount window, therefore, is not the place for banks to satisfy all their liquidity needs.

In summary, it can be said that capital plays its proper role as a buffer for temporary setbacks in operations if banks have sufficient liquidity to overcome the market's psychologically induced reactions. Every bank faces some limitations on complete liquidity because of the market restriction on the amount of assets it has. Only a few banks can, under most conditions, escape this by having liability markets in which funds are supplied elastically. Since even the Federal Reserve does not supply liabilities under these conditions, other banks, with restricted liability markets, are forced to carry smaller loan portfolios than they otherwise would because they run the risk of having to provide for liquidity out of assets. Therefore, a bank's capital must support more than just the risk inherent in financial leverage.

OPTIMAL CAPITAL STRUCTURE

Earlier it was argued that banks may have an unconstrained optimal capital structure, and Figure 5-1 depicted how this optimal capital structure related to the bank's cost of capital. Now it is necessary to see what conditions must exist for there to be an optimal capital structure and, as nearly as possible, to determine the amount or at least the constraints on this optimum.

Capital as a Variable in the Model

The model used is the same as that presented in Chapters 2 and 3, except that capital is now allowed to vary, that is, to become a decision variable. In specifying the role of capital in the bank's optimization process, care must be taken to allow for the fact that equity capital may not be supplied elastically to the bank and that some other costs, such as flotation costs, must be included to account for imperfections that might exist in the capital markets. Consideration of these factors will be general enough that the traditional cost of capital can be assumed—that is, the average cost of capital schedule will be U-shaped, as in Figure 5-1—or it can, as an extreme case, be horizontal, which would imply that there is no optimal capital structure for the firm. Economies or diseconomies of scale in issuing capital can also be introduced. Equations (5-1) and (5-2) can now be given. Equation (5-1) describes the supply curve of capital to the bank. It says that the cost of capital, r_K, is functionally related to the amount of capital the bank demands, K. Equation (5-2) describes the expense curve of

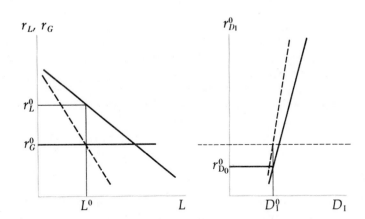

FIGURE 5-2   Determination of the Optimal Portfolio and

capital and relates the average cost of flotation and servicing bank capital, b_K, to the quantity of capital needed.

$$r_K = r_K(K) \qquad\qquad (5\text{-}1)$$

$$b_K = b_K(K) \qquad\qquad (5\text{-}2)$$

These two equations can then be introduced into the process of maximizing the terminal cash flow received by the owners of the bank. This was done earlier, in Chapters 2 and 3. The explicit mathematical solution of the problem is presented in the appendix to this chapter. The following discussion summarizes the conclusions reached in the appendix. Figure 5-2 graphically summarizes the more important points.

General Results

First, the bank can be an asset manager or a liability manager. The crucial magnitude is, as explained earlier, the optimal level of loans the bank is willing to take, shown in Figure 5-2 as L^0. If $L^0 < D_I^0 + K^0$, then the bank is an asset manager; if $L^0 > D_I^0 + K^0$, then the bank is a liability manager. This assumes, of course, that the bank has a market in which D_{II} deposits are elastically demanded.

Second, the optimal values on the vertical axes of the figures, the interest rate measures, are really a combination of things. Basically, these values include not only the interest cost, r, but also the administrative and overhead costs associated with the variables under consideration and an

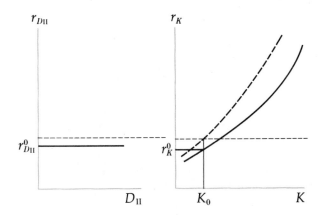

Optimal Capital Structure Under Certainty

adjustment for risk. This adjustment is handled in exactly the same way as it was in Chapter 2. Thus, the levels of r_L^0, $r_{D_I}^0$, and r_K^0 shown in Figure 5-2 are exclusive of expenses and risk. In actuality, r_K^0 may exceed r_L^0 because of these expenses and risk factors; these cannot be graphically shown in the accompanying diagrams.

Third, the optimal capital structure, if one exists, depends on whether the bank is an asset or liability manager and whether imperfections exist in asset, liability, and capital markets. The results of the study pertaining to capital structure can be divided into five distinct categories. All five may not be empirically relevant, but theoretically they are all possible.[9] It should be noted that possible variations in demand and supply are taken into consideration in the derivation of these results.

Specific Conclusions

1. All markets are perfectly competitive, and all b's are equal to zero. In this case banks would cease to exist or would never have existed. This would be the case where the demand for loans, the supply of Type I deposits, and the supply of capital were all perfectly elastic, and the market would take the rate in each case to r_G or $r_{D_{II}}$.[10]

[9] These results are derived in the appendix. A more complete presentation of the same material can be found in J. J. Pringle, "Capital Decision," p. 789, and J. M. Mason, "The Bank Capital Decision," Finance Department Working Paper, The University of Pennsylvania, 1978.

[10] Note that Pringle does not obtain this result because he has assumed deposits to be inelastically supplied. Thus, his first case is more like case 2(b).

2. Imperfections exist on the asset side of the balance sheet, deposits of Type I are supplied inelastically, but capital is supplied elastically.

(a) In an asset-management world, the bank would dichotomize its decisions. First, it would take all Type I deposits and invest them in government securities earning the spread between r_G^0 and $r_{D_1}^0$. Second, it would issue capital up to the point $K^0 = L^0$. Since the supply of capital curve is perfectly elastic, $r_K^0 = r_G^0$ and loans will be made up to the point where the marginal revenue on loans is equal to r_K. This determines an optimal capital structure, but a rather peculiar one.

(b) In a liability-management world, the bank would exist but would have no optimal capital structure. This is because both D_{II} and capital are supplied elastically and $r_K^0 = r_{D_{II}}^0$. Thus, no optimal combination of the two exists.

3. Imperfections exist in both asset demands and capital supplies, as well for deposits of Type I, but the loan markets have greater imperfections than the capital markets. In this case there will be an optimal capital structure in which $0 \leq K^* \leq L^*$, where the asterisks imply optimal values. The exact value will depend on the relative elasticities of demand and supply as well as administrative and overhead costs. Up to the point where the marginal revenue of loans is equal to the marginal cost of capital, the greater imperfections in the loan markets allow the bank to arbitrage between the capital market and the loan market. Until this point the bank will certainly take advantage of the disparity in relative prices.

4. Imperfections exist in both asset demand and capital supply, as well as in the supply of deposits of Type I, but the imperfection in the capital market is equal to or greater than the imperfection in the loan market. In this case there will be a corner solution to the maximization process at $K^* = 0$. If the degree of imperfection is the same in asset markets and capital markets, then $r_L^0 = r_K^0$ and there will be no opportunity for banks to arbitrage the situation. That is, they will not obtain capital to lend out at the same rate as they are paying for the capital. If the imperfections in the capital markets exceed those in the asset markets, then $r_K^0 > r_L^0$. This will mean that the marginal revenue of loans will never be equal to the marginal cost of capital at a positive level of capital, so the optimal amount of capital must be zero. These results will hold in both asset- and liability-management banks.

5. Imperfections exist in the capital markets and in the Type I deposit market but not in the asset markets. This is really similar to the second part of case 4. A negative spread will exist between r_K^0 and r_L^0, so that the optimal level of capital is again zero. Again, this result holds for both asset- and liability-management banks.

Analysis of Results

Empirically, it seems that only cases 2(b) and 3 are relevant in a practical sense. Since financial intermediaries do exist, it seems that case 1 can be dismissed without much argument. Case 2(a) presents a little more difficulty. The crucial condition there is that individual banks must be able to obtain as much capital as they need without affecting their cost of capital. This would imply that banks had access to financial markets that were "efficient" in the sense that the price on these markets truly reflected all the information that was available to the market at the time the price was determined. In general, the markets must have sufficient information disseminated to participants and many active traders with an adequate capital base. In other words, the securities of these banks must be traded in markets that are "broad and deep."

Only a relatively minor proportion of the banks in the U.S. banking system qualify in this sense, and these are the large banks centered in major metropolitan areas. Furthermore, even these banks did not meet this standard until the middle of the 1960s. The reason for this is that they were generally local or regional banks before that time and were able to finance their expansion plans through retained earnings. However, as the banks became more national or international in character, they could not obtain sufficient capital through either retained earnings or deposit liabilities to support the growing demands for funds. Thus, to obtain capital to support growth they had to raise funds externally, which meant that they had to operate in more efficient markets if they were to get the funds as cheaply as possible. They began listing their common shares on the New York Stock Exchange and actively seeking investor interest.[11]

Note that a second factor was needed. Banks had to obtain funds in excess of those supplied in the local or regional area to support their growing loan base. This satisfied the first condition for the existence of liability management. Since this condition is satisfied for most of the very large banks that have elastically supplied capital, few if any banks, in practice, satisfy the requirements of case 2(a); that is, most banks that operate in efficient capital markets are liability-management banks. Hence, case 2(a) lacks empirical relevance.

It seems that cases 4 and 5 can be dismissed quite easily. Only in the smaller banks might the imperfections in the capital markets be expected to exceed the imperfections in the loan markets. Even so, this does not

---

[11] Citicorp, then First National City Bank of New York, was the first to achieve listing on the New York Stock Exchange.

seem likely, since many of these banks operate in the most geographically isolated loan markets or lend to specialized borrowers. In either case, the loan markets served by these banks would be highly imperfect. Moreover, the banks would not generally need to raise capital externally, and if the stock were closely held, the cost of retained earnings would not be extremely high. It is very unlikely, therefore, that situations exist like cases 4 and 5, where imperfections in the capital market force $r_K^0 > r_L^0$.

The more likely cases, then, are cases 2(b) and 3. In both, it is expected that $r_L^0 > r_K^0$, that is, the loan rate exceeds the return on capital, when the marginal revenue of loans will be equal to the marginal cost of capital. Thus, arbitrage opportunities exist for the bank to issue capital in support of loans. The only difference between the two cases is that in 2(b) banks can obtain all the capital they need at the going cost of capital, whereas in case 3 they will face a rising cost of capital if they attempt to obtain additional amounts.

It should be remembered that in case 2(b) the banks are liability managers and there is no optimal capital structure. Basically, this represents a situation in which banks are indifferent between raising funds in the market where liabilities are supplied elastically and raising funds in the market in which capital is supplied elastically. From the discussion in the preceding section, it is obvious that the solvency of the bank is not a major question unless it becomes badly managed, as in the case of the Franklin National Bank. The liabilities markets in which Franklin dealt became aware of the riskiness of the bank, and the participants in these markets became unwilling to supply funds elastically to Franklin. The condition of being a liability manager was therefore violated.

Investors—and, for that matter, borrowers and lenders—care very little about the capital position of these banks. In most cases they will be among the most highly leveraged banks and yet still be considered excellent credit risks. The capital they do keep on hand is mostly for ownership purposes and, to some extent, to satisfy the regulators. Thus, many large banks have only 5 to 6 percent of their assets protected by bank capital.[12] Case 3 applies to most banks whether they are listed on regional exchanges or in markets that are less than perfectly efficient or whether the stock is closely held and is traded only "in the president's desk." The point is that these banks do not face an infinitely elastic supply of capital funds. There is, as mentioned above, an optimal amount of capital for these banks,

---

[12] This in some sense will result in game playing. The banks will continually test the waters to see how far the regulators can be pushed in terms of a minimum amount of capital. The regulators can use the argument that the banks are "undercapitalized" to prevent acquisitions or mergers or branch expansion.

which seems for the "normal" case to be somewhere between zero and the amount of loans outstanding, whenever the marginal revenue of loans is equal to the marginal cost of capital. In addition, this will hold true whether the bank is an asset manager or a liability manager. In the latter case, there will be a relevant tradeoff between the amount of capital issued and the need for money in the purchased funds market.

It can be concluded that, with the exception of the large liability-management banks, there will exist an optimal capital structure for banks. This is because most of these banks operate in highly imperfect loan markets but also cannot obtain capital elastically from their investment sources.

THE NEXT STEP

The question now arises as to the ability of the market to determine the optimal capital structure and whether it takes into account all the factors necessary, particularly the risk of multibank failures, for the determination. This is discussed in Chapter 7. Its importance lies in the fact that if the market cannot adequately determine the optimal quantity of capital, then the regulators must and will. The importance of this for the management of an individual bank is that often regulatory standards become standards for "good bank management." If these standards are inadequate, a misallocation of economic resources can result.

SELECTED REFERENCES

Crosse, H. D., and Hempel, G. H. *Management Policies for Commercial Banks.* Englewood Cliffs, N.J.: Prentice-Hall, 1973.

Mason, J. M. "The Bank Capital Decision," Finance Department Working Paper, The University of Pennsylvania, 1978.

Pringle, J. J. "The Capital Decision in Commercial Banks." *The Journal of Finance* (June 1974).

Robinson, R. I., and Pettway, R. A. "Policies for Optimum Bank Capital: A Summary." *Policies for Optimum Bank Capital,* Association of Reserve City Bankers, Chicago (February 1967). Reprinted in P. Jessup, ed., *Innovations in Bank Management: Selected Readings.* New York: Holt, Rinehart and Winston, 1969.

REVIEW QUESTIONS

1. What do you feel defines the riskiness of the bank you keep your money in or borrow from? Do you worry about it? Does the possibility of multibank failures bother you? What do you feel about your bank or banks in general when you read about Congressional concern over "problem" banks?
2. Is the potential riskiness of any one bank different from that of any one nonfinancial firm? Why or why not? Explain your answer as well as you can in economic terms.
3. How great a problem would a "collapse of the payments mechanism" be for the operation of our economic system? Discuss.
4. What does "market regulation" mean to you? As a nonexpert, would you feel better if some "expert," or regulator, regulated your bank's capital position than if some indeterminate collection of people, the "market," regulated it? Why?
5. Why can psychological factors have only a short-run impact on banks?
6. What role does a liquid portfolio or a liquid market play in determining a bank's capital adequacy?
7. Do banks really have an "optimal" capital structure, or is this just a theoretical construct having little to do with the real world? What role do the characteristics of asset/liability markets play in determining banks' capital structure?
8. Identify the costs associated with issuing equity capital and maintaining bank capital. Are they very large, or can they generally be ignored?

APPENDIX

Mathematical Formulation of Models
Presented in Chapter 5

The model of the banking firm in this chapter is the same as the one presented in the appendixes to earlier chapters. The demand for loans is

$$L_i = f_i(r_i^a, u_i); \quad E[L_i] = L_i^*; \quad E[(L_i - L_i^*)^2] = \sigma_{Li}^2$$
$$\text{for all } i = 1, 2, \ldots, m \quad (5A-1)$$

and the supply of deposits is

$$D_h = g_h(r_h^d, w_h); \quad E[D_h] = D_h^*; \quad E[(D_h - D_h^*)^2] = \sigma_{D_h}^2$$
$$\text{for all } h = 1, 2, \ldots, n \quad (5A-2)$$

L and D are loans and deposits, respectively, and r_i^a and r_h^d are loan rates and deposit rates, respectively. The u_i and w_h are random error terms with means zero and variances $\sigma_{u_i}^2$ and $\sigma_{t_h}^2$.

The profits of the bank, π, are

$$\pi = \sum_{i=1}^{m} (r_i^a - b_i^a)L_i - \sum_{h=1}^{n} (r_h^d + b_h^d)D_h - b_K K \quad (5A-3)$$

where the b_i^a and b_h^d are cost of administration, overhead, etc., per dollar of asset (a) or liability (d). The quantity b_K is the administrative and overhead costs per dollar of capital, K. The value of the firm to wealthholders is the risk-adjusted expected terminal cash flow earned by the bank less the initial outlay of the shareholders, i.e., the original capital invested in the bank, K.

$$V = \frac{1}{1 + R_f} [E(T) - R\sigma_{\pi m}] - K \quad (5A-4)$$

Here, R_f is the risk-free rate of interest, T is the terminal cash flow of the bank, $\sigma_{\pi m}$ is the covariance of the bank's profits with market returns, and R is the market price of risk. For R, if R_m represents the market return and σ_m^2 the variance of market returns, the following equation is obtained:

$$R = \frac{E(R_m) - R_f}{\sigma_m^2} \qquad (5A\text{-}5)$$

Terminal cash flow, T, is composed of profits, π, and capital, K. Since K is the same as the capital initially invested in the bank, it is known with certainty. Hence, $E(T) = E(\pi) + K$. Substituting this into (5A-4) and rearranging yields

$$V = \frac{1}{1 + R_f} [E(\pi) - R_f K - R\sigma_{\pi m}] \qquad (5A\text{-}6)$$

The imperfections of the capital market (given as equations (5-1) and (5-2) in the body of the chapter) are now introduced:

$$r_K = r_K(K); \quad b_K = b_K(K); \quad r'(K) \geq 0 \qquad (5A\text{-}7)$$

Now equation (5A-6) becomes the objective function the shareholders of the bank wish to maximize subject to the balance sheet constraint,

$$\sum_{i=1}^{m} L_i = \sum_{h=1}^{n} D_h + K \qquad (5A\text{-}8)$$

which is expressed as

$$\max_{r_i^a, r_h^d, K} \Phi = V + \lambda \left[\sum_{i=1}^{m} L_i - \sum_{h=1}^{n} D_h - K \right] \qquad (5A\text{-}9)$$

where λ is the Lagrangian multiplier.

When derivatives of Φ are taken with respect to r_i^a, r_h^d, K and the results set equal to zero, the following optimal results are obtained:

$$\frac{\partial \Phi}{\partial r_i^a} = \frac{1}{1 + R_f} \left[(r_i^a - b_i^a) \frac{\partial L_i^*}{\partial r_i^a} + L_i^* \left(1 - \frac{\partial b_i^a}{\partial L_i^*} \frac{\partial L_i^*}{\partial r_i^a} \right) - \frac{R \partial \mathrm{Cov}(\pi, R_m)}{\partial r_i^a} \right]$$
$$+ \frac{\lambda \partial L_i^*}{\partial r_i^a} = 0 \quad (5A\text{-}10)$$

$$\frac{\partial \Phi}{\partial r_h^d} = \frac{-1}{1 + R_f} \left[(R_h^d + b_h^d) \frac{\partial D_b^*}{\partial r_h^d} + D_b^* \left(1 + \frac{\partial b_h^d}{\partial D_b^*} \frac{\partial D_b^*}{\partial r_h^d} \right) - \frac{R \partial \mathrm{Cov}(\pi, R_m)}{\partial r_b^d} \right]$$
$$- \frac{\lambda \partial D_b^*}{\partial r_h^d} = 0 \quad (5A\text{-}11)$$

$$\frac{\partial \Phi}{\partial K} = \frac{1}{1 + R_f} \left(-R_F - b_K + K \frac{\partial b_K}{\partial K} - \frac{R \partial \text{Cov}(\pi, R_m)}{\partial K} \right) - \lambda = 0 \qquad (5A\text{-}12)$$

The equations can be simplified by introducing elasticities, which will be denoted e. Thus, $e_i^a = -(r^a/L^*)(\partial L^*/\partial r^a)$, $e_i^b = (L^*/b^a)(\partial b^a/\partial L^*)$, $e_h^d = (r_h^d/D_h)(\partial D_h^*/\partial r_h^d)$, and $e_h^b = (D_h^*/b_h^d)(\partial b_h^d/\partial D_h^*)$. Solving for equilibrium values yields

$$r_i^a \left(1 + \frac{1}{e_i^a} \right) - b_i(1 + e_i^b) - \frac{R}{\partial L_i^*/\partial r_i^a} \left(\frac{\text{Cov}(\pi, R_m)}{\partial r_i^a} \right)$$

$$= r_h^d \left(1 + \frac{1}{e_h^d} \right) + b_h^d(1 + e_h^b) - \frac{R}{\partial D_h^*/\partial r_h^d} \left(\frac{\text{Cov}(\pi, R_m)}{\partial r_h^d} \right) \qquad (5A\text{-}13)$$

$$= r_f + b_K(1 + e_K) + R \left(\frac{\text{Cov}(\pi, R_m)}{\partial K} \right)$$

If the elasticities are known along with the effect each decision variable has on $\text{Cov}(\pi, R_m)$, then the series of equations can be solved for the r_i^a, r_h^d, and K. With knowledge of these values and use of the loan demand equation (5A-1), the deposit supply equation (5A-2), and the cost of capital equation (5A-7), the quantities of L_i and D_h can be obtained.

As noted earlier, some markets serve as residual markets that allow a bank to fill in their balance sheets. These are markets in which the elasticity of supply of funds or the elasticity of demand for funds approaches infinity. It is assumed that banks will operate at quantities of these assets or liabilities where the adminstrative and overhead costs are extremely small; they will, in fact, be assumed to be zero. Thus, costs in each of these markets reduce to the interest cost. The two markets generally assumed to meet these qualifications are the government securities market, denoted by the subscript g, and the market for negotiable certificates of deposit, denoted by CD. Thus, from equation (5A-13)

$$r_g = r_{\text{CD}} \qquad (5A\text{-}14)$$

Obviously, the way the model is set up now the bank would not buy certificates of deposit to invest in government securities. Thus, the bank would either be an asset manager, if the loan demand did not exceed the amount of deposits supplied inelastically, or it would be a liability manager, buying no government securities and funding the loan demand that exceeded the inelastically supplied deposits with money obtained by selling certificates of deposit.

Now the conclusions reached in Chapter 5 can easily be derived from the above results.

1. If no imperfections existed and there were no transactions costs, i.e., if $b_K = b_h^d = b_i^q = 0$, then elasticities would be infinite and equations (5A-13) would collapse to

$$r_i^q = r_h^d = R_f \tag{5A-15}$$

There would be no banks.

2. Imperfections exist in the loan demand and deposit supply, but not in the capital market.

(a) The asset-management case: In this case it can easily be seen that $r_g = R_f = r_K$. Thus, the bank would not obtain capital funds to put into government securities. However, since in general $r_L > r_K$ and $r_g > r_D$, the bank will obtain deposits to invest in government securities and will obtain capital to invest in loans. Thus

$$K = \sum_{i=1}^{m} L_i - L_g \quad \text{and} \quad \sum_{R=1}^{n} D_h = L_g$$

(b) The liability-management case: In this case it can easily be seen that $r_{CD} = r_K$. Thus banks will be indifferent to whether they use CD money or capital money to fund the loans demanded in excess of inelastically supplied deposits.

3. Imperfections exist in all markets, but the imperfections that exist in the loan markets are greater than those that exist in the liability markets. In general, this would mean that in equilibrium $r_L > r_K > r_g = r_{CD}$. There will be an optimal capital structure in this case somewhere between zero and $\sum_{i=1}^{m} L_i - L_g$. The exact amount of capital that is optimum depends on the various elasticities and cost considerations. It makes no difference whether the bank is an asset or liability management bank.

4. Imperfections exist in all markets, but those that exist in the loan market are no greater than those that exist in the capital market. Solving equations (5A-13) would yield the relationship $r_K > r_L = r_g = r_{CD}$. Here the optimal amount of the capital held by the bank would be zero, and whether the bank was an asset or liability manager would make no difference.

5. Imperfections exist in the capital markets and the deposit markets, but the asset markets are perfectly competitive. In this case, solving equa-

tions (5A-13) would give the relationship $r_K > r_L = r_g = r_{CD}$. Capital would again be zero, regardless of whether the bank were an asset manager or a liability manager.

APPENDIX REFERENCES

Mason, J. M. "The Bank Capital Decision." Finance Department Working Paper, The University of Pennsylvania, 1978.

Pringle, J. J. "The Capital Decision in Commercial Banks." *The Journal of Finance* (June 1974).

6

Internal Sources of Bank Capital

Until recently, most banks in the United States obtained the capital they needed for operations from retained earnings. The amount of retained earnings a bank had depended on three factors: the bank's earnings, the effective tax rate paid on those earnings, and the bank's dividend policy.

Since most U.S. commercial banks were regional or local firms, their rate of growth was determined primarily by regional or local economic conditions. A bank in a growing area where loan demand and deposit supply were increasing rapidly could generally expect growth in earnings and hence sufficient internally generated capital to support expansion. A bank in an area that was not growing as rapidly could expect slower growth in loan demand, in deposits, and in earnings. However, since it required less capital, its earnings also were sufficient to satisfy its needs. Because the needs and availability of internal bank capital were usually the product of local or regional economic patterns, banks were generally independent of capital markets. They rarely if ever experienced a portfolio situation in which the demand for loans exceeded or grew faster than the supply of inelastically supplied deposits. Profitability could be improved by good management regardless of what markets the bank operated in.

Twenty to twenty-five years ago, taxes and dividend payouts were not very important considerations for commercial banks. The banks generally operated in highly imperfect markets and thus were able to obtain large spreads between the rates they charged on loans and the rates they paid for deposits. As a result, profit margins were more than adequate and the banks could generate sufficient capital for growth without devoting much effort to tax planning and, since they did not need to raise capital externally, without paying more than minimal dividends.

As banks moved into more competitive markets, they found it necessary to purchase some funds that were supplied elastically. Profit margins fell, and it became more important for management to control taxes and to weigh the costs and benefits of dividend payouts because of their effects on internal funding.

This chapter takes a closer look at the factors that influence the amount of bank capital that can be raised internally. First, the sources of earnings are examined and the portfolio factors that contribute to "high performance" are reviewed. Then the tax shelters available to banks are presented, and finally the impact of dividend payment decisions is discussed.

EARNINGS

Aggregate Results

In order to place the factors influencing earnings in proper perspective, it is desirable to reproduce the income statement presented in Chapter 1. Now, however, this equation will be net of taxes:

$$\hat{\pi} = (1 - T)\left[\sum_{i=1}^{m-p} r_i^a L_i - \sum_{i=1}^{m} b_i^a L_i - \sum_{h=1}^{n} (r_h^d + b_h^d)D_h\right] + \sum_{i=p+1}^{m} r_i^a L_i \quad (6\text{-}1)$$

$$= (1 - \hat{T})\left[\sum_{i=1}^{m} r_i^a L_i - \left(\sum_{i=1}^{m} b_i^a L_i + \sum_{h=1}^{n} b_h^d D_h\right) - \sum_{h=1}^{n} r_h^d D_h\right]$$

$$= (1 - \hat{T})(R - OE - IE)$$

The variable $\hat{\pi}$ is net income after taxes, T is the tax rate applied to taxable income, and $\hat{T}$ is the effective tax rate applicable to the bank. All other variables are as defined earlier. The only other difference is that the first p assets are considered to have taxable returns, whereas the assets from $p + 1$ to m are assumed to bear nontaxable returns.

In bank planning, the banks are assumed to consider the portfolio composition as shown in the first line of equation (6-1). The goal is to maximize net income by rearranging assets so as to make full use of the nontaxable status of some operations. The reported earnings are more like the second line of equation (6-1), where all interest revenues are aggregated as well as interest expense and operating costs. The gross income is then adjusted by an effective tax rate, rather than the actual rate applied to taxable revenues. In the third line of the equation, these factors are summarized as R for gross revenues, OE for operating expenses, not including interest expense, and IE for interest expense.

Thus, anything that raises R or lowers OE, IE, or $\hat{T}$ will raise $\hat{\pi}$. This is, of course, the objective of bank planning.

Commercial banks earn about 70 percent of their gross revenues, R, from interest revenues and fees and income from federal funds sold and securities purchased under resale agreements. The rest comes from securities income, approximately 20 percent of R, from other areas such as the trust department, and from other service charges. As to the general makeup of expenses, there has been a substantial change in recent years as high-cost deposits have been purchased more frequently by banks. Salaries, wages, and other benefits have also increased rapidly, but whereas these expenses, primarily those defined in OE, accounted for approximately 50 percent of total expenses ($OE + IE$) in the early 1950s, they now account for only about 25 percent of total expenses. Interest expense (IE), on the other hand, has moved from approximately 15 percent of total expenses in the early 1950s to about 45 percent now. All other factors contributing to total expenses have roughly maintained their relative proportion of the total.

In the aggregate, bank revenue has increased by over 300 percent since the early 1960s, but bank expenses, led by the growth in interest expense, have increased by over 400 percent. This gives some credence to the fall in the profit margin of banks in general.

The profit margin of a bank can be defined in terms of the symbols used in the third line of equation (6-1). Specifically, it is income before income taxes (and securities gains and losses)[1] divided by total operating income:

$$\text{Profit Margin} = \frac{R - OE - IE}{R} \qquad (6\text{-}2)$$

As can be seen in Table 6-1, the profit margin of all insured commercial banks has dropped substantially since 1970. Specific comparisons with earlier periods are impossible because of a revision in the series that makes the pre-1970 data inconsistent with the post-1970 data.

---

[1] Securities gains and losses are excluded because they are generally assumed to be random over time and gains tend to offset losses, so that gain from sale of securities is zero.

TABLE 6-1   Selected Data for All Insured Commercial Banks, 1969–1976

Year	Profit Margin	Asset Productivity	Rate of Return on Bank Assets	Effective Tax Rate (percent)[a]	Capital–Asset Ratio
1969	21.85	5.97	1.30	32	7.1
1970	20.53	6.38	1.31	30	7.0
1971	18.46	6.03	1.11	25	6.9
1972	18.02	5.93	1.07	23	6.5
1973	16.42	6.83	1.12	24	6.5
1974	13.57	7.82	1.06	24	6.6
1975	13.49	7.20	0.97	20	6.8
1976	12.29	7.18	0.88	20	7.1

Source: FDIC, Annual Report, 1976.
[a] Approximate

Two things work to counteract a declining profit margin: (1) higher productivity in the use of assets, that is, greater earnings per dollar of assets, and (2) a lower effective tax rate.

Asset productivity can be calculated as total operating income divided by total assets:

$$\text{Asset Productivity} = \frac{R}{\sum_{i=1}^{m} L_i} \tag{6-3}$$

From Table 6-1 it can be seen that although asset productivity fluctuates with changes in general economic conditions, there is some indication that it increased slightly as interest rates rose in the 1970s. However, the increase has not been sufficient to offset the decline that has taken place in the profit margin.

The latter fact can be verified by seeing what has happened to the rate of return on the total assets of the insured banks before taxes over the same period of time. Rate of return on assets before taxes can be obtained by multiplying profit margin by asset productivity:

$$\begin{array}{c} \text{Rate of Return on} \\ \text{Assets before Taxes} \end{array} = \frac{\pi}{\sum_{i=1}^{m} L_i} = \frac{R - OE - IE}{R} \times \frac{R}{\sum_{i=1}^{m} L_i} \tag{6-4}$$

where π is net income before taxes. In Table 6-1 it can be seen that the before-tax rate of return on bank assets has in fact declined rather substantially during the time period under review.

To see the effect of taxes on this rate of return, the profit margin equation must be adjusted to an after-tax basis. This results in the following formula:

$$\text{Rate of Return on Assets after Taxes} = \frac{\hat{\pi}}{\sum_{i=1}^{m} L_i} = \frac{(1 - \hat{T})(R - OE - IE)}{R} \times \frac{R}{\sum_{i=1}^{m} L_i} \quad (6\text{-}5)$$

Again, Table 6-1 shows that the banks have been relatively effective in reducing their effective tax rates. Consequently, this has cushioned the decline in the after-tax rates of return on assets earned by insured commercial banks since 1970.

Since it has been maintained all along that, at least for the stockholders, rate of return on equity is a better measure of return to wealthholders than rate of return on assets, it is desirable to convert equation (6-5) into a return-on-equity equation. By comparing return on bank assets with the return on bank equity, an analyst can see the effects of a change in firm leverage on bank returns. A bank that is more highly leveraged than another and has the same return on assets will have a higher return on equity. If the capital–asset ratio $K/\sum_{i=1}^{m} L_i$ is denoted by k,

then

$$\text{Rate of Return on Equity after Taxes} = \frac{\hat{\pi}}{K} = \frac{1}{k}\left(\text{Rate of Return on Assets after Taxes}\right) \quad (6\text{-}6)$$

As Table 6-1 shows, the capital–asset ratio fell during the early 1970s and has risen only recently. As a result, the after-tax rate of return on equity rose in the early part of the decade and fell slightly in the most recent period as the after-tax rate of return on assets remained relatively constant.

Relative Performance of Commercial Banks   There are longer, more consistent series on bank returns than the series available on the individual income and expense items presented above. These data are reproduced in Table 6-2. As can be seen from this table, the after-tax rate of return on assets remained fairly constant throughout most of the 1960s and then jumped to a new plateau in about 1969 or 1970. This level was maintained for several years but has declined drastically in the most recent reporting periods.

TABLE 6-2   Rates of Return to Insured Commercial Banks and to Durable
and Nondurable Goods Producers, 1965–1976

| | After-Tax Rate of Return on Assets | After-Tax Rate of Return on Equity | | |
Year	Commercial Banks	Commercial Banks	Durable Goods Producers	Nondurable Goods Producers
1965	.70	9.2	13.8	12.2
1966	.69	9.2	14.2	12.7
1967	.74	10.1	11.7	11.8
1968	.72	10.3	12.2	11.9
1969	.84	12.0	11.4	11.5
1970	.89	12.4	8.3	10.3
1971	.87	12.4	9.1	10.3
1972	.83	12.3	10.7	10.5
1973	.85	12.9	13.1	12.6
1974	.81	12.5	12.6	17.1
1975	.78	11.8	10.2	12.9
1976	.70	11.4	13.6	14.3

Source: FDIC, *Annual Reports,* and Department of Commerce, *Statistical Abstracts of the United States,* various years.

The after-tax rate of return on equity seems to move from a low in the period 1964–1966 to a period of sustained growth through 1970. These were the years in which the banking industry was considered a growth industry. This interpretation can be verified by comparing the results for the banking industry with the after-tax returns on stockholders' equity for total durable goods producers and total nondurable goods producers. As can be seen in Table 6-2, through 1971 the rates of return on both types of producers were declining, although the nondurable goods industry did not experience as much volatility or as great a degree of decline as did the durable goods industry. Commercial banks were thus prime performers at this time and were recognized as such by investors.

However, after 1970 the growth of the banking industry slowed down, and the rate of return on equity stabilized and then declined. Investors could not count on the spectacular results of the previous four or five years. The events of 1974–1975, with the specter of multibank failures hanging over the market, even caused some analysts to expect the banking industry to experience negative growth rates. Fortunately, events did not develop along those lines.

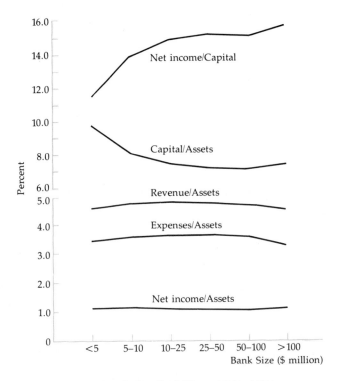

FIGURE 6-1 Bank Profitability, 1954–1974

(After Edward C. Gallick, "Bank Profitability and Bank Size," *Monthly Review*, Federal Reserve Bank of Kansas City (January 1976) and FDIC, *Annual Reports*.)

Performance and Bank Size Another way to look at the developments of aggregate bank performance is to examine how results were distributed according to size of bank.[2] To help explain the results as they pertain to different sizes of banks, the reader is referred to Figures 6-1, 6-2, and 6-3. First, in Figure 6-1 it can be seen that in the period 1954–1974 the rate of return on assets was roughly constant for all banks, regardless of size. This is explained by a roughly constant ratio of expenses to revenues throughout the spectrum of bank sizes. However, rate of return on equity seems to increase constantly with size. The increased leverage of larger banks obviously accounts for the increase.

[2] The results reported here are taken from the paper by Edward C. Gallick, "Bank Profitability and Bank Size," *Monthly Review*, Federal Reserve Bank of Kansas City (January 1976), pp. 11–16.

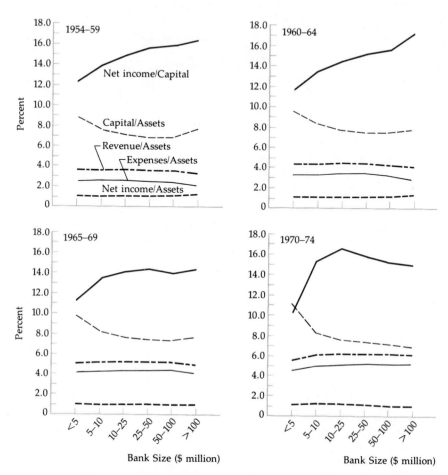

FIGURE 6-2   Bank Profitability in Subperiods, 1954–1974
(For source, see Figure 6-1.)

If we look at subperiods within this time span (Figure 6-2), a different pattern emerges. In the early years the results described in the previous paragraph, in general, hold up. However, for 1965–1969 and 1970–1974, the picture is entirely different. In the earlier period, except for banks under $25 million in asset size, leverage does not seem to play an important role and the rate of return on equity does not seem to vary with the bank size.

The most substantial differences are seen in the 1970–1974 period. Again, the general results hold for banks of less than $25 million; those

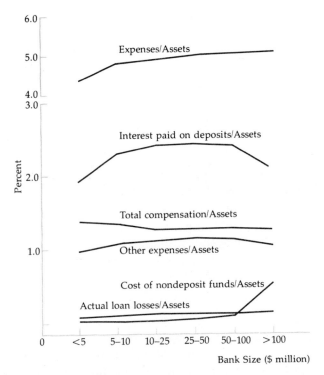

FIGURE 6-3   Expense Component of Aggregate Bank Performance, 1970–1974

(For source, see Figure 6-1.)

with assets of more than $25 million show results that are just the opposite. As bank size increases from $25 million, the rate of return on equity becomes smaller rather than larger, even in the light of evidence that the larger banks were more highly leveraged than their smaller counterparts. The reason for this can be seen in the decline in the rate of return on assets experienced by the larger banks. This decline was a result of the increasing ratio of expenses to revenues.

As described earlier, a large part of the decline in the profit margins of banks can be attributed to the interest cost of more expensive money. Figure 6-3 brings this out even more clearly, as the higher interest cost of funds is centered in the larger banks. Whereas banks that run in size from $25 million to $100 million do not rely as heavily as the largest banks on nondeposit sources of funds, they are more aggressive than smaller banks in their attempts to obtain time accounts. They are willing to pay higher interest rates on time accounts and also are more likely to have a more extensive menu of longer-term certificates and accounts that also cost more than a normal passbook account. Thus, as can be seen, interest paid on deposits as a proportion of total assets increases with the size of the bank for all but the very largest banks.

The very largest banks, however, are those most likely to deal in the purchased funds markets. Because these markets are more competitive, interest rates are generally higher. Figure 6-3 shows very clearly the remarkable increase in interest expenses experienced by these large commercial banks due to the cost of nondeposit sources of funds.

Thus, it appears that whereas profit margins generally declined, owing to the increased cost of personnel and the increased cost of liabilities, the decline was centered primarily in the large banks and thus tended to dominate the overall banking statistics. These results will again be borne out in the micro data presented next.

Micro Results

The micro results are taken from a study done by the research staff at the American Bankers Association.[3] In the study, banks were first arbitrarily segregated on the basis of size into small, medium, and large banks and then were split into high-performance banks (HPB) and others solely on the basis of highest return on capital. This sample showed that high-performance banks earned around 23 percent on capital while the industry average was around 13 percent.

Some preliminary effort was made to eliminate local or regional influences that might bias the results. However, the various local-regional considerations tested showed that high performance (or low performance) was not a result of the area in which a bank was located. Two seemingly important factors, the competition from thrift institutions and the state of the local economy, had no significant influence in achieving the better than average performance.

In light of the aggregate analysis described in the previous section, one very interesting result is present in the micro study. High-performance banks generally were more highly leveraged than the other banks in the

---

[3] W. F. Ford, "Profitability: Why Do Some Banks Perform Better Than Average? An In-Depth Analysis," *Banking* (October 1974), pp. 29–54; D. A. Olson, "How High-Profit Banks Got That Way," *Banking* (May 1975), pp. 46–58.

sample. However, high leverage seemed to contribute little to the differentiation of the banks; the research showed that with the leverage factor held constant, return on equity only dropped to about 20 percent. The major difference in performance came from the return on assets earned by the high-performance banks: 1.60 percent to an industry average of approximately 1.00 percent. This contradicts the aggregate results, in that rates of return on assets seemed relatively constant across all asset sizes, whereas differences in capital structure accounted for the higher earnings on equity.

Aside from this result, the data conform reasonably well to what might be expected. In terms of interest returns, high-performance banks received higher loan yields, primarily because of their mix of loans, and higher loan revenues than other banks in the sample. They also had fewer dollars of assets invested in Treasury bills and U.S. government agency securities, holding greater proportions of their asset portfolios in either loans or tax-exempt securities. Thus, in general, revenues (R) were higher because of higher-yield before-tax and after-tax interest rates and fees (r_i^a) and fewer holdings of low-yield assets, such as government securities (r_G^a).

High-performance banks also had lower effective tax rates $(\hat{T})$. Part of this was due to their greater investment in tax-exempt securities.

Interest expenses (IE) were lower for small and medium-sized high-performance banks, although, as expected, this was not the case for the larger high-performance banks.

Perhaps the most substantial contribution to performance was the way the high-performance banks seemed to control operating expenses (OE) and fixed assets. They employed fewer people than their group average, and hence their employees seemed to be more highly productive than those in other organizations. They also held one-third fewer dollars in fixed assets than the other banks in the sample. There was not enough information to determine whether all fixed assets were treated properly in an accounting sense—that is, whether leases on bank premises were capitalized or not, or whether bank premises were entered at economic values or not—but the evidence seems to be fairly strong that even if the results were adjusted, the high-performance banks operated on fewer fixed assets than banks that did not perform as well.

In summary of this section, it can be said that high-performance banks seem to be those that manage their costs and taxes well and fully exploit the market opportunities available to them. Thus, they earn a higher rate of return on assets than less well managed banks; and this, when combined with more leverage (since a well-managed bank is less risky than one that is poorly managed), leads to substantially higher rates of return on equity than the average. High performance banks experienced higher net income growth and a larger expansion of capital than the rest of the sample. This would seem to indicate that the banks determined by the study to be high-performance banks have been so for several years. Furthermore, the original study has been updated, with similar findings.[4]

DIVIDEND POLICY

As stated in the introduction to this chapter, bank dividend policies have gained increasing attention in recent years. This is because bank managers have found that achieving a higher price for the bank's stock (which reduces the bank's cost of capital) is consistent with the best interests of the owners of the bank. On the one hand, a higher stock price means that if the bank needs to raise funds in the capital markets to support growth, it will be cheaper to do so. On the other hand, if management wants to merge with or acquire another bank, it will be cheaper to do so. Moreover, if the owners want to sell the bank to another organization, they will get a better price. In the latter two instances, this will be particularly true if acquisitions or mergers take place through an exchange of stock. The price of the merger will be determined as the ratio of the number of shares of one bank to be exchanged for a share of stock of the other.

The major question confronting bank management is whether the dividend payout ratio, the ratio of dividends paid to net earnings after taxes, that a bank chooses has a significant effect on the price of the bank's stock. This was a moot point when bank ownership was tightly controlled, the bank's stock was not traded, and there was no need for external capital or for using stock in acquisitions or mergers. However, many bank stocks today are widely held and traded on national or regional stock exchanges. For these banks it is important to know whether or not dividend policy affects their stock price. If the dividend payout the bank chooses does affect its stock price, then the decision to change the amount of dividends paid becomes very important.

Residual Theory of Dividends

There are two theories as to how an organization's dividend payout ratio affects, or fails to affect, the price of its common stock. The first, called

[4] W. F. Ford, "How the 1,000 High-Performance Banks Weathered the Recent Recession," *Banking* (April 1978), pp. 36–48.

the *residual theory of dividends,* states that only the investment decisions of the firm are important in determining stock prices, because these decisions affect the risk classification of the firm. Shareholders are assumed to have no innate preferences for dividends or retained earnings; they are simply interested in their shares yielding the highest return for a given level of risk.

As long as corporate investment opportunities promise a return greater than that available to shareholders in alternative investments, the shareholders prefer that the corporation retain earnings. When corporate investment returns drop below the shareholders' alternative investment returns, they will wish the firm to distribute the remaining portion of earnings in the form of dividends.

This theory implies that if investment opportunities that provide a return greater than the firm's cost of capital are available, and the firm pays out dividends, the firm will have to go to the equity market to raise the funds, and the result will be that everyone will be just as well off as if the dividends were not paid. The new equity capital raised would be equal to the dividend payments, and the increased equity outstanding would dilute the price of existing shares by an amount equal to the dividends obtained from the ownership. Investors, in the absence of taxes, would therefore be indifferent between dividends and retained earnings.

Theory of Dividend Relevance

In contrast to the residual theory of dividends is the *theory of dividend relevance,* which states that numerous factors may create a preference between dividends and retained earnings. For example, dividends may be preferred for their "information content," whereby an increase in dividend payments signals that the firm anticipates a significant and stable growth in earnings. Or investors may simply prefer dividends for the relative certainty of their payment in the present, as opposed to the vagaries of a promise of future dividends resulting from current earnings retention. Shareholders also seem averse to selling their shares to generate income because of the market risk and brokerage costs involved.

One factor that may cause investors to prefer retained earnings is the lower taxes they would have to pay on capital gains income. Another relates to the flotation costs of new stock issues. Moreover, new stock issues may lower the price of the existing shares because of the dilution of earnings per share that results from stock dividends.

Every investor must weigh these considerations and arrive at a position either of net preference or of disdain for dividends at a given level of dividend payout. When aggregated, these attitudes may have important effects on a bank's cost of equity capital. It is conceivable that at lower levels of dividend payout, investors will have a net preference for dividends and will tolerate a lower overall return on their stock holdings as dividends are gradually increased. However, at high dividend payout levels, investors will become more concerned about their potential tax liabilities and will desire lower returns on their stock holdings as dividend payments increase. The task of the bank, therefore, is to pinpoint the dividend payout ratio that minimizes its cost of equity capital.

Empirical Studies of Dividend Relevance   The first analysis along these lines concluded that the dividend payout ratio at banks is very important in determining stock prices. Sherman Adams concluded from his study that "if banks as a group were to move up to an appreciably higher average payout ratio, this would probably be reflected in a significant enhancement of the market value of outstanding bank stocks."[5] This study was published in late 1967 and drew inferences from data for 1966.

The assumption that dividend policies affect stock prices became a generally acknowledged fact in banking circles. For example, two authorities on banking, Roland I. Robinson and Richard H. Pettway, reported in a study for the Association of Reserve City Banking in the same year as the Adams study was published that "[t]he most important part of an individual bank's capital planning is its dividend policy. The evidence seems clear and unmistakable that bank share prices are influenced by dividend payout. If a bank retains earnings to increase its rate of capital growth, it increases its cost of external equity capital."[6]

Since the Adams study was so loosely done and since there existed a body of evidence for the nonfinancial firm that was somewhat contrary to this result,[7] others began to examine the dividend question as it pertained to commercial banks. The results presented here are drawn from the study

[5] E. Sherman Adams, "Are Bank Dividend Policies Too Conservative?" *Banking* (November 1967).

[6] R. I. Robinson and R. H. Pettway, "Policies for Optimum Bank Capital: A Summary," reprinted in P. F. Jessup, ed., *Innovations in Bank Management: Selected Readings* (New York: Holt, Rinehart and Winston, 1969).

[7] F. Black and M. Scholes, "The Effects of Dividend Yield and Dividend Policy on Common Stock Prices and Returns," *Journal of Financial Economics* (May 1974), pp. 1–22; E. Fama, L. Fisher, M. Jensen, and R. Roll, "The Adjustment of Stock Prices to New Information," *International Economic Review* (February 1969), pp. 1–21.

TABLE 6-3   The Effect of Dividend Payments on Stock Price[a]

Regression Equation: $P_t = a + bD_t + cR_t^n + d(E/P)_{t-1}^n$

Year	D_t	R_t^n	$(E/P)_{t-1}^n$	R^2	D.W.
		New York Stock Exchange			
1969	15.30	9.37	−286.14	0.9870	1.86
	(1.03)	(1.28)	(42.96)		
1972	10.37	11.50	−415.76	0.9664	1.60
	(1.04)	(1.02)	(50.76)		
1974	5.81	8.90	−376.03	0.9169	1.93
	(1.70)	(1.09)	(47.06)		
		Over the Counter			
1969	13.01	9.01	−319.01	0.9836	1.96
	(1.46)	(1.15)	(45.25)		
1972	10.15	10.64	−396.52	0.9561	2.57
	(1.27)	(1.28)	(50.77)		
1974	7.15	6.23	−295.16	0.9302	2.45
	(1.32)	(0.71)	(38.43)		

[a] Standard errors are in parentheses. Earnings are computed after taking extraordinary items into account.

Definitions:

D = dividends per share

R_t^n = retained earnings normalized by taking a moving average

$(E/P)_{t-1}^n$ = earnings/price ratio normalized by taking a moving average

D.W. = Durbin-Watson statistic

done by Mason and Hill.[8] The methodology of this research was originally developed by Friend and Puckett.[9]

Mason and Hill tested whether investors seemed to prefer dividends or retained earnings by examining, through regression analysis, whether the coefficient attached to dividends was statistically different from the coefficient of retained earnings once most of the biases were removed from the tests. Two samples of 20 banks were taken, one from those companies listed on the New York Stock Exchange and one from those companies traded over the counter. The study covered two years when the stock market declined sharply (1969 and 1974) as well as a year when stock prices generally increased (1972). The major results for the individual years are presented in Table 6-3.

[8] J. M. Mason and D. Hill, "Dividends, Risk and Commercial Bank Stock Prices," Finance Department Working Paper, University of Pennsylvania, 1977.

[9] I. Friend and M. Puckett, "Dividends and Stock Prices," American Economic Review (September 1964), pp. 656–82.

Analysis of Results   The conclusion drawn by Mason and Hill was that in 1969, for both the New York Stock Exchange and the over-the-counter market, investors placed more weight on dividend payments than on retained earnings. In 1972 and 1974, however, the market seemed to be indifferent between the two. This implied that during the late 1960s dividend payouts were relevant, which was consistent with the Adams study, but that they became irrelevant in the 1970s.

The best explanation for this result comes from interpreting the latter part of the 1960s as a period when banking was considered a growth industry and increases in dividends carried some "information" as to which banks were experiencing the growth. That is, it was assumed that a bank would not cut into its major source of capital, retained earnings, just to pay dividends unless earnings were expected to grow to cover the increased dividend payments. Thus, those organizations that raised their dividend payout ratios were signaling to the market that they anticipated an increase in earnings. Investors incorporated this information into their valuation of bank stock prices.

The data on rates of return on equity presented in Table 6-2 lend credence to this interpretation. That is, the expectations of increased earnings on capital were fulfilled, and this gave additional reason for the market to interpret announcements of increased dividend payouts in that way. There is evidence that if these expectations had not been borne out in practice, the higher stock prices or the higher price–earnings ratios would not have been maintained.[10]

In the early 1970s, the banking industry ceased to be a growth industry. The rate of return on equity leveled off and failed to grow further; increases in dividends did not carry any more information to the market. This meant that, other things remaining the same, investors should be indifferent to whether the bank paid dividends or not. This is clearly the result Mason and Hill obtained for 1972 and 1974.

The conclusion that can be drawn from this is that the dividend question may be important for a commercial bank and thus must not be summarily dismissed by bank management. The bank must assay its situation and make a judgment as to its ability to grow and then attempt to present this story to the market. If management feels fairly confident that the bank will experience increasing growth in the future—by, say, changing its

---

[10] R. R. Pettit, "Dividend Announcements, Security Performance, and Capital Market Efficiency," *Journal of Finance* (December 1972), pp. 993–1007.

customer base or by acquiring new firms—then part of its effort to convey this information to the market should consist of overtly raising its dividend payments.

On the other hand, if management feels that the bank does not have the possibilities for this future growth, it should not alter its dividend policy, for any increase in stock price that might result from higher dividends would be short-lived. If future events do not warrant the higher stock price, then it will drop back to its former level. The bank will have lost some capital in paying out a higher rate of dividends and will receive nothing in return.

The dividend policy of a bank is important. But the policy may be one of not changing the dividend rather than one of changing it. Bank management must be aware of its economic situation before it chooses one or the other.

TAX SHELTERS

As implied in the introduction to this chapter, tax management has become a very important part of bank profit planning and hence of internal capital accumulation. Banks have had several opportunities to reduce their taxes, but either the tax savings would not be worth the administrative and overhead costs incurred, or tax rates for the bank were low enough that the bank could not reduce taxes by using the tax shelters. Tax shelters are defined as means of reducing actual tax payments. Legislation in the past decade or so has opened up several more possibilities to banks. Hence, with their growing need for capital, banks have generally become much more careful in planning their asset allocation to reduce their effective tax rate.

Five types of tax shelters will be considered here: securities gains and losses, loan-loss writeoffs, tax-free securities, the investment tax credit, and the foreign tax credit.

Securities Gains and Losses

Securities gains and losses have not always been treated as taxable additions to or subtractions from ordinary income and thus taxable at the rate applicable to other earned income. Before the Tax Reform Act of 1969, long-term gains were treated as capital gains, whereas losses were treated as an ordinary expense. Thus, commercial banks had a built-in tax break that favored portfolio switching (selling one security and buying another) to gain the benefits of capital appreciation. However, this switching was limited to investments, and the law tended to encourage banks to stay in securities rather than move into loans.

The Tax Reform Act of 1969 removed this incentive. Since interest and fees earned on loans are taxed at the same rate as interest and/or capital gains on securities, there is no incentive to sell securities that have a capital loss and put them into other securities.

However, if opportunities are available and interest rates are expected to decline, there is incentive to sell loss-producing securities and move into loans or into other securities. First of all, the bank gets a tax saving immediately. Thus, it can offset some current income. Second, the bank can invest in higher-earning loans or securities and will then receive the income or possibly, if interest rates decline, capital gains, in the future. The bank must, of course, consider the cost of taking a capital loss now and the income it shelters against the discounted present value of future earnings and taxes. As with any capital budgeting problem, the securities should be sold at a loss up to the point where the net present value of the transaction becomes zero.

It should be noted that the benefits of taking tax-reducing losses are limited by the amount of taxable income available to offset the loss. However, like nonfinancial corporations, banks can carry losses forward for five years. Thus, this year's losses can be used to offset income not only for the current year but also for the next four years.

Loan-Loss Reserves

Lending always involves the possibility of loss. Although actual losses do show regularity in their occurrence, there is some degree of variance around the expected amount of loss from year to year. Thus, since commercial banks do not know exactly what losses will be in any one year but only that extraordinary losses or lack of losses will offset one another over time, a reserve is set up that allows a bank to make regular provision for these losses but shelters the income statement from variations due to the timing of the loan losses.

The loan-loss reserve is, therefore, an asset valuation account in that it helps to maintain asset values as opposed to supporting or financing the holding of assets. This has raised some questions as to the loan-loss reserve account being considered a part of a bank's capital. Theoretically at least, the account should be zero over time; it is greater than zero only when the bank has had less than expected loan losses so that the account is not depleted. Technically, then, this reserve account could be less than zero if the bank had loan losses greater than expected. Recently, regulatory officials have allowed banks to carry their valuation reserves, described below, on the asset side of the balance sheet in the loan account.[11] In practice, however, this is not how it works. There are several complicating factors.

First, the rules used to govern writeoffs for loan losses allow some leeway for the bank to write off more than it expects to use. Since these writeoffs are accounted for as ordinary income, they are not taxed and hence represent tax-free additions to capital. (This will be explained more fully later by means of an example.) There are incentives, however, to build up loan-loss reserves in excess of what the bank feels it needs.

Second, the issue is clouded by the fact that three accounts are involved in the whole process of preparing for loan losses. There is the *valuation reserve*, against which the bank can charge off loans. Allocations to this account are reported in the accounting statements released publicly. However, there are two other accounts, the *contingency reserve* and the *deferred tax reserve*. These accounts arise because commercial banks can allocate greater amounts to their loan-loss reserve in the statements they report to the Internal Revenue Service than they do in their public statements. Thus, they can reduce their effective tax rate on reported income.

Essentially, funds going into the valuation reserve come from operating expenses; funds going to the contingency reserve come from publicly reported retained earnings. The tax savings from these additions to capital go to the deferred tax account.

Only funds in the valuation reserve can be used to charge off actual loan losses. The contingency reserve and the deferred tax reserve represent tax-free capital to the bank but cannot be used to charge off loans. The only way the contingency reserves can be used is to restore the funds to retained earnings via the income statement and pay the necessary taxes on them, accumulated through the deferred tax account. This will be explained in more detail in the example given below.

The methods used to allocate funds to the loan reserve accounts are in the process of change. The schedule for tax changes results from the Tax Reform Act of 1969, which allows a bank to shelter a loan-loss reserve whose ratio to eligible loans is based either on experience or on a legal maximum. The amount that can be allocated to the loan-loss reserve is 0.6 percent of

---

[11] This would be a negative value, however, something to subtract from total loans on the books.

eligible loans. The maximum reserve allowed the bank is 1.2 percent of eligible loans. This is much in excess of general bank experience. However, before 1976, the ratio stood at 1.8 percent. In 1982, the ratio will drop to 0.6 percent, and in 1988 banks will go entirely on an "experience" basis. The law lays out how experience is to be computed:

> Banks will be limited to a tax-free reserve no larger, as a function of their eligible loans, than the ratio of uncollected loans to eligible loans on an average basis over the prior six years.[12]

Thus, banks will be less able to obtain tax-free reserves in the future.

The way the loan-loss accounts are used can be explained with an example. Assume that a bank has $10,000 in gross revenue from a loan portfolio of $100,000 and its operating expenses are $8,000. If the bank decides, as a result either of actual loan losses or of its tax planning, to transfer $300 to its valuation reserve, then the $300 is charged to bank expenses and allocated to the valuation reserve account. The bank now reports to the public that its net income before taxes is $1,700. However, it has the option to report a larger figure to the Internal Revenue Service. That is, it can allocate up to 1.2 percent of eligible loans into its loan-loss reserve account. If it takes the full 1.2 percent, then it can report to the IRS a charge of $1,200, or $900 more than reported to the public. Taxable income is now reported to the government as $800 ($1,700 minus $900). If the bank's tax rate, for simplicity, is 50 percent, then taxes will be $400 rather than the $850 they would be if they were computed on the net income reported to the public. There is a $450 saving in taxes.

Now, the $450 that the bank saves in taxes is allocated to the deferred tax account. The remaining $450, the difference between the extra $900 allocated to loan-loss accounts on the report to the Internal Revenue Service and the $450 tax saving, is channeled to the contingency reserve account.

All told, the bank has charged off $1,200 to its loan-loss reserve accounts. The public only sees the $300 charged off to the valuation reserve. The rest results in a reduction in the bank's effective tax rate from 50 percent to $400/$1,700 $\cong$ .24, or 24 percent.

In practice, banks generally take the full amount allowed by law when reporting to the Internal Revenue Service. This only makes sense since the chargeoff represents a way of obtaining tax-sheltered capital. The amount that is charged to the valuation reserve has generally depended on two

---

[12] Stuart A. Schweitzer, "Bank Loan Losses: A Fresh Perspective," *Business Review*, Federal Reserve Bank of Philadelphia (September 1975), pp. 18–28.

things. First, the actual amount of losses expected by the bank will form a lower limit for the amount allocated to the valuation account. Thus, in years of high loan writeoffs, such as 1976 and 1977, banks generally allocated much more to their valuation reserves than in other years.

Second, banks have used their allocation to the valuation account as a means of achieving growth targets. For example, if, in the above example, the bank wanted reported earnings after taxes to be higher than $1,300, then by charging off $200 rather than $300 to the valuation reserve account it would have had net income before taxes of $1,800, with taxes still at $400. Net income after taxes would then be $1,400 rather than $1,300. In this way, banks can manipulate their after-tax income to achieve their targeted goals for income or earnings per share, or for some other purpose.

Tax-Free Securities

Tax-free securities have provided one simple means of obtaining tax-free income. As mentioned earlier in the chapter, high-performance banks have almost invariably held higher proportions of assets in tax-free securities than other banks. However, tax-exempts have not been uniformly used in bank portfolios. There seem to be several reasons for this.

First, banks must have sufficient taxable income to make tax-exempt investments. A small bank's tax rate may not be large enough to warrant their use. To many large banks in recent years, tax-exempts have been less useful because of the availability of other tax shelters, such as the investment tax credit and the foreign tax credit; effective tax rates have been reduced to a low enough level to make tax-exempt securities less attractive than before.

Second, tax-exempt securities are not as "liquid" as some types of investments, such as U.S. government securities. If banks are looking for the ability to earn more than they would holding cash but want to be able to get in and out of the securities rapidly without suffering a substantial capital loss, then tax-exempt securities are not the ideal investment. The use of tax-exempt securities is dependent on "long-run" tax planning considerations. Many investment portfolios are not constructed in such a way.

Third, tax-exempt securities are riskier than many of the other securities in which the bank deals. Particularly in the mid-1970s, when many states and cities had financial crises, many investors were concerned that their investments in state and municipal issues were not as safe as they were once thought to be. Thus, some banks have become reluctant to purchase these securities because of the uncertainties connected with the solvency of these fiscal units.

Investment Tax Credit

As banks have increased their leasing activities, their ability to use the investment tax credit has also increased. Again, the decision to go into leasing is a long-run decision that affects both before-tax and after-tax earnings and must be justified on an economic basis. The impact of the investment tax credit is discussed more thoroughly in the appendix to Chapter 9.

Foreign Tax Credit

The foreign tax credit is not really a tax shelter. It is an effort by the government to limit the double taxation of bank income by both the United States government and the governments of foreign countries. Since 1962 commercial banks have been able either to deduct foreign taxes from net income or to claim a credit for foreign income taxes actually paid or accrued during the tax year. The first method is the easier to use, since it requires only a simple deduction on the income statement. The second, however, seems to provide the greater tax benefits, since it is more flexible.[13]

The foreign tax credit has been particularly useful for the larger U.S. banks that have expanded overseas in the past 10 to 15 years. Early in the 1960s, when the federal government imposed the voluntary credit restraint program, restraining the amounts American banks could lend outside the United States, banks were forced to branch, expand, or otherwise enter into banking operations in foreign countries in order to service their multinational clients. Since income earned abroad is subject to foreign taxation, the foreign tax credit has protected earned income from being taxed a second time as it appears on the income statement of the U.S. bank.

---

[13] There are limitations on the amount of the foreign-tax credit a bank can use. These limitations come from either a per-country constraint or an overall constraint. They generally relate to the ratio of foreign taxable income to U.S. taxable income, whether from one country or from all foreign sources. There are carryover or carryback provisions that help banks to smooth out large variations. For more on this, see M. E. Bedford, "Income Taxation of Commercial Banks," *Monthly Review*, Federal Reserve Bank of Kansas City (July–August 1975), pp. 3–11.

REVIEW QUESTIONS

1. Declining profit margins seem to have been associated predominantly with large banks that became liability managers during the last 10 to 15 years. Was it rational for these banks to subject themselves to a declining profit margin when retained earnings serve as the major source of bank capital?
2. What constrains some banks from using tax-sheltered income, even from municipal securities? Why might a small bank pay the full tax rate?
3. Give some reasons why geographic region or the degree of local competition might not play a role in determining whether a bank is a high performance bank.
4. Explain, in terms of the dividend theories presented in the chapter, how a cut in dividends might affect a bank's price-earnings ratio. Trace through the effects of the announcement of a dividend cut on the performance of a bank's stock.
5. What contributes to making an industry a growth industry? How does this apply to commercial banking?
6. Given the tax shelters available to banks, how much credence can be given to banks' reported earnings? Is sufficient information provided to the public in a bank's annual report to make possible an adequate analysis of the bank's performance? Examine the annual reports of a number of banks to determine what information is presented in them.

7

External Sources of Bank Capital

Raising capital from external sources has become more of a necessity for commercial banks in recent years. As described in Chapter 6, until the 1960s almost all banks grew using retained earnings, and so questions of "going to the market" and "meeting the demands of the market" posed no problem to the banker. Most banking operations were local or regional, and as local industry prospered or languished, banks followed suit. Retained earnings were usually sufficient for their capital needs; growing areas generally provided ample earnings, and although banks in declining regions had only small earnings, they also had small capital needs.

Today, however, the growth of national and international banking has generated a greater need for external capital funds. Banks need capital to support the increased demands for loans and other services requiring assets. Retained earnings are no longer sufficient to provide all the capital a bank requires.

In this chapter the sources of external bank capital are examined. First what bankers mean by capital must be examined as well as the bank's potential entry into the markets for capital. Next, the efficiency of these markets must be questioned; this includes an examination of how effectively participants in these markets can evaluate bank performance and risk. Finally, there is a discussion about who plays a role in determining the financial structure—managers, investors, and regulators; the methods used to determine financial structure in practice; and the effects these decisions have on a bank's cost of capital.

DEFINITIONS OF BANK CAPITAL

Regulators' Definition of Bank Capital

There are several ways to define bank capital; to avoid confusion, the reader must be aware of which definition is being used in a given instance. The most comprehensive definition of bank capital is the one regulators use in determining a bank's capital adequacy. Most regulators at the federal level include the preferred stock and common stock of the bank, reserves on loans and securities, and long-term subordinated debt in their definition of capital. It should be noted, however, that the amount of long-term debt is limited by most regulatory bodies. For example, issues must have maturities of at least seven years to qualify as long-term, and total long-term debt must not exceed one-third of total capital. Thus, for every $10 in capital, as just defined, the bank can obtain a maximum of $3.33 by issuing long-term debt.

The Comptroller of the Currency has the strictest rules pertaining to the use of long-term debt in capital accounts. In addition to the two constraints on maturity and debt-to-capital ratio, the Comptroller's office also requires a bank to meet an earnings coverage test and a retained earnings test. If these tests are not satisfied, the ceiling on debt issue is reduced below one-third of capital.

Book Value

Other definitions are somewhat more restrictive. Many analysts define bank capital in terms of the book value of the bank. Book value consists of the bank's common stock (at par value), paid-in surplus, retained earnings, and the equity reserve accounts. Subordinated debt and preferred stock are not included because of their fixed commitments. This definition represents an easy way to arrive at a value that does not involve a lot of guesswork or manipulation.

The major difference between the two definitions is that long-term debt is included by the regulators. There is, of course, some debate over including long-term debt in capital, both sides having some valid reasons for its inclusion or exclusion. The regulator regards long-term debt as capital that will help to keep the bank open. One of the major problems in maintaining a "going" banking system is to see that the banks do not have to convert assets into cash at a capital loss that might impair their book value. A loss of liabilities due to either withdrawal of deposits or the failure of investors to renew maturing issues can lead to a situation where the bank would need to sell assets.

Long-term debt, however, because its maturity is relatively far in the future, is not subject to withdrawal within the near future. Therefore, the regulators feel that a reasonable amount of long-term debt, up to one-third of capital, provides protection for asset positions that enhances the safety of the bank. Greater amounts would impair earnings and make the firm riskier.

Others do not feel that this protection from withdrawal is of much value to the bank. The bank has an obligation to make interest payments on the debt, and failure to meet the obligation would force it into bankruptcy. Furthermore, in the case of a failure, the bank would be obligated to pay off the principal of the debt issue, something that would not be required in the case of other forms of capital. These people feel that debt contributes little or nothing to the ultimate protection of either the depositor or the owner and hence must be excluded from the capital accounts of the bank.

Residual Definition of Bank Capital

Bank capital can also be defined as the difference between total assets and total liabilities. In considering the bank to be a "going" concern, this definition requires a judgment on how to value the different assets that appear on the bank's balance sheet.[1] The three alternative methods of valuation are (1) historical cost, (2) market value, and (3) maturity value. The particular value chosen by the analyst often depends on the purpose of the analysis.

A problem that is connected directly with the valuation of assets is the treatment of the reserve accounts. The bank may not be able to realize the book value of all its assets. Some loans will go into default. Some securities may not be kept until maturity and will be sold at a capital loss. To prepare for these contingencies the bank sets aside funds in its equity reserve or asset valuation accounts in order to be able to charge off losses without depleting current earnings.

[1] If a bank is a "going" concern, then liabilities are valued at their recorded value on the books. Thus, the analyst need worry only about properly valuing the bank's assets.

However, the equity reserve accounts and the asset valuation accounts are both technically asset valuation accounts and are not components of capital; they cannot be used to absorb unexpected short-run losses from operations so as to keep the bank open. Theoretically, if the bank sets aside the exactly correct amount of funds to meet loan or security losses, then the funds kept in the equity reserve and asset valuation accounts would average zero. To the extent that they do represent tax-sheltered additions to capital,[2] they should truly be counted as part of the bank's available capital.[3]

Valuation of the physical assets of the bank is also associated with this method of determining capital. Here the question is whether the physical assets should be valued at purchase price or at replacement cost. Obviously, what seems to be a very simple method of determining bank capital—as a residual, total assets minus total liabilities—is not so simple when it comes to putting it into practice.

Present Value of Future Earnings

A final way to determine the capital of a bank is to determine the present value of the bank's future earnings. This involves setting up an economic balance sheet where the value of the assets is equal to the discounted interest revenues and other fees the bank expects to receive (net of loan and security losses) and the value of the liabilities is equal to the discounted interest costs of the liabilities. The capital of the bank, or its economic value, would be the difference between the two discounted income streams.

If investors are rational and the markets in which its equities are traded are efficient, the bank's economic value should be the market value of its stock. More will be said on this later. This value is particularly interesting when compared with the firm's book value, because it gives some indication of how the bank is performing in relation to the accounting values that are already on its books. The relationship between market value and book value has been of great concern to many analysts in recent years as the stock of many banks has been selling below book value. This has been regarded as especially strange because most bank assets and liabilities are in fixed claims; that is, the contract rates and terms of the

---

[2] See the section on the loan-loss account in Chapter 6.

[3] Often in bank acquisitions where the value of a bank is set in terms of the acquired bank's book value, one-half of the equity reserve accounts is considered to be true capital. However, this is just a convenient rule of thumb.

items are set. However, the market must make estimates about future chargeoffs and securities sales that are not yet recorded on any books, and these estimates may be entirely different from what the bank has been prepared for. If there is a difference between market estimates and what the bank has allocated to the equity reserve accounts or the asset valuation accounts, then it is easy to see why market values may fall below book values, because the claims and contracts may be fixed but their actual realization is subject to some uncertainty.

There is a great deal of debate as to whether or not the economic value definition of bank capital is sound. Theoretically, the concept is correct, because if all future inflow and outflow streams of the bank are properly accounted for, the difference represents the funds available to the owners or the funds available to take care of unexpected short-term losses and still keep the bank open. The approach does raise some questions: Does the market have all the information necessary to make an accurate evaluation of these future flows? Does the market have the correct model to use the information? And is the market rational enough and free of the fads and herd psychology that might make the evaluation at any one time incorrect? Analysts have shied away from using the present value approach because they have felt that these questions must be answered in the negative.

For practical reasons, then, most discussions of bank capital use either the regulators' definition (that is, the definition that includes preferred stock, common stock, reserves on loans and securities, and long-term subordinated debt) or the book value of the bank. Later, the question of whether the economic value may ever be used and if so for what banks and under what conditions will be examined. Perhaps this will lead to a better idea of the meaning of bank capital and capital adequacy. First, however, the types of external capital must be discussed a little more thoroughly to familiarize the reader with the alternatives particularly available to banks and their use in raising bank capital.

EXTERNAL SOURCES OF BANK CAPITAL

Capital Notes and Debentures

Nature of Capital Notes and Debentures   Capital notes and debentures are fixed-claim, interest-bearing obligations due at some time in the future. They are not secured by any of the bank's assets, and their claims must be subordinated to those of bank depositors. As mentioned earlier, there are some constraints on the role these securities can play in the capital structure of a bank. However, within these limits, banks can exhibit some creativity in their use. For example, when credit conditions were relatively tight in the mid-1970s, some banks offered small-denomination capital notes to raise capital, and others issued floating-rate notes.

Convertible Debt   Another recent bank practice has been to use convertible debentures (long-term debt convertible into the common stock of the bank) to raise long-term funds. Convertible debentures have many desirable properties for banks. First, they can be issued at lower interest rates than nonconvertible issues. In attempts to maintain interest rate spreads, this is particularly desirable, since banks have generally had to pay a premium on straight debt over nonbank organizations because not enough bank debt has been rated by rating agencies like Standard and Poor's or Moody's to warrant wide market interest, and because of the high leverage position of banks, the subordinated position of long-term debt, and the psychological regard for bank debt.[4]

Second, the debentures will be converted into common stock at higher prices per share than the bank could obtain if it issued common stock at the current market price. If the bank needs funds for expansion at a time when stock market prices are low, it can issue a convertible bond with the hope that when the market improves bond holders will convert their holdings to stock at a higher price. A higher stock price reduces the bank's cost of capital.

An alternative to this is that banks must often raise capital in advance of investment in order to be able to convince regulators that they are capable of supporting expansion. This is opposite to the way a nonfinancial corporation usually operates. The nonfinancial firm will generally begin projects using short-term bank loans and the commercial paper market, unless the long-term markets are particularly favorable, and then fund the debt picked up here and there with long-term debt or equity when enough debt has been incurred to make recourse to the market worthwhile. Thus, the firm may already be receiving some of the benefits of the investment by the time it goes to the market. The bank cannot do this so easily. Hence, it must obtain funds before the results of the expansion effort can be clearly foreseen. If its growth possibilities or the reduction in risk that comes from the investment have not affected the price of the bank stock, then the cost of capital may be higher than it will be in the future because the market has not fully anticipated these favorable events. Issu-

---

[4] This is discussed further later.

ing a convertible debenture will allow the bank to get the project under-way, and if earnings improve or risk is lowered, as the bank foresees, then the stock price will rise and the owners of the convertibles will convert them to the bank's common stock.

A final point on convertibles is that the dilution of ownership shares created by issuance of stock is delayed by the use of convertible securities. In some instances—for example, to the owners of a closely held bank—this may be a particularly desirable feature because of the decline in the price of the bank's stock that could result from dilution.

Psychological Aspects of Bank Debt The psychological regard for bank debt was mentioned in Chapters 5 and 6. This was considered a very important reason why banks in the 1950s and early 1960s did not issue much long-term debt. Long-term debt was first issued by commercial banks in the 1930s, when banks that failed or otherwise found themselves in some sort of financial difficulty such that they needed capital but could not raise it by issuing common stock often issued subordinated debt instead. Thus, the debt issues of banks became associated with troubled banks, and, the argument goes, healthy banks shied away from issuing debt instruments, so that the feeling was reinforced.[5]

In 1962 the Comptroller of the Currency ruled that capital notes and subordinated debentures could be included in the computation of bank capital in determining a bank's lending limit. This made subordinated debt more attractive, and the dollar volume of bank-related debt issues increased.[6] This increase, however, should not be entirely attributed to the Comptroller's ruling. Whereas it certainly played a part in moving the banking industry toward the issuance of greater volumes of long-term debt, there is evidence that economic conditions dominated bank decisions. If economic conditions in the 1950s had been more like those of the 1960s, no doubt the increase would have taken place in the 1950s.

It is true that banks needed more capital funds in the early 1930s. Loan losses had depleted the capital accounts of many banks, which then had to raise funds in external financial markets in order to remain in business. Other banks were able to remain adequately capitalized through retained earnings in the stagnant economy of the 1930s. The only organizations that had to go to the market were banks that were troubled.

The 1940s were dominated by wartime finance. In the 1950s commer-

---

[5] A more complete examination of this point is made in P. F. Jessup, "Bank Debt Capital: Urchin of Adversity to Child of Prosperity," *The Bankers Magazine* (Summer 1965).

[6] See Y. E. Orgler and B. Wolkowitz, *Bank Capital* (New York: Van Nostrand Reinhold, 1976), p. 43, for a discussion of this point.

cial banking was subject to two major influences: (1) Since the growth rate in the industry was not very great, most banks found that their retained earnings were sufficient for their capital needs. (2) The term structure of interest rates had a pronounced upward slope during most of the decade[7]; long-term rates were much higher than short-term rates.[8] Since banks lend on short-term maturity and borrow on an even shorter term, this spread made the issuance of long-term debt a moot point.

In the 1960s banks got more favorable regulatory treatment of long-term debt, but this would not have had much of an impact if economic conditions had not changed. Commercial banks became national and even international in scope and needed more capital than could be raised internally to support their growth. To balance the capital structure and take as much advantage of leverage as they could, they issued more long-term debt. In addition, the term structure of interest rates flattened out. Debt became much more attractive vis-à-vis equity financing because of the fact that the interest cost of debt is a tax-deductible expense whereas dividend payments are not.

Thus, the avoidance of capital notes and debentures in the 1950s can be attributed to the relative economic incentives in existence at that time, whereas the increased use of debt in the 1960s can be seen as a response to a different set of economic incentives. There is no reason why conditions may not revert to those of the 1950s.

Psychological reasons are not adequate to explain the long-run avoidance of a particular debt instrument if there are economic incentives for its use. If even one or two creditworthy banks issue such an instrument, the psychological barrier will start to crumble. Expectations must adjust to the economic realities of the situation, even if the adjustment process takes a relatively long time.

Preferred Stock

Preferred stock has a preferred claim on assets and usually has a stated dividend payment. The asset claim and the dividend claim are subordinate to deposits and all other indebtedness of the bank but have priority over dividend payments on common stock. Although the bank, at the least,

---

[7] For an explanation of the term structure of interest rates, see Chapter 12.

[8] Economic evidence of this situation was the striking growth of savings and loan associations in the 1950s, since savings and loans borrow short and lend long. In the 1960s, when the term structure flattened out, these firms did not fare so well. Long-term debt, as will be explained, became more attractive to the banks.

feels a moral obligation to pay the dividend, it may omit dividend payments[9]; a missed dividend payment may be a signal to the market that the bank is in serious financial trouble. Although preferred stock has no maturity, many issues contain call provisions that allow the bank to reduce the amount of preferred stock it has outstanding by calling it in and repurchasing it at a prearranged price. Preferred stock convertible into common stock may also be issued. Preferred stock does not usually carry voting privileges, so banks that are closely held may issue it rather than common stock in order to maintain voting control by certain owners.

Historically, the use of preferred stock has paralleled that of capital notes and subordinated debt. That is, preferred stock was used in the early 1930s, again primarily by troubled banks. After the trouble of the 1930s subsided, bankers retired their preferred stock. Very little was issued in the 1950s, and its use picked up again in the 1960s when bank demand for capital from external sources increased considerably. In 1962 the Comptroller of the Currency also ruled that preferred stock may be considered part of a bank's capital for purposes of determining loan limits. The reader is cautioned again, as with debentures, that reliance on psychological factors to explain the use or nonuse of preferred stock is on somewhat shaky grounds; explaining the changing usage by changes in economic conditions is a much firmer argument.

Common Stock

Only the common stock portion of the equity position will be treated here, since most of Chapter 6 was devoted to a treatment of earnings, retained earnings, and equity reserves. Common stock outstanding represents, of course, the existing residual claims on ownership. The common stock account is divided into two parts: (1) the par value of the stock and (2) the surplus over the par value the original stockholders paid for the stock plus any amount of retained earnings that have been transferred into the surplus account from retained earnings. Funds may be shifted from retained earnings to the surplus account either when management wants to increase its recognized capital[10] or when a stock dividend is declared.

Issuance of common stock has historically been the most frequently

---

[9] If the stock is cumulative preferred, then missed dividends must be paid before any further dividends can be distributed.

[10] Most regulatory bodies include retained earnings in the computation of a commercial bank's lending limit. However, some state agencies still do not; in these states, a bank may transfer funds from retained earnings to its surplus account to raise its legal lending limit.

used method of raising long-term capital. Its major advantage is that common stock has no set dividend payments and, unlike debentures, stock has no maturity value. Thus, funds raised from a new equity issue truly represent a cushion that can absorb unexpected short-term losses.[11] The major disadvantages are the dilution of the ownership rights of the current owners of the bank and the dilution of earnings per share, which can bring about a decline in the price of the stock. As will be discussed later, equity capital is also the most expensive form of long-term funds.

MARKET EVALUATION OF BANKS

Raising capital funds externally raises questions about the markets in which commercial banks sell their debt and equity. It also raises questions about the information that the market can give people about the bank. These are questions of market efficiency.

Concern about the efficiency of the market for bank securities is fairly recent for the banking industry, although it has a long history in the area of the nonfinancial firm. This is because banks have not been steady participants of any size in the capital markets until the last 15 to 20 years, with their issues listed on the major market exchanges only in the last decade. Furthermore, the banks that do come to the capital markets regularly and are listed on major exchanges are only a small handful out of the approximately 14,000 that comprise the banking universe in the United States.

It is helpful, for purposes of exposition, to separate banks into three groups, based on the markets in which they are capable of raising capital funds. The first, which will here be called the Tier I group, comprises the banks that list on one of the major exchanges and thus sell their debt and equity in relatively efficient markets. The exact number of banks that meet these qualifications is extremely uncertain—at most perhaps 100 banks, and at the least only 40. Tier II banks are those that list their securities on local or regional exchanges but are not able to tap the efficient national markets. Tier III banks do not have their stock listed on any exchange. Most of these are small local or regional banks that find retained earnings sufficient for growth and thus do not need to go to the capital markets for funds. They raise new capital by selling new stock to existing owners or by

---

[11] Or, if earnings are quite variable, the firm may be very reluctant to pay out dividends or to raise dividends in the face of improved earnings. This is because the firm will not be able to generate much in the way of retained earnings if it must maintain the higher level of dividend payments when earnings decline. This may limit its ability to grow.

bringing in a new owner, generally a prominent local businessperson or lawyer.

Obviously, market efficiency and the ability to place securities are not of great concern to banks in the Tier III group. They do not have to "serve" the capital market; market evaluation of these banks must come from their depositors and borrowers. Since they deal in very closed markets and reveal very little information to their customers or to their owners, it is questionable that the market can provide much in the way of regulation. These banks need some form of outside regulation to control their riskiness; public regulation will raise social welfare in this case.

Tier I banks are a different story. Since their stocks are listed on major exchanges and their customers are national and in many cases multinational, theories pertaining to market efficiency are applicable to them, and they are subject to market regulation. Market participants, if the theory holds, have the information and models necessary to evaluate the banks and determine the appropriate risk-return requirements for bank decisions on asset composition and capital structure. The performance of a bank's stock relative to that of the stocks of other banks provides bank managers and customers, as well as regulators, with the information necessary to judge the relative health of the bank.[12] Subsequent behavior on the part of customers, both borrowers and depositors, can reinforce the evaluation of the participants in the capital market.[13]

If a bank does not react to the market in controlling the riskiness of its loan portfolio and its leverage factor, then it will have to pay more for capital in the open market or pay higher interest rates on the liabilities it sells. This is the market cost of risk or of a nonoptimal capital structure.[14] It is a cost similar to that attributable to the regulatory constraint that would be forthcoming if the regulators found the bank too risky. The market makes the cost explicit, whereas most regulatory costs are implicit.

Tier II banks are between the two extremes. Whereas the market may be capable of regulating Tier I banks, the Tier II banks do not quite meet all the conditions for market regulation. The exchanges on which their stocks are

[12] Some unpublished work completed in 1978 by Joseph Vinso of The University of Pennsylvania and Richard Rogalski of Dartmouth University indicates that for major listed firms stock price information is sufficient to predict the potential failure of an organization several years in advance of any actual failure. This study was of nonfinancial firms, but many studies that have duplicated tests done on nonfinancial firms with financial firms have indicated that the results are transferable.

[13] Customers have played a much more aggressive role in the evaluation of banks in recent years. An example of this is given in a *Wall Street Journal* article of September 9, 1976, called "The Examiners: Now the Customers Check Out the Banks; So Do Other Banks."

[14] For more on the optimal capital structure, see Chapter 5.

listed do not require as much disclosure as the major exchanges. Tier II banks are not as willing as Tier I banks to disclose information to analysts or others interested in their operations. Furthermore, there are fewer traders in Tier II stocks than on the major exchanges.

One consequence of their market position is that the stocks of Tier II banks generally sell at lower multiples of earnings than similar bank stocks listed on major exchanges. Thus the cost of raising additional capital through the market will be greater for Tier II banks than for Tier I banks in the same risk class. Any customer or regulator using the market evaluation of the bank's stock to judge its riskiness would infer that Tier II banks are riskier than similar banks listed on the major exchanges. This lower price–earnings ratio was one reason many of the larger banks switched to the major exchanges in the late 1960s.

Since there are fewer traders in local and regional exchanges, stock prices can vary more in response to a given piece of information. Thus, a Tier II bank's stock may not be traded for days at a time, but new information or a rumor can set off substantial activity in the price of the stock. In addition, since information is sparse and traders few, the stock's market price can last longer than if the stock were selling in a more efficient market. Hence, at any one time, and even over an extended period of time, the market may be valuing the bank incorrectly. At times this may make it more expensive to raise funds in the market than if the stock traded in a more efficient market when the price tended to be closer to its "correct" value, and it can also lead investors to misinterpret how risky the bank really is.

In general, Tier II banks cannot be regarded as operating in very efficient markets and hence cannot be expected to be regulated by the market. A sharp decline in stock price may convey little or no information to the management, customers, or regulators about the performance of the bank, either absolutely or relatively. Furthermore, raising long-term funds in these markets poses a very serious problem of timing and impact for the bank. Any Tier II bank whose management expects to use the markets on a fairly regular basis must devote time and resources to publicizing its services and its stock to the investment community. The reduction in its cost of capital may be well worth the effort.

THE RISK OF MULTIBANK FAILURES

Bank performance and bank risk have been discussed so far in terms of the individual bank or firm. However, regulators—and, at times, management, customers, and analysts—are also concerned with the risk of multibank failures. As was mentioned earlier, banking is a relatively homogeneous industry: The customers of many banks are customers of other banks; loan syndicates join many banks to a single borrower; correspondent balances unite many banks with other banks; almost all banks have the same marginal cost of funds and the same availability of reserves.[15] Hence, when one bank experiences difficulties, many others may also be put into a precarious position.

This is the major concern of the bank regulators. They speak of it in terms of the "failure of the payments mechanism." They recognize that there is a business risk associated with the operation of any profit-making enterprise. However, the failure of one bank affects only those directly connected with the failed bank. In contrast, multibank failures affect people in a wider area, may cause some perfectly sound banks to collapse, and may even bring the soundness of the whole banking system into question. No other industry faces this risk to the same degree as the banking industry.

In discussing the potential market regulation of commercial banks, a major question is whether the market can adequately evaluate the possibilities of multibank failure. Analysts generally agree that the market can evaluate fairly well the risk of the individual bank in the Tier I group. They are not so sure, however, that the market takes fully into account the potentiality of many banks failing as a result of one bank's failure.

To analyze the potential for multibank failures, the analyst needs several pieces of information:

1. How tight will the Federal Reserve be in providing reserves to the banking industry? If, as in 1974, the Federal Reserve causes the nonborrowed reserves of the banking system to contract at a 33 percent annual rate over several months, there is a substantial probability that several banks will fail. At any given time there is an extremely small likelihood that the Federal Reserve will conduct such a policy. However, this possibility must be taken into account in the analysis of an individual bank.

2. What loan syndications and participations exist? Large lines of credit to major corporations are common knowledge. Perhaps these are the only ones that should be matters of concern, because the failure of a large company will have the greatest impact on the industry. However, in the case of the collapse of an industry, several syndicates can be affected, and this will do considerable damage to banks. The situation in real estate in the early 1970s is a case in point.

---

[15] See Chapter 2 and the appendix to Chapter 8.

3. What are the compensating balance relationships and other inter-bank relationships? This is perhaps the area where the least information is available and the largest dollar amounts are involved. The failure of a large bank that is a correspondent to many small and medium-sized banks may send shock waves throughout the country.

One example of recent experience in interbank effects is the 1974 failure of Bank Herstatt in Germany. Many U.S. banks had open lines of credit and deposits with Herstatt. As a result of the speed with which Herstatt failed, U.S. banks were not able to foresee its demise soon enough to protect themselves. The failure brought into question the viability of several American banks because of their correspondent balances with or outstanding loans to Herstatt. Fortunately, no U.S. bank failed in this instance, but several experienced some anxious moments.

Whether it is possible to determine the probability of multibank failures will continue to be questioned regardless of empirical evidence that it is not. There is no empirical evidence as to the ability of the market to analyze this potentiality, and it is even questionable whether appropriate statistical tests can be derived. However, if such tests did exist, they would be of questionable validity because of the limited number of sample periods over which they could be made. The validity of generalizations reached from so few experiences would always be questionable.

Thus, a case may be made for bank regulation as long as there exists the possibility of multibank failures. It is not clear that the market has all the current information[16] needed for a proper evaluation of this risk. Until such time as the market does have this information and can adequately process it, it cannot be relied on to measure appropriately the total risk faced by the bank individually and as a member of the banking industry.

---

[16] The problem here is that managers, regulators, investors, and customers put things out of mind as they recede into the past. Whereas they may have had personal experience with multibank failures, it may have occurred so long ago that it is no longer given very much weight. Bankers were very concerned about multibank failures in the 1950s, because many of them went through the bank failures of the Great Depression. They kept capital standards high and were very conservative. The events of the 1930s receded further in memory in the 1960s, and standards for capital and banking in general were liberalized. The early 1970s saw an even more liberal attitude.

The specter of multibank failures arose again in the mid-1970s after the experiences of 1974–1975. Banking standards became more conservative. However, the attitudes of bankers apparently did not return to those of the 1950s, and the fear of multibank failures has even eased somewhat since 1976.

PARTICIPANTS

There are several groups of participants in the banking process who must be concerned about the safety of a bank and hence of the amount of capital the bank has. These are depositors, investors, managers, and regulators. Each group has its own objectives and needs, which the bank must be aware of satisfying in its choice of the amount of capital it keeps on its balance sheet.

Small Depositors

This group does not present much of a problem to the bank in its demands for bank capital. Small depositors do not generally worry about the soundness of any particular bank, and the bank consequently does not have to be overly concerned about them because their deposits, on average, are relatively stable. Of particular concern to these depositors is whether the bank has its deposits insured by the Federal Deposit Insurance Corporation. Otherwise the bank's size, reputation, and location seem to be the variables that affect choice. In the aggregate, these deposits (regardless of whether they are demand deposit accounts or savings accounts) are not very responsive to interest rate movements. These customers are generally not inclined to seek out information on the bank and to analyze it. When they do move their deposits from one bank to another, it is more often in response either to dissatisfaction with bank service or to aggregate happenings, such as the threat of multibank failures or large discrepancies in market interest rates and bank rates, than to the perceived riskiness of an overleveraged bank.

Large Depositors

The typical customer in this class wants a safe, negotiable investment that earns a market yield and thus purchases large-denomination certificates of deposit. These depositors have many alternative places to put their money and are very responsive to changing yields and risks.[17] They give

[17] They are also not covered by deposit insurance. Some analysts have tried to analyze the need for capital to protect large uninsured depositors. See, for example, B. M. Friedman and P. Formuzis, "Bank Capital: the Deposit-Protection Incentive," *The Journal of Bank Research* 6 (Autumn 1975).

considerable effort to analyzing the banks in which they place their money. The larger organizations tend to limit themselves to the larger banks, because they feel that government regulators will not allow a major bank to fail. [18]

They can also obtain information on banks from commercial rating services. These institutions take advantage of economies of scale in collecting data and in analyzing it for customers, thus forming a mechanism that helps make the market more efficient. In general, only the largest banks— the top 100—are analyzed regularly by the rating services, because they are the primary issuers of large-denomination CDs and their stocks are traded actively on major exchanges.

Banks analyzed as being more risky than others will end up paying higher interest rates to depositors. Organizations will lend to them only if a risk premium is added onto the pure payment for the time value of money. Moreover, a bank whose risk increases may find that the supply curve of money from the CD market, which used to be perfectly elastic, now has a positive slope. In other words, the bank that becomes too risky may lose its ability to be a liability manager.

Paying higher interest rates on deposits may decrease earnings and thus increase the price–earnings ratio of the bank's stock. Of course, a higher price–earnings ratio implies that the bank's cost of capital has risen.

Large Borrowers and Depositors

This category is slightly different from the previous one because the organizations that fit into this class are interested more in the total customer relationship with the bank and not just the highest yield they can earn on their excess funds. Although many large borrowers may also purchase CDs, their banks will generally not look on these CD funds as a part of the customer relationship. These funds are "hot money" and are treated independently of other business with the bank.

Large borrowers are generally large depositors, either because of compensating balance requirements or simply because borrowers *tend* to do business with the banks that lend to them. It should be noted that customers can be other banks as well as nonfinancial institutions.

---

[18] Franklin National Bank was kept open for approximately six months after the regulators would normally have closed it, to allow for large CDs to run off so that large corporations could recover their funds.

This is a separate group because of the importance of the loan relationship. Borrowers want to deal with banks that will be around to lend to them when they need funds. Open lines of credit or revolving lines of credit will not necessarily be honored by another bank that acquires a failing bank. Whereas the bank that initiated a line of credit would feel a very strong moral obligation to honor its commitment even if it were in trouble, the new bank reserves the right to review all previous arrangements.

Hence, it is very important for a potential borrower setting up a line of credit to have confidence that the bank granting the line will still be a going concern when the organization needs to borrow. A potential borrower, therefore, has a very strong reason for investigating the bank before it establishes a relationship.

Borrowers will therefore analyze the bank in much the same way as the large depositor would,[19] either engaging in a screening process themselves or subscribing to a commercial rating service.

The major effect on the bank of a loss of confidence is a withdrawal of some loan demand, although there will also be some shift in the supply curve of deposits. But losing these loan customers may lead to more than loss of revenue. The customers the bank loses will be the biggest and best customers, the ones with many alternative sources of funds. This affects the loan demand curve of the bank in two ways. First, it will become less interest elastic. Since the lost customers have alternative sources, their demand for funds was relatively elastic. Thus, the demand curve of the remaining customers will in general be more inelastic, resulting in a higher average yield and offsetting to some extent the fall in yields caused by the decrease in demand.

Second, however, the borrowers leaving the bank will be the less risky borrowers. Thus, the average risk of the bank's asset portfolio will rise, reducing the net yield earned on loans. Whether this decline in yields offsets the increase brought about by the added average imperfection of the portfolio is an empirical problem: No *a priori* solution is possible. Overall, the loss of customers can be expected to reduce revenues and hence reduce bank profits. The net effect on the cost of capital will, as in the previous case, be negative; that is, the loss of customers will raise the bank's cost of capital.

---

[19] Indications are that one of the major industries that analyze banks carefully or obtain ratings from the information services is the banking industry itself. See the *Wall Street Journal* article (page 22) cited in footnote 13.

Investors

As in most industries, investors rely heavily on stock analysts for their information and in grading of investment opportunities. It is the stock analysts who generally make or add to the efficiency of any market, since, as noted previously, they can specialize and take advantage of economies of scale in obtaining and disseminating information.[20]

Several organizations specialize in the analysis of bank stocks. Two of these are Keefe, Bruyette and Woods and David C. Cates and Co., Inc. Brokerage houses and mutual funds have analysts specifically assigned to the banking industry. As mentioned before, however, these organizations do their most thorough analysis on the largest 60 to 100 banking firms. Other banks get less thorough and less regular treatment. The implication of this coverage is that the firms that are scrutinized closely enough to possibly warrant being regulated by the market are the largest ones. Only these banks are continually probed for facts and information by analysts attempting to determine the correct price of their stock. It can be expected that these stocks will be fairly accurately priced most of the time. Because there are too few investors seeking information on small and medium-sized banks, market valuation of their stocks may be inaccurate. The banks do not encourage investigations, so much less is known about them. For the individual analyst or organization, the benefits to be gained from additional information on these banks is not worth the expense of obtaining it.

Managers

Bank managers want to make as much profit as possible, given the level of risk they are willing to assume. Thus, they are concerned with increasing revenues, decreasing costs, and increasing leverage. However, to achieve the highest price for the bank's stock, management must respond to market conditions. In the noncapital area, obviously, a loss of deposits or of loan customers will lower the price of a bank's stock by either reducing revenues or increasing risk. This, of course, increases the bank's cost of capital.

Furthermore, particularly in the largest banks, investors are very aware of the bank's capital position, and if it strays too far from its optimal

---

[20] Information about the specific tools of analysis is presented in the appendix to this chapter.

capital structure they will sell the stock, causing its price to fall and raising the bank's cost of capital. Thus, management must be responsive to both its customers and its owners, especially if it foresees a need to go to the capital markets. Managers of the smallest banks may be immune to this type of situation.[21]

Regulators

The bank regulators are important to the process being described here because they often set the standards on which bank managers and bank analysts base their conclusions. In this sense, the standards of bank regulators can become the example of what "good bank management" should be. Thus, the extent to which the regulators' guidelines differ from those determined by the operation of the market is crucial for the effective functioning of banking institutions.

Regulators are most interested in two aspects of bank operations. Their first concern is with whether or not the balance sheet accurately represents current asset and liability values. Unexpected withdrawals, changes in loan demand, and unusual loan losses can lead to variations in these figures. In examining a bank, regulators attempt to determine the volatility of deposits, noting particularly the percentage of deposits being obtained from interest-sensitive sources. The geographic proximity of depositors is important here also, because even if the bank loses some interest-sensitive money, the likelihood of its returning in some form is greater if the funds are from a local depositor than from one further away. These matters are analyzed in the light of the individual bank and the characteristics of its business and location.

The regulators also examine the quality and maturity of the bank's loans and classify them as to probability of loss. These classifications are somewhat subjective and may vary among examiners. With the information gathered in this manner, the examiners calculate the expected loss on the bank's assets. Recent efforts to gather information on the extent of bank loan commitments have not had widespread cooperation from the banking community.

---

[21] The easy answer to the failure of the smallest banks to respond to market pressures is competition. The lack of competition may not be entirely the fault of the bank regulators. Because of the economies of scale that exist for small banks, the market may not be large enough to support two or more banks. These economies may even keep branches of larger banks out of an area.

The second factor the regulators are interested in is the bank's capital position. This area perhaps gets the most public attention, because a decision affecting capital may require a bank to take some kind of overt action in the market to improve its capital position. The threat of regulatory action almost always causes banks to raise capital before it is needed. The reason for this is that the regulators may not permit a bank to expand, acquire other banks, or establish branches unless it is "adequately" capitalized. The process is entirely different for a nonfinancial firm, because it will often build up short-term debt as it expands and then pull all the short-term debt together in a long-term issue. Bank regulators frown on this.

The most familiar model for judging the adequacy of a bank's capital is the one that has been used by the Federal Reserve. This form is presented in Figure 7-1. Conceptually, the Federal Reserve is concerned with two types of contraction of assets: (1) the contraction caused by default on loans and (2) the loss that can come from a forced sale of assets. Forced sales can be brought about by a reduction in liabilities caused by a loss of demand deposits or a runoff of certificates of deposit in a period of disintermediation, or by an unexpectedly high demand for loans to the bank's "good" customers. As mentioned earlier, it is difficult to discern the risk of unexpected loan demand from customers to whom the bank has extended lines of credit because of the scarcity of information on these lines.

The Federal Reserve calculates the liquidity available to the bank by applying percentage "costs" to the various categories in the balance sheet to determine the credit risk of the bank's assets. The calculated liquidity is then compared with a liability measure that estimates the bank's potential loss of deposits under rather severe economic conditions. If the deposit loss figure exceeds the liquidity figure, then the market risk—the sales value of other nonliquid assets—is computed to see how the bank would fare under a forced liquidation of these assets.

Capital must be equal to the aggregate risk of the bank's assets adjusted for nonbanking areas such as the trust department and for nonquantitative factors such as asset quality and quality of bank management. The Federal Reserve has no direct means of enforcing its capital requirements; however, it uses several indirect means of achieving its goals if it feels strongly that a bank should improve its capital position. It can alter the amount it will grant to the bank at the discount window; it can refuse to approve the bank's applications for branches; and it may not allow the bank to acquire any other bank or business until it obtains more capital. Although these means of control are not direct, they may be just as effec-

FIGURE 7-1 Federal Reserve Form for Analyzing Bank Capital

FR 363 (Form ABC)
Rev. 3/72

FORM FOR ANALYZING BANK CAPITAL
(Amounts in thousands of dollars)

BANK _____ CITY _____ STATE _____

IDENTIFICATION: __ABC 2__   District   State   Bank   Exam. Date Yr. Mo. Day
                   File

LIQUIDITY CALCULATION

	Amount Outstanding	Per Cent	Calculation
Demand deposits, IPC		35	
Savings deposits		25	
Time deposits, IPC, under $100,000		30	
Time deposits, IPC, $100,000 & over		80	
Deposits of banks		80	
Other deposits		80	
TOTAL DEPOSITS			
Borrowings		100	
Other liabilities (a)		100	
Special factors:		100	
TOTAL LIQUIDITY CALCULATION (b)			

MEMORANDA

(a) "Other liabilities" and "Loans: Consumer instalment" are shown net of:
   Dealers reserves ....

   Income collected
   but not earned ....

(b) "LIQUIDITY AVAILABLE FROM ASSETS" is to be aggregated only until it equals "TOTAL LIQUIDITY CALCULATION."

(c) "Cash assets" are shown net of:
   Required reserves ....

(d) "TOTAL ASSETS" are shown net of assets classified as:
   Doubtful ....
   Loss ....

	AMOUNT OUTSTANDING	CAPITAL CALCULATION CREDIT RISK		CAPITAL CALCULATION MARKET RISK		LIQUIDITY AVAILABLE FROM ASSETS (b)	
		Per Cent	Amount	Per Cent	Amount	Amount	Aggregate
(1) PRIMARY RESERVE							
Cash assets (c)		0	0	0	0		
Federal funds sold		0	0	0	0		
(1) TOTAL			0		0		

(Continued)

FIGURE 7-1 (continued)

(2) SECONDARY RESERVE

Commercial paper & bankers acceptances	1		1
Securities maturing under 1 year:			
U.S. Treasury	0	0	*
Government agencies	0	0	*
State, county & municipal	0	0	*
Other Group 1	0	0	1
(2) TOTAL	0	0	1

(3) MINIMUM RISK ASSETS

Securities maturing 1-5 years:			
U.S. Treasury	0	0	*
Government agencies	0	0	*
State, county & municipal	2		*
Other Group 1	2		8
(3) TOTAL			

(4) INTERMEDIATE ASSETS

Securities maturing 5-10 years:			
U.S. Treasury	0	0	*
Government agencies	0	0	*
State, county & municipal	3		*
Other Group 1	3		15
Loans specially secured or guaranteed			
(4) TOTAL	3		15

(5) PORTFOLIO ASSETS

Securities maturing over 10 years:			
U.S. Treasury	0	0	*
Government agencies	0	0	*
State, county & municipal	5		*
Other Group 1	5		25

Loans: Real estate _____ | 5
       Consumer instalment (a) _____ | 5
       All other _____ | 5
       (5) TOTAL _____ | 25 25 25

(6) FIXED, CLASSIFIED & OTHER ASSETS

Bank premises _____ | 50
Furniture & fixtures; other real estate _____ | 100
Group 2 securities _____ | 50
Groups 3 & 4 securities _____ | 100
Assets classified substandard _____ | 20
Accruals & other assets _____ | 0 | 0
       (6) TOTAL _____

(7) TOTAL CAPITAL CALCULATED FOR MARKET RISK _____

(8) TOTAL CAPITAL CALCULATED FOR CREDIT RISK _____

(9) TOTAL ASSETS (d) _____ | 2

(10) TRUST DEPARTMENT GROSS EARNINGS _____ | 200

(11) SPECIAL FACTORS: _____

(12) TOTAL CAPITAL CALCULATION (sum of lines 7 through 11) _____

(13) ADJUSTED CAPITAL STRUCTURE[1] & CAPITAL STRUCTURE INDEX (Adjusted capital structure divided by line (12)) . . . . . . $ _____ | _____ %

(14) ADJUSTED EQUITY CAPITAL[2] & EQUITY CAPITAL INDEX (Adjusted equity capital divided by line (12)) . . . . $ _____ | _____ %

* See reverse side for securities computations which take account of quality, yield and narrower maturity ranges.

CAPITAL RATIOS

Adjusted capital structure as a percent of:
total assets _____ %; total assets minus primary reserves, U.S. Treasury and Agency securities _____ %; total deposits _____ %.

Adjusted equity capital as a percent of:
total assets _____ %; total assets minus primary reserves, U.S. Treasury and Agency securities _____ %; total deposits _____ %.

[1] and [2] Footnotes appear on reverse side.

tive in the long run. The possibility that the Federal Reserve may exercise this form of control is also the reason why members of the Federal Reserve System attempt to raise capital before they begin expansion rather than after. Of course, the potential liquidity of the bank in terms of the amount of funds it could purchase in the open market cannot be calculated.

Other agencies carry out similar analyses to gauge the capital position of the banks they examine, and their standards may be tougher or looser than those of the Federal Reserve. One problem is that it is difficult to estimate the managerial ability of the people running the bank. Since examiners differ, some attempt is made to routinize the process by using objective forms such as the Federal Reserve form shown in Figure 7-1. Some agencies have tried to make qualitative judgments about management practices, looking for imbalances and judging their possible impact on the basis of expected economic and industry behavior. Thus, if interest rates are expected to rise and the maturity composition of the bank's liquid assets is structured inappropriately, with assets having longer maturities than liabilities, then the agency would call management's attention to the situation. It would then observe the bank's response to see whether adequate attempts were being made to correct the imbalance.

This highlights the direction that modern regulation is taking with respect to bank capital. The regulators are coming to believe that there is no "correct" amount of capital for a bank and that the best thing they can do is act as industry analyst in the marketplace by keeping management on its toes, asking hard questions, and generally providing guidance where the market cannot. In this respect regulators feel they should supplement bank management, as an efficient market does, and not supplant it. They do provide some consistency across a large number of banks that do not have an effective market mechanism to keep them in line with appropriate banking practices.

EMPIRICAL EVIDENCE OF MARKET EFFICIENCY

It would be desirable to have a body of empirical evidence on the efficiency of the markets in which banks operate. There is a relatively large body of literature relating to nonfinancial institutions, and there is some evidence that the results pertaining to nonfinancial firms also apply to financial institutions. However, it would be comforting if more studies were available on banks. A few research efforts have attempted to determine how efficiently the markets evaluate banks, but these do not provide conclusive evidence in any form.[22]

[22] Several studies are D. Durand, *Bank Stock Prices and the Bank Capital Problem* (New

The following are the only generalizations that can be made at this time:

1. Banks that deal in national or international markets and list their securities on major exchanges can be considered to operate in relatively efficient markets. Thus the efficient market results that were obtained for nonfinancial firms apply to these commercial banks. It is to be expected that the managements of these banks will also be sensitive to market forces and will respond to them reasonably quickly. Approximately 50 to 100 U.S. banks are in this category.

2. Other banks do not meet the test of market efficiency and hence are less subject and less responsive to market forces. Efficiency, or inefficiency in this case, is a matter of degree, and some banks will be more subject to market forces than others. However, the generalization still holds.

3. There are no studies, for either nonfinancial firms or financial institutions, that consider the possibility of multifirm failure. As discussed earlier, this is not a major problem for nonfinancial organizations. There is, however, little evidence of any kind on this point, and until some information becomes available it must be assumed that regulation is necessary for all banks.

4. There is no empirical evidence that regulation reduces the riskiness of firms, either financial or nonfinancial. This factor does not seem to be a problem for regulated nonfinancial institutions; the nature of public utilities, for example, does not lend itself to the choice of risky asset portfolios. There is some evidence that bank regulation may force aggressive banks into riskier portfolios than they would hold without regulation.[23] However, it is not clear how this affects the riskiness of the industry.

York: National Bureau of Economic Research, 1957); D. P. Jacobs, H. P. Beighley, and J. H. Boyd, *The Financial Structure of Bank Holding Companies,* A Study Prepared for the Trustees of the Banking Research Fund (Chicago: Association of Reserve City Banks, 1975); S. D. Magen, *The Cost of Funds to Commercial Banks* (New York: Punellen, 1971); J. C. Van Horne and R. C. Helwig, *The Valuation of Small Bank Stocks* (East Lansing, Mich.: Michigan State University, Graduate School of Business Administration, 1966); R. A. Pettway, "Market Tests of Capital Adequacy of Large Commercial Banks," *The Journal of Finance* (June 1967), pp. 865–75.

Some evidence pertaining to the efficiency of the markets for bank stocks is gleaned from the market reaction to dividend payments. Thus, the study by Mason and Hill described in Chapter 6 provides some circumstantial evidence about efficiency.

[23] Two articles that deal with this problem are Y. Kahne, "Capital Adequacy and the Regulation of Financial Intermediaries," *The Journal of Banking and Finance* (October 1977), pp. 207–18, and M. Kochne and A. M. Santomero, "Regulation of Bank Capital and Portfolio Risk," Working Paper No. 15-77, Rodney L. White Center for Financial Research (The University of Pennsylvania, 1977).

5. There is no evidence that regulation is a good substitute for the market.

These results leave one with the impression that there is a lot that is not known about the banking industry and banking markets. This is not a false impression. Much of what has been done in banking has been in the form of "gut" reactions to events. "Bank failures show the need for regulation." "Bank expansion must be controlled." Responses like these have led to the present state of regulation. More concrete evidence is needed before it can be decided whether market forces should be granted more control over bank operations or whether current regulations are justified.

A BANK'S COST OF CAPITAL

One of the major decisions bank management faces is the choice of the capital structure. As stated in Chapter 5, the bank should attempt to choose the capital structure that minimizes its cost of capital. The bank gains knowledge on this optimal capital structure by varying its debt–equity ratio over time and observing how costs change. There are three possible results:

1. The bank may find its optimal capital structure defined within a narrow range.
2. The bank may find that it has no optimal capital structure. This is an extreme result and implies that the tradeoff between debt and equity financing has no overall effect on the aggregate cost of funds.[24]
3. The bank may find that there is a range of capital structures in which no optimal capital structure exists. However, outside this range the cost of capital does rise. The cost-of-capital curve is horizontal over some range of values, not U-shaped with an absolute minimum.

Experience and consultation with investment bankers will help to define the limits around which the bank may find its optimal capital structure. In reality, it cannot be expected that the bank will always achieve this optimal structure. The bank management, however, will always be tending toward it as it attempts to maximize the price for which its stock sells.

The capital structure the market determines must then be compared with that required by the regulations. If the two do not differ greatly, then the bank can choose the market-determined amount. The regulators will

---

[24] For the theoretical results that support this, see the appendix to Chapter 5.

probably not enforce their objective standards against small deviations. However, if the deviations are large (and if the regulators require a larger capital–asset ratio), then the bank had better make plans to obtain more capital so that it will have the amount required by the regulators or it will find that the regulators will not approve its future plans. Otherwise, the bank must build a solid justification for being so highly leveraged.

Small and medium-sized banks that do not have enough market information to judge their optimal capital position must rely more heavily on the regulators' assessment of their needs. Firms that go to the market more regularly than others will have some information to supplement the regulators' views. However, those that go to the market infrequently or not at all will have very little information on which to base capital structure decisions except rules of thumb and regulatory guidelines.

Once this optimal capital structure is determined, it is assumed that the bank maintains the structure in its future financing. Since the optimal structure is a ratio rather than an absolute amount, maintenance of that ratio is sufficient for the maintenance of the minimum cost of capital. If this is true, then the cost of capital can be determined to be the weighted average of the cost of each of the components that make up the capital structure.

Two other assumptions must be considered before the actual computation of the cost of capital is discussed. First, it is assumed that the riskiness of the asset portfolio remains constant as the capital structure of the bank is varied. For the nonfinancial firm, the risk incorporated in the asset portfolio is called the *business risk*. The business risk of the bank is assumed to be constant. Changes in capital structure have to do with the *financial risk* of the firm. Thus, the discussion of optimal capital structure and the minimum cost of capital refer solely to the bank's financial risk. The *total risk* of the firm is a combination of business risk and financial risk.

In the finance literature, the concept that the bank's business risk and financial risk are independent of each other is called the *separation principle*. That is, decisions pertaining to asset composition can be made independently of decisions about how to raise funds to support those assets. This is not a bad assumption for a nonfinancial firm, since assets are generally physical assets and liabilities are paper claims. The covariance of these items is not expected to be very great. However, for a bank, whose assets and liabilities are both paper claims, the independence assumption does not seem to be as good a picture of reality. If the covariance of loans and deposits is high, business risk will not be separate from financial risk. Some liabilities do not have as high a covariance with assets as do others. Thus, the appropriate combination of liabilities must be determined before the bank can choose its minimum cost of capital and optimum capital structure.

Analysts have suggested that, in determining the liabilities that go into the computation of the firm's cost of capital, the "free" liabilities of the nonfinancial firm be excluded from the measure. Thus, accounts payable and accruals are excluded from these calculations. [25] Another way of describing these liabilities is in terms of their characteristics. Items like accounts payable are derivable from the production process and are not explicitly obtained by a capital structure decision. In other words, the supply of these funds is very inelastic with respect to interest rates and is determined by the transactions necessary for the production process. Very inelastic curves have very low average costs—perhaps zero in the case of a completely inelastic curve.

This result can be carried over to commercial banking. As was shown earlier, much of the right-hand side of the bank's balance sheet is supplied to the bank inelastically, or at least the funds supplied are not very responsive to the own rate of interest or, for that matter, to other interest rates. These funds can be excluded from calculations of the cost of capital. Thus, a good portion of a bank's liabilities are left out of the calculation of its cost of capital. This is an example of the imperfections in the market overriding everything else.

What about liabilities like federal funds, negotiable certificates of deposit, or Eurodollars? Should their cost be included in a bank's calculation of its cost of capital? The immediate response is to say that they should be included if the funds coming to the bank through this market are supplied elastically or nearly so. As shown in Chapter 5, this is the only practical way a bank may find itself without an optimal capital structure.

There are two problems in including these costs, however. First, the bank must consider the term structure of interest rates. Its purchased funds may have an average maturity of only three to four months. This is obviously much shorter than the average maturity on capital notes or subordinated debt and certainly shorter than the expected life of preferred stock or common stock. If the pure expectations hypothesis of the term structure of interest rates holds, [26] then, given the information available, the long-term interest rate represents the best guess as to the cost of debt over the maturity span of the long-term debt. Thus, the cost of these other liabilities would be the bond rate, not the CD rate or the Eurodollar rate.

---

[25] Weston and Brigham, *Managerial Finance*, 6th ed. (Hinsdale, Ill.: The Dryden Press, 1978), p. 714.

[26] The term structure of interest rates is explained more fully in Chapter 12.

However, if there is a permanent liquidity premium in the market, then banks can continue to sell CDs or buy Eurodollars at rates below the rates they would pay on long-term issues. All available information would be expressed in the short-term and long-term rates, including the liquidity premium, and the bank should use the appropriate rates for these instruments in calculating its cost of capital.

If funds are supplied efficiently in both the short-term market and the long-term market, the banks would not choose long-term debt if the short-term rates were always lower than the long-term rates. Moreover, there are other costs of short-term borrowing that make it less desirable as a "permanent" source of funds than long-term debt or equity. For one thing, experience has shown that the Federal Reserve (as well as other agencies) will, at times, allow or cause interest rate ceilings to become effective, almost entirely closing off this portion of the money markets to the banks. Furthermore, history has also shown that when money and credit become scarce, many banks that previously found these markets accessible find themselves being rationed or paying rates that are above other open market rates or above what some other banks are paying for funds.

Another possibility is that a bank that was a liability manager when loan demand was strong reverts to being an asset manager when loan demand drops off. In this case, there would be no reason to continue to purchase funds, and the cost-of-capital calculation would change.

In the opinion of this author (and it must be stressed that this is only an opinion), the cost of purchased funds should be excluded from computing a bank's cost of capital except for those ten or fifteen very large banks that use purchased funds as a "permanent" source of funds and that will continue to have funds supplied elastically to them in these markets even in times of the most severe credit restraint. There are three reasons for this conclusion.

1. The pure expectations hypothesis is a relatively good "first" approximation of the relationship between interest rates on securities of different maturities. Thus, the rate on long-term bonds is a better approximation than the rate on short-term instruments for the expected life of the bank.

2. Most banks are liability managers only on a temporary basis, depending on demand conditions.

3. The actions of the policy makers may force many people out of liability markets for a time. Thus, the analyst should concentrate on the longer-term sources of capital, starting with capital notes, when computing the cost of capital.

Computing a Bank's Cost of Capital

The means of computing a firm's weighted cost of capital is well known and will not be developed completely here.[27] It must also be realized that not all banks will have all sources available. The cost of capital notes and debentures is calculated according to the equation

$$\frac{\text{Interest payments}}{\text{Principal amounts}} = k_b \qquad (7\text{-}1)$$

Interest payments must be the payments associated with the instruments being considered. Public information may not be disaggregated enough to make this computation; that is, data may be available on total interest payments but not on the interest cost of capital notes and debentures. Thus, it may be necessary to include other liabilities as well as capital notes and debentures in the calculations. This figure must then be put on an after-tax basis by multiplying (7-1) by 1 minus the bank's marginal tax rate, T:

$$\text{After-tax cost of debt} = k_b(1 - T) \qquad (7\text{-}2)$$

For preferred stock, the cost of capital is found from

$$k_{ps} = \frac{\text{Dividend payments on preferred stock}}{\text{Price of preferred stock}} \qquad (7\text{-}3)$$

There are two methods for obtaining the cost of equity capital. First it should be noted that two kinds of equity are being considered: retained earnings and new issues of common stock. It is assumed that the owners are in portfolio equilibrium with the yield they are earning on their present equity position. Thus, the current yield that the bank is providing to its owners is as good a yield as the owners could receive, for a given level of risk, on alternative investments. Otherwise, they would invest in the other opportunities. Thus, the "cost" of retained earnings is the opportunity cost of retaining the earnings, which in the case of a bank with listed stock is the yield now being earned on the stock.

If the bank raises capital by issuing more common stock, it will issue the new stock to yield the same return to the owners as the outstanding

---

[27] For a complete description, see Weston and Brigham, *Managerial Finance*, Chapter 19.

stock, so that the immediate "cost" to the bank of a new issue of common stock is the same as that of retained earnings. However, the flotation cost of the new issue will push the cost of a new equity issue above the cost of retained earnings.

The first method of obtaining the yield on retained earnings and on common stock is to estimate the *security market line* of the firm. Although the security market line has not been developed specifically in this book,[28] its framework was presented in Chapter 2 as the objective function of the bank in the case of uncertainty [see equation (2-4)]. If this equation is solved for the rate of return on equity instead of value, V, and then rearranged, the following can be obtained:

$$k_{cs} = \rho + \beta[E(R_m) - \rho] \qquad (7\text{-}4)$$

where ρ is the risk-free rate, $E(R_m)$ is the expected return on the market portfolio, and β is the measure of the *systematic risk*[29] of the firm and can be computed as

$$\beta = \frac{\text{Cov}(R_m, R_B)}{\text{Var}(R_m)} \qquad (7\text{-}5)$$

where R_B is the rate of return to the bank. Information is available on ρ and $E(R_m)$, so that once the value of β is known the required rate of return for the bank can be easily computed.

As an example, the cost of capital for J. P. Morgan and Co., the holding company for Morgan Guaranty Trust Company in New York, will now be computed. The holding company owns only the one bank and has not diversified extensively, so it fairly well represents the bank. The *Value Line Investment Survey* has computed the β for Morgan to be 1.20.[30] That is, when the market moves by 1 percent, Morgan's stock responds with a 1.2 percent move in the same direction. Historically, the expected return on the market has varied between 9 percent and 13 percent, and the risk-free rate from 5 percent to 7 percent.[31] If averages of 11 percent and 6 percent are used for the expected market return and the risk-free rate, respectively,

---

[28] A complete development of the security market line can be obtained from Weston and Brigham, *Managerial Finance,* Chapters 11 and 17.

[29] Systematic risk is the risk of the firm that cannot be diversified away in a portfolio. This is the risk that the stock will vary with the market.

[30] *Value Line Investment Survey,* June 30, 1978.

[31] Figures taken from Weston and Brigham, *Managerial Finance,* p. 630.

then the required return on Morgan's equity would be approximately 12 percent:

$$k_{cs} = 0.06 + 1.2(0.11 - 0.06) = 0.12 \qquad (7\text{-}5)$$

If the expected return on the market or the risk-free rate were higher, Morgan's cost of equity would be higher. Thus, if the risk-free rate was expected to be 8 percent and the expected market return was forecast to be 12 percent, Morgan's cost of equity would be 12.8 percent. This figure would then be used as the cost of retained earnings. The cost of new equity could be obtained by adjusting this figure by the flotation costs of new equity.

The second method for obtaining the cost of equity capital is to use the valuation formulation

$$P_0 = \frac{d_1}{(1 + k_{cs})} + \frac{d_2}{(1 + k_{cs})^2} + \cdots \qquad (7\text{-}6)$$

where P_0 is the current price of the bank's common stock, the d's are the dividend payments, and k_{cs} is the required return on the bank's common stock, given the risk of the bank. If dividends are expected to grow constantly at the rate g, and if $k_{cs} > g$, then equation (7-7) can be reduced to

$$P_0 = \frac{d_0}{k_{cs} - g} \qquad (7\text{-}7)$$

and since k_{cs} is being sought, (7-7) can be rearranged to give

$$k_{cs} = \frac{d_0}{P_0} + g \qquad (7\text{-}8)$$

The required rate of return on the bank's stock is thus found to be equal to the dividend yield on the stock plus the expected growth rate of dividends.

This can be translated into a usable formula if it is assumed that the past is a good guide to the future and that required rates of return are equal to expected rates of return. Thus, the cost of equity can be obtained by using the current dividend yield of the bank and a historical estimate of the growth rate, based on, say, five or ten years' data on growth of dividends or, as a proxy, earnings, since dividends are not always raised in line with earnings.

In the case of J. P. Morgan and Co., Value Line estimates the current yield on Morgan stock to be 5 percent. The five-year growth rate of dividends is 7 percent, and the ten-year growth rate is 6.5 percent.[32] The required rate of return on Morgan equity determined with these figures is 11.5 to 12 percent. If future growth is expected to be higher or lower than the historical figures, the required return will vary accordingly.

Flotation costs can be taken into account more easily in this formulation. Adjusting equation (7-8) for flotation costs, f, gives

$$k_{cs} = \frac{d_0}{(1-f)P_0} + g = \frac{\text{Dividend yield}}{(1-f)} + g \qquad (7\text{-}9)$$

If flotation costs are about 10 percent of the selling price, P_0, then the cost to Morgan of issuing new common stock would be 12.1 to 12.6 percent (0.056 + 0.065 or 0.056 + 0.07).

The smaller bank that does not have its stock listed and does not regularly issue new quantities of common stock can estimate its cost of retained earnings only by obtaining an estimate of the alternative opportunities of its stockholders. A survey could be made of the owners to obtain this figure, or bank management could use the historical estimates for return to the market, assuming that the owners' alternative was to hold the market portfolio. In addition, since these banks have no capital notes, subordinated debentures, or preferred stock and plan no new issues of common stock, this value would serve as the bank's cost of capital.

Organizations that have these other alternatives, however, must compute the weighted cost of capital. For J. P. Morgan and Co., the capital allocation must be determined next. On March 31, 1978, Morgan had $623 million in long-term debt and $1,630 million in net worth. Purchased funds are excluded from the determination of Morgan's weighted cost of capital because no information is available on their cost. Morgan has no preferred stock outstanding. The effective tax rate is 39 percent. Interest on long-term debt is $39 million.[33]

The before-tax interest on debt is found to be about 6.3 percent ($39 million/$623 million). The after-tax cost of debt is approximately 3.8 percent, or 6.3(1 − 0.39).

If it is assumed that there is no new common stock issue and if the figure of 12 percent is used as the cost of retained earnings, then the weighted cost of capital to the bank can be computed as follows:

$$0.038\left(\frac{623}{2,253}\right) + 0.12\left(\frac{1,630}{2,253}\right) = 0.011 + 0.086 = 0.097 \qquad (7\text{-}10)$$

[32] *Value Line Investment Survey*, June 30, 1978.
[33] *Value Line Investment Survey*, June 30, 1978.

Thus it is found to be 9.7 percent. If the bank needed to make a new common stock issue, the cost would be slightly higher. In recent years, Morgan has paid out roughly 40 percent of net profits in dividends. If net profits after taxes are expected to be around $100 million, then Morgan would retain approximately $60 million. With the capital structure just given, Morgan could increase debt by $23.3 million and retain the same capital structure, a total of $83.3 million of new capital ($23.3/$83.3 = $623/$2,253). If the bank wanted to raise more than this amount, it would have to issue some common stock. If the "cost" of a new issue of common stock is 12.5 percent, then to raise $150 million of new money Morgan would have a weighted average cost of capital of

$$0.038(0.28) + 0.122(0.72) = 0.011 + 0.088 = 0.099 \qquad (7\text{-}11)$$

The 0.122 is the weighted cost of retained earnings and the new issue of common stock.

It should be noted that since historical data were used, the cost-of-capital figure computed here is probably understated by a percentage point or two. This is because some of Morgan's debt is rather old and was issued when interest rates were much lower than they are today. A more accurate figure would be obtained if the estimated yield on a new issue of debt were used. Only under circumstances where interest rates had not changed much over time would historical figures give an accurate estimate of the cost of capital.

RISK OF RUIN

Recent advances in finance have contributed to the understanding of how to estimate the probability that a firm will fail. Some of these techniques have been extended to the banking firm and so are of great interest to those in the banking industry. As yet, the techniques rely on data that are available only to insiders or to the regulators. Nevertheless, they are extremely valuable because bank managers and regulators can more accurately evaluate the bank's potential for failure than in the past. It is hoped that this information will help prevent some of the problems of bank examination discussed earlier in this chapter. [34]

[34] The next step, of course, is to develop methods of evaluating the potential failure of banks on the basis of regularly available market data. Joseph D. Vinso of The University of Pennsylvania and Richard Rogalski of Dartmouth (unpublished) have attempted to do this with stock market data. Obviously, this technique would not be useful for banks that do not

The major work in this area is that of Vinso and Santomero,[35] who specify a model of the movement of the total capital accounts of the bank in which are included capital notes, subordinated debentures, preferred stock, paid-in capital and surplus, retained earnings, and equity reserve accounts. The size of the capital accounts is assumed to be a result of the various changes taking place in all the other accounts of the bank including loan losses and capital losses due to security sales. A time series of the capital accounts can be used to obtain a statistical estimate of the expected time to ruin. A distribution of possible times to ruin can be estimated. A second, more general, measure is also computed. This second process tries to estimate the probability of failure at any time in the future. Using these two pieces of information, bank managers or regulators can have some objective means of determining how close a given bank is to exhausting its capital accounts and how this measure moves over time so that banks that are drifting toward a greater probability of failure at a given time, or find that the distribution of time to ruin is moving closer to the present, can be singled out for special help and consideration.

These tests can be made on weekly observations and so provide a current and relatively quick updating of the position of the bank with respect to potential failure. Vinso and Santomero provide a test of this method by examining the weekly report of condition of banks in the Federal Reserve System. This information is readily available to the regulators and the banks themselves but not to the general public. Thus it provides a reasonably good test of how the method can be used.

The tests were compared with some traditional analytical ratios in the hope of finding some "early warning" device that would help to detect banks that were vulnerable to failure. The finding of the study, although quite tentative, was that the capital–asset ratio and the coefficient of variation of capital account charges might be effective in pinpointing the banks with some potential difficulty.

In conclusion, the study points to more sophisticated ways in which the potential failure of a bank can be flagged, either by management or by bank regulators. The technique can be used with data that are regularly available to the analysts. It is to be expected that more techniques like this one will be developed and applied to the banking industry. One note of comfort can be taken from this research effort. Some of the traditional

---

have their stock listed on some exchange or that have their stock listed in relatively inefficient markets. Again, these techniques do not eliminate the need for regulators if appropriate market conditions for the banks involved are not available.

[35] A. M. Santomero and J. D. Vinso, "Estimating the Probability of Failure for Commercial Banks and the Banking System," *Journal of Banking and Finance* (September 1977).

methods of analyzing capital adequacy seem to be valid rules of thumb for such an analysis. Therefore, analysts outside the bank can be relatively confident in using these methods to determine the capital position of the bank.

REVIEW QUESTIONS

1. Does the "regulators' definition" of bank capital really relate to regulators' reasons for capital requirements? Why don't other definitions satisfy the regulators?
2. How can the book value of a bank differ from its market value when the bank deals only in paper claims that usually have fixed maturities?
3. How important is the term structure of interest rates in determining whether a bank finds it feasible to issue long-term debt? Do taxes play a role in the decision?
4. The conditions of the markets in which banks operate are related to the awareness of the bank's customers and the people who supply long-term capital to the bank. Is it worthwhile to the bank to provide more information? Under what conditions would supplying more information be beneficial to the bank, and under what conditions would it be harmful?
5. What responsibility does a newspaper or other communications medium have to publish or withhold information about a troubled bank? Could a newspaper report cause a bank to fail?
6. What is the difference between business risk and financial risk? How might the size of a bank affect the covariance existing between assets and liabilities and hence the riskiness of the organization?
7. Should short-term liabilities be excluded from calculations of the cost of capital? Will the size of the bank affect your answer?

APPENDIX

Analyzing Bank Performance

Bank managers, investors, depositors, and regulators must constantly monitor bank performance if they are to make decisions consistent with the objectives under which they each work. One method of keeping current with bank performance is to use financial ratios that give some indication of the bank's financial condition and the changes that are taking place in its operations. There are several standard ratios that have been used for years to analyze a bank. Depending on the viewpoints of the persons doing the analysis, these ratios have been considered everything from adequate to grossly inefficient.

One problem of delving more deeply into a bank's balance sheet and income statement has been the lack of adequate information. The data the banks must publish have never been found particularly useful because of their aggregate nature and the lack of disclosure required on many important items such as loan losses, maturity distribution of loans or securities, and interest charges. However, one must make do with what one has, and financial analysis can at least be indicative of problems, leading managers, analysts, and regulators to areas that may need to be investigated further.

Ratio analysis provides certain static information that can help to highlight the performance of a bank. Care must be taken in the analysis and interpretation of the various measures computed so that the interested party does not read too much into the ratios. Ratios are summary measures and are very useful to the experienced and skillful analyst. However, they can be misleading to the casual user. There are several reasons for this. First, balance sheet and income statement information is a result of accounting, legal, and management practices; it may consist of artificial figures and may not have any relationship with economic reality. For example, loan-loss figures may be derived from legal limit computations and may bear no relationship to actual loan-loss chargeoffs. Securities may be entered at purchase price and differ considerably from the amounts the bank could obtain from their sale. Second, accounting practices are not standardized, and a comparison of one bank with another may be a comparison of two entities that are not comparable. Third, the organizational structures of banks vary, and this can also complicate or preclude comparison. For example, the data on a bank holding company cannot be compared with data on an individual bank.

Even though these problems exist, financial ratios are still useful in analyzing a bank. The best way to analyze the data is to compare them with historical data of the bank being reviewed, similar banks, and the industry as a whole. Tracking the movements of these ratios over time gives some indication of the direction in which the bank is going. For example, a declining capital–asset ratio *may* indicate that the bank is becoming riskier because capital expansion is not keeping up with overall growth. Comparing the bank with industry averages or with other banks whose size, markets, or structure are similar gives an indication of the relative position of the bank. A lower capital–asset ratio than the industry average *may* mean that the bank is one of the riskier banks in the industry. The analyst should investigate this possibility, keeping in mind that it is a possibility, not a foregone conclusion.

Several types of ratios can be studied: liquidity ratios, leverage ratios, earnings ratios, and loan quality ratios. It should be stated again that the ratios presented here can be computed from readily available data. The number of ratios that can be analyzed from more disaggregated data grows with the amount of data available. These data can vary substantially from organization to organization.

LIQUIDITY RATIOS

Information on the liquidity of a bank is generally inadequate. Thus, the analyst must collect circumstantial evidence. First, if the information is available, the analyst can compute the amount of cash, deposits, and short-term assets the bank has available to handle unexpected movements in assets or liabilities. This amount can be divided by total assets, loans, or deposits to determine the ability of the bank to handle unexpected cash outflows. The larger the ratios, the more liquid the bank and the better equipped it is to cope with a sudden cash outflow. Three useful ratios are

$$\frac{\text{Short-term assets}}{\text{Total assets}}$$

$$\frac{\text{Short-term assets}}{\text{Total loans}}$$

and

$$\frac{\text{Short-term assets}}{\text{Total deposits}}$$

where short-term assets equals cash plus deposits plus high-grade securities with a maturity of less than one year.

It should be noted that these do not completely measure the asset liquidity of the bank. Short-term assets include the amounts the banks must keep on hand to satisfy reserve requirements. These cannot be reduced as deposits are withdrawn, because the bank still has other deposits, for which it must hold reserves. Furthermore, some cash on hand is needed to handle daily transactions. If these stocks are depleted, they must be replaced in order to continue business. Finally, some of the government securities included in the short-term securities figure may be pledged as collateral for federal or municipal deposits. These cannot be sold to meet the bank's need for funds. Thus, the ratios derived above must be used with the utmost caution.

Furthermore, these measures only attempt to assess asset liquidity; they do not in any way measure the liquidity that the bank gets from the liability market. Liability-management banks will generally have relatively low values for these ratios but may still consider themselves extremely liquid. Although the analyst can never know the amount of funds the bank could borrow, it may be possible to discern if it would have some trouble in purchasing funds. Two ratios that reveal whether the bank has relied too heavily on purchased funds in the past are

$$\frac{\text{Total loans}}{\text{Total deposits}}$$

and

$$\frac{\text{Total loans}}{\text{Total assets}}$$

The ratio of loans to deposits tells how much of the loan portfolio is financed by purchased funds. A ratio of 1.00 or greater indicates that short-term purchased funds are being used to fund longer-term loans, which is considered to be relatively risky. As a result, the bank may have to pay a premium for additional funds or may actually face some rationing of needed money.

Another guide to the precariousness of the bank's position is the percentage of its deposits or total assets represented by "hot money." Hot money is very interest sensitive; its supply curves are very elastic, and thus it can move in or out of the bank very rapidly. Hot money consists of large-denomination CDs, Eurodollars, and federal funds purchased and securities sold under repurchase agreements. The ratios are

$$\frac{\text{Hot money}}{\text{Total deposits}}$$

and

$$\frac{\text{Hot money}}{\text{Total assets}}$$

LEVERAGE RATIOS

The most common leverage ratios are

$$\frac{\text{Total capital}}{\text{Total deposits}}$$

$$\frac{\text{Total capital}}{\text{Total assets}}$$

and

$$\frac{\text{Total capital}}{\text{Risk assets}}$$

where total capital is defined to include equity capital, debt capital, and reserve accounts. Risk assets are total assets less cash and government securities. The reason for the use of risk assets is that the bank can be assured of receiving almost 100 percent of the balance sheet value of cash and government securities. Since capital is supposed to provide a cushion for unexpected losses and these losses can be expected to come only out of assets other than cash and government securities, the third ratio is considered a better measure of the financial riskiness of the firm than the first two.

A measure used to determine the long-run leverage used by the bank can be obtained by dividing the long-term debt of the bank by total capital:

$$\frac{\text{Capital notes} + \text{Subordinated debentures}}{\text{Total capital}}$$

This ratio gives some indication of the amount of bank capital that is subject to fixed charges.

Two other sets of ratios have been devised in recent years to account for the fact that some capital, primarily from common stock issues—paid-in capital and surplus—originally was obtained to provide for fixed investment and startup costs. Since these represent permanent assets, they were not originally designed to handle temporary or unexpected losses that need to be charged off against equity accounts. The first two are called the *excess capital ratios:*

$$\frac{\text{Equity capital} - \text{Common stock}}{\text{Total deposits}}$$

and

$$\frac{\text{Equity capital} - \text{Common stock}}{\text{Risk assets}}$$

Two others that have been developed to examine basically the same thing are called the *free capital ratios:*

$$\frac{\text{Total capital} - \text{Debt capital} - \text{Fixed assets}}{\text{Total deposits}}$$

and

$$\frac{\text{Total capital} - \text{Debt capital} - \text{Fixed assets}}{\text{Risk assets}}$$

The higher these four ratios are, the less risky the bank.

EARNINGS RATIOS

There are three basic earnings ratios that are widely used. The first, the net return on assets, shows asset efficiency or asset productivity:

$$\text{Net return on assets} = \frac{\text{Net income}}{\text{Total assets}}$$

The earning power of the bank represented by the rate of return on equity

$$\frac{\text{Net income}}{\text{Total capital}}$$

is the best measure of the return that should be of most concern to the owners.

The third basic earnings ratio is the profit margin:

$$\frac{\text{Net income}}{\text{Total revenues}}$$

The spread the bank earns on its loans and investments can be estimated as the difference of two ratios:

$$\frac{\text{Interest revenues}}{\text{Earning assets}} - \frac{\text{Interest expense}}{\text{Interest-bearing liabilities}}$$

The two ratios give the average interest earned and the average interest cost of funds, and their difference is thus the average spread earned by the bank. Note that the numerator of the first term can be separated into loan income and securities income if the data are available.

As mentioned in Chapter 2, one should be very careful in interpreting average figures. The analyst should not attribute the qualities of marginal variables to average variables. Doing so could lead to a serious misinterpretation of the bank's performance.

LOAN QUALITY RATIOS

There are three ratios that are often used to estimate the loan quality of the bank's loan portfolio:

$$\frac{\text{Loan losses}}{\text{Total loans}}$$

$$\frac{\text{Loan losses}}{\text{Net income}}$$

and

$$\frac{\text{Net loan recoveries}}{\text{Total loans}}$$

An increase in the first two of these represents a worsening of the quality of the loan portfolio. A fall in the last measure also represents a decline in portfolio quality.

OTHER MEASURES

The position of the bank can also be analyzed with other measures, some quantitative and some qualitative. Qualitative factors include the type of institution the bank is attempting to be, its customer base, the geographic market it serves, the quality of its management, the consistency of earnings, and so on. Other things an analyst should examine if the information is available are the maturity structure and quality of the securities and loan portfolio. A bank that holds all 25-year bonds of CCC quality is not well managed. Although this is an extreme example, some banks, particularly small ones, can get into difficulty with their portfolios by purchasing securities of "good customers" like their local government even when the securities are considered risky by rating services.

Two additional areas need special attention. First, analysts today are giving greater emphasis to bank overhead costs. It may take some effort to obtain information on these costs, but with the growing importance of non-funds-using operations, such as service areas, and electronic funds transfer systems, cost control has become an important consideration in analyzing a bank's progress. For example, some analysts compare the net change in overhead expense to the net change in interest income. The implication is that, since overhead cost is more or less fixed, if its growth exceeds the growth of interest income there may be some ultimate danger to the firm due to the possibility of interest income dropping off or growing more slowly in the future.

Another concern is the parent company–lead bank relationship that exists within the holding company framework. Several measures have been suggested for use in analyzing the strength of the holding company. These are the lead bank dividend as a percentage of lead bank net income, the holding company dividend as a percentage of affiliate dividends, and the "double-leverage" ratio. The latter ratio measures the amount of debt the parent company pyramids downstream to the affiliates based on its own equity. It gives an idea of how earnings of the parent might be affected by the fixed charges that have been set against the potential earnings of the affiliates. The larger this ratio is, the riskier the parent is; and the riskier the parent is, the less able it is to issue its commercial paper or debt in the future to help the affiliates or, in particular, the lead bank.

SOURCES AND USES OF FUNDS

The analyst can also gain some insight into the performance of the bank by computing a flow-of-funds statement for the bank. A flow-of-funds statement tells the analyst the *net* sources and uses of funds of the bank during the time period under review. It is composed from two balance sheets. An income statement can also be used to provide some added information but is not necessary.

To construct a sources and uses table, subtract from the most recent balance sheet of the bank the balance sheet for the last period. This will give the net changes in the balance sheet over that period of time. Then the figures can be collected as follows:

1. Sources of funds are net additions to liabilities or to net worth or net reductions in assets. Each of these generates funds for the bank.

2. Uses of funds are net increases in assets or net reductions in liabilities or net worth. Each of these represents a purchase of an asset—cash, a loan, a security, or a purchase of a liability of the bank.

If used correctly, a flow-of-funds analysis can give insight into the pressures a bank faced during the time period under review and how management has responded to the pressures. It cannot tell what went on, however, within the period. Thus, the only thing that can be said is that certain types of transactions occurred on average during this time. But it can isolate important factors. For example, an increase in loan demand serviced would be shown as a net use of funds. The sources of funds for this increase may be a reduction in U.S. government securities held, an increase in purchased funds, such as negotiable CDs, an increase in demand deposits, or a combination of some or all of these factors.

On the other hand, a decrease in loans may result in an increase in holdings of U.S. government securities and very little change in purchased funds or other liabilities, since the bank may feel that the decline in loan demand is a temporary phenomenon and may not want to cut off its sources of funds if loan demand is expected to pick up again. This situation should be watched by the analyst. The bank obviously cannot earn much by selling, say, negotiable CDs and investing in U.S. government securities. Thus, if the dropoff in loan demand is finally deemed to be permanent, the bank will have to reduce its holdings of government securities and also reduce the amount of purchased funds it is using.

A lot of information on the bank can be obtained from a flow-of-funds statement. However, expertise and skill are needed in performing such an analysis, and even then the researcher must be careful not to read too much into the figures. All these efforts must be accompanied by a study of the statements of the bank management, a further analysis into the bank's markets, and a constant awareness of the general conditions of the money market and the economy.

8

The Commercial Loan Portfolio

The composition of the long-run loan portfolio initially is a problem of strategic planning for the commercial bank. The crucial question that must be asked in long-term planning concerns the customer base of the bank—to whom is the bank going to lend? Careful consideration must be given to this decision, because the impact of decisions made in this part of the planning process will be reflected in the performance of the bank for a long time to come. For example, if the bank chooses to lend on an installment basis to persons purchasing automobiles through car dealerships, the choice entails a major commitment of financial, physical, and human resources. The success or failure of this effort will affect the bank for many years.

Thus, over the long run, the bank must choose which customers and markets it is going to serve. It must then set its relative prices and terms so as to be a factor in the markets it decides to enter.[1] After determining the viability of the various loan markets and customer classes, it must decide on the optimal number of loan classes.[2] Consistent with this planning is, of

---

[1] Deciding not to go into a market is the same as deciding to set an infinite price in that particular market. Thus, the bank is still setting prices. It simply sets them high enough to exclude all borrowers in that loan class.

[2] See Chapter 3 for a more detailed examination of this point.

course, the long-run risk-return tradeoff that management desires to achieve for the bank and for the loan portfolio.

The effort to make the long-run plan operational, in a shorter-run sense, is examined in this chapter. First, the relationship between the long-run plan and the annual budget is discussed. Along with the need for a plan, the uses of this plan for control are also analyzed. Following this, a discussion of the actual budgeting process is presented along with a description of how this process might be implemented. The sources of information necessary for the efficient functioning of such a planning process are discussed. The final sections of the chapter deal with the types of commercial loans a bank may offer commercial borrowers and explain the uses of a number of common loan terms.

THE LONG-RUN PLAN

The concept of long-run planning was presented in Chapter 4. The lending function of the bank gets information pertaining to the loan types and markets with which it will be dealing, the degree of risk the bank will accept, the relative prices necessary to maintain the desired loan groups, and the return it expects to receive on each group. However, these will be formulated in terms of what the top management of the bank feels it can achieve in five to seven years, given the efforts it is allocating to marketing, building, and so on. What goes on within this period (that is, the day-by-day and month-by-month happenings) is not a major factor to the long-run planners. [3]

In making these plans, the members of top management know that there will be variations within the long-run horizon. Profits will vary, sometimes running below plan and sometimes above. Risk exposure will change over the credit cycle. Some borrowers will be rationed out of the market at certain times and given loans gladly at other times. However, these things do not change the nature of the plan. In a world of uncertainty this does not mean that the desired results will be achieved, and this is why short-run plans or targets and control are necessary.

The bank needs as much feedback as possible. Feedback provides

---

[3] It is not of concern if the movements around the projected trends balance out or are random. A path continuously below or above trend may affect what the decisions are. However, since the major influence on loan demand (or deposit supply) within this time horizon is the credit cycle, a five- to seven-year planning horizon is long enough, in most instances, to allow a complete cycle to take place. Hence, it is to be expected that the variations around the trend will be somewhat offsetting.

answers to the questions: Is the growth in loan demand being achieved? Are loan classes as profitable as they should be? Has the bank been too restrictive in defining its loan classes, thus losing legitimate customers? Is risk exposure greater than anticipated?[4]

The long-run plan not only provides information necessary to the operational short-run effort but also provides a tracking path. Actual results can be compared with expected results to check on whether assumptions are being fulfilled. For example, many banks entered the 1970s assuming that the U.S. economy would sustain a relatively high economic growth rate. As events unfolded, the bankers found that this assumption was incorrect and that a more modest projection of economic growth was called for. At the beginning of the 1970s, the assumption of a lower economic growth rate was inconceivable to most economists; continued rapid growth was the consensus forecast. However, as the economy went into a slower growth pattern, loan demand slowed, and banks had to adjust their plans to achieve smaller loan portfolios over time than they would have held if the original assumption had been correct. Banks that had plans and traced shortfalls back to the paths implied by the plans were able to adjust to the evolving economic environment more quickly than those that did not use such a procedure.

The long-run plan, therefore, provides important information to be used in short-run planning. It also provides a check on the achievement of the plan. The long-run and short-run efforts of the bank should be thoroughly integrated. The maximization of the price of the bank's stock, given risk, for the short run should be consistent with the maximization of the price of the bank's stock over the long run.

THE SHORT-RUN BUDGET

In most banks the next step is the formation of the one-year plan or the annual budget. The most important items to the annual budget are forecasts of loan rates, loan quantities, and loan terms for the different established loan classes and markets, consistent with both the long-run plan and short-run economic conditions. What the bank hopes to achieve in this plan is a set of target rates, terms, and quantities that will help it meet both its long-run and short-run[5] goals.

---

[4] Such as loans to Real Estate Investment Trusts (REITs).

[5] This does not mean that these items are inflexibly set for the time period being considered. As with the long-run plan, the annual plan must be continuously monitored to make

The present discussion is not concerned with the organizational format within which the planning process takes place but with the information that must be collected to make the plan. Hence, it will abstract completely from institutional arrangements.

Interest Rate Forecasts

In most efforts at annual planning, interest rate forecasts are the first information gathered. This is because the loan portfolio is highly sensitive to the credit cycle and therefore to interest rate levels and movements in interest rates. In addition, most other parts of the annual budget are in some sense based on interest rate levels and relative interest rates.

The bank must therefore have some knowledge of short-term open-market rates (those that are not administered by some group or organization within the economy and that are of particular importance to the bank's pricing structure). The rates that are particularly important to the bank are the Treasury bill rate and the rates on commercial paper and negotiable certificates of deposit. The latter, of course, can be controlled by the Federal Reserve System through the imposition of an effective Regulation Q ceiling. [6] These rates, in a sense, are the pivot on which all bank rates depend.

Next, the bank must determine what relationship its prime rate should bear to these open-market rates. Many factors, some of them mentioned in Chapters 2 and 3, enter into the relationship between the prime and open-market rates. Management must concern itself with the varying relationship between these rates, or otherwise prime customers will not be priced correctly relative to the market. If prime customers are not priced correctly, then the whole loan portfolio will be unbalanced. First, due to the competitive nature of the prime loan market, there will be too many or

---

sure that its purpose is being achieved and that the underlying assumptions are correct. Various banks have used different methods to keep on top of loan pricing: These methods include asset/liability committees or loan review committees. The point is that the plan and the market must be constantly observed so that, if needed, the bank can adjust as rapidly as possible to changing market conditions.

[6] Regulation Q allows the Federal Reserve to set maximum interest rates on time and savings accounts at member commercial banks. Although the Federal Reserve does not have authority to control rates in nonmember banks, the Federal Deposit Insurance Corporation (FDIC) is authorized to set rates for banks that have FDIC deposit insurance. Thus, almost all banks in the country experience some control over the rates they pay on time and savings accounts. The FDIC also administers rates to mutual savings banks. The Federal Home Loan Bank Board has the same authority for member savings and loan associations. Generally, these institutions all act in concert with one another.

too few prime loans, given economic conditions. Second, it is the usual practice of banks to base their whole pricing structure on the prime loan portfolio, and a bank's risk-return structure depends on how the prime is set.[7]

Moreover, the bank must forecast the term structure of interest rates.[8] This is needed in pricing long-term commitments such as term loans and mortgages. Whereas the term structure is usually developed for one particular type of instrument, such as for U.S. government issues, the bank needs to translate the term relationship into loan spreads so as to plan allocations to appropriate loan classes of appropriate maturities. A maturity imbalance can make the loan portfolio undesirably risky.

Furthermore, the bank needs to project the interest rates on tax-exempt securities. The relationship between these and taxable instruments also changes over the credit cycle. However, this information is more important for the investments portfolio than for the loan portfolio, so not much attention will be given to it at this time.

Forecasting Loan Demand

To forecast loan demand the bank needs input on the state of the local, regional, national, and perhaps the international, economy. It also needs an estimate of the loan demand in each individual loan class. It is assumed that the number and type of loan classes are given; since these are a long-run decision, they will not be added to or subtracted from in the short run.

In addition, it is assumed that the bank knows the riskiness of each loan class. That is, from previous experience or *a priori* estimation, it knows the variances and covariances of each loan class and liability class. This is important, because in computing expected return on either assets or capital, the figure used is *net* of loan losses. The bank is assumed to have the information it needs to compute this net amount. Thus, although loan demands and yields will be determined on a *gross* basis in setting up the budget, the bank must set its objectives in terms of *net* returns.

Using macro information on the state of the economy and the expected configuration of interest rates, the bank must determine the level of loan demand in each loan class. Conceptually, Figures 2-1 and 2-2 can be used

---

[7] Instead of attempting to project levels of interest rates, some banks have attempted to forecast spreads between assets and liabilities. Technically, to do a good job, great effort must be expended to determine both levels and spreads.

[8] Those needing a refresher on the term structure should turn to Chapter 12.

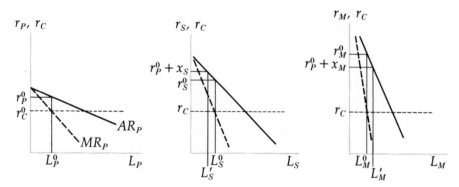

FIGURE 8-1   Optimal Composition of the Loan Portfolio with Three Loan
Classes

to illustrate precisely what the bank must do. In Figure 8-1, three loan classes can be observed, the prime class, P, the satisfactory class, S, and the marginal class, M. The "marginal cost" of funds is r_C^0, which may or may not be an opportunity cost; the prime rate is r_P^0; and the rates charged on loans of types S and M are r_S^0 and r_M^0, respectively.

Assume for the present that the market-clearing rates, r_S^0 and r_M^0, and quantities L_S^0 and L_M^0 are not available. The bank has information only on r_P^0, and hence $r_P^0 + x_S$ and $r_P^0 + x_M$, where the x's are the interest rate mark-ups over prime for the individual loan classes. The planning process must then come up with the corresponding quantities L_S' and L_M'. How this may be done is discussed later. The important thing is that in order to make a reasonable budget these figures must be forecast in some way. Since there will be uncertainty as to both the slope and the position of the demand curves, the amounts estimated will, of course, be uncertain.

It must be remembered that the positions of the demand curves are dependent on the nonprice terms charged each class of loans. At this stage of the budget process, it is desirable for top management to keep the other terms of the loan constant at current levels. These other terms, of course, include fees, compensating balance requirements, collateral require-ments, down payments, and maturity, among other items. The reason for keeping them constant is that at the present stage no one would have any idea about how they ought to be changed, because no decision has been made concerning the makeup of the whole portfolio with regard to either return or risk. Until this is done, these terms must be kept at existing amounts.

The bank planners can now compute the return to the bank, if they have sufficient information on the liability side. With the use of contract rates and terms, the yields on the various loan classes can now be obtained.[9] These will be yields before losses are taken into account and will be designated Y_P^G, Y_S^G, and Y_M^G, which stand for the gross yields on prime loans, satisfactory loans, and marginal loans, respectively.[10] To obtain net yields the expected default rates must be subtracted. Thus, if δ_i is the default rate on the ith loan class, then the net yields on prime loans, satisfactory loans, and marginal loans, respectively, are

$$Y_P^N = Y_P^G - \delta_P, \qquad Y_S^N = Y_S^G - \delta_S, \quad \text{and} \quad Y_M^N = Y_M^G - \delta_M$$

Calculating the Bank's Rate of Return

The focus must now shift from the individual loan and deposit classes to the performance of the bank as a whole. It should be remembered that the bank has an overall target rate of return, $\hat{Y}_B$, determined in conjunction with its long-run plan. Before this is translated specifically into a target for the annual budget, two things must be considered. First, the long-run target is assumed to be achieved linearly. That is, the credit cycle is not taken into account in the construction of this return. Therefore, in determining the actual target level for the coming year, the bank planners must take cognizance of the stage of the credit cycle the economy is now in and adjust the target yield accordingly. The bank's target rate of return adjusted for the credit cycle, which will be designated $\hat{Y}_B^*$, may be lower or higher than $\hat{Y}_B$.

There is another problem in setting $\hat{Y}_B^*$, however. One of the objectives of top management may be to have a low variance of bank returns because the stockholders prefer steady returns to ones that are highly variable. Thus, the bank may want to set $\hat{Y}_B^*$ fairly close to $\hat{Y}_B$, so as to maintain the low variance.

A low variance may be achieved in practice in one of two ways. The bank may use the accounting practices available to it to achieve stable reported returns,[11] or it may restructure its loan portfolio to do the same thing. However, if the bank is listed on a relatively efficient stock exchange, it would be expected that market participants would take into

[9] Formulas for computing these yields are presented in Chapter 10.

[10] At present we are not concerned with whether these are rates of return on assets or on capital.

[11] For example, the bank may use the loan-loss reserve accounting procedure to smooth out reported earnings. For how this is done, see Chapter 6.

account the bank's practice and would not rely on reported figures. Thus, efforts to show stable returns for a bank that is in reality not very stable would achieve very little in the long run, for investors would eventually catch on and adjust their behavior accordingly. The only ones that would be fooled would be the management who thought they could fool investors.

It is assumed, regardless of what management tries to do, that some $\hat{Y}_B^*$ is chosen. Associated with this rate of return is some level of risk consistent with the long-run risk class of the bank and the particular stage of the credit cycle projected for the coming year. As with the expected return, the acceptable level of risk assumed by the bank must reflect current economic realities. Thus, it is assumed that this figure is available to the bank management team constructing the annual plan.

To keep things relatively simple, other revenues, R, and costs, C, are assumed to be fixed. That is, they are the result of assets or liabilities fixed in amounts and costs because their lifetimes exceed the one-year time horizon of the annual budget or because some assets and liabilities that are obtained in imperfectly elastic markets do not have nonprice terms that can be manipulated to shift demand or supply curves to achieve different quantities of the assets or liabilities. The balance sheet of the bank is completed by using appropriate residual markets for an asset- or liability-management bank.

In this case, the expected yield to the bank (Y_B) is

$$Y_B = \frac{Y_P^N L_P^0 + Y_S^N L_S^1 + Y_M^N L_M^1 + r_G^0 G + R - C}{Z} \tag{8-1}$$

This is an asset-management bank, so it expects to buy the quantity G of U.S. government securities and earn the rate r_G^0 ($= r_C^0$ in Figure 8-1) on them. The variable Z is either the total dollar amount of bank assets or the total dollar amount of the bank's capital accounts, depending on whether the rates of return are figured on assets or on capital.

This estimated return, Y_B, must now be compared with the appropriate target yield, $\hat{Y}_B^*$, and the riskiness of the bank's portfolio must be compared with the desired risk. It is unlikely that either of these desired figures will be achieved in the first effort.

Adjustments to Achieve Targets

If $\hat{Y}_B^* \neq Y_B$, or the risk of the portfolio is not what is desired, then some adjustments must be made. If $\hat{Y}_B^*$ and the desired risk level are correct, given market conditions and long-run plans, then the hypothetical market-clearing conditions shown in Figure 8-1 are more correct than those determined by the administered pricing mechanism. That is, the market-clearing rate for loans of type S would be $r_S^0 < r_P^0 + x_S$, which would give an expected amount of loans equal to $L_S^0 > L_S^1$, and the market-clearing rate for loans of type M would be $r_M^0 > r_P^0 + x_M$, which would result in an expected amount of loans of type M equal to $L_M^0 < L_M^1$.

Given the apparent relative elasticities of the two curves, it can be argued that the return to the portfolio will be at least as high as desired, or $Y_B \geq \hat{Y}_B^*$, and that the riskiness of the portfolio may be greater than can be tolerated by the bank. Although the first point may be arguable, because the elasticities are not known with certainty, the second is not. If loans of type S are less risky than loans of type M, then the effort at portfolio planning will result in less S than desired and more M than desired, thus making the riskiness of the portfolio greater than management desires.

A situation of this type may result in a case of pure credit rationing similar to that described in Chapter 3. That is, the amount of loans made at the going combination of interest rate and nonprice terms may be restricted, with the bank refusing some credit demands. In practice, this would not be done by cutting back on credit lines outstanding or "calling" existing loans. Rationing would affect only new loans and requests for increases in lines. Banks may reduce lines of credit to existing borrowers when they come up for renewal, but not before. There have been rumors, from time to time, that some banks have reneged on lines of credit, but such examples, if they exist, are rare. Thus, the marginal credit demand is the one affected by the rationing procedure; existing commitments will continue to be honored.

Furthermore, the bank would probably not alter any of the terms on loans of type S. This is not the most desirable situation for the bank to be in, since it would like to have more type S loans in its portfolio because they are less risky than type M loans. It is more likely that the bank will try to reduce the riskiness of the portfolio by reducing the quantity of the type of loans that are demanded in excess; it would choose to lend only L_M^0 dollars of type M loans while still lending L_S^1 dollars of type S loans.

As described earlier,[12] the bank will not, in general, vary the markups, in this case the x_S and x_M. Thus it is faced with the following decision: Should it maintain nonprice terms as they are and hope that the situation will be a temporary one? If top management believes this to be the case, it will ration credit for a while in the expectation that interest rates will fall in

---

[12] See Chapter 3.

the near future. Alternatively, should the bank alter nonprice terms and attempt to alleviate the disequilibrium. The managers would do this if they felt that the likelihood of a reversal of economic conditions was small. How quickly management reacts depends on their reading of the situation. Sometimes they will move nonprice terms very rapidly; at other times they will move more slowly. It depends on how uncertain the environment is.

If the bank desires to make further adjustments, new values must be derived for Y_P^N, Y_S^N, and Y_M^N. These, along with new quantities, if they are obtained, will be substituted into equation (8-1) and a new Y_B will be computed. This yield and the riskiness of the new portfolio will be compared with the owner's desired level of yield and risk.

This process should continue until a combination of yields on loans and portfolio composition is found that will achieve the desired yield and risk level consistent with the long-run plan. The annual planning process is now complete, and what remains is to put the plan into operation, translating the budget into yields and terms that can be used by loan officers to actually price borrowers.

The budget should then be transmitted to the lending areas in terms of the target yields or expected returns loan officers are to earn on each type of loan, the loan terms applicable to the various loan classes, and the quantities (including any plans for rationing) of loans to be given that class. The contract rates are given because the markup x_i is set for each class. The budget should now be operational; that is, loan officers should have enough information to price loans correctly in order to achieve the objectives of the annual plan and contribute to the long-run performance of the bank.

Capital Allocation

The job of top management, however, has not been completed. In implementing their plan there must be some way to control the allocation of funds to borrowers and ultimately to control the risk-return attributes of the loan portfolio. One common technique has been to allocate the bank's scarce supply of capital among its various asset classes. Requiring that each dollar of assets be backed by so much capital places an ultimate limit on the amount of assets, or loans, the bank can hold.

An alternative to capital allocation is to set lending limits. It can easily be recognized that if the capital–asset ratio is expected to remain constant, it does not make any difference which approach is used as long as the ratio is kept constant. There are some very good reasons, however, for basing loan policies on capital allocation rather than on limiting loans.

First of all, capital allocation is easier to deal with, because there is only so much capital to go around. To be consistent with long-run goals, the bank must stop when its capital is exhausted.[13] In other words, the long-term plan determines the asset makeup of the bank, its optimal capital structure, and hence its risk class. If the bank does not stop lending once its has effectively allocated all of its capital, then it will be threatening to change its risk class. It should not do this as a response to the current economic environment. To do so may mean maximizing short-run returns at the expense of long-run returns.

This does not mean that the bank's capital structure may not need changing.[14] The current situation should continually provide feedback to the long-run plan to signal evolving trends that may call for a revision of the assumptions that underlie the long-run plan. Any changes that take place in the capital structure, however, must not be made only for the purpose of maximizing short-run profits.

The second advantage to capital allocation is that the bank can use it to achieve desired changes in its capital structure. It can set its capital–asset ratio to the value it hopes to achieve rather than at historical levels. Then, as loans are booked, the actual capital–asset ratio will move toward the desired ratio. Working with loan amounts does not necessarily achieve this result.

Third, although bankers have historically considered return on assets the most important measure of the yield on a loan, the return on capital is more appropriate from the standpoint of financial management. There are two reasons for this. First, loan decisions are, in a sense, capital budgeting decisions, and capital budgeting techniques compare returns with the cost of capital. Second, if owners want their wealth maximized, the appropriate measure for wealth maximization is the return on capital, not the return on assets.

Thus, it will be assumed throughout the next few chapters that top management allocates the bank's capital among the profit centers or loan officers in the bank. A given dollar amount of capital will be given to each loan officer, and the allocation may continue on down the line to the officers' subordinates. The dollar amount will then be allocated to areas in the bank or to loan classes on the basis of the desired capital allocation ratio

---

[13] If the bank operates in imperfectly competitive markets, then there is an optimal capital structure for the bank. For the conditions describing whether a bank has an optimal capital structure, see Chapter 5 and its appendix.

[14] This depends on the markets the bank faces for raising capital and whether or not it has an optimal capital structure.

and the relative allocation of loans by loan classes as determined in the annual plan. If these areas fully use their capital in the desired ratio, then the bank not only will obtain the asset size it desires but also will achieve its desired asset portfolio.

Capital can be allocated in one of two ways. It can be allocated as a fixed proportion of loans, for example, five cents for every dollar of loans made by the officer, regardless of the quality or type of loan. Alternatively, the proportion of capital allocated to a loan can depend on the riskiness or type of the loan. In that case the bank might allocate, say, four cents of capital for every dollar of prime loans and ten cents for every dollar of marginal loans. Either way, capital is "used up" as loans are booked. When a loan area allocates all its assigned capital, it must usually stop lending. It may be able to "buy" additional capital from the central source of internal capital if the purchase can be justified by the return it can receive on its use or if the capital is needed to service a good customer.

Allocated capital can also serve as a control device, since a loan area must earn a given yield on its capital. That is, in assigning capital to a profit center, top management expects it to earn at least an amount consistent with the annual plan and with the specific loan types and risks for which the center is responsible. If these explicit quantitative standards are not set up, then there is no way to measure performance consistent with optimization of return for a given risk.

Lack of adequate control variables has caused banks to rely on very unsatisfactory measures of portfolio performance. For example, the number or amount of loan losses attributable to a loan officer has frequently been used to judge his or her performance. Rules like these have the tendency to lead banks into unduly conservative portfolio construction with unduly conservative personnel. It is assumed that banks are averse to risk, but if a bank considers only losses without considering the potential earnings it could receive, it is taking into account only half of the problem of portfolio construction.

Return on capital can, therefore, be used to measure the profitability of individual loans as well as to judge the performance of lenders. The former will be discussed later, in the chapter on customer profitability analysis. In the latter case, all that can be said is that, given risk-return targets, loan officers can be held accountable for meeting or missing their targets and hence contributing or not contributing to the achievement of the annual plan and the long-run goal of the bank. Thus, the allocation of capital provides a means not only of evaluating personnel but also of achieving the long-run objectives of the firm. The difficulty in constructing and using a system of capital allocation should not be minimized. This is one reason why the technique is not widely used: The added cost of implementing this type of system may be too great relative to the benefit that many banks would receive from applying the technique. The capital allocation technique, however, is the correct theoretical approach to the problem and thus should be seriously considered.

Collection of Budget Information

The Role of the Economist   There are several sources of the information needed for making loan portfolio plans and several methods of determining the optimal combination of terms for arriving at targets. The budgeting process will generally start with the bank economist, not because the economist is the most important person in the exercise, but because most annual plans start with a forecast of interest rates and interest rate spreads.

Thus, the annual effort starts with the charge to the economics staff to prepare interest rate forecasts for the upcoming period. The economist should be able to present levels of open-market rates for such issues as commercial paper, negotiable CDs, and U.S. Treasury bills, the prime rate, and, if the bank deals in the Eurodollar market, the Eurodollar rate. Furthermore, rough estimates of the term structure of interest rates should be made, so that reasonably intelligent expectations can be formed about possible maturity structures of the portfolio. The economist should also point out any possibility that ceiling interest rates may become effective or be made effective by, say, the monetary authorities. These would include such ceilings as the Federal Reserve System's Regulation Q ceiling on time deposits or state ceilings on mortgages or consumer loans.

In many banks this is where the economist's role ends. In other banks, the economist may provide forecasts of deposits and loans and may even be in charge or second in charge of the entire budgeting process.

If a bank does not have an economist, the general procedure is to make use of some service that provides interest rate forecasts or to rely on the economist of the bank's correspondent bank. This is, of course, one of the many services larger banks can provide through a correspondent relationship.

The Role of Line Officers   Once this information is attained, most banks proceed down the line from top management to the officers in charge of the various lending and deposit-collecting departments. The assignment of these officers is to determine the volume of assets or liabilities to come from their area of responsibility, given the interest rate forecast, pricing conventions, and terms. Depending on the size of the bank, the planning process, and the support it receives, this charge may filter further down through the line management. This would achieve a finer breakdown of loans and deposits into smaller categories and also bring into play those who are "closer" to the market, who have a special expertise in their respective areas.

The reports prepared in all these areas must be collected by one person, either the chief planning officer or, in some banks, the controller, who then must assemble all the diverse numbers into a relatively consistent and meaningful format. This is a very difficult part of the budgeting process, because there may be no unifying strand to the collected data. The interest rate forecast provided by the economist may be the only consistent factor in the various reports, and in all likelihood it will have been interpreted differently by the various participants in the process.

Furthermore, estimates of loans and deposits usually have an upward bias. There are two reasons for this. First, the participants are generally optimistic about their own areas, seeing their market in the most favorable light even in the depths of a recession. Thus, forecasts obtained in the manner just described are a little higher than they perhaps should be. Second, everyone knows that budgets will be trimmed. Thus, a certain amount of game playing occurs. Planning officers know that there will be an upward bias to the projections, so there will naturally have to be some scaling back of forecasts. Department heads know that their estimates will be cut, so they attempt to compensate. The result is an extra upward bias.

The person in charge of assembling and coordinating these inputs must be a magician and a politician as well as a planner. Although some very important information is contained in the departmental estimates, the planner must overcome the interplay of internally competitive forces to draw up a realistic and worthwhile plan.

Other Information Aids In some cases, independent estimates are made of some or all loan and deposit categories. This can be done with the use of econometric models. This is where the economist's office comes in once again, for the economist, being in a staff position, has no axe to grind and also has the tools and qualifications to form independent judgments.

The bank economist may or may not use national or regional econometric data provided by a modeling service. Such organizations exist, with quite detailed national and industry models and large data bases that can be used by banks to construct their own models of bank loan demand and deposit supply. There are also several useful regional models.

A smaller bank that does not have the financial or human resources to use a modeling service may build its own simple model. All it requires are regression equations based on historical data from the bank and some other relevant time series. In many cases the simpler the effort, the better the results, because it is often easier to compute an aggregate amount than the aggregate's components.

Thus, a bank may estimate its commercial and industrial loans, mortgage loans, and consumer loans, or break them out into finer classifications. For example, if lending to textile mills is an extremely important part of its loan business, then loans in that category should be separated from other commercial and industrial loans and estimated as an independent equation. Actual equations may show that a bank variable, such as commercial and industrial loans, is explained by a combination of national, regional, and local factors as well as interest rate levels. The bank must experiment to find the "best" set of explanatory factors; that is, the variables that explain the largest amount of movement in the quantities of the loan classes it is attempting to estimate.

The estimates obtained from econometric models are valuable for two reasons: (1) They are not subject to the biases of interdepartmental competition. (2) They are consistent, in that the assumptions are treated similarly in all estimates, whereas assumptions may mean different things to different people when collected from line management.

There are still problems, however, with this kind of forecasting. For one thing, the estimates are based on historical relationships that may break down at any time. Also, they do not take into account any special knowledge of markets or customers that bank personnel may have.

Whereas the use of econometric models may be valuable in constructing an annual plan, the people in charge of putting the plan together must use a judicious combination of bank personnel and statistical techniques to arrive at their final result. Being aware of the benefits and costs of both approaches is the first step toward solving this dilemma. Econometric models may be used, but bank personnel must feel that they have a part in the process and that their advice is not being ignored in favor of an electronic machine.

Finally, to help the planner there are several simulation models that can be used to find "best" solutions. These models do not forecast or "create" data; the collection process is still necessary. They do, however, input user data and assumptions and then output balance sheet and income data. The primary benefit of simulation models is that they allow numerous changes in assumptions and policy decisions to be entered into the model relatively efficiently and quickly. However, the results obtained

from them are no better than the data, assumptions, and decisions that are
put into them.

TYPES OF COMMERCIAL LOANS

Commercial loans can be constructed to meet the needs of individual customers. However, there are five "basic" types: (1) the open line of credit,
(2) the transaction loan, (3) the working capital loan, (4) revolving credit,
and (5) the term loan.

Open Lines of Credit

Many borrowers experience seasonal or cyclical swings in their need
for funds. It is inconvenient and costly for these borrowers to go to a bank
and apply for a loan every time they need funds. It can be costly and
unnecessary for banks to go through the application, examination, and
lending process every time a steady customer needs money. There are
good economic reasons for developing the more regular relationship
known as the open line of credit.

Open lines of credit are generally given to good, creditworthy borrowers who have borrowed regularly at the bank in the past or are expected to be regular borrowers in the future. Because this is to be a long-
term relationship and because no collateral can be required (for this would
make the line legally binding), banks must examine the potential borrower very carefully before making such a commitment. In the terms developed in Chapters 2 and 3, the customer firm usually has a lower variance of demand than other borrowers, that is, it is a steady borrower and is
not expected to default, and it must provide sufficient future loan demand
to make the arrangement worthwhile. Now, this does not mean that loan
demand cannot have seasonal or cyclical patterns. It does mean that borrowers that have established more regular borrowing habits with the bank
will be preferred.

After the bank decides that the relationship is desirable, the customer
is told what its line of credit is, that is, the maximum amount it can
borrow; the price it will pay on the amount of the loan used; and the need,
if any, to "clean up" or pay off all its borrowings once a year. Agreements
for lines of credit are very informal; they may or may not include a letter,
and they are not legally binding, although banks feel a very strong moral
obligation to honor them.

Commercial banks have not established strong controls over the number or amounts of lines of credit in the past. Much to the frustration of regulatory authorities who have desired such information, banks have not always known what the full extent of their commitment has been. There have been efforts in recent years to control the extent of these commitments, but it is still not evident that the banks have been greatly successful in doing so.

In general, loans arising out of lines of credit are not very risky from a default standpoint. Lines of credit are usually given only to the "best" credit risks and to firms that have had a long-standing relationship with the bank. Since bank lines are the most important source of credit to many of their regular customers, these firms will pay off the bank to keep the credit available even if they are in trouble elsewhere and must slow down payments somewhere. Thus, line-of-credit loans are relatively safe investments for the bank.

Transaction Loans

The purpose of the open line of credit is to satisfy temporary needs of a recurring nature. Transaction loans are for temporary needs that occur only once; hence, they give rise to one "transaction." Since the demand is infrequent, the terms of the loan are negotiated each time a need arises and the loan can be tailored to the particular situation. This loan is usually secured by the asset, say inventory or accounts receivable, that gives rise to the application for the loan. Since the need is temporary, the repayment is expected to come from the use of the asset being financed; that is, as inventory is sold or accounts receivable are paid off, the money to repay the bank is generated. Since the need for the loan is not a recurring problem, transaction loans do not give rise to a continuing relationship as do other types of loans.

Working Capital Loans

The working capital loan is usually used by smaller, riskier firms to finance "permanent" increases in current assets. It can be used for either the acquisition of current assets or the repayment of debt incurred in their increase. Since these credits are for longer periods of time and the repayment is not expected to come from selling an asset, as in the case of inventories, but with the production of goods by means of the capital assets, the lender must be concerned with the cash flow generated by the production and sale of goods or the ability of the firm to fund the bank loan with longer-term debt. Because the payoff of the loan may not occur for some time (a matter to be negotiated), the loan is usually secured, with the current assets being financed, generally inventories or accounts receivable, used as collateral.

Revolving Credit

Revolving credit is much like the open line of credit, except that it is a formal agreement set up for a longer period of time, frequently two to three years. It is a flexible arrangement in that a borrower can borrow up to a certain amount whenever the need arises. It is almost always given only to creditworthy, large companies. Thus, this type of loan is suitable for firms that expect to experience greater uncertainty with respect to cash needs over the period of the loan than, say, those that would obtain a working capital loan. However, since these are for "permanent" needs, either permanent additions to current assets or the purchase of fixed assets, repayment comes out of cash flow or through funding with longer-term debt. As stated earlier, these are formal agreements, with the terms, prices, and responsibilities of the parties explicitly set down on paper.

Term Loans

Term loans are generally used for the purchase of fixed assets, so their maturities run for several years. Most often maturities will run from three to five years, but terms have sometimes gone to as much as seven to ten years. The borrower can usually "take down" the loan as needed or obtain the funds all at once. Repayment is specifically expected to be out of cash flow, so most term loans are repaid on an amortized basis.

Combinations

Commercial bankers have been more innovative in recent years and have tried to tailor loans or combinations of loans to meet the specific needs of their borrowers. For example, banks frequently give revolving credit that is convertible into term loans. This affords flexibility to those who are planning to expand their physical facilities during the earlier years when the exact amount needed may vary, and a fixed commitment when the new plant and equipment are finally in place. Another type of arrangement, called "evergreen credit," grants the borrower a revolving credit or short-term loan with the option to convert the credit into a new revolving credit or a term loan at a particular time each year. A creative bank can devise many other combinations to meet the needs of its borrowers. Creativity in the construction of loan types may play an important part in the development of a bank's customer base.

LOAN TERMS

Although many loan terms have been discussed in reviewing the various loan types, it is desirable to consider them individually in order to gain better insight into their use. Eight such terms will be treated here.

Interest Rates

The contract rate of interest is the most obvious term of the loan, because it includes the payment for the actual use of funds. However, one must be careful when examining interest rates in a world of imperfect competition, because these rates will include much more than just the payment for the use of the money. The most important addition to the pure use of money is the payment to the bank for undertaking the risk of lending to a particular borrower. Second, some of the interest payment received by the bank results from the imperfect nature of the market in which the bank operates. That is, the interest return on a loan will be higher if the demand curve the bank is facing is downward sloping than if the curve were horizontal, holding risk and other payments constant. A third component that may be included in the contract rate of interest is the payment for the "insurance" contract, that is, for the guaranteed availability of funds if and when the borrower wants them. Use of explicit fees may reduce this component. In the opposite direction, the bank may charge a smaller rate of interest to a borrower who provides compensating balances as a part of the loan arrangement. However, these compensating balances may be used to reduce the loan rate on the use of funds[15] or the risk of the

---

[15] In modern terminology, in funding the loan the bank first purchases funds from the borrower and then goes to the market to purchase the needed money for the rest of the loan. See Chapter 10, on loan pricing.

loan,[16] or they may serve as a commitment fee for the future availability of funds.[17]

Thus, the precise interest rate charged by most banks today represents a "package" of payments. This is, of course, what those who want banks to "unbundle" services see as the problem with present pricing practices.[18] For example, when the borrower pays a rate on a line of credit, it does not know whether the interest rate it pays is just for the money it uses or includes an insurance fee for the potential future use of money. If an insurance fee is embedded in the contract rate, then those who borrow a lot—the "good" customers—actually subsidize those who borrow very little and hence are not considered to be good customers. Modern practice is moving in the direction of separating the items being purchased and pricing them explicitly, but banks can unbundle much faster than they already have.

In recent years, some innovative techniques have appeared in the application of loan rates. As the banks have experimented with longer-term loans and combinations of loan types, greater concern has arisen over the long-term nature of the loan and the possible adverse movements in the general level of interest rates. Banks have, therefore, responded by using variable-rate loans. Since 1970, major U.S. banks have used floating rates on almost all corporate loans. In order to provide some protection to borrowers, they have experimented with "collars," placing limits on the maximum or minimum levels the loan rate on an individual loan can reach. Another new gimmick has been the "cap rate" loan. On "cap" loans, the interest rate is allowed to float, but as the loans mature the total interest paid is computed against the amount borrowed; if that exceeds a "cap" rate that is set relative to existing bond rates, the excess interest cost is refunded to the borrower. The borrower's cost could, however, be lower than the cap rate. "Step rates," allowing for graduated markups over prime, have also been used to encourage different types of loans and also to protect the bank against possibly rising interest rates.

Variable-rate techniques have arisen because bank asset portfolios have carried longer maturities than liability portfolios. Variable rates have

---

[16] Because it raises the covariance between assets and liabilities. This is discussed in Chapter 3.

[17] J. M. Guttentag and R. G. Davis, "Compensating Balances," in *Essays in Money and Credit* (Federal Reserve Bank of New York, 1964).

[18] See L. L. Bryan, "Put a Price on Credit Lines," *The Bankers Magazine* (Summer 1974); L. L. Bryan and S. G. Clark, *Unbundling Full Service Banking* (Boston: Harcomm Associates, 1973).

the effect of "shortening" asset maturities, because the loan rate can change over much shorter periods of time than the loan maturity would allow. An alternative approach is to try to "match" the maturity of liabilities with the maturity of a fixed-rate loan. This locks in a given spread or gap between the interest rate the bank earns on the loan and the interest rate it pays for the money it uses to fund the loan.[19]

Fees

Explicit fees have a relatively long history in the banking industry. However, they have been used much more frequently since the early 1970s as a response to the large number of revolving credit arrangements established in the late 1960s by firms attempting to guarantee their sources of funds in preparation for future periods of tight money. These lines were almost costless to the potential borrowers because no fees existed, and compensating balances, at that time, were based on the average amount borrowed. Thus, if nothing was borrowed, no balances were required and yet the firm had borrowing power up to the maximum amount of the commitment. In addition to changing the manner in which compensating balance requirements were computed, banks began assessing commitment fees or usage fees to raise the cost to these firms. Thus, these fees represent payments for the cost to the bank of being liquid enough itself to honor the line of credit if it is drawn on some time in the future. If priced correctly, the fees would discourage firms from obtaining more commitments than are economically justifiable. Furthermore, an explicit charge for these "insurance" services is consistent with the argument for unbundling.

Compensating Balances

As implied earlier, compensating balances have been collected as payment for various services provided in the lending relationship. They are a payment in the sense that their presence in the bank reduces the cost that would otherwise be incurred in funding the loan, and also because they are funds over and above what the bank would otherwise have and thus can be invested at the market rate of interest.

[19] Two references to this type of financing are A. Dill and G. Gaffney, "The Effects and Implementation of Spread Management Banking," *The Journal of Commercial Bank Lending* (April 1975), pp. 38–45, and D. C. Cates, "Interest Sensitivity in Banking," *The Bankers Magazine* (January–February 1978), pp. 23–27.

A compensating balance can also be considered a form of collateral that reduces the riskiness of the loan, if a borrower does not increase its loan usage from the bank. If, as expected, a firm that maintains deposits at a bank will also borrow from the bank, the firm's funds will be on hand and may be applied to the bank to pay off the loan if the need is felt.[20]

The balances may also be considered a source of funds to support the loan. If balances are computed on the average loan of the customer, the balances will increase as the actual amount borrowed increases and fall when the loan quantity falls. Since the bank would have to buy more funds or sell another asset to support a larger loan amount, the bank either saves money by not having to borrow these funds or continues to earn interest on its existing assets. Thus, the compensating balances reduce the cost of obtaining more funds.

Finally, a compensating balance may be considered a payment for the bank's willingness to provide funds when the firm needs them. If balance requirements are set at an absolute amount or as a percentage of the total commitment, the assumption is that a cost is incurred that is not simply for the loan of the funds. Thus, a compensating balance may be considered an "insurance fee" or a "commitment fee."

Collateral

In most cases, unless the credit rating of the firm or the purpose of the loan makes it unnecessary, commercial banks prefer to have their loans secured. Although they really do not want to take ownership of collateral, collateral does provide some assurance that the loan will be repaid. Second, the borrower does lose a part of its ability to produce or function if the bank takes over its assets. This might prevent it from continuing to be a going concern and hence encourage it to meet its obligation. Finally, asking for security places a limit on the amount the firm can borrow from the bank and from others. That is, if the bank does not use the asset being financed as collateral, the borrower can use it as collateral for further borrowing elsewhere. In all cases, the bank tries to protect the asset values it carries on its balance sheet either by having a lien on something tangible it could sell, by encouraging repayment, or by limiting the additional debt the borrower can secure.

---

[20] It should be remembered that this was described earlier in terms of the covariance of the loan and a liability account. The net effect was that the compensating balance reduced the riskiness of the loan to the bank, and hence the bank was willing to charge a lower loan rate.

Maturity

One of the major principles of bank lending is that the purpose for which the loan is used should contain within it the time period needed to repay the loan. In other words, loan maturities should never exceed the life of the assets financed by the loans. Temporary but recurring needs can be handled with some kind of credit line, whereas "permanent" working capital needs or fixed asset purchases require a longer payoff period.

Repayment

Using a very similar argument, bankers say that the schedule of re-payments should also relate to the purpose for which the funds are being used. A seasonal buildup in inventories may be financed with a line of credit, with loans repaid as inventory levels are reduced. Lines of credit need to be "cleaned up" at least once a year; otherwise, it would seem that some permanent needs were being financed.

A term loan used to buy a fixed asset generates cash over the lifetime of the asset. Payment on term loans should be made periodically, therefore, as cash flows into the firm. A loan expected to be refinanced may be amortized as cash is received, but the contract may include a "balloon payment" at the end, the amount the borrower hopes to refinance. This is basically the idea behind bankers declaring that all loans should be "self-liquidating": They should carry within their uses the means of repayment.

Loan Commitments

A loan commitment is the total amount of credit the borrower can receive. The amounts loaned or committed, therefore, must also bear a relationship to use or need: The bank does not want to lend money to a firm for purposes that are not consistent with the type of loans the bank offers. Commitments on lines should change as the borrower's need changes. In practice, apparently, banks do not closely follow this rule. It has been estimated that during times of adequate credit availability, lines are only 25 to 30 percent used; in periods of tight credit, this figure moves to 50 to 60 percent. Part of the problem is that borrowers want to have more funds committed than they expect to use because this protects them from uncertainties. However, banks should try to control the extension of lines not only to protect themselves during periods of credit restraint but also to protect themselves from firms using lines for purposes for which they were not originally intended.

Loan Covenants

As maturities have become extended, commercial banks have increasingly written into agreements terms to strengthen their present and future positions. These covenants include restrictions on issuing other debt or stock and limitations on asset sales, mergers and acquisitions, dividends, capital expenditures, and salaries, among other things. In this way the bank uses its lending position in an effort to secure its creditor position in the future.

REVIEW QUESTIONS

1. Net yields should be used in the bank's annual plan, and not gross yields. Why?
2. How do you reconcile the long-run plan, which is usually determined by a trend, with the annual plan, which has to take the credit cycle into account? What assumptions about credit cycles are incorporated into the long-run plan?
3. In its annual planning, is a bank a rate setter or a quantity setter? Does it make any difference which it is?
4. In what ways is the technique of allocating capital better than concentrating on assets and return on assets for achieving a desired portfolio composition and capital structure?
5. Who is better able to forecast loan demand, the head of the lending department or a bank economist? Who is better able to forecast deposit levels?
6. Should a bank change its customer base in the annual planning exercise? If a bank stops lending to construction firms—that is, if it completely rations their loans—does this mean that it is changing its customer base?

7. Should a bank aim at hitting its target rate of return every year? What will stockholders want the bank to do? What will investors in the stock market want the bank to do?
8. How can the bank control the riskiness of its loan portfolio in the annual plan?
9. "The purpose of the loan should define the type of loan a bank makes." Is this true? Explain.
10. How does a bank decide whether or not to ration some borrowers? What kinds of information should management seek?

APPENDIX
Forecasting Interest Rates and Bank Reserves

In planning its loan portfolio, the management of a commercial bank needs information not only on loan demands, but also on interest rates and the availability of bank reserves. In this appendix a closer look is taken at forecasting interest rates and bank reserves.

Forecasting interest rates is important for two reasons. First, banks need an estimate of market levels in order to be able to set the prime rate with respect to open-market rates. Unless the prime rate is set correctly with respect to the market, the bank will not only have too much or too little prime loan demand, owing to the competitiveness of the prime loan market, but, because most other loan rates are set by markups over the prime rate, it will find its entire pricing scheme out of line. This may cause the intertemporal balance of the bank to be something other than desired.

The second reason for forecasting interest rates is to get some idea of interest rate spreads. Since the bank's profitability depends on the spread it earns between what it pays for funds and what it can lend them out at, an idea of future spreads will help in profit and tax planning. In fact, many bankers feel that forecasting interest rate spreads is more important than forecasting interest rate levels. Spread forecasts enable the bank to rearrange its portfolio to achieve earnings targets, whereas rate levels are not so helpful unless translated into relative rates.

Forecasting bank reserves is another important task; as pointed out earlier, banks should be more concerned about quantity movements than about interest rate movements. Available reserves (along with reserve requirements) are the constraint on the ability of the banking system to expand. A recent study has shown that the expansion of bank credit depends heavily on what bankers expect to happen to bank reserves.[1]

A bank should not adjust immediately to changes in bank reserves, because some changes are merely temporary. For example, a seasonal swing in float may increase reserves, but this is a temporary movement that will be reversed in the near future. Operating transactions of the

---

[1] J. M. Mason, R. J. Rogalski, and J. D. Vinso, "Expectations, Commercial Bank Adjustment, and the Performance of the Monetary Aggregates." Working Paper, The Rodney White Center for Financial Research, The University of Pennsylvania, 1978.

Federal Reserve may cause a temporary increase or decline that may be offset at a later date. The bank must attempt to distinguish between temporary shifts in its reserve position and changes that are permanent and reflect a new "dynamic" posture of the central bank.

Movements in bank credit and demand deposits do not always coincide. There are two ways the bank may break the link between these two items: discount borrowings from the Federal Reserve[2] and time accounts.[3] Thus, in forecasting reserves, the bank analyst should not expect that bank credit and the demand deposits of the bank will always move together. However, if reserve levels change, these other items will eventually change as well.

There does not seem to be a direct relationship between interest rates and aggregate bank reserves. However, a causal relationship apparently does exist between these two variables and two other reserve measures. Once understood, this relationship can help the bank to forecast both of the first two items.

There is empirical evidence that variations in free reserves, which are defined as the excess reserves of the banking system less member bank borrowings from the Federal Reserve, affect the federal funds rate.[4] When the Federal Reserve attempts to tighten credit, for example, the first thing to happen is that the excess reserves in the banking system decline. Either banks reduce their own excess reserve positions or they borrow excess reserves from other banks through the federal funds market. The additional demand coupled with a smaller supply of excess reserves in the federal funds market tends to put upward pressure on the federal funds rate.

As the federal funds rate goes up, the Federal Reserve generally maintains the existing discount rate, thus creating a larger spread between the cost of money in the open market and that at the discount window. This gives member banks incentive to obtain funds from the discount window. There is, therefore, a more contemporaneous movement in member bank borrowings and the federal funds rate than between free reserves and these other two items. In fact, there is a definite time lag between free reserves and member bank borrowing and the federal funds rate.

[2] The study by Mason et al. cited in footnote 1 emphasized this point.

[3] A study that concentrates on this aspect of reserve forecasting is B. M. Friedman and K. C. Froewiss, "Bank Behavior in the Brunner-Meltzer Model," *Journal of Monetary Economics* (April 1977), pp. 163–78.

[4] The results reported here are from D. A. Pierce, "Relationships—and the Lack Thereof—Between Economic Time Series, with Special Reference to Money and Interest Rates," *Journal of the American Statistical Association* (March 1977), p. 17.

This result appears to be symmetrical. That is, when the Federal Reserve loosens up, the first effect is on free reserves, followed by movements again in member bank borrowings and in the federal funds rate. Interested readers can work out the mechanism for this adjustment themselves.

There is also a connection between free reserves and nonborrowed reserves or the nonborrowed monetary base. Nonborrowed reserves are the basic raw materials of the banking industry, for they represent the unencumbered reserves the banking system has available to it to expand deposits and loans. The nonborrowed monetary base is composed of nonborrowed reserves and currency outside the banking system. Empirical studies have shown, however, that nonborrowed reserves are the only component that needs to be discussed because all the measurable variation in the nonborrowed monetary base seems to be contained in nonborrowed reserves. The reason for this is that the currency follows no distinguishable pattern; that is, changes in currency are random and convey no relevant information for economic analysis.[5] Therefore, it is only necessary to examine movements in nonborrowed reserves to obtain all the information contained in either nonborrowed reserves or the nonborrowed monetary base.

Free reserves seem to bear a very strong causal relationship to nonborrowed reserves. If free reserves begin to decline, this is a good indication that nonborrowed reserves will either experience slower rates of growth in the future or begin to decline absolutely. The reverse is also true for an increase in free reserves.

Thus, the basic conclusion that can be drawn from the preceding discussion is that movements in very short-term interest rates and movements in reserve aggregates can be forecast if the bank is capable of forecasting the direction of free reserves. Note that the *level* of free reserves is not precisely under the control of the Federal Reserve, because excess reserves depend on the portfolio decisions of the banking industry. However, the *short-run direction* of free reserves is almost certainly under the control of the Federal Reserve. Thus, the *direction* of movements in the federal funds rate and nonborrowed reserves can be surmised by forecasting the *direction* in which the Federal Reserve is aiming to move free reserves.

The bank's next concern is with the relationship between the federal funds rate and other market interest rates. Studies have shown that there is a very strong contemporaneous relationship between all market rates of

---

[5] This was found to be true by both Pierce, "Relationships Between Economic Time Series," p. 18, and Mason et al., "Expectations."

interest;[6] that is, adjustments take place in a time period no longer than one month, often in as little as a week. To put it simply, when the short-term rate moves, all rates move, but those associated with longer maturities move much less than those associated with shorter maturities.[7] Thus, an upward movement of the federal funds rate will be translated very rapidly to other market rates. Rates on items that are very close in maturity will show similar changes. Thus, it can be expected that the three-month Treasury bill will respond rapidly and in similar magnitude to the change in the federal funds rate; the commercial paper rate and the rate on negotiable certificates of deposit will also respond rapidly.

The information contained in the changes in free reserves will. give very clear direction to the movements expected in rates that are very important to commercial bank operations.

What about other factors that may have an impact on interest rates and reserves? Two that are particularly important are the rate of economic activity and the expected rate of inflation. For example, an increase in economic activity is expected to increase the demand for money balances to satisfy transaction needs, which will squeeze liquidity positions and put upward pressure on interest rates. Alternatively, nominal interest rates are assumed to be composed of an expected real rate of return, which is determined by full-employment economic activity, and a price expectations amount. If inflation is expected to worsen, then nominal interest rates will rise, expected real rates remaining constant.

Over the longer run these factors are an important determinant of interest rates. Real economic activity has a particularly strong and regular effect on the demand for money.[8] However, the relationship in periods shorter than a quarter is less close.

Inflationary expectations have also been shown to have an important influence on the level of interest rates, but the relationship appears to have been quite unstable and irregular.[9] This may be due to the fact that people

---

[6] Of particular interest here are, once again, Pierce, "Relationships Between Economic Time Series," p. 17; and also R. H. Cramer and R. B. Miller, "Dynamic Modeling of Multivariate Time Series for Use in Bank Analysis," *Journal of Money, Credit, and Banking* (February 1976), pp. 85–96, and J. R. Brick and H. E. Thompson, "Time Series Analysis of Interest Rates: Some Additional Evidence," *The Journal of Finance* (March 1978), pp. 93–103. For further references, see the bibliography of the Brick and Thompson article.

[7] See Brick and Thompson, "Time Series Analysis," p. 99.

[8] S. M. Goldfeld, "The Demand for Money Revisited," *Brookings Papers on Economic Activity*, 1973:3, pp. 577–646.

[9] For evidence on this, see Brick and Thompson, "Time Series Analysis," p. 101, and T. F. Cargill and R. A. Meyer, "Intertemporal Stability and the Relationship Between Interest Rates and Price Changes," *The Journal of Finance* (September 1977), pp. 1001–1016.

respond to inflation differently in different time periods, depending on their current and past economic history. The weak relationship may also be due to the inability of researchers to model and measure inflationary expectations adequately.

In either case, the controlling factor over interest rates in the short run appears to be the Federal Reserve System. Even though economic activity or inflationary expectations may be exerting an upward push on interest rates, if the Federal Reserve wants to fight this pressure, it can control short-term rates indefinitely. However, it can do so only at the cost of increasing bank reserves more and more rapidly.

These additional pressures on interest rates must be incorporated into any forecast of interest rates and reserves, because the forces themselves or the Federal Reserve's response to them will bring about changes in either interest rates or the rate of growth of reserves. Either result has important implications, not only for current bank operations but also for the future environment in which the bank will be operating.

If interest rates are allowed to rise with economic activity or inflationary expectations, then some investment expenditures, both durable goods for business and consumer durable goods, will be choked off and economic growth will be slowed. If the Federal Reserve fights the pressure on interest rates by supplying reserves, then the resulting increase in the money supply will lead to greater economic activity or inflationary pressures in the future. In either case, the Federal Reserve's response will foreshadow future economic events.

The question to be asked now is, Which is it more important for the bank to forecast, interest rates or reserve measures? It is the author's opinion that the forecasting of reserve movements is perhaps the most important forecasting the bank can do. Reserves are the raw materials of bank expansion: Without adequate reserve growth the banking system becomes continuously pressed for funds to meet loan demands. If the Federal Reserve is going to tighten up or loosen up on credit, it will do so by altering the reserves available to the banking system. Thus, the ability of the banking system and the individual bank to grow and adjust depends on the availability of reserves.

On the other hand, banks usually have adequate spreads built into their markets because of the imperfectly competitive nature of their loan and deposit markets. The narrower spreads the banks face under liability-management conditions appear to argue against this, but the reader must remember the argument developed in Chapter 2, which showed that a bank would not be maximizing its profits if it did not take advantage of the opportunities offered under liability-management conditions.[10] If the bank is flexible in moving its prime rate with the market, taking into account the direction in which interest rates are expected to move, then it will generally be relatively successful.

[10] The liability-management bank may even operate at negative spreads in some markets during tight money periods, but this would represent a time when the cost of liabilities was greater than expected. If this situation were not a result of the potential variability of interest rates, then the banks would not be as reliant on management of their liabilities as they have been. Remember that in the case of liability management a potential variation of interest rates is not an important risk to the bank. If banks can still buy all the funds they need at the going rate, they will be able to live with the situation. This result was derived in Chapter 2.

9

Evaluation of the Borrower Before Lending

The evaluation of the potential borrower should not be restricted to a credit analysis of the firm's riskiness. Much more is involved, and to price the borrower correctly, with appropriate contract rate, fees, and terms, the bank must be able to identify the multiple characteristics that make up any one loan customer. Risk is only one of these characteristics.

Essentially, every customer is a composite of characteristics. If it is assumed that the bank has a matrix of various borrower and loan types, the objective of evaluating the borrower is to determine its correct classification—its appropriate cell in the bank's matrix of borrower classes and loan types.

What information does the bank need and where can it get it? In the following pages an attempt is made to answer these questions. The theory of loan classification presented in earlier chapters will be essential to the development of the material discussed here.

One word of caution: This is not a chapter on how to conduct a credit check on a potential borrower or how to set up and organize a credit department. There are many sources that explain these procedures.[1] As

[1] D. A. Hayes, *Bank Lending Policies* (Ann Arbor: The University of Michigan Press, 1977), Chapter 12. E. W. Reed, R. V. Cotter, E. K. Gill, and R. K. Smith, *Commercial Banking*

described earlier, one task of the bank is to categorize borrowers into different loan classes. The student of financial management should be interested in the economic rationale for making such choices. Distinctions based on risk are but one basis of choice; analysis is the means of making this type of distinction.

IS THE APPLICANT A BANK CUSTOMER?

The first thing that must be checked when a loan officer receives a loan application is whether or not the potential borrower is a customer. If the applicant has previously borrowed from the bank, the loan officer proceeds to an analysis of the application. If not, the loan officer must determine whether or not the applicant is likely to become a good customer. Since good customers are vital to the bank's success, better credit terms will be given to a good customer than to someone who contributes less to the bank either in quantity or steadiness of loan demand or as a user of other bank services.

Lending to an Established Customer

If the applicant has borrowed from the bank before, the bank already has an internal record of the applicant's credit rating, previous loan amounts and terms, repayment habits, and use of other bank services. Larger firms may provide a steady flow of information to the bank, such as periodic balance sheets and income statements, pro forma balance sheets and income statements, and other information pertinent to the firm and the industry. A small borrower or one that borrows infrequently from the bank may not be required to submit this additional information.

The loan officer may or may not, therefore, run a credit check on the customer, depending on the circumstances. For example, if an inexperienced loan officer runs a credit check on a "good" customer, the firm's management may be offended and take its business elsewhere. On the other hand, if it seems possible that the credit check could bring about an improvement in the firm's credit rating, and hence a lower interest cost, the customer may be very willing to commit itself to such an examination.

Besides the fact that the bank may already have a good record on the

(Englewood Cliffs, N.J.: Prentice-Hall, 1976), Chapters 9 and 10. R. J. Robinson, *The Management of Bank Funds* (New York: McGraw-Hill, 1962), Chapters 8 and 9.

applicant, the bank also has other information of a very desirable nature. First, it has a history of the customer's payment habits. Most customers protect their borrowing power with the bank, because it is their most important source of credit. Therefore, if a payment record is at all suspicious, the bank has some reason to worry. If the firm has borrowed extensively in the past, questionable payment habits will readily show up.

The quantity of funds the firm has borrowed in the past can be used as a guide to its probable future demand. Since loans are a bank's main source of revenue, it is important to be able to judge what future demand may be.

Previous experience, however, may not be an adequate guide. The conditions facing the firm may have changed, and the customer may intend or need to borrow more in the future. This is something the loan officer must attempt to determine.

The historical record of borrowing may also provide information about how steady the customer's loan demand will be. Low variance of borrowing is a desirable trait in a borrower. Again, the loan officer should seek hints as to changes in behavior with regard to this characteristic.

Finally, the officer needs to have information pertaining to the other services the firm uses and the fees charged for them. This is necessary for two reasons. First, the officer wants to assess the contribution these services make to the bank or to the customer.[2] Since most profitability analysis systems lump the cost of these services into the evaluation of the borrower *after* the loan is made, the loan officer must be careful to incorporate them into the pricing agreements *before* the loan is made. There is no reason why the provision of these services should not be profitable.

Second, the bank loan officer may be able to cross-sell some other services that were unknown to the customer or that are new to the bank. For example, many banks have added cash management programs to the services offered their customers, and the customer may have a strong need for such a program. The intelligent loan officer will be constantly on the lookout for the needs of customers and ways in which the bank can service these needs, preferably at a profit.

The fact that an applicant has borrowed at the bank before does not mean that the arrangements it had were as desirable as possible for it or for the bank. However, a long-time customer generally will find it easier to get accommodations from a bank in which it has built up a substantial record of experience.

---

[2] Providing services at less than cost is one way banks have competed for customers. For more on this, see D. Hodgman, *Commercial Bank Loan and Investment Policy* (Champaign, Ill.: University of Illinois Press, 1963).

Evaluating a New Applicant

If the applicant has not borrowed or deposited at the bank before, the loan officer must make some effort to determine the contribution the applicant will make to the future performance of the bank. For example: Is it likely that the loan will be a one-time arrangement? Is the potential borrower dissatisfied with the bank it has been dealing with, so there is some likelihood that it will become a good customer of this bank? Is the applicant only looking for an "insurance" line of credit to protect its liquidity during periods of credit restraint, and not very likely to become a steady customer? Is the applicant a new company, just getting started and hopeful of setting up a relationship with the bank that will benefit both borrower and lender over the future?

Loan officers must keep these questions in mind when they begin to analyze credit applicants. The factors the loan officer looks for are no different from the criteria used for defining a "good" customer: future loan demand and steadiness of that demand.

The important thing to remember is that the bank values more demand, steady demand, and a positive return on its other services. The loan officer should be willing to grant concessions in the form of a lower interest rate or better terms to induce the applicant to do business with the bank. Thus, the current yield on a loan to a potential "customer" will be lower than it would be to an applicant that does not seem as promising. Concessions made to attract desirable borrowers are as good a reason for a loan to be underpriced as any. However, it is up to the loan officer to justify the favorable terms on which the loan is granted. Thus, the loan officer must try to establish the value of the applicant's business at an early stage of the relationship.

ANALYSIS OF RISK

The bank personnel who analyze the application of a potential borrower spend the greater part of their time and effort analyzing the riskiness of the applicant. Most banks devote many hours to collecting data on the firm, spreading and analyzing statements, and studying industry trends, what other firms in the industry are doing, and how the firm or its industry is being affected by the local, regional, or national economy. The effort has primarily been to establish which risk class a firm is to be placed in.

Even though tremendous technological advances have been made in many other areas of banking, this is one area in which things are done much as they were in the past. Efforts have been made to construct credit scoring techniques,[3] but these techniques have not apparently gained wide usage in the industry.

The reason credit scoring techniques have not been used more frequently in practice is that the techniques developed to date seem to work best on the major firms in mature industries. This is because of the general stability and regularity of these firms and industries. However, a large proportion of the bank lending in this country is to firms that are neither large nor very creditworthy and that are also in very unstable industries. The future of a firm is always uncertain, and it is not altogether clear what the historical records of the firm mean in relationship to its future.

Thus, analysis of risk consists in examining three items: the firm's immediate industrial environment, management capabilities, and the firm's general economic environment.

1. The nature of the industry or industries in which the firm operates. The characteristics of the industry or industries often are overriding factors in the determination of firm behavior and performance. Are there large seasonal patterns? Do the firms in the industry or industries rely on specialized sources of raw materials or energy? Is the firm susceptible to cyclical influences? These factors help to define or at least put constraints on the individual choices of a firm. That is, the industry within which a firm operates has its own riskiness.

2. The ability of the firm's management. Is the firm doing better or worse than others operating in the same industry or industries, or is it achieving the industry average? This is where most of the statement analysis comes in. What can the bank determine from historical data or from pro forma data about the management capabilities of the firm? The results of this analysis are not always clear-cut. There might be conflicting evidence on the balance sheet: too high a current ratio, too low a leverage factor. The balance sheet data may be different from industry standards and yet the firm may be very adequately managed. Uncertainties such as these make a large number of risk classes impractical. Banks are simply not able to divide borrowers finely on the basis of risk; there are too many gray areas. This is one reason that credit scoring techniques have never been very popular.

This analysis of credit scoring brings up another important part of the analysis process. Lending is, in a sense, a function of people. The owners of the bank, as well as the people within the bank, determine what degree

[3] See Y. E. Orgler, *Analytical Methods in Loan Evaluation* (Lexington, Mass.: Lexington Books, 1975), particularly Chapter 4.

of risk is acceptable to the bank. But part of determining the creditworthiness or risk class of many borrowers is knowing the people who are doing the borrowing. Hence, personal calls are an extremely important part of commercial lending. Getting to know customers—management teams and their strengths and weaknesses, potential shortfalls, and potential management succession problems—is part of really understanding the ability of the firm to meet its obligations.

3. The relationship of the industry or industries of the applicant to other industries and to local, regional, national, and international factors. In a sense, the analyst is trying to obtain information on the covariance of the potential customer with the market or with economic activity. A bank that deals mostly in farm loans may be very susceptible to seasonal swings in both deposits and loans; in most cases the swings do not occur at the same time. If the bank could also become involved with, say, the food processing industry, it might be able to offset some of the variance in loan demand or deposit supply by industry diversification. Thus, the analysis of the firm must take account of how the firm's borrowing and lending activity will mesh with that of the bank's other customers.

To put it in technical terms, the risk analysis of the firm includes determining as well as possible the variance of loans due to default risk (variance due to unsteady demand has been discussed) and the covariance of the applicant with other potential borrowers in the bank's loan portfolio. Whereas this is necessary information for any type of lending institution, it is of particular importance to commercial banks because of the imperfectly competitive nature of many of the markets in which the bank operates.

PURPOSE OF THE LOAN

The bank is interested in the purpose of the loan because the use to which the borrowed funds are to be put usually defines both the means of repayment and the collateral required against the loan. In banking terms, loans should generally be "self-liquidating" in the sense that the working down of the assets financed by the loan should be capable of repaying the loan. For example, the seasonal loan used to finance inventories should be paid off as the inventories are sold.

Finding out the purpose of the loan allows the loan officer to determine the type of loan needed by the borrower,[4] whether the loan is consis-

---

[4] For the different types of loans, see Chapter 8.

tent with bank policy (the bank may not be willing to give the appropriate loans, because of current economic conditions or because it never gives that type of loan), and whether the firm is using the funds for an appropriate reason. Furthermore, it can be determined whether or not the assets financed can be used as collateral. The farmer borrowing to plant a crop has nothing initially to pledge against the loan; a toy manufacturer has inventories to pledge while it is building up its stock of toys for the Christmas season. Conceptually, different loan purposes make for different loan classes, and hence this information is very necessary for the correct pricing of a customer and for optimal loan portfolio construction.

ELASTICITY OF DEMAND

Theoretically, the elasticity of demand is required for the correct pricing of a borrower. Practically, the banks have little or no idea about elasticities, with perhaps the exception of one class of loans. Even this exception may not hold for smaller banks. Rules of thumb have been created to help banks operate, however imperfectly, in this world of incomplete information. As described earlier, these rules of thumb have generally taken the form of markups over prime.

Even though a bank does not estimate the elasticity of demand for particular loan classes, and for that matter could not realistically estimate it even if it tried, some effort is made to get information that contains implications about elasticities.

For example, a customer that is a national firm and an excellent credit risk will, in all probability, get better terms on a loan than a customer that is a local firm and has the same credit rating. Technically, the reason is that the national firm has a more elastic demand for funds than the local firm. An alternative way of expressing the situation is that the national firm has more alternative sources of funds.

Moreover, the demand for loans is a derived demand for the financing of the production process. The characteristics of the firm or industry will often have a substantial effect on the elasticity of the demand curve for loans. Thus, the demand for loans to farmers will be quite inelastic because the production process causes farmers to borrow at one or two specific times every year. Borrowing for the construction of residential housing may be bunched seasonally or, since construction is one of the industries most severely hit by stringent credit conditions, cyclically. Firms whose borrowing is more regularly spread throughout the year may be able to postpone some types of borrowing by slowing production processes and speeding up collections throughout the year. Hence, their demand for funds will be more elastic.

Although somewhat ambiguous and indefinite, this information is useful and should be funneled into the lending and pricing process by the loan officer.

DETERMINATION OF YIELD

All the information collected so far is enough to determine the loan class of the applicant, i.e., which cell it belongs to in the matrix of borrower characteristics. If the bank has adequately done its homework on the risk-return construction of its loan portfolio, it should now be possible to determine the required yield for the borrower. The loan officer, therefore, goes to his or her source of target yields and selects the one appropriate for the customer under review.

DETERMINATION OF TERMS

More will be said in the next section on the precise combination of terms needed to give the bank its required yield. However, the good loan officer should be constantly on the alert to work out arrangements that are helpful to the customer. For example, a firm that keeps smaller balances at the bank may prefer a higher loan rate to keeping larger compensating balances on hand. On the other hand, the customer may wish to keep larger balances rather than pay a facility fee for the line.

Some arrangements could be helpful to the bank. For example, a customer that does not actively use its compensating balance could be induced to hold some of its balances in non-interest-bearing or low-interest-bearing time deposits. The bank could even split the opportunity cost of the released reserves with the customer; the bank could increase its yield on the customer relationship while the effective cost of the relationship to the borrower would be reduced.

The point of this is that the creative loan officer, in evaluating customers' needs and demands, must use this evaluation not only to protect the bank and earn a higher return but also to help customers better solve their own problems. Providing this help may have as great a long-run impact on customer borrowing as the availability of funds. To the economist, providing these services without cost is a way of granting concessions or underpricing a loan. This activity is, of course, consistent with establishing greater future loan demand or steadier loan demand.

UNBUNDLING

Much has been written about whether or not banks should unbundle loans and services.[5] In unbundling, the loan officer or analyst determines exactly what the borrower is receiving and then prices each facet of the relationship so as to earn a profit for the bank. That is, each service offered must be independently profitable.

If banks unbundle services, some things will be easier for the loan officer and some things more difficult. Unbundling will eliminate the need for loan officers to get involved in matters over which they have no control, such as payroll services and trustee services. Whereas the loan officer may arrange for the customer to be provided with these services, their costing and pricing will be entirely out of the officer's hands.

On the other hand, the loan officer will need to know precisely which services each customer is using (buying) and which it is not. The most important determination here is between the actual amount of money borrowed and the "insurance" contract for future availability of loans. For example, if a customer has a line of credit that appears to the loan officer to be far out of line with its needs, the loan officer should raise the commitment fee on the line to encourage the customer to seek a smaller commitment. The loan officer who is unbundling services must be correct in his or her analysis, or customers will be lost to banks that are pricing their relationships more correctly.

For illustrative purposes, the distinction between bundling and unbundling has been more finely drawn than the reader will find in practice. However, if banks do make a greater effort to unbundle services, better cost accounting systems and loan analysis procedures will have to be developed. This will not necessarily be bad for borrowers, because it may lead to better, more accurate pricing of loans and services.

SUMMARY

The evaluation of the borrower must help the loan officer to make correct decisions about the contribution the customer will make to the bank and

---

[5] L. L. Bryan and S. G. Clark, *Unbundling Full Service Banking* (Boston: Harcomm Associates, 1973).

the risk to which it will expose the bank. Whether or not the bank unbundles services, the officer must be aware of the economics of each individual borrower, the borrower's potential loan demand, the stability of demand, the risk of the borrower, both systematic and unsystematic, and the exact conditions of repayment and protection the bank is receiving. Then loan officers must be sure that they understand how they are pricing the customer and whether the customer's "price" is consistent with its "cost." Only in this way can a bank hope to prosper and grow.

REVIEW QUESTIONS

1. Why is it difficult for banks to estimate the elasticity of demand of borrowers?
2. How can a bank tell whether or not a potential borrower will become a good customer? What types of information should the bank look for?
3. An established customer generally tends to pay off the bank before it pays off other creditors. Why? Is this rational?
4. What can accounting ratios tell loan officers about the riskiness of a borrower?
5. Calling on businesses is an important part of a loan officer's duties. How would you explain this activity in terms of the bank model developed in earlier chapters?
6. Why is it important for a loan officer to determine whether a loan applicant is a customer before knowing the purpose of the loan?
7. Why might a customer resent a credit check?

APPENDIX

Leasing

The leasing decision, for both the bank and its customers, is very much like the borrowing decision. In the borrowing decision the customer purchases the capital good and then, to avoid having its financial resources tied up by the purchase, or because its own funds are insufficient, enters into a financing arrangement with the bank. For the borrower, the decision to borrow is justified if the project bears a positive net present value. For the lender (the bank), the loan is also justified by a positive net present value or by an interest return that exceeds the bank's interest expense on the funds it invests in the loan.

The leasing decision also depends on positive net present values, but in this instance the bank purchases the asset and then leases it to the customer. Note that the bank cannot, technically, initiate the transaction. The customer, the lessee, must request that the bank, the lessor, purchase the asset and then lease it. This makes the transaction like a loan; the borrower approaches the lender rather than the other way around.

The lessee has a cash flow from its use of the leased asset, but it also has a series of lease payments that must be subtracted from the cash flow. A positive net present value again is a necessary condition for a profitable choice. When the net present value of the leasing opportunity exceeds the net present value of the loan alternative, it is not only worthwhile for the firm to obtain the asset or the use of the asset but also appropriate to finance the asset by means of a lease.

For the bank, the decision is more like the borrowing decision of the firm. The leasing of the asset sets up a net cash flow of lease payment receipts for the bank. How the bank itself pays for the asset, of course, plays an important part in the value of the lease arrangement for the bank. Again, if the net present value of the two alternatives is positive and the lease alternative has the higher net present value, then the bank should choose to lease.

If the two types of arrangements are similar economically, then the question is: Why should one opportunity be favored over the other? The answer to this is that legal and accounting practices often dominate the decision. For example, the bank may be limited in the amount it can lend to a borrower (the legal lending limit constraint), and it may also be limited in the maturities it can offer. The borrower must then anticipate refinancing of the loan and a change in loan terms if the asset is to be financed by the bank.

In general, a lease can be made for a greater amount of funds, for a longer time periods, and for fixed terms, or at least terms in which changes are stated before the fact, so that the lessee can plan on the maximum changes if changes are expected. The firm achieves additional flexibility because, in general, it need not appropriate funds to acquire the asset and financing is available when the asset is needed. A business must often borrow various amounts by several different methods, such as the bank line, commercial paper, and the bond market, before it finally puts together a suitable financing package.

A second, perhaps more important, reason for choosing the lease arrangement is the distribution of tax benefits associated with the purchase of the asset. Whoever purchases the asset obtains not only the tax advantages of the depreciation attributable to the asset, usually at an accelerated rate, but also the use of the investment tax credit.[1] The investment tax credit is an immediate credit against taxes equivalent to a percentage of the purchase price of the asset. This is particularly valuable because of the time value of the credit.

The tax benefits have been especially important in large transactions when the lessee has no taxable income. This situation may occur when the borrower-lessee has a large loss carryover or is taking advantage of all available tax credits.[2] This may set up a "wedge" between the cost of the lease to the lessee and the return to the bank. The existence of this wedge may not change the position of the bank customer (that is, the customer may be indifferent between borrowing and leasing), but it may make the lease arrangement more profitable to the bank. In such cases the bank may make arrangements because after-tax returns, especially with a "good" customer, are raised by splitting the difference and charging the customer less than if it had just borrowed the money.

The "wedge" may be described in the following way: Whereas the bank computed the net present value of the alternatives in the previous example, it now should compute the internal rate of return for each opportunity. Thus, the potential customer will determine what its internal rate of return will be (a) if it purchases the asset and (b) if it leases the asset, and it will not lease the asset if the rate of return on the lease is below that of the

---

[1] This discussion ties in with the tax-planning portion of Chapter 6.

[2] In the past, a firm could use the shelter from the investment tax credit up to 50 percent of taxable income. Recently, proposals have been made to increase the amount of taxable income the tax credit can be applied to.

loan contract. The tax benefits of purchasing the asset will often lead to a higher rate of return from the borrowing alternative, but other factors may be important enough to override this choice.[3]

However, if there are no tax advantages to either, the firm may find that the internal rates of return on the two alternatives are relatively close. In that case, the bank's position may dominate the choice of method.

The bank, too, should determine its internal rate of return on each alternative. Which one will have the higher rate of return depends on several things. First, the lifetime of the loan must be compared with that of the lease, and the possibility of refinancing the loan must be considered in the decision. Second, the availability of other income must be considered. If the bank does not have other taxable income, the investment tax credit and accelerated depreciation will do it very little good. Third, the residual value of the asset must be estimated; this may play an important part in the return on the lease. Fourth, the expenses connected with each alternative must be determined. In general, the lease will be more expensive than the loan to originate and maintain, because of the legal expenses, sales expenses, and operational expenses associated with the leasing function. Finally, the internal rates of return for the loan case and the leasing alternative must be compared with the appropriate cost of capital.[4]

In general, if other taxable income is available, the rate of return to the bank on the lease will be greater than the rate of return on the loan. This is the "wedge" discussed earlier: It represents the difference in the returns on the two alternatives. Given the perceived difference in risk between the two, the bank could offer a lower cost on the lease arrangement and still receive a larger return than it could on a loan. If the customer has other taxable income, then the loan will be by far the better alternative and the bank could not make a sufficient concession in price to induce the customer to lease rather than borrow. However, if the customer does not have other taxable income, the bank can probably make it worthwhile to lease and both could benefit by the lease arrangement.[5]

[3] See Weston and Brigham, *Managerial Finance*, 6th ed. (Hinsdale, Ill.: Dryden, 1978), Chapter 15, for some reasons why the firm may not want to borrow even though that may initially seem the more profitable decision.

[4] This is a highly unsettled area in finance literature at the present time. The general argument is that leasing is more risky than straight lending, and hence the future cash flows of the lease must be discounted at a higher rate than those of the loan, or the internal rate of return on the lease must be higher than that on a loan because the cost of capital applicable to the lease is larger than the cost of capital related to the loan. The argument has not been satisfactorily resolved at the time of writing.

[5] The firm would benefit from the lower borrowing cost, and the bank would benefit from the higher rate of return. This double benefit is a subsidy given by the government to the

The bank must consider some subsidiary benefits of leasing that may affect it in the long run. One benefit is that leasing may increase its customer base. Adding a leasing operation to its other services might attract organizations that have not dealt with the bank previously. Leasing may also allow the bank to diversify its portfolio further and develop new areas in which to market products and services that were not previously available. These considerations may be very important in the bank's overall effort to expand and grow.

Regulatory officials, while recognizing the legitimate role of bank leasing activities, have attempted to keep the leasing arrangement as much like the loan relationship as possible. This is why banks cannot initiate a lease contract. The lessee, like a borrower, must approach the bank with a financing need. Regulators also limit types of contracts a bank may enter into in order to reduce the risk of leasing.[6]

Thus, banks and bank-affiliated leasing companies are limited to what are called "financial leases," which are noncancelable full-payout leases. The full price of the asset must be returned to the bank over the lifetime of the lease, and the early termination of the lease must meet certain criteria that eliminate the bank's exposure to risk. For example, in case of early termination, most financial leases force the lessee to pay an amount equal to or greater than the lessor's costs, including the cost of the leased asset during the base term of the lease. Most are also "net" leases, which require the lessee to pay all taxes, maintenance, insurance, and other necessary service costs of operating the asset. In other words, the lessee assumes all responsibilities of ownership.

Banks and bank affiliates are allowed to issue *leveraged leases,* whereby the bank puts up a portion of the cost of the asset and borrows the rest of the funds from one or more long-term lenders. The lessor receives an origination fee but must pay interest costs on the funds used to finance the asset. The benefits to the lessor are those of any leveraged arrangement— the possibility of leveraging itself into greater returns for the money it

---

private sector. If an economy were at full employment, there would be a welfare transfer between sectors depending on who bore the taxes and who received the ultimate benefits, the increase in net worth of the subsidy. If the economy were at less than full employment, there could be a net increase in welfare as the purchase of the asset led to more employment and higher real income.

[6] Banks are almost forbidden to enter into "real" contracts, such as stocks and real estate ownership. This is, of course, to protect the depositor. If prices declined and a bank owned real assets, the value of these assets would decline, threatening the solvency of the bank. Thus, banks have been limited to holding "nominal" assets (except for bank buildings), i.e., assets that are denominated in current dollar values like most loans, bonds, and bills.

contributes to the financing. In this case, the bank may put up only 20 to 40 percent of the cost of the asset, receive the lease payments, make use of the investment tax credit and accelerated depreciation, and have available for use the fees received for initiating the lease arrangement minus the interest cost of the debt. This results in substantial tax losses but large cash inflows in the early years of a lease contract, so that the bank has higher internal rates of return because of the timing of the deductions. The bank also assumes greater financial risks.

The choice of an appropriate organization to handle leasing business has been a difficult one for banks in recent years. The alternatives have been to put the leasing operation within the bank organization itself or to create a leasing affiliate associated with a holding company. At the beginning of the movement into the leasing business, the scale seemed to be more heavily weighted toward forming an affiliate of the holding company. The reasons are as follows:

1. The "double-leverage" argument for the holding company form of organization has been very persuasive.

2. A holding company affiliate often found it easier to do business in other states. For example, legal restrictions in one state might prohibit a bank from entering into a legal lease arrangement, so if a bank desired to create leases in many states, it was better to do it outside through a holding company.

3. A holding company affiliate can borrow from a bank or a group of banks to obtain funds for leases. It can also issue commercial paper to lend to its leasing affiliate. These opportunities may not always be so readily available to banks.

4. A leasing company will usually be subject to less regulation than a bank's leasing operations.

5. In the case of suits arising out of the use of leased property, the bank's assets will be better protected if the leasing operation is in the affiliate rather than in the bank.

6. Compensation may be a problem. Banks have typically paid relatively low salaries, but the situation is changing. To attract the necessary trained leasing personnel, the bank may have to pay salaries that would disrupt its salary structure.

Two factors militate against locating the leasing business in an affiliate. First, it is argued that the bank cannot provide as many resources to an affiliate as it could to a leasing organization within the bank because of the legal limit on what it can lend to another organization. This limit does not exist for bank funds transferred internally.

Second, banks do not transfer funds to a leasing affiliate at the same rate they transfer funds internally: An incremental cost is attached to lending to outside affiliates. Many banks have entered the leasing business in recent years and have placed their leasing operations within the bank to take advantage of the lower cost of funds. The number of participants in the industry has led to increased competition, which has put substantial pressure on the margins of bank-affiliated leasing companies. To be able to compete with the banks, the leasing companies have had to reduce their cost of borrowed funds. This has forced some banks—Citicorp Leasing is a notable example—to shift their holding company subsidiary to their lead bank. Thus, there has been a trend toward more bank-operated leasing business and less bank-affiliate leasing.

If the bank is to reap the benefits of ownership for tax purposes, the lease must be legally structured as a true lease. If it is not, the IRS will consider that the property has been sold to the lessee and pledged to the lessor as security for a loan. Several conditions must be satisfied for a lease to qualify as a true lease:

1. The lessor must bear all the risks of ownership.

2. The lessee cannot build up any equity interest in the asset. When the lease is fully paid out, the asset will belong completely to the bank.

3. The rental charged by the bank cannot exceed a "fair market" rental. If it did, the lessee would build up an implicit equity interest in the asset.

4. The lease term must be less than the economic life of the asset.

5. The accounting treatment must be consistent with proper accounting methods for a lease.

Other areas of uncertainty exist with respect to bank leasing activities. First, the Federal Reserve, in its role as regulator of holding companies, has not fully decided on the extent to which banks and bank holding company affiliates should be allowed to enter into leasing activities. Second, the accounting profession is rethinking many of its practices, among them the treatment of leasing arrangements. Finally, banks are expected to become subject to disclosure rules similar to those affecting other corporate entities. As they become forced to reveal more data about their lending and leasing practices, and as accounting rules and tax regulations affect the desirability of the two types of financing, changes will doubtless be made in the way many banks conduct their business in this area.

10

Loan Pricing

In this chapter the concept and practice of loan pricing are examined. In contrast to the theoretical work of Chapters 2 and 3, explicit account is taken of nonprice loan terms. Nonprice terms were introduced implicitly in Chapter 2, where it was shown how they affected the demand for loans, but where their effect on loan yield was ignored.

Handling nonprice terms in this way did not do too much damage to reality when the only nonprice term considered was the compensating balance requirement. Compensating balances may increase the cost of the loan to the borrower, but from the bank's standpoint they add to the supply of deposits and increase the covariance of deposits with some assets. This effect, it was shown, is valuable to the bank, which will therefore encourage the use of compensating balances. However, treating nonprice terms implicitly does not provide answers to how banks should explicitly value nonprice terms and how they should incorporate them into their pricing practices.

The concern here, therefore, is with the yield the bank receives on the loan arrangement when all aspects of the arrangement are taken into consideration. The bank gives credit to the borrower for the funds it has deposited with the bank as a compensating balance, fees are charged for explicit services the bank is providing the customer, and other considerations such as the maturity of the loan, the maximum amount of the loan, and collateral requirements are accounted for.

Before proceeding, however, it is necessary to clear up one point of interpretation. Some bankers, as well as some analysts, have argued that banks make loans to obtain deposit balances. These people, therefore, emphasize the compensating balance requirement in the loan relationship, because they feel that making loans will bring new deposits to the bank so that the bank can make additional loans. Since the acquisition of deposits is of crucial importance to a bank, the proponents of this theory give undue allegiance to the use of compensating balances in the lending process and have helped to maintain the practice, even in the face of changing market conditions. The more modern concept is that banks obtain deposits so they can make loans. This transfers the emphasis, and correctly so, to lending as the major function of the bank. This has helped in the pricing of loans as well as in making banks more willing to give up compensating balances and develop such techniques as pure spread pricing. The latter concept is closer to the European practice of lending and to current international borrowing arrangements. With this shift in viewpoint, bank managers now tend to place their loans first and then find the money to fund them. This is quite new to American banking.[1]

PRELIMINARIES

Introduction to the Pricing Scheme

The pricing formula developed in this book is derived from the balance sheet and income statement of the bank with respect to the individual borrower. Each loan is considered a capital budgeting decision, and each case must be decided on its own merits. The bank allocates scarce capital to each loan; therefore it must determine whether that capital contributes sufficiently to its profits or whether it might be more profitable to put this capital to other uses.

It is assumed that the bank draws up a balance sheet on each individual customer. It then considers the amount of loan each customer is ex-

---

[1] This does not mean that banks must become liability managers. The asset-management bank still faces loan demands that are less than inelastically supplied liabilities and funds its loans out of these liabilities. The importance of the concept is that emphasis is placed on the bank's main source of revenue, interest income from loans, whereas the earlier concept placed the emphasis on deposits. The asset-management bank's problem is not obtaining deposits; it is obtaining loans that fit into the bank's risk-return plan for its portfolio. As will be shown in the appendix to this chapter, the concentration on obtaining deposits has led to a misinterpretation of the pricing formulas used by bankers.

pected to need and allocates capital to each.[2] The deposit balances the customers will keep at the bank are estimated. Pricing proceeds in a way that will allow the bank to achieve a yield on each customer commensurate with the required yield for the customer's particular loan class.

When these individual balance sheets are aggregated (added together), the bank should obtain the balance sheet for the bank as a whole. In deriving the pricing formula used by the bank, the strict prime plus markup scheme will be used, although a percentage markup over prime could be used just as well. What markups are used and how they are determined are of no concern here. These are a part of the decision on the customer base of the bank analyzed in Chapter 4. As mentioned there, markups will depend on what markets the bank chooses to serve, the conditions in these loan markets, and the competition of others in the area.

The Customer Balance Sheet

The individual balance sheet of the ith customer can be depicted in T-account format as follows:

Loan Customer i

C_i	D_i
L_i	T_i
	K_i

Capital letters represent the bank's balance sheet accounts that are relevant to the customer's dealings with the bank; the subscript identifies the customer account under review, in this case a particular commercial borrower. The variable L_i refers to the average loan outstanding for customer i; D_i is customer i's compensating balance.

It is assumed that each customer keeps on deposit just the amount required and that the figure D_i is net of float or any balances used to pay for services not incorporated into the current loan arrangement.[3] The capital

---

[2] The specific process of allocation of capital will be discussed later in this section.

[3] This assumes that only the loan is considered in loan pricing. It should be noted that the loan officer may be held accountable for more than just the loan arrangement. Current practices of customer profitability analysis (see Chapter 11) lump all the services the borrower buys from the bank into one statement. The original reason for this was to avoid double

funds allocated to customer i are denoted K_i, and the residual amount of funds needed to support the loan is T_i. More will be said on the quantity T_i later.

It should be noted that the borrower is assumed to borrow its own funds first. That is, D_i supports L_i. This is consistent with the modern practice of making the loan first and then funding it; the first funds used are the customer's own.[4] The other concept assumed that the funds for the loan were already available and that the compensating balances D_i were over and above what the bank had. Thus, the bank made loans in order to obtain deposits.

Reserves and Capital Allocation

The variable C_i represents the cash reserves needed to support the liabilities requiring them. It is assumed that the bank allocates no excess reserves.[5] Thus, required reserves can be separated into appropriate categories depending on the respective reserve requirements, r_D and r_T:

$$C_i = r_D D_i + r_T T_i \qquad (10\text{-}1)$$

---

counting of compensating balances, i.e., the practice of using the same balances to pay for, say, payroll services, as well as to serve as compensating balances supporting a loan. If the relationship is bundled to determine profitability, then the loan officer must have and use all this information in pricing the borrower; if each item is treated separately, then the loan officer must be sure that balances applied to the loan are not being used to pay for other services as well.

[4] This clears the way for two modern concepts of lending. First, the bank is now free to engage in lending without compensating balances. This is because the bank now must seek funds elsewhere if the borrower does not provide them. However, these funds are now substitutes, not complements. Second, the bank can give credit to its customers for these funds, i.e., can pay an implicit market rate for their deposits, thus making it worthwhile for them to keep their funds on deposit. This is consistent with unbundling; see L. L. Bryan, "Put a Price on Credit Lines," *The Bankers Magazine* (Summer 1974). For what the other concept means for loan pricing, see the appendix to this chapter.

[5] Technically, there are two reasons for holding excess reserves. First, to provide liquidity when the individual borrower's loan demands are greater than expected. Second, to protect against deposit withdrawals that are greater than expected. The former could be included in the individual balance sheet of the borrower. The second, however, gives rise to an independent balance sheet for "excess reserves." In practice, an independent balance sheet can be used for both, and a "cost" can be allocated to the borrower that is consistent with the exposure it forces the bank to protect against. How this cost might be treated is discussed in Chapter 11. The latter method will be the one used in this chapter; thus, excess reserves as allocated to the individual borrower will be assumed to be zero.

Further examination of the compensating balance requirement reveals the following points: First, the D_i need not relate only to demand deposits. Modern practice allows for the use of some low-interest or non-interest-bearing time deposits in compensating balances. This is done for two reasons: It reduces reserve requirements, and it also protects the bank against the use of float, since checks cannot be written against time balances. If time deposits are used, the reserve requirement against these accounts, r_D, will be a weighted average of the reserve requirements relevant to the amounts in the two types of accounts.

Second, if it is assumed that the borrower, on average, keeps just its compensating balance requirement on hand, then the amount of this balance can be stated as a percentage of L, the average loan outstanding.[6] Thus,

$$D_i = dL_i \qquad 0 \le d \le 1 \tag{10-2}$$

The next item to be considered is how capital will be allocated to this account. Although there are several methods used for this, the most common approach is to allocate capital at a fixed percentage of the average loan outstanding. Thus,

$$K_i = kL_i \qquad 0 \le k \le 1 \tag{10-3}$$

The exact proportion used can be determined in several ways. For example, the bank can use the existing capital-to-loan ratio as determined historically on the bank's balance sheet. Or it can use a desired capital-to-loan ratio, in which case, at the end of the period in which the loan portfolio turns over, the actual capital-to-loan ratio should be close to the desired ratio. Pricing can thus be used to help structure the bank's balance sheet.

Purchased Funds

With this additional information the balance sheet of the individual customer can be rearranged and rewritten in more convenient form. Thus, subtracting the required reserves from both sides of the balance sheet and then collecting the accounts together and substituting dL_i and kL_i for D_i

---

[6] Other ways of determining compensating balance requirements are presented later in the section on compensating balances.

and K_i, respectively, as given by equations (10-2) and (10-3), the following balance sheet is obtained:

Loan Customer i

L_i	$(1 - r_D)dL_i$
	$(1 - r_T)T_i$
	kL_i

Since the two sides must be equal, this can be rewritten in equation form:

$$L_i = (1 - r_D)dL_i + (1 - r_T)T_i + kL_i \tag{10-4}$$

Rearranging terms yields the following relationship:

$$T_i = \left(\frac{1 - (1 - r_D)d - k}{1 - r_T} \right) L_i \tag{10-5}$$

A word needs to be said about the variable T_i and the reason for solving the balance sheet equation for it. As described above, T_i represents "the residual amount of funds needed to support the loan"; it is the amount of noncapital funds allocated to the loan from other funds-collecting areas in the bank. Its amount depends on the average loan outstanding, the compensating balance requirement, and the capital allocation. Since it is the amount left over after these other amounts are determined, it requires no behavioral or institutional relationship to define it, as d and k do for compensating balances and capital. Thus, T_i is solved for in equation (10-5) and will be eliminated later, since its determination adds nothing to the final pricing arrangement. In practice, T_i can be considered to be the amount of *purchased funds* needed to support the loan.

Some banks refer to this amount as "pool funds." Pool funds are liabilities that are present on the aggregate balance sheet of the bank. Since these funds have been deposited at the bank, the bank has already committed itself to a cost of funds, the "pool rate." This is undesirable for two reasons. First, the concept of a pool is not consistent with the philosophy of lending presented in this book. A pool of funds implies that deposits preceded loans, and hence deposits rather than loans should represent the most important part of banking. It was argued earlier that the bank should make loans and then purchase funds. Second, as described in Chapter 2, the pool rate understates the marginal cost of funds and leads to a misallocation of resources within the bank.

Thus, T_i represents purchased funds, and the appropriate rate that should be charged, then, is the marginal cost of funds, in this case R_T.

The Customer Income Statement

The discussion now turns to the income statement of the individual borrower. With R as the general symbol for interest rates, R_L^i, R_b^i, and R_k^i represent the interest rates on loans and compensating balances and the rate of return on capital, respectively, all related to the ith borrower. R_T, the interest cost of purchased funds, is common to all borrowers. It is assumed that the bank sets these loan rates and deposit rates in accordance with the principles presented in Chapters 2 and 3 so as to maximize the rate of return on owners' equity. Thus, the profit on the ith customer will be assumed to be a maximum; that is, the expected R_k^i will be assumed to be as large as possible. The income statement can be described as follows:

$$
\begin{aligned}
\text{Interest Revenue on Loan} &= R_L^i \times L_i \\
\text{Interest Cost of Deposits} &= -R_b^i \times D_i \\
\underline{\text{Interest Cost of Purchased Funds}} &= \underline{-R_T \times T_i} \\
\text{Profit} &= R_k^i \times K_i
\end{aligned}
$$

This relationship, which expresses the residual nature of profits, can also be written in equation form:

$$R_L^i L_i - R_b^i D_i - R_T T_i = R_k^i K_i \tag{10-6}$$

Rearranging to solve for the rate of return on capital yields

$$R_k^i = \frac{R_L^i L_i - R_b^i D_i - R_T T_i}{K_i} \tag{10-7}$$

Pricing the Loan

The two summary equations, (10-5) and (10-7), can now be combined to obtain the full pricing relationship. This is done by substituting the relationships described in (10-2) and (10-3) into (10-5) and (10-7) and rearranging:

$$R_K^i = \frac{R_L^i - dR_b^i - R_T\left(\dfrac{1 - (1 - r_D)d - k}{1 - r_T}\right)}{k} \tag{10-8}$$

This relationship is said to be an optimal one if loan and deposit rates are set so that marginal costs are equal to marginal returns. In other words, R_K^i should be the largest possible return on capital that can be achieved by the bank on the ith loan customer.

The difficulty now is in making this a working pricing equation. It must be realized that in making the jump from theory to reality a lot of assumed knowledge and continuity are given up and other imperfections of various sorts are introduced. Therefore, the first thing that is done is to switch R_K^i from the optimal return on the ith borrower to a target return determined by bank management for the borrower's loan class. The R_K^i now becomes R_K^j, where the j stands for the borrower's loan class. This target is determined by the management, before the actual lending decision is made, in a manner similar to the planning exercise described in Chapter 8. This R_K^j is also important for customer profitability analysis, covered in Chapter 11.

The next factor to consider is the loan rate. If the customer under consideration is a prime customer, then R_P, the prime rate, is substituted for R_L^i. If the customer fits into a nonprime loan class and the bank uses some type of markup system of pricing, then R_L^i is replaced by either $R_P + x_j$, where x_j refers to the absolute markup for the jth class, or $R_P(1 + \hat{x}_j)$, where $\hat{x}_j$ is the percentage markup for the jth loan class.

The compensating balance requirement, the rate paid by the bank on these deposits, and the corresponding reserve requirement are decision variables that are all determined more or less together. If the bank requires that all balances be kept in demand deposits, then the matter is simplified. In that case, $R_b^i = 0$ and the reserve requirement r_D becomes the reserve requirement appropriate for demand deposits.

On the other hand, if the bank decides to have the borrower deposit some of its compensating balance in time accounts, then R_b^i may or may not be equal to zero and r_D will be a weighted average determined by the proportion of these funds kept in time deposits and the reserve requirements on the accounts.[7]

---

[7] This is one instance in which the creative loan officer can benefit both the bank and the customer. If, for example, the borrower is not using all of its deposit balances, then the loan officer might suggest to the customer that some of the funds be put into time accounts. For example, if the bank allows compensating balances to be computed on the average balance

The variables R_T, r_T, and k are more or less set for each loan arrangement. As described above, R_T is the marginal cost of funds, some market-determined rate such as the rate paid on negotiable certificates of deposit or commercial paper. The r_T is set by the Federal Reserve, and k is determined by top management and is assigned by formula.

It can be easily seen, therefore, that the only factor, so far, that loan officers can vary in any way is the compensating balance requirement. Unless a loan officer has some control over the markup charged to a particular borrower, the only variable that can be used to assure the target rate of return on capital is the amount of funds the borrower must keep on deposit at the bank.

In some banks, loan officers are allowed some limits in which they can trade off balances for loan rates and vice versa, in the interest of making a more acceptable loan package for a customer. If this is allowed, however, it will usually be tightly controlled by guidelines within which the loan officer must work.

There are exceptions to pricing strictly according to the target rate of return. Good customers of the bank may, and in many cases do, receive a better package than a borrower that is not considered a good customer. This makes sense, and it will be remembered that the discussion of the customer relationship in Chapter 3 indicated that a bank can find economic justification for such concessions if there is a good chance that the borrower will either help to reduce the variance of the bank's loan demand or present the possibility of additional future loan business to the bank.

COMPENSATING BALANCES

Compensating balance requirements can be figured in several ways. Up to now balances have been computed as a percentage of the average loan outstanding. Two other methods will be presented.

Rather than vary the compensating balance as the customer's loan varies, the bank may require that the borrower keep a fixed amount of

---

the customer keeps on hand, then the minimum balance that the firm always maintains could be moved into a time account. A quick look at equation (10-8) will show that if none of the other terms of the loan arrangement change, the yield on the loan will rise. This situation will not normally last, but the bank can now change some other term or price of the loan to accommodate the customer's needs better. This is a situation where both the borrower and the lender can profit. The assumption is that the deposits were not that volatile; thus, there is really no cost to society from the reduction in required reserves. Both can benefit because given resources are being used more efficiently.

funds on deposit. That is, $D_i = \overline{D}_i$, so that D_i/L_i will vary as the size of the loan varies. This will affect two components of the pricing equation (10-8). As the size of the loan increases, and d decreases, the exact effect on the rate of return on the relationship will depend on two factors: The expense of deposits (dR_b^i) is made smaller, and since relatively more purchased funds will be needed to support the loan, the total expense of purchased funds will increase. In general, the latter effect will be greater than the former, particularly if R_b^i is institutionally set equal to zero. Thus, if nothing else changes, the rate of return on a loan with a fixed deposit amount for the compensating balance will decline as the average loan outstanding increases and will rise as the loan size decreases.

Another method of computing compensating balances is to charge the customer a percentage of the loan commitment. Thus, the dollar amount of balances stays constant if the commitment remains constant. The effect on the rate of return of the loan will be the same as in the case where the absolute amount of the deposit is fixed. However, in the pricing formula, equation (10-8), the term d'/U can be substituted for d, where d' is the percentage of the commitment kept in deposits and U is the expected utilization of the commitment. The variable U is equal to the average loan outstanding divided by the loan commitment. The effect that usage has on the rate of return on the loan can thereby be estimated as the loan is being priced.

In modern practice, loan officers use a combination of these methods. For example, a bank will frequently combine the percentage of line and percentage of loan outstanding methods. The borrower may then be charged 10-and-10. That is, the borrower will be required to maintain deposit balances in the amount of 10 percent of its total line of credit and 10 percent of its actual borrowing. Thus, there is an expense for having the line open, but some of the expense of the credit is deferred until actual usage takes place. This means a cheaper arrangement to the borrower than if the compensating balance is levied on the entire commitment.

Historically, the percentage of line was the most popular method of assessing balances until the 1960s, when banks became more competitive. The banks then moved to assign compensating balance requirements on only the amounts borrowed.

In the late 1960s and early 1970s, however, borrowers began to obtain "insurance" lines of credit. Firms have always tended to obtain commitments in excess of needs. At this time they were even more aggressive than usual in seeking commitments. Insurance lines of credit are lines obtained by customers that intend to use them only in times of scarce money when other sources of funds are nonexistent. Fees are not charged on open lines of credit, and the fees charged on revolving credit were kept low by the competitive pressures at that time.[8] Moreover, since compensating balances were only a percentage of the loan outstanding or a minimal percentage of the line, obtaining these lines required little or no outlay on the part of the potential borrower.

Banks, in general, suffered in the credit crunch of 1974–1975 from the commitments made earlier. Firms made extensive use of bank lines as other sources of funds dried up. The banks also were pressed for funds, so bank earnings suffered drastically. After this experience, banks became much more cautious in granting lines of credit. Furthermore, they raised fees and reinstituted percentage-of-line compensating balance requirements to discourage borrowers from abusing their willingness to provide credit. They realized that they had been providing a very valuable commodity, the ability to obtain funds at any time they were needed, but had underestimated the cost of providing it. In terms of the arguments developed in Chapters 2 and 3, the banks reduced costs to obtain future loan demand. However, they implicitly assumed that the variance of loan demand would remain constant. They got the increased future loan demand, but they also got a greater variance of loan demand. The reduction in the cost of these lines was not warranted.

FEES

To incorporate fees, the income statement must be revised. For the present, F^i will be the general symbol for the contribution made to earnings by fee charges; this is denominated in percentage terms. Rewriting the income statement to include fees results in

$$
\begin{array}{lll}
\text{Interest Revenue on Loan} & = & R_L^i \times L_i \\
\text{Fee Revenue from Loan} & = +F^i & \times L_i \\
\text{Interest Cost of Deposits} & = -R_D^i & \times D_i \\
\underline{\text{Interest Cost of Purchased Funds}} & = -R_T & \times T_i \\
\text{Profit} & = & R_k^i \times K_i
\end{array}
$$

---

[8] It appears, after the fact, that banks underestimated future loan demand from the lines or the variability of loan demand from the lines, or both. This led them to underprice the arrangement.

Substituting as before gives the new pricing equation:

$$R_k^j = \frac{R_P + x_j + F^i - dR_b^i - R_T \left(\dfrac{1 - (1 - r_D)d - k}{1 - r_T} \right)}{k} \tag{10-9}$$

The computation of fees can take one of two forms or a combination of the two, as was done with compensating balances earlier. The first fee is a commitment or facility fee that is charged the borrower on the front end of the loan arrangement, that is, when the loan agreement begins, or periodically if the line is a revolving line. The second is the usage fee based on the portion of the line not used by the customer.

The commitment fee or facility fee is a flat percentage of the total line of credit given to the customer. Thus, if CF is the commitment fee, then $CF \times$ Total Line is the revenue earned on fees. This must be converted into a yield figure for the term of the loan so that in pricing the loan the contribution this fee makes to the rate of return on the loan is accurate; the borrower is given full credit for the payments it makes to the bank.

The important point here is that the commitment fee is paid at the front end of the loan. All the other payments are received at the end of the period when the loan matures or when settlement takes place. The commitment fee is therefore available to the bank for the full time period the relationship is on the books. The revenue earned from the fee must be adjusted by the rate at which the bank can put those funds to work for the period of the loan. Technically, this rate should be the bank's internal transfer rate, R_T.[9]

The second adjustment that needs to be made is to convert the fee revenue into an interest yield. This is done by dividing the future value of the fee revenue by the expected average loan outstanding over the loan period. The formula for F_c^i, the yield on commitment fees from the ith customer, is

$$F_c^i = \frac{CF(1 + R_T)}{U} \tag{10-10}$$

The usage fee is a little simpler. The revenue from this fee is computed by multiplying the fee on the unused portion of the line of credit (CU) by

[9] Some banks have used rates that have been "historically" determined. See, for example, the presentation of Bank of America's pricing relationship in G. Severson, "Determining Pricing Alternatives," *Journal of Commercial Bank Lending* (November 1974). Although no more information than this is given in the article, one can assume that the "historically" determined rate is the pool rate.

the portion of the line not used. Thus, $CU \times$ (Total Line of Credit − Average Loan Outstanding) is the revenue earned. Since this is received at the end of the loan or at the time of settlement, adjustment does not have to be made for the availability of funds over the life of the relationship.

As before, the fee revenue must be put on a yield basis. This is done by dividing the fee revenue by the average loan outstanding. The formula for F_U^i, the yield on nonusage of the line from the ith customer, is

$$F_U^i = \frac{CU(1 - U)}{U} \qquad (10\text{-}11)$$

The bank can use either the formula presented in equation (10-10) or the one in equation (10-11), or it can use the two in combination. That is, the general way to write the fees into the pricing equation (10-9) is

$$F^i = F_C^i + F_U^i$$

OTHER SERVICES AND FEES

One thing more must be considered. This is the problem of including services other than those strictly related to the loan agreement in the loan pricing formula. By including other services in the loan arrangement, the bank is, in effect, bundling bank services. Many analysts feel that the loan relationship should be kept separate from any other bank services or products the borrower buys from the bank and that each should be priced on its own merits alone.[10]

Other analysts feel that bundling services and products together is a major outlet for competitive pressures that would not otherwise be attainable. Hodgman,[11] for example, feels that the loan arrangements, including prices, are so homogeneous among all banks that the only way banks can compete is by offering services and underpricing them to compensate for

---

[10] This is, of course, the recommendation of the "unbundlers," who feel that each service or product should be priced so as to maintain its own profitability. Bundling causes cross-subsidization of services and products, allowing banks to offer some unprofitable items to customers and overpricing others to compensate for this shortfall. For more on this, see Chapter 11.

[11] D. R. Hodgman, *Commercial Bank Loan and Investment Policy* (Champaign, Ill.: Bureau of Economic and Business Research, The University of Illinois, 1963).

their inability to alter loan rates or loan terms. Thus, banks compete on services offered, such as lock boxes, trust services, account reconciliation, payroll, and computer facilities, rather than on price.

A less theoretical but more practical reason for bundling is that customer profitability analysis as it is set up now in many banks includes all the relationships a customer has with the bank. This has happened historically, as banks have tried to eliminate double and triple counting of deposit balances. Thus, in designing customer profitability analysis systems, banks combined all relationships between a customer and the bank into one account to make sure they were receiving enough compensation on the total package of services they were providing to the customer.

The point of this is that if a customer is going to be judged on the basis of all the services it receives from the bank, then the pricing relationship should also be based on these factors. To judge a relationship by different criteria than were used in its development is not only unfair to those being held responsible for developing the relationship but leads to a misallocation of resources within the bank because of the differing standards.

Until customer profitability analysis changes or banks fully unbundle services, all customer services and any payments received for them will be included in the pricing scheme.

The cost of these services, therefore, must be estimated and made available to the loan officer at the time the loan agreement is established or renewed. This assumes, of course, that the bank has a good cost accounting system so that it can compute unit costs of services and can allocate them to the appropriate customers. Furthermore, information on service charges and other remuneration required by departments other than the loan department must be made available to the loan officer. Whereas at one time all this information might have been very expensive to obtain and disburse, most banks today should not find the cost excessive because of the computer information systems now available.

Two new entries will now be made in the income statement. First, revenues, FR^i, which consist of all fees and charges relating to other services the customer buys from the bank, will be added, and services, S^i, consisting of the expenses associated with these items and attributable to the customer, will be subtracted. The following pricing formula is then obtained:

$$R_k^i = \frac{R_P + x_j + F^i + \dfrac{FR^i - S^i}{L_i} - dR_D^i - R_T \left(\dfrac{1 - (1 - r_D)d - k}{1 - r_T} \right)}{k} \qquad (10\text{-}12)$$

SPREAD FINANCING

Spread financing has increased in the United States as a response to the movement of U.S. companies and banks into international financial circles and the competition coming from foreign banks in the United States. Equation (10-12) can be changed to give a spread financing formula. The following changes must be made: First, in spread financing no compensating balances are required. Thus, dR_D^j and $(1 - r_D)d$ drop out of equation (10-12). Second, no other services are purchased from the bank—spread financing is a pure loan arrangement—so variables FR^i and S^i drop out. This leaves

$$R_K = \frac{R_L^j - \dfrac{R_T(1 - k)}{1 - r_T}}{k} \tag{10-13}$$

where $R_L^j \; (= R_p + x_j)$ is the contract rate of interest to the jth loan class.

Generally, spread financing is based on the return on assets as opposed to the return on capital as presented here. The assumption is that the full loan is supported by purchased funds. Thus, loans financed this way conform most closely to "lend first, fund later." Equation (10-13) can be rearranged by multiplying both sides by $k = K/L$. This makes the left side of the equation

$$\frac{K_i R_K^j}{L_i} = \frac{\text{Profit}}{L_i} = R_A^j \tag{10-14}$$

where R_A^j is the required return on assets of the jth loan class. That is, K is no longer included in the profit function of the firm.

Since no capital is explicitly allocated to the loan, the total amount of financing is through purchased funds and k vanishes from the numerator of equation (10-13). This leaves

$$R_A^j = R_L^j - \frac{R_T}{1 - r_T} \tag{10-15}$$

Rearranging gives

$$\frac{R_T}{1 - r_T} + R_A^j = R_L^j \tag{10-16}$$

where R_A^j represents the spread on the loan over the adjusted open-market rate. It is not technically correct to ignore the reserve requirements on purchased funds if such reserve requirements exist. This is, of course, why domestic American banks cannot price competitively with foreign banks in the United States; the funds purchased by the foreign banks are not subject to the reserve requirements.

The U.S. banks either have to overprice and rely on the full-service banking arrangement or accept a lower profit margin. An example will clarify this point.

If the marginal cost of purchased funds, R_T, is 8 percent and the reserve requirement on purchased funds is 5 percent, then $R_T/(1 - r_T) = 0.0842$. If R_A^j is expected to be 0.0075, or $3/4$ of 1 percent, then R_L^j, the loan rate, is 0.0917. The foreign bank, with no reserve requirements, could earn the same rate of return and offer loan rates of 0.0875. For the U.S. bank to charge the same rate, its required return on assets would have to be $1/3$ of 1 percent, or 0.0033 instead of 0.0075.

AN EXAMPLE OF LOAN PRICING

A loan-pricing example will indicate how the various terms described above fit together. Information available to the loan officer includes a prime rate of $8\frac{1}{2}$ percent and a marginal cost of funds of 8 percent. Reserve requirements on demand accounts and purchased funds are 15 percent and 5 percent, respectively. No interest payments are made on demand deposit accounts. The bank's capital allocation ratio is 10 percent, and it requires a compensating balance on this customer class of 15 and 5, that is, 15 percent of the total line of credit and 5 percent of the amount borrowed. For the specific customer in question the bank provides services to the customer costing $57,580 and is remunerated for these services in the amount of $42,800. With the symbols presented earlier, this can be translated as

$$R_P = 0.085$$

$$R_T = 0.08$$

$$r_D = 0.15$$

$$r_T = 0.05$$

$$k = 0.10$$

$$R_D^j = 0.00$$

$$FR^i = \$42,800$$

$$S^i = \$57{,}580$$

$$d = 0.15$$

$$d' = 0.05$$

The customer's loan class requires a 50 basis-point (0.005) markup over the prime rate. The total commitment is for \$4,000,000, and the expected usage, U, is \$2,000,000. The commitment fee is 0.0025, or ¼ of 1 percent of the total line, and the usage fee is 0.0025, or ¼ of 1 percent of the unused portion of the total commitment.

First, the compensating balance requirements are computed:

$$\hat{d} = d + \frac{d'}{U} = 0.15 + \frac{0.05}{0.5} = 0.25 \qquad (10\text{-}17)$$

Next the commitment fees are computed. From (10-10),

$$F_C^i = \frac{0.0025(1 + 0.08)}{0.5} = 0.0054 \qquad (10\text{-}18)$$

and from (10-11),

$$F_U^i = \frac{0.0025(1 - 0.5)}{0.5} = 0.0025 \qquad (10\text{-}19)$$

Therefore, total commitment fees are $F_i = F_C^i + F_U^i = 0.0054 + 0.0025 = 0.0079$.

Note that services and charges as a percentage of the average loan outstanding work out to a negative 0.0079 [$= (42{,}800 - 57{,}580)/2{,}000{,}000$]. Note also that the effective interest cost is

$$0.08 \left(\frac{1 - (1 - 0.15)(0.25) - 0.10}{1 - 0.05} \right) = 0.0579$$

When all this information is put into equation (10-12), the before-tax yield obtained for the ith customer is

$$R_k^i = \frac{0.085 + 0.005 + 0.0079 - 0.0074 - 0.0579}{0.10} = 0.326 \qquad (10\text{-}20)$$

Now this may be too high or too low. For example, if the before-tax return to the bank on the jth loan class, the class to which customer i belongs, were 30 percent instead of 32.6 percent, the loan officer would have to reduce the cost somewhere. Now assume that the borrower does not want to keep as large a compensating balance as is required by the 15-and-5 in the original example. Assume that the loan officer changes it to 20 percent of the loan and nothing on the line. This would increase the amount of purchased funds needed, so that the effective interest cost would be

$$0.08 \left(\frac{1 - (1 - 0.15)(0.20) - 0.10}{1 - 0.05} \right) = 0.0615$$

This would reduce the bank's return on the customer to 29 percent.

To make up the 1 percent needed to hit the target, the usage fee could be raised to 35 basis points, that is, $CN = 0.0035$, or CF could be raised by 5 basis points to 0.0030. The logic behind this is that the bank originally wanted the compensating balances behind the total commitment to provide some return against the unused commitment. Since it is more desirable to the customer to have smaller balances at the bank, the "commitment fee" could be made explicit by substituting the charge into the explicit fees from the compensating balance requirement.

Note how sensitive the yield is to changes in the assumption about usage. For example, if usage increases from $2,000,000 to $2,400,000, an increase of 10 percent of total commitment, the yield on the loan drops to 30.9 percent. If usage drops 10 percent to $1,600,000, the yield rises to 35.2 percent. Hence, the loan officer should try to estimate as closely as possible the expected usage of the commitment. The more accurately this amount is known, the more consistent the *ex ante* efforts will be with the *ex post* analysis of the loan and the greater the contribution the loan officer can make to the bank in terms of both profits and reasonably satisfied customers.

MARKET RELATIONSHIP

Before closing this chapter, it is desirable to depict how the various terms of the loan fit together and particularly how the loan rate relates to the market rate of interest. Of special interest is the relationship between the prime rate and the marginal cost of funds, R_T. To see this relationship most clearly it is desirable to assume that k, the capital-to-loan ratio, is constant and work with return on assets. Thus, rearranging equation (10-12) to obtain the return on assets, and ignoring for the time being the fees, R_b^i, other services and payments, S^i and FR^i, and interest payments on deposits, gives

$$R_A^i = R_L^i = \left(\frac{R_T}{1 - r_T}\right)\left[1 - \frac{1 - r_D}{L_i/D_i}\right] \tag{10-21}$$

Note that L_i/D_i is just the inverse of the compensating balance requirement.

By rewriting (10-21), an equation is obtained that is quite useful in examining the relationships that are to be studied:

$$R_L^i = R_A^i = \left(\frac{R_T}{1 - r_T}\right)\left[1 - \frac{1 - r_D}{L_i/D_i}\right] \tag{10-22}$$

In Figure 10-1 the various combinations of R_L^i and $L_i/D_i = 1/d$ are charted for given values of R_A^i, R_T, r_T, and r_D. The curve CC shows the loan rate R_L^i the bank must charge, given compensating balances, to earn the required return on assets R_A^i.

In examining curve CC it can be seen that as compensating balances

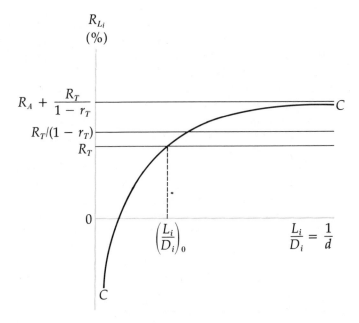

FIGURE 10-1   Relationship Between the Loan Rate and Compensating Balance Requirement on the *i*th Loan Class

become very small—that is, as L_i/D_i becomes very large—the pure spread financing result is approached; R_L^i approaches $R_A^i + R_T/(1 - r_T)$. The curve CC approaches the upper line. This is the result shown in equation (10-16).

As the compensating balance becomes larger, that is, as L_i/D_i becomes smaller, the quantity in brackets in equation (10-22) approaches zero and even becomes negative where compensating balances become large enough. This means that R_L^i can become zero and even negative for large enough values of balances. Although unrealistic, this result simply carries out the logic of the pricing equation.

The loan rate lies above the open-market rate, R_T, over a large portion of the curve. Calculations can be made to find the compensating balance requirement, $(L_i/D_i)_0$ in Figure 10-1, that would make $R_L^i = R_T$. On the assumption that $r_D = 0.15$, $r_T = 0.05$, and $R_A^i/R_L^i = \frac{1}{8}$, the compensating balance comes out to be approximately 20 percent. If $R_A^i/R_L^i > \frac{1}{8}$, then the compensating balance requirement increases, and quite rapidly. If $R_A^i/R_L^i < \frac{1}{8}$, then the compensating balance declines quite rapidly. The larger the rate of return on assets is relative to the loan rate, the larger the compensating balance must be to determine the point where CC intersects the R_T line. As compensating balances decline from $(L_i/D_i)_0$, R_L^i will exceed R_T.

Next, services are introduced, without the bank achieving any remuneration. Since the cost of services, S^i, enters negatively into equation (10-12), it will enter positively when the rearrangement just described takes place. Thus, the relevant loan rate curve, now $C'C'$, will lie above the old curve. This is seen in Figure 10-2. Now, the loan rate must cover not only the cost of funds, reserve requirements, and a required profit figure, but also the cost of the services provided to customers. Hence some cross-subsidization may take place as borrowers that do not use many services will pay for those that do, because all those customers that do borrow pay something to cover service costs.

The bank can charge for these services. Depending on what the services are, the bank can either assess service charges and other fees that would be included in FR^i or, if the services are in terms of the "insurance" contract of having funds available to borrow, it can assess a commitment fee or a usage fee, which would be included in F_i. These fees or service charges would cause $C'C'$ to fall, and if the payments just offset the cost of services, including a return to the bank, it would fall all the way back to the original CC curve. In this case the interest rate on the loan would be a payment only for the use of money, the riskiness of the loan, and monopoly payments due to the imperfections in the market.

The unbundlers desire to achieve this last state, where payments are for the exact services the customer is buying. In such a world no cross-

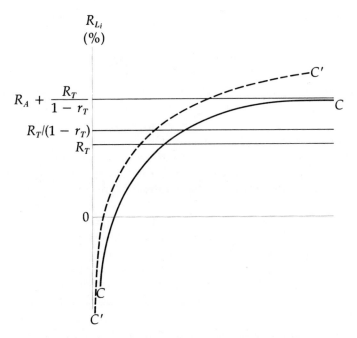

FIGURE 10-2   Shift in the Loan Rate–Compensating Balance Relationship
Due to a Change in Customer Services

subsidization would occur, and each service or function would stand or fall
on its own profitability or lack of profitability. More will be said on this in
the next chapter. The important thing to be gained from this discussion is
how the loan rate varies to take into account the various services and terms
included in the loan arrangement and how other payments help to offset
these costs.

REVIEW QUESTIONS

1. The pricing relationship presented in this chapter is said to be optimal "if loan and deposit rates are set so that marginal costs are equal to marginal returns." How can this be achieved in practice? How does the bank know when rates are optimal?
2. What happens to the pricing relationship if the borrower decides to keep more deposits at the bank than the compensating balance requirement? How should a loan officer take this into account in pricing the loan?
3. Why would a loan officer use the "percentage of loan" compensating balance requirement as opposed to other techniques?
4. How could a loan officer persuade the potential borrower to keep some of its compensating balance in a low-interest savings account?
5. How much flexibility should a loan officer have in setting rates, terms, and fees? Should the officer have this flexibility on all types of loans?
6. How should the maturity of a spread-priced loan compare with the maturity of the purchased funds used to finance the loan?
7. Set up a hypothetical loan, and price it to give the bank a yield of 25 percent on allocated capital. Assume the prime rate is 11 percent, and let $FR^i = \$102,740$ and $S^i = \$110,120$. Try different combinations of balances and fees to achieve the 25 percent yield.
8. Does the fact that the prime rate lies above the commercial paper rate mean that the prime rate always includes payments other than just the fee for borrowing money?
9. When a full EFTS is in place, people are expected to be more aware of the time value of money. If this turns out to be the case, what do you expect to happen to bank pricing schemes, particularly with respect to price markups and bundling?

APPENDIX
Other Loan-Pricing Schemes

Some published pricing schemes differ from the one described in the body of this chapter. Specifically, the two best known published pricing schemes are those of G. Severson, "Determining Pricing Alternatives" in the *Journal of Commercial Bank Lending* (November 1974), and D. R. Hodgman, *Commercial Bank Loan and Investment Policy* (Champaign, Ill.: Bureau of Economic and Business Research, The University of Illinois, 1963). Except for the symbols used, the two pricing systems are precisely the same. In this appendix Severson's formula will be examined, since it is the one Bank of America is reported to have used. The development will proceed according to Hodgman, since he provides the background for the pricing scheme.

Loans come from the funds already on deposit at the bank. These deposits are assumed to be obtained by the loan department costlessly in terms of both interest costs (marginal costs) and reserve requirements. Compensating balances put on deposit by the borrower are assumed to be over and above the funds already on deposit at the bank. These deposits less reserve requirements can be lent out at the market rate of interest, the commercial paper rate. The balance sheet of the ith customer, therefore, appears as follows:

Loan Customer i

$C_i = RR \times D_i$	D_i
CP	O_i
ALO_i	

Here C_i refers to reserves, where RR is the reserve requirement on deposits, CP is commercial paper purchased with the customer's deposits, ALO_i is the average loan outstanding, D_i is the compensating balance deposit, and O_i is the amount of other funds supplied by the bank to support the loan.

Rearranging the balance sheet, it should be noted that two equalities hold within the balance sheet. First, $CP = D_i(1 - RR)$, and second, $ALO_i = O_i$.

Loan Customer i

CP	$D_i(1 - RR)$
ALO_i	O_i

The income statement for the ith customer is now constructed. Following Severson, Y is used as the yield on commerical paper and R is the contract rate on the loan.

Income Statement
Customer i

Interest Revenue on Loan	$R(ALO_i)$
Derivative Revenue from Deposits	$Y(CP) = YD_i(1 - RR)$
Profit	

Now the income statement can be put into the form of an equation:

$$R(ALO_i) + YD_i(1 - RR) = \text{Profit} \qquad (10A\text{-}1)$$

Next, (10A-1) is divided by the average loan outstanding to obtain a rate of return on the "customer relationship." Note that the rate of return on the "customer relationship" includes the derivative income from investing the compensating balances of the customer in commercial paper. The variable d is again the compensating balance requirement D_i/ALO_i.

$$R + Y(1 - RR)d = \frac{\text{Profit}}{ALO} \qquad (10A\text{-}2)$$

The next assumption made is that the bank must earn as much on the "customer relationship" as it could if it invested directly in the open-market paper of the company. In this instance, it must be assumed that the type of customer being dealt with is the prime customer. Thus, $R + Y(1 - RR)d = Y$ and

$$\frac{R}{1 - (1 - RR)d} = Y \qquad (10A\text{-}3)$$

which is precisely the pricing formula given by Severson.

The balance sheet constraint plays no role at all! Remember that in the pricing formula developed in Chapter 10 the residual amount of funds was eliminated in the income statement by substituting for it the solution for residual funds in the balance sheet equation. Here the cost of residual funds, O_i, is zero, so it makes absolutely no difference how great the amount of residual funds is because they are free!

Equation (10A-3) can be rearranged to derive the relationship between the loan rate, R, and the commercial paper rate, Y. This should be compared with equation (10-22).

$$R = Y \left(1 - \frac{1 - RR}{1/d}\right) \qquad (10A\text{-}4)$$

A contract curve can now be drawn between R and $1/d$ as it was earlier. This is done in Figure 10A-1. Here it is seen that the prime loan rate can never lie above the commercial paper rate. Hodgman pointed this out and was mystified by it because the prime rate often did exceed the commercial paper rate. He assumed this result was due to the fact that his study was "static" in the sense that nothing was expected to change.

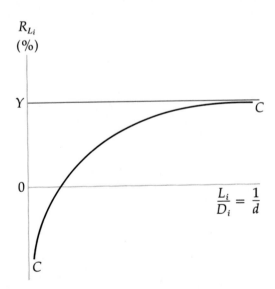

FIGURE 10A–1 Hodgman-Severson Loan Rate–Compensating Balance Relationship

If the cost of other services were included, as it was in Chapter 10, the CC curve would rise and thus it is possible for the prime rate to lie above the commercial paper rate. Of course, one of these services could be the "insurance" service and introduce some "dynamic" aspects into the model. However, it is not very satisfactory to introduce these items into the argument to explain something as lasting as the fact that the prime rate lies above the commercial paper rate.

Two assumptions are crucial to the results of Severson and Hodgman. The first assumption is the costless nature of the funds used to support the loan. The second is that the bank must earn the going market rate of interest on the "customer relationship" in order to make direct lending to the customer worthwhile.

It was shown in Chapter 2 that even if the residual funds used to support the loan have a very low average cost, the marginal cost to the deposit-collecting department should be the transfer price at which that department would be willing to sell the funds to the loan-making depart-ment. Thus, the cost of O_i should, in this example, be Y and not zero. If this is the case, the bank would not want to borrow from the deposit-collecting department at a cost of Y to buy commercial paper with a return of Y. Thus, the customer's deposits should be applied to the loan because then the loan-making department would need to buy fewer funds from the deposit-collecting department. The balance sheet and income state-ment look more like those presented in the body of the chapter.

Loan Customer i

ALO_i	$D_i(1 - RR)$
	$O_i(1 - r_T)$

Income Statement
Loan Customer i

$R(ALO_i)$
$-YO_i$
——————
Profit

Now

$$R(ALO_i) - YO_i = \text{Profit} \qquad\qquad (10A\text{-}5)$$

or

$$R - \frac{YO_i}{ALO_i} = \frac{\text{Profit}}{ALO_i} = R_A^i \qquad \text{(10A-6)}$$

and R_A^i is obviously not equal to Y. Rearranging the balance sheet so that $O_i = [ALO_i - D_i(1 - RR)]/(1 - r_T)$ and substituting into (10A-6) gives

$$R = \frac{Y}{1 - r_T} [1 - d(1 - RR)] + R_A^i \qquad \text{(10A-7)}$$

which is obviously the same as equation (10-21).

Thus, Severson and Hodgman leave out the cost of funds in deriving their pricing formula. Perhaps this was not such a bad assumption in an asset-management world where things were very stable and investment opportunities were not very great. However, their formula still is incorrect and should lead to a misallocation of resources.

11

Evaluation of the Borrower After Lending

The evaluation of the borrower after lending, which has commonly become known as customer profitability analysis, is an examination conducted to determine whether the borrower has been priced correctly and is contributing to the bank the yield expected of the borrower's loan class. Customer profitability analysis is a tool of control. It is used to maintain surveillance on the bank lending and pricing process and can also serve as a feedback mechanism to enable the lender to improve the way its loan officers grant terms and price loans.

Banks, however, need two things to achieve an adequate control system. First, they need a cost accounting system that can collect all relevant data and then allocate costs appropriately. The banking industry has been slow in developing adequate cost accounting systems, although some improvement has been made in recent years.

Second, banks must organize for control. Just to evaluate customers is not enough. Evaluations must be consistent with the other bank practices, such as loan pricing. In many banks, loan evaluation has been included in the accounting function, separated entirely from the lending function. Control requires coordination in planning and implementation. In addition, a feedback mechanism must exist that allows for the processed information to be returned to the people who can use it.

Unfortunately, it has often been the case that customer profitability analysis systems have been created because it was the thing to do and, since no one particularly wanted to administer the system, it was given to the accounting department or made an entirely separate unit within the organizational framework. Consequently, customer profitability analysis systems have perhaps caused as many problems as they have solved.

Accounting techniques and organizational structure are not treated here. What will be discussed are the methods of customer profitability analysis and the important decisions that must be made to evaluate the customer correctly.

A WORD ON UNBUNDLING

Perhaps nowhere is the correct allocation of costs and prices as important to analysis as in customer profitability analysis. If costs and prices are not allocated correctly, biases will be introduced into the system that, on a micro level, lead to false evaluations. A good customer may appear to be a poor risk, and a mediocre customer may be given an undeservedly high rating. Bias can also make a good lending officer seem to be pricing incorrectly, whereas a poor lending officer might appear to be pricing correctly. On the macro level, if such biases exist, the analytical results may imply that the bank is misallocating resources and therefore not performing as well as it could be. These errors obviously should be avoided.

Complete unbundling, therefore, plays the role within bank analysis that the perfect market concept plays in economics. Although complete unbundling is perhaps as impossible in reality as a perfect market, the concept provides a logical testing ground in seeking better means of pricing and allocating costs.

Unbundling will thus serve as the extreme case when examining for biases in the treatment of various items. An attempt should be made to unbundle costs and prices, but in many cases complete unbundling cannot be achieved. This does not mean that it is not useful to compare present practices with what should be if complete unbundling were possible. In fact, the examination of current procedures in this way may be quite helpful in developing a more correct approach to customer profitability analysis.

HISTORY[1]

Customer profitability analysis grew out of the practice of account analysis. Account analysis was a method of assuring that compensating balance requirements were being met by customers and that the most profitable customers could be serviced adequately. The accounts originally treated in this way were not loan accounts but accounts relating to other services of the bank such as payroll accounting, computer services, or trust services. Fees may have been collected for bank services, but in most cases compensating balances were required instead. An earnings credit was then allowed on customer balances, and the revenue thus computed was compared with the expenses incurred by the bank in providing the services to determine whether or not the account was profitable—that is, whether the bottom line of the account was positive or negative. The bank compiled an income statement for its service relationship with the customer.

Analysis of the customer's loan account extended only to determining whether or not the loan was being paid according to the agreed-upon terms. Very little consideration was given to whether a loan was contributing to bank profitability or whether the assets allocated to the loan could be put to better use somewhere else.

On the surface, this type of procedure should ideally suit the unbundlers. Each item or account was seemingly treated on its own. The methodology of treatment may not have been the most desirable, but that could always be remedied.

Bank analysts noted that customers were using their compensating balances to pay for two, three, or more services, i.e., the banks were double-counting or triple-counting the balances. This meant, of course, that the banks were not being fully remunerated for the services they were providing the customer. Their reaction was to try to consolidate all the accounts of each customer into one account and examine whether or not the *total* activity the customer had with the bank was profitable. This trend toward the consolidation of accounts led to the current practices of customer profitability analysis.

The banks thus got away from double- and triple-counting compensation balances. However, the price they paid was to scramble the results for individual services to the customer. This, of course, the unbundlers find very undesirable, because instead of each service being independent of all

[1] A more complete description of the history of customer profitability analysis is found in Robert E. Knight, "Customer Profitability Analysis, Part I: Alternate Approaches Toward Customer Profitability," *Monthly Review*, Federal Reserve Bank of Kansas City (April 1975), pp. 11–20.

others with regard to its profitability or lack of profitability, profitable units are often overpriced to subsidize unprofitable units. In addition, customers that do not use some services often subsidize those that do, because the cost of such services is generally allocated to all who borrow.

This, however, is the system that has come into general use. It has been expanded in many multinational banks to include all the relationships the bank has with a multinational customer, both domestic and international. Hence, in many instances the complexity has multiplied. The system that will be analyzed here includes these defects, but it is similar to the ones actually used by banks.

PRICING AND CUSTOMER PROFITABILITY ANALYSIS[2]

The natural starting point for customer profitability analysis is the pricing formula developed in Chapter 10. Since the pricing arrangement sets the standard that the loan officer, among others, attempts to achieve, the objective of customer profitability analysis should be to observe whether or not the standard was, in fact, achieved.

The Pricing Formula and the Accounting Framework

The final pricing formula, equation (10-12), was stated in terms of proportions or percentages. Since the framework for customer profitability analysis is accounting, the formula must be converted into quantities. Rewritten, the pricing relationship of equation (10-12) becomes

$$R_k^j = \frac{R_i + F^i + \dfrac{FR^i - S^i}{L_i} - dR_b^i - R_T\left[\dfrac{1 - (1 - r_D)d - k}{1 - r_T}\right]}{k} \tag{11-1}$$

where R_k^j is the rate of return on capital for the jth loan class, R_i is the loan rate on the ith customer, F^i is the fee charged the ith customer, L_i is the average loan outstanding, FR^i and S^i are the bank charges for services rendered and costs of services rendered, respectively, d is the compensating balance requirement, R_b^i is the interest cost of compensating balance

    [2] For the most complete description of customer profitability analysis and the practices of commercial banks see Robert E. Knight, "Customer Profitability Analysis, Part II: Analysis Methods at Major Banks," Monthly Review, Federal Reserve Bank of Kansas City (September–October 1975), pp. 11–24.

deposits, R_T is the marginal cost of funds, r_D and r_T are the reserve requirements for compensating balances and purchased funds, respectively, and k is the capital-to-loan ratio.

Two things are needed to put this into a form acceptable for customer profitability analysis. First, multiply the numerator and denominator of the right-hand side of (11-1) by the average loan amount, L_i, and then multiply both sides by capital, K. This yields

$$\pi_i = R_i L_i + F^i L_i + FR^i - S^i - D_i R_D^j - R_T \left[\frac{L_i - (1 - r_D)D_i - K_i}{1 - r_T} \right]$$

$$= R_i L_i + F^i L_i + FR^i - S^i - D_i R_D^j - R_T T_i \qquad (11\text{-}2)$$

where π_i is the profit of the ith customer. This is the proper format for customer profitability analysis.

The Customer Worksheet

In translating equation (11-2) into a workable framework, the reader is referred to Table 11-1. This table represents the worksheet a bank can use for analyzing a customer. The first section of the table presents a sources and uses of funds statement for the customer. First, the average loan outstanding is computed. If customer profitability statements are prepared monthly, the average balance for the period may be more meaningful than if these statements are prepared every six months, because the variance of usage is probably less within the shorter time period. Regardless, relatively steady usage is assumed, and the average loan balance reflects this usage.

Average demand deposits serving as compensating balances are then computed. To measure the funds available to the bank (investable balances) accurately, these deposits must be adjusted for float (they must be collectible balances) and must also be net of reserve requirements. The bank determines investable balances because some of the customer deposits are not usable; the reserve requirements impose a cost that must be absorbed somewhere in the bank. The correct place is with the deposits with which the requirements are associated. Investable balances are shown in line 2'.

The average amount of time deposits used to satisfy compensating balances is then entered along with a computation for the reserve requirement on these deposits. More and more banks use non-interest-bearing or

TABLE 11-1 Customer Profitability Analysis Form

XYZ Bank
Customer Profitability Analysis

Account: ABC Discount Stores   Date:_____
Affiliated Accounts:_____   Period:_____
_____   Type of Loan:_____
_____

Sources and Uses of Funds	Current Period	Last Twelve Months
1. Average Loan Balance, L_i	\$_____	\$_____
2. Average Collected Balance, D_i	\$_____	\$_____
2′. Investable Balances, $(1 - r_D)D_i$	\$_____	\$_____
3. Average Time Balances, D_i'	\$_____	\$_____
3′. Investable Balances, $(1 - r_{D'})D_i'$	\$_____	\$_____
4. Total Investable Balances (2′ + 3′)	\$_____	\$_____
5. Allocated Capital, $K_i = kL_i$	\$_____	\$_____
6. Free Purchased Funds $[1 - 4 - 5 = T_i(1 - r_T)]$	\$_____	\$_____

Income Statement

Revenues

	Current Period	Last Twelve Months
7. Gross Interest Income on Loans, $R_i \times L_i$	\$_____	\$_____
8. Fees on Line, $F^i \times L_i$	\$_____	\$_____
9. Fees Generated by Services, FR^i		
a. Service charges	\$_____	\$_____
b. Data processing	\$_____	\$_____
c. Other	\$_____	\$_____
d. Total	\$_____	\$_____
10. Total Income (7 + 8 + 9d)	\$_____	\$_____

Expenses

	Current Period	Last Twelve Months
11. Interest on compensating balances, $(D_i + D_i')(R_b^i)$	\$_____	\$_____
12. Cost of Services Provided, S^i		
a. Activity costs	\$_____	\$_____
b. Loan handling expense	\$_____	\$_____
c. Cost of fee services	\$_____	\$_____
d. Data processing	\$_____	\$_____
e. Other costs	\$_____	\$_____
f. Total	\$_____	\$_____
13. Charges on Bank Funds Used, $R_T \times T_i$	\$_____	\$_____
14. Total Expenses	\$_____	\$_____

Net Income

	Current Period	Last Twelve Months
15. Profit before taxes (= 10 − 14)	\$_____	\$_____

Profitability Measures

	Current Period	Last Twelve Months
16. On Allocated Capital (15 ÷ 5) × 100	_____ %	_____ %
17. On Bank Funds (15 ÷ 5 + 6) × 100	_____ %	_____ %
18. On Assets (15 ÷ 1) × 100	_____ %	_____ %

low-interest-bearing time accounts to satisfy compensating balance requirements. There are three reasons for this. (1) Customers often keep a larger bank balance than they need for transactions purposes. Thus, the chance to earn interest on these funds is attractive to them. (2) Because the bank faces a smaller reserve requirement on time deposits than on demand deposits, it will have a larger free balance with time accounts than with the same quantity of deposit balances. (3) Since customers cannot write checks on time accounts, there can be no problem of float using up these funds.

The bank must also allocate capital to the loan. In Chapter 10 capital was allocated to the loan as a proportion of the average loan outstanding. This method is not used in all banks. Some banks, for example, do not allocate any capital at all. Of course, this precludes computation of the rate of return on capital for individual loans or services. Other banks allocate capital to loans on the basis of the riskiness of the customer. More capital is allocated to a riskier customer than to a less risky one. As would be expected, the formula used for capital allocation has a significant effect on the computed rate of return on capital. This raises important questions about how capital is allocated, which will be treated later in this chapter.

Finally, the sources and uses statement is completed by computing the residual amount of funds needed. This residual has been termed *free purchased funds*. The actual amount of purchased funds allocated to the loan is T_i, but, as with other sources of funds, the bank must pay the cost of holding idle funds as required reserves. As in the case of demand deposits and time deposits, it is correct to allocate reserves to these funds where they are used. Thus, required reserves must be calculated for purchased funds and allocated to the customers that borrow the purchased funds. This has not been common banking practice, but it is obvious that to allocate the required reserves elsewhere (unless the transfer price accounted for this) is to misallocate costs. Thus, to compute free purchased funds, total purchased funds is adjusted for required reserves.

The middle section of Table 11-1 is the income statement of the customer, divided into revenue and expense sections. The reasons for the inclusion of most of the items in this part of the table are straightforward. The main problems come in lumping the loan transaction together with all the other accounts the customer has with the bank. Although heavily criticized by the unbundlers, this method has been the general practice of most customer profitability analysis systems.

Some Minor Points

Some points do need clarification.

1. Some banks include an earnings credit for compensating balances maintained with the bank.[3] This would figure as a separate positive entry in the revenue section of the income statement. However, this represents double counting. The reason for this is clear if the reader will look at the pricing formula shown in equation (11-2). There the borrower's compensating balance shows up in brackets on the right-hand side of the equation. It has a negative sign in front of it, but the whole bracketed expression is multiplied by the negative marginal cost of funds. Hence, the customer is given credit for compensating balances at the bank's marginal cost figure, and the relationship is positive—the larger the compensating balances, the larger the expected yield on the loan.

The customer profitability worksheet does not show this directly. This seems to be why many banks include a credit for compensating balances. However, as can be seen in the second part of equation (11-2) and in line 13 in Table 11-1, charges for purchased funds enter as an expense in the income statement, which gives the customer credit for its compensating balances. As compensating balances go up, purchased funds go down, and hence expenses go down. Thus, it is easy to see that either an earnings credit can be given to the customer in equation (11-2), or expenses can be reduced as shown by a reduction in purchased funds in the bracketed portion of equation (11-2) and by line 13 in the customer profitability worksheet. It is incorrect to do both!

2. The bank must decide whether or not each expense item should include its own profit margin. Some banks more or less assume that the profitability of services comes from the total bundle of services provided to the customer. In this case, costs do not include a necessary return for each service, but this return will obviously be built into the required yield of the borrower. This is the result shown in the last section of Chapter 10. In this way, if costs are allocated across loan classes on the basis of average usage, then the required yields of each class will be pushed upward to reflect these costs. However, subsequent analysis of customers will be biased in favor of borrowers that do not use many bank services. The reason for this is that all customers pay for the services in higher loan rates, whether they use the services or not. The customers that do not use the services pay for something others are getting; in other words, they will pay the price but will not be allocated the costs.

The alternative is to include a profit figure in the cost of each service provided. In this way, customers that use many services will be charged

---

[3] Knight does this. See "Customer Profitability Analysis, Part I," p. 14. L. L. Bryan, "Put a Price on Credit Lines," *The Bankers Magazine* (Summer 1974), also recommends that the bank give credit, at the marginal cost of funds, for its deposits.

for them, whereas those that do not will not be charged. The major difficulty with this is that few banks have had sufficiently good accounting systems to allocate costs and profits adequately. Hence, if a good cost accounting system does not exist, inaccuracies will still creep in. In this case, the bank perhaps is better off not charging a profit figure to each individual service or product offered.

3. Some banks will include a figure for risk in the expense section. This, in a sense, would make the yield on the loan the risk-free yield. However, as with the allocation of profit to the various service or transaction accounts, the bank must be able to allocate risk to the various loan classes correctly.

All too often, banks that have attempted to allocate risk have used an average default rate either computed from bank experience or collected from data obtained from some banking agency such as the Federal Reserve or the Federal Deposit Insurance Corporation.[4] The problem with this approach is that it biases results against both the most creditworthy customers and the least creditworthy. That is, taking an average figure means that customers with little chance of default will be charged a higher expense for risk than is correct, whereas a borrower with a much higher probability of default will be undercharged. Using this information as feedback into the future lending plans of the bank would tend to lead the bank to construct a riskier portfolio than it would desire.

What are the alternatives? If the bank can break out the risk cost of each loan class, then it can expense this cost to each customer. If the bank does not have adequate information to determine the allocation of risk, it should not try to expense it. In the latter case, the bank should simply adjust the target yield for the risk class to generally incorporate this expense, so that different risk classes will have different target yields (aside from imperfections). This would seem to create fewer biases in the absence of an adequate accounting system.

4. Some commercial banks will also include a figure for the cost of capital in their profitability calculation.[5] In Table 11-1 an expense for capital has not been included. However, if it is to be included, it can be figured in one of two ways. First, the bank can compute its cost of capital from its own experience (see Chapter 3) and multiply this by the quantity of capital allocated to the loan (line 5 in Table 11-1). Alternatively, it can establish a pretax target return it wishes to earn on capital. This is something like the "hurdle" rate of return used by nonfinancial firms. This figure is then

[4] Knight, "Customer Profitability Analysis, Part II," p. 21.
[5] Knight, "Customer Profitability Analysis, Part I," p. 14.

multiplied by the capital allocated to the customer, and the total is entered in as an expense.

If this capital costing is done correctly, the net profit before taxes (line 15 in Table 11-1) for a correctly priced relationship should be zero. Hence, all the profitability measures, if capital is allocated, would show a zero percent return, and thus the target return would be zero percent.

This method of including a capital cost is not inconsistent with the method implicit in Table 11-1. The difference is that the method used in the table introduces capital costs implicitly into the target yields used for pricing and control. The other method introduces capital costs explicitly, which means that the bank must have the ability to measure them correctly. If the cost is measured too high, many good loans will appear to be unprofitable; if measured too low, the bank will have more loans than optimal. Again, consistency of approach is important, and the ability to measure what the bank wants to measure is absolutely necessary.

5. A word should be said about whether large-denomination negotiable certificates of deposit bearing competitive interest rates should be included in the customer profitability analysis. Many banks do not include these because they consider them investments of the borrower and not a part of the customer relationship. These funds are, in a sense, "hot money" and can be taken out of the bank to chase higher interest rates. If this is not the case—if the bank has other knowledge of the customer's intentions—then it may include them. Again, it is the bank's responsibility to justify inclusion or exclusion of the item.

6. The expense of providing the insurance contract to lines of credit may also be included in the expense section. As described earlier, in providing a line of credit to the customer, the bank assures the borrower that it can borrow up to a certain amount whenever desired within the time limits of the agreement. The bank must incur a cost, either by forgoing interest returns to have liquid assets available to support loans or by maintaining positions in liability markets so as to be able to buy funds to support loans. How much "liquidity" the bank must buy depends on the bank's judgment of how likely its customers are to use up their lines of credit. Thus, one could make the case that this cost should be allocated to customers on the basis of the probability of their making additional use of their lines. This point will be discussed more fully later.

Banks have found that if they do not expense this potential usage of a line, or recognize the expense of maintaining the needed liquidity, customers that borrow only a little appear to be more profitable than those that borrow a lot. This is not a desirable result; in most cases, one would assume that the bank would consider a customer that borrowed more to be a "better" customer than the customer that borrowed less. If, for example, balances are charged a customer either as an absolute amount or as a percentage of the total line, the same earnings credit will be given customers that borrow a little or a lot. The same would be true of fees assessed on the line and not on usage. However, the customer that borrows only a small amount (less than another with the same balance and fee costs) will have a larger numerator in any of the profitability measures presented in lines 16 to 18 of Table 11-1, relative to its denominator, than the customer that borrows more. This is similar to the situation of leverage, where the fixed costs are roughly the same for both borrowers, but the variable costs relative to funds supplied by the bank make the borrower who borrows a greater amount of funds less profitable. Both have paid a fee for the line. However, the expense of the insurance contract has not been assessed to offset the fee. Since the customer that borrows less has an opportunity to borrow more, the expense of maintaining liquidity to service this customer is greater than it would be for the one that borrows more.

Again the problem arises that this expense must be costed out correctly. A method for doing this will be presented later. If this costing is done correctly, then the fees and balances charged for the insurance contract should be sufficient to cover the insurance contract plus any profit that should be made on the arrangement. That is, the insurance contract would be able to stand on its own, independent of the pure loan.

AN EXAMPLE OF CUSTOMER PROFITABILITY ANALYSIS

An example of customer profitability analysis will enable the reader to feel more comfortable in analyzing some of the current problems troubling the banking industry. Table 11-2 presents data on ABC Discount Stores. Note that the analysis is for one quarter, so that in computing interest payments or rates of return, the figures must be adjusted for the appropriate time period. ABC Discount Stores has a line of credit of $5 million, is charged a commitment fee of ¼ of one percent, and pays prime plus ½ percent on all borrowings. Compensating balances are determined on an average basis and relate to the average loan outstanding. No time accounts are included in the balance relationship.

ABC Discount Stores has been put in the Class A loan category, and the budget exercise of the bank, described in Chapter 8, has set target returns for this class at 3.28 percent on assets, 32.80 percent on capital, and 4.69 percent on purchased funds. Reserve requirements are assumed to be 15 percent on demand deposits, 6 percent on time deposits, and 6 percent

TABLE 11-2 Customer Profitability Statement

Account: ABC Discount Stores		Date:	March 31, 198X
Terms:		Rate:	Prime + ½
Commitment:	$5,000,000	Loan Class:	A
Commitment fee:	¼ of 1%		

Target Returns:

On allocated capital	32.80%
On bank funds	4.69
On assets	3.28

Sources and Uses of Funds, First Quarter, 198X

1. Average Loan Balance	$3,000,000
2. Average Collected Balance	638,000
2'. Investable Balance @ 15%	542,300
3. Average Time Balance	-0-
3'. Investable Balance	-0-
4. Total Investable Funds	542,300
5. Allocated Capital @ 10%	300,000
6. Free Purchased Funds	2,157,700

Income Statement

Revenues

7. Gross Interest Income on Loan	$ 55,356
8. Fees on Line	7,500
9. Fees Generated by Services	
a. Service charges	-0-
b. Data processing	-0-
c. Other	-0-
d. Total	-0-
10. Total Income	62,856

Expenses

11. Interest on Compensating Balances	-0-
12. Cost of Services Provided	
a. Activity costs	37
b. Loan handling expenses	15
c. Cost of fee services	104
d. Data processing	-0-
e. Other costs	499
f. Total	655
13. Charges on Bank Funds Used	37,301
14. Total Expenses	37,956

Net Income

15. Profit Before Taxes	24,900

Profitability Measures (annualized)

16. On Allocated Capital	33.20%
17. On Bank Funds	4.34
18. On Assets	3.32

Profitability Index

19. Capital (33.20/32.80)	1.01
20. Bank Funds (4.34/4.69)	.925
21. Assets (3.32/3.28)	1.01

on purchased funds. The capital allocation coefficient is 10 percent.

The average loan balance for the quarter ended has been $3 million. The borrower has kept, on average, collected balances of $638,000. Multiplying this figure by one minus 15 percent gives the bank $542,300 in investable deposit balances. Allocating bank capital equal to 10 percent of the loan asset, the bank sets aside $300,000 for ABC Discount Stores. This means that the bank must also channel $2,157,700 in *free* purchased funds to this account to support the loan. Adjusted for reserve requirements, the total amount of purchased funds charged to this loan is $2,157,700/(1 − .06), or $2,295,426. This, of course, will affect the computation of profitability figures.

Gross revenues from the loan amounted to $55,356 over the quarter in question. Since the borrower was charged the interest cost monthly and the prime changed during the quarter, the amount of interest paid corresponds to no listed interest rate. The fees collected amount to $7,500, so that the total income received from this customer during the period was $62,856.

Next the analysts would collect all the relevant usage charges from other parts of the bank. A computer information system makes these data readily available to loan officers or analysts on a timely basis. The analyst simply collects this information, since services and charges are decided upon elsewhere in the bank and are independent of the actions of either the analyst or the loan officer.

The charge on bank funds used is obtained by multiplying the *total* amount of purchased funds used by the average transfer rate for the period under review. In this case, the average transfer rate was assumed to be 6.5 percent, so that the total cost of funds used was $37,301. Total expenses are now figured at $37,956, which leaves $24,900 as net profit before taxes.

In computing the profitability measures, all figures are multiplied by 4 to annualize them. Once this is done, it is seen that ABC Discount Stores returns the bank 33.20 percent on allocated capital, 3.32 percent on total assets, and 4.34 percent on allocated funds.

Next, the profitability indexes are computed with the use of the target yields listed earlier in the table. Return on capital and return on assets both show the loan relationship to be slightly overpriced. The return on bank funds shows that the customer is slightly underpriced. In all, returns indicate a relatively good performance; the loan pricing relationship has been very close to what was expected.

There is a difference in the three measures because the compensating balance kept at the bank by ABC Discount Stores was less than the target figure. If the average collected balance is divided by the average loan outstanding, it is seen that the customer kept only 18 percent of its average loan outstanding on deposit. The expected norm for this loan class is 20 percent. Thus, more purchased funds were allocated than planned. This raised the amount attributed to expenses over what was expected and thus reduced profits before taxes.

A larger numerator or a smaller denominator would raise the rate of return on bank funds and improve the profitability index. Note, too, that an increase in profits before taxes would also raise the rate-of-return figures for capital and assets, implying that the loan is slightly more over-priced than previously thought. There are several reasons for this, one being that the borrower still "owes" something to the bank for having another $2,000,000 in funds available for borrowing. This point is dis-cussed further in the section on the insurance contract.

The amount of deviation from target here is not substantial. If the profitability indexes showed that the customer was considerably more profitable or less profitable than expected, then the loan officer should first analyze the account to see where deviations occurred. This is easily done by computer. In pricing the loan, the loan officer estimates the various revenues and costs the customer can be expected to incur (this was de-scribed more fully in Chapter 8) and enters them into the customer's file in the computer. Then when profitability analysis is performed, the actual amount for the period under consideration is compared with the targeted amounts and the computer can be asked to compute deviations from target and print out all three sets of data. This saves a great deal of collection effort and puts most of the information needed by the reviewers right in front of them for determining why they overpriced or underpriced the loan and what improvements could be made in the future.

CURRENT QUESTIONS

Risk allocation, capital allocation, and the cost of the insurance contract are three areas at the forefront of current discussions about customer profit-ability analysis. All three were briefly discussed earlier. In this section they will be examined more closely, and examples will be presented to show how they may be correctly treated.

Risk Allocation

As mentioned earlier, risk may be treated as an expense. Since the bank does not know which loans in a given loan class are going to fail, it must allocate, across the loan class, a fee associated with the probability that any one loan may fail. Since the loan class, as defined in Chapter 2, is homogeneous with respect to all borrowers within it, all borrowers in the class must be assigned the same probability of defaulting.

The figure to be entered for a given loan class should therefore be one computed for that loan class and no other. Calculations can be based on historical data of the loan class, aggregate data from the banking system, or the bank's expectations.

Since the probability that a given loan in a given loan class will default changes over the credit or business cycle, the expense the bank enters into the customer profitability analysis should also vary. Thus, to do their job correctly, bank analysts must constantly be conscious of the risk exposure of each class of loans and how this risk exposure will change over time. Otherwise the loan portfolio will show poor-quality loans being relatively more profitable in recessions or periods of tight money than good-quality loans, whereas the reverse will be the case during a boom period or a period of loose money.

Technically, this expense should be allocated to the loan-loss reserve account. As was described in Chapter 6, this is an asset valuation account against which bad loans are charged. It should be noted that the sum of all risk expense items, obtained by adding together all asset accounts, will not be equal to the amount the bank actually charges off. This sum will be the "actuarial" amount the bank will set aside to protect itself. However, since banking laws allow commercial banks to charge off more than this amount, they can accumulate "tax-free" capital. The actual amount charged off is a question for aggregate profit planning and tax planning and should not be included in an analysis of the individual customer.

Finally, the contract rate on the loan will not be reduced relative to the risk-free rate even if the bank does expense the riskiness of the loan customer in pricing and analysis. The contract rate is composed of several things: (1) the risk-free rate, (2) the risk component, (3) any charges for services and the insurance contract that are not paid for explicitly by fees (see the last part of Chapter 10), and (4) the effect of imperfections in the market. Even if risk and services and other products are correctly and explicitly priced, what is left will not be the risk-free rate, because of the imperfections in the various loan markets. This is not a major problem except for the fact that target or required rates of return on the different loan classes that are net of risk and fees and service costs should not be equal. Target rates must reflect the relative imperfections that exist within the loan markets. If this adjustment is made correctly, then the interpretation of the relative loan rates, that is, the rate relationship due to the relative imperfections in the different loan markets, will be correct.

Capital Allocation

Capital, if it is allocated at all, can be allocated according to a fixed proportion of loan size or "risk asset" size, or according to a schedule dependent on the risk or loan class of the customer. Most of the discussion up to this point has been in terms of fixed proportions. Scheduled allocation uses the same information but rearranges it a bit to emphasize different characteristics of the loan or the borrower, such as customer risk. The reason for concentrating on these other factors is that banks feel they can stimulate loans or control risk better by using the information on risk rather than applying a fixed proportion of capital to all loans.

In order to allocate capital according to risk, the bank must know (1) what rate of return it wants to earn on its capital and (2) the makeup of its portfolio in terms of the quantities of various asset classes or loan classes it will achieve to make the target rate of return. When allocating a flat proportion of capital, the bank needs to know both the desired rate of return on capital and the relative returns that must be earned on the various asset and loan classes to achieve the target return.

In either case, the knowledge of quantities and returns comes out of the planning or budgeting process described in Chapter 8. In one case, relative quantities are used to control, while in the others, relative interest rates are used to control.

TABLE 11-3   Determination of Return on Capital as a Basis for Loan Targets

Loan Class	Loans	Capital	Capital as a Percent of Loans	Profit Before Taxes	Return on Assets	Return on Capital
Total Portfolio	$2,000,000,000	$200,000,000	10.00%	$70,000,000	3.50%	35.00%
A	400,000,000	37,486,000	9.37	13,120,000	3.28	35.00
B	800,000,000	77,714,000	9.71	27,200,000	3.40	35.00
C	600,000,000	60,858,000	10.14	21,300,000	3.55	35.00
D	100,000,000	23,942,000	11.97	8,380,000	4.19	35.00

Changes in Sources and Uses		Changes in Income Statement	
Capital	$ 281,100	Charges on Bank Funds Used	$37,627
Free Purchased Funds	2,176,600	Profit Before Taxes	24,574

Return on Allocated Capital (annualized) = 34.967

If a bank allocates capital according to risk, the general procedure is to require the same rate of return on capital on each loan class. This means that a poorer-quality loan that does not go into default will provide a greater net income figure than a better-quality loan that does not go into default. In order to earn the same rate of return on capital, the poorer-quality loan must have more capital allocated to it than the better-quality loan. Once target rates of return are determined for each loan class, the relative capital allocation ratios can be determined.

The example presented earlier can be used to clarify this procedure. In Table 11-3 it can be seen that the bank is planning for $2 billion in loans in the coming period. This amount is divided into the four loan classes shown, with the division based on relative loan demands, relative yields, and the return bank management would like to earn for the risk exposure it feels the bank can maintain. The management has decided that, on average, capital will be allocated at 10 percent of loans and the average return on assets before taxes on the portfolio is to be 3.50 percent. Return on capital is thus expected to be 35 percent.

Next, since interest rates and costs are allocated as a percentage of loan amounts instead of a percentage of capital allocated, the bank determines the expected rates of return on the various loan classes. This information comes out of the budgeting process. As can be seen from Table 11-3, the bank expects to have net earnings of 3.28 percent on class A loans, 3.40 percent on class B loans, 3.55 percent on class C loans, and 4.19 percent on class D loans. If the bank allocates 10 percent of capital behind all loans, the process stops here and the technique for customer profitability analysis described earlier can be executed because all the target data are now available for analysis.

Several additional steps must be performed if capital is to be allocated according to loan class. In the last column of Table 11-3 it can be observed that the bank targets a 35.00 percent return on capital for all classes of loans. This means that it assumes that *if capital is allocated correctly* and the appropriate return is earned on each class of loans, it will, on average, earn 35.00 percent before taxes on total capital available.

This means that profit before taxes, a figure computed by multiplying the loan amount in each class by the return on assets for that class, divided by an as yet unknown amount of capital, is equal to .35. That is, for class A loans, $13,120,000/x = .35$. When this equation is solved for x, allocated capital is found to be $37,486,000, which is the amount entered into row 2 for class A loans.

Now, the amounts in row 2 are divided by the loan amounts in each class of loans to obtain the percentage allocation of capital for that loan class. That is, for class A loans, $37,486,000/$400,000,000 = .0937; thus, the amount of capital that is allocated to class A loan customers is 9.37 percent of the loan amount.

This will change the figures in Table 11-2 slightly, as shown at the bottom of Table 11-3. The capital allocated to the loan of ABC Discount Stores is $281,100 instead of $300,000. Free purchased funds now amount to $2,176,600, and the charges on bank funds used now rise to $37,627. Profits before taxes drop to $24,574. Return on capital, annualized, is 34.967 percent, or approximately 35 percent. Thus, the loan is priced, as indicated before, at approximately the appropriate level. If a smaller amount of purchased funds had been needed (for example, if ABC Discount Stores had kept up its level of collected deposits), then the return would have been in excess of 35 percent and the loan would have appeared to be slightly overpriced, as before. Otherwise, the results are pretty much the same in the two cases.

The Insurance Contract

The bank must calculate the expense it incurs in promising to lend a customer up to a certain amount of money regardless of the timing of the borrowing. Otherwise it will be underpricing customers that borrow only a small proportion of their line of credit and overpricing those that borrow a larger proportion of their line. This can be shown very simply. Assume, for example, that ABC Discount Stores borrowed only half the amount shown in Table 11-2, that is, $1,500,000. Also suppose it reduced its balances by 30 percent, to $446,000. If the use of all other services does not change, then ABC would provide the bank with a net profit before taxes of $17,748. Since only $150,000 of capital is now allocated to the account, the annualized rate of return of this borrower is now 47.33 percent, the annualized return on assets committed is 4.73 percent, and the annualized return on bank funds is 6.88 percent. The customer now appears to be in "overpriced" relation to the bank's targets, whereas before it was seen that the customer was just on target.

The reason for this is that the customer is borrowing much less than was expected when the line was originally given. And because the bank expected the customer to borrow more, it arranged (at least implicitly) to provide liquidity on its balance sheet by holding liquid assets or by maintaining its position in liability markets to be able to buy funds when they were needed to support the loan. Thus, in borrowing $3,000,000 the customer is forcing less of an implicit cost on the bank than when it borrows

$1,500,000. The fact that this cost is not included in the customer profitability analysis means that costs are not being correctly assessed, and therefore neither are the profits from that customer. Some adjustment must be made.

The cost of this contract can be expensed in two ways. It should be noted, however, that the computed expense in either method should not determine, once and for all, the cost to the bank of supporting a given customer or class of customers. The analysis must be carried out over relatively short intervals of time, not only because of the customer's changing habits, but also because of the changing value of the insurance contract. Moreover, the insurance contract will be more valuable to the customer and more costly to the bank during periods of tight money or during boom economic conditions; it will have the least worth during periods of loose credit or recession.

In either case the bank must make some analysis of its additional exposure. Its analysts must estimate not only the customer's expected usage but also the distribution of that usage and the probabilities attached to the different outcomes. Once this is done the analysts will have some idea not only about how much the customer is expected to borrow but also the contingencies the bank must face should the customer not borrow the amount expected.

These expectations must always be kept current, of course, to take account of a change in the customer's financial situation so that the bank can adjust rapidly to a change in the underlying strength or weakness of the customer.

Thus, if a customer borrows less than expected, the firm must allocate a cost to the firm's account to charge it for the liquidity the bank has maintained to support its line of credit. If a customer borrows more than expected, it may not be charged at all, because the bank is now having to keep nothing in the way of liquidity to meet these contingencies.

One way to charge a customer is to charge its asset balance for the availability of the line. For example, on the basis of the distribution of expected usages of the line by ABC Discount Stores, the bank assesses the company a charge of 3 percent of the unused portion of its line. This charge will be paid by means of additional deposit balances the bank has to have on hand to support the additional part of the line that ABC *might* use.

This means that the bank now must tie up some additional capital to support the additional funds. Furthermore, the bank must allocate more purchased funds to the relationship. The changes that take place in the sources and uses statement for ABC Discount Stores are shown in Table 11-4, case I. Balances amounting to $60,000 are now set aside to account for the additional $2,000,000 availability. Allocated capital rises to $306,000,

TABLE 11-4   Effect of Insurance Contract on Customer Profitability

Case I:

Sources and Uses Statement

Average Loan Balance	$3,000,000	Investable Balances	$ 542,300
Balances for Line	60,000	Allocated Capital	306,000
	$3,060,000	Free Purchased Funds	2,238,700
			$3,060,000

Changes in Income Statement

Charges on Bank Funds Used	$38,234
Profit Before Taxes	23,967

	Rate of Return	Profitability Index
Capital	31.33%	0.96
Bank Funds	4.07	0.87
Assets	3.13	0.96

Case II:

Changes in Income Statement

Other Costs (0.0022 × unused portion of line/4)	$ 1,100
Profit Before Taxes	23,800

	Rate of Return	Profitability Index
Capital	31.73%	0.97
Bank Funds	4.15	0.88
Assets	3.17	0.97

and free purchased funds rises to $2,238,700. (Purchased funds allocated now increase to $2,238,700/.94 = $2,381,596.) Charges on bank funds used are now $38,234 [$2,381,596 × (.065/4)], and profit before taxes drops to $23,967.

As would be expected, all rate-of-return figures drop and the profitability indexes for all measures fall below 1.00. The indication is that the loan relationship is now slightly underpriced, whereas before it had been priced to provide the target return. If this adjustment makes the analysis more accurate, then the bank must consider whether or not it should reprice this customer, or whether there has been a fundamental change in the borrower's financial situation.

A second method of costing the insurance contract is to charge the customer an implicit fee that represents the cost to the bank of maintaining a liquid enough position to support the borrower's opportunities. This is shown in Table 11-4, case II. In this case the customer is charged $1,100 for the unused portion of its line of credit. This is calculated by multiplying the unused portion of the line, $2,000,000 in this case, by .0022/4 to put the fee on a quarterly basis. The result is then entered as an expense that reduces profit before taxes to $23,800.

As in case I, all rate-of-return values drop and the profitability indexes again show that the customer relationship is underpriced. Both adjustments result in approximately the same answers. Both are theoretically correct. The problem, as usual, comes in the practice. To estimate these costs and then continuously apply them is difficult given all the complex and ambiguous relationships that exist. However, if a bank is going to allocate its resources correctly, price its customers right, and maximize its owners' wealth, it must make the effort to identify and appropriately apply all its costs of operations.

UNBUNDLING ONCE AGAIN

Although commercial banks moved to unbundling in the 1970s, they have not progressed very far in applying a completely unbundled approach. In the first place, their cost accounting systems have been inadequate to the task of determining and allocating costs in sufficiently disaggregated terms. Second, the process of unbundling has not had the full support of top banking management. Finally, the pressure to unbundle seems to be greatest when there is a seller's market, that is, when banks do not have to be concerned about their demand for loans. If demand is slack, the pressure on the bank is to bundle and cross-sell services in the same package. Thus, the greatest pressure to unbundle came in the early 1970s; then, with the slack loan demand that followed the 1974–1975 recession, banks retreated and began once again to practice bundling.

In studying customer profitability analysis, however, the need to unbundle becomes apparent. Not only do the practitioners of customer profitability analysis want to determine whether customers are contributing adequately to bank profitability; they also are concerned about the biases that exist when costs are not allocated correctly. Thus, they push to obtain better data and better information on cost allocation; hence, by seeking these improvements, they are pushing (if only implicitly) for unbundling costs and prices.

Furthermore, there is some indication that sophisticated borrowers prefer more explicit pricing. There was some evidence of this in the mid-1970s; the practice has received greater publicity in more recent times.[6]

---

[6] See, for example, the article on Manufacturers Hanover Trust in *The Wall Street Journal* (January 11, 1978), p. 2.

These borrowers want to know the cost of the various services they are receiving so they can make decisions about doing business in the cheapest way. Therefore, pressures do exist inside and outside of the bank to unbundle to a greater extent. It is likely that with electronic funds transfer systems, pressures to unbundle will grow, because these customers will be even more sensitive to earning opportunities.[7]

In contrast, middle-sized and smaller borrowers still seem to desire packaged loans and services from the bank. One reason is that the opportunities to find cheaper methods to do the same thing are not as great for them as for a larger firm. Another is that they may actually be getting a "better deal" from the bank than if the package were unbundled, and the costs of finding out may be too high. Thus, in this segment of the market, pressure to unbundle is slight.

[7] M. J. Flannery and D. M. Jaffee, *The Economic Implications of an Electronic Monetary Transfer System* (Lexington, Mass.: Heath, 1973).

REVIEW QUESTIONS

1. How can you analyze a bank customer if the customer relationship does not include a loan, that is, if there are no "assets" on the balance sheet the bank draws up for the customer?
2. If a bank "bundles" its products and services, how can it include a profit margin for each product and service provided when it analyzes the profitability of a particular customer? How can it determine whether the total relationship is really profitable?
3. If the bank includes a cost-of-capital figure in the customer profitability analysis so that the target rate of return is zero, how can it compute a profitability index?
4. Should the relationship of the bank with the officers of a borrowing firm be included in the customer profitability analysis of the firm? For example, if the president of a company has a loan, deposits, and other dealings with the bank from which his company borrows, should the accounts of the two be analyzed together?

5. What changes would have to be made in a customer profitability analysis system if a bank were to unbundle? Would the new system be feasible?
6. Why is it easier to control the riskiness of the loan portfolio by allocating capital according to the riskiness of the borrower than by using a fixed allocation?
7. Could the bank alter the way it charges compensating balances to cover the insurance contract instead of changing its fees?

SHORT-TERM MANAGEMENT

12

Asset and Liability Markets

The short run and intermediate run pose entirely different problems for the bank than the long-run questions discussed in previous chapters. This chapter examines the problems and constraints a bank faces in the short run and intermediate run. Specific problems will be treated more thoroughly in the following two chapters. Once the environment of these time horizons is introduced, the various instruments and lenders with which the bank deals and the relevant markets will be discussed.

Since seasonal and cyclical factors are so important to the time horizons included in this discussion, the term structure of interest rates becomes a crucial element for bank performance. Thus, the chapter closes with a brief presentation of the theory of the term structure of interest rates.

THE SHORT RUN AND INTERMEDIATE RUN

The main difference between the matters treated in this section of the book and those dealt with in previous chapters is the time horizon within which the bank works. In previous chapters the main concern was with the long run, variously described as anywhere from four to seven years in length.

The matters under consideration were those that could not be changed rapidly and that dealt with the general structure and image of the bank. These included the customer base, on both the asset and the liability sides of the balance sheet, and the bank's capital structure. Branch systems, national loan departments, debt issues, and dividend policies were specific decision areas confronted within the long-run horizon.

Now it is assumed that decisions have been made regarding these issues. That is, the bank has decided on its capital base, its dividend policy, its loan customers and pricing system, and its sources of funds. Although loan and deposit amounts may vary over the shorter run, the bank will not alter its image or its relative pricing scheme.

The variations that take place in the demand for loans and the supply of liabilities are the source of the major difficulties with which the bank must cope in the shorter run. There would be no problem, however, if these variations were known with certainty; the bank would have to try to match the maturities of assets or liabilities it bought or sold, but that could be handled simply. The uncertain timing of these variations causes some difficulty in planning bank operations. Thus, the bank's task within this shorter time horizon is to manage the assets and liabilities over which it has control in a way that will contribute to the maximization of the value of the bank.

The situation is not the same for all banks, because the assets and liabilities available to them and the maturities of the different components of their portfolios may vary. In the context of this discussion, a bank is considered to have control over its assets or liabilities if it can exactly determine the quantity of the item it wants without changing the price it pays or receives on the item. This was explicitly stated in Chapter 2 in terms of the elasticity of supply of funds or demand for loans (or supply of securities). The bank faces perfectly elastic supply or demand curves for these assets and liabilities and can therefore choose the quantity of the particular assets or liabilities it takes from the market.

On the basis of the mix of assets and liabilities and their demand/ supply characteristics, commercial banks are strictly divided into three classes: asset-management banks, liability-management banks, and banks that do not quite meet all the requirements for full management of their liabilities.[1] Asset-management banks are those that do not have sufficient loan demand to exhaust the deposits that are supplied less than perfectly

---

[1] Banks may not be classified by people in the industry and in industry publications precisely as is done in this book. This specific division is followed here purely for expository purposes.

elastically. These banks will generally be small or medium-sized and operate in local markets.

Banks that deal in national or international markets and have a loan demand that exceeds their local or regional supply of funds generally can be considered liability managers. Some of these banks (the large regional banks, for example) will not or cannot count on even a few of the markets that supply funds being perfectly elastic at all times. Hence, they cannot fully manage their liabilities in the sense defined above, whereas the others (the large New York banks) will be able to obtain funds elastically from these liability sources at all times.[2]

The portfolio management problems of these banks will be different both with respect to instruments used and with respect to the importance of various time constraints. Thus, the next two chapters deal with two different time horizons and the management problems each type of bank has with regard to each time horizon.

Reserve Management

The reserve management time horizon refers exclusively to the bank's need to meet the reserve requirements on its liabilities established by federal or state banking authorities. For banks that are members of the Federal Reserve System, the time horizon for reserve management is two weeks, for this is the time lag over which the bank has to satisfy reserve requirements as determined by the technicalities of the Federal Reserve's operating procedure.

Reserve management follows a different philosophy from management over longer time periods. Since reserve requirements establish an "effective" constraint on portfolio construction,[3] and since the normal obligation to meet the constraint is so great, banks tend to operate conservatively in attempting to satisfy their reserve requirements. Thus the philosophy is one of minimization of losses rather than maximization of bank

---

[2] This division must, of course, be taken with a grain of salt. A large New York bank would not be able to obtain amounts of funds substantially larger than normal using one particular instrument or instruments of a particular maturity within a very short period of time without making price concessions. As will be discussed later, these banks may go to the Federal Reserve for the funds rather than to the open market in such a situation. Thus, when it is said that a bank will be able to obtain funds elastically at all times, this should only be taken in the sense that a bank will obtain the needed funds within a reasonable period of time.

[3] Effective in the sense of forcing the bank into a portfolio it would not otherwise maintain.

value. Although minimization can often be considered the other side of the coin to maximization,[4] it conveys more clearly the conservative nature of reserve management operation. Minimization also considers the potential implicit loss to the bank that can be included as a constraint if reserve requirements are not satisfied. Reserve management will be treated in Chapter 13.

Asset/Liability Management

The time horizon for asset/liability management is somewhat longer than that of reserve management. Because of this, reserve requirements are not a vital constraint on bank operations; the bank will always have time enough to convert assets or purchase liabilities to satisfy reserve obligations. Thus, banks will be concerned about structuring their asset/liability portfolios in a way that will maximize bank value within the uncertain variations that are expected to take place in loans or deposits.

Differentiating this from the reserve management horizon, one could say that asset/liability management deals with seasonal and cyclical investments in loans and deposits, whereas reserve management must protect against random or unexpected changes that would cause the bank either to fall short of its needed reserve or to have too much of its portfolio in low-interest-bearing assets. Thus, in asset/liability management considerable time must be spent trying to determine the seasonal pressures to be expected as well as the changes occurring in the national and international economies, including the policies likely to be followed by the Federal Reserve System and the U.S. Treasury Department.

Although the time horizon used for asset/liability management may differ among banks, there exist some outside constraints on what this time horizon may be. It can be as short as 30 days, the minimum maturity of negotiable certificates of deposit. Although the bank can use federal funds and repurchase agreements to meet asset/liability management needs, there is a term structure problem to consider relative to the needs of the bank to fund assets or use liabilities. The 30-day CD market represents the minimum maturity for obtaining funds elastically that contains all the term structure information available for that time period.

The maximum horizon varies considerably from bank to bank. The figure that will be used in the following discussions will be six months, or

---

[4] Loss minimization is the dual solution to profit maximization in a mathematical programming problem.

180 days. The reason for the choice of this cutoff period is the condition of the market for negotiable CDs with maturities greater than six months. Whereas banks can sell CDs with maturities of one to six months in markets that have many participants and a great deal of money, so that large amounts of funds can be obtained without significantly affecting interest rates,[5] markets in maturities greater than six months have neither the width nor breadth to meet this condition. Although they can obtain funds in the longer-term markets, when managing their asset or liability portfolio to handle seasonal or cyclical swings in loan or deposit flows or in the term structure of interest rates, banks are primarily restricted to CD maturities of six months or less. Asset/liability management will be treated more completely in Chapter 14.

CONTROLLABLE ASSETS AND LIABILITIES

The assets and liabilities described in the following pages are those whose demand and supply curves are elastic, or nearly so, to the bank. The bank can therefore exert considerable control over its portfolio holdings of these items, adjusting their quantities to maintain the desired balance and liquidity. Not all of these instruments are available to all banks, nor may it be assumed that the demand/supply is always completely free of constraints. For example, negotiable CDs will not be available to a $10 million bank, and borrowing from the Federal Reserve discount window cannot be maintained indefinitely without some pressure being brought upon the bank by the Federal Reserve System.

The six instruments or techniques that will be discussed here are borrowings from the Federal Reserve System, federal funds, U.S. Treasury bills, repurchase agreements, negotiable certificates of deposit, and Eurodollars.

Borrowing from the Federal Reserve

Borrowing from the Federal Reserve is considered a right and not a privilege. Nonetheless, the attitude taken by both the regulators and the participants is that this right should not be abused. Consequently, implicit costs and limits are recognized in practice even though they are not present in theory. Bankers tend to act, in general, in a very conservative

---

[5] See footnote 1.

fashion with respect to obtaining funds from the Federal Reserve. In fact, some will take fairly large losses on selling their assets rather than risk the displeasure of the Federal Reserve by borrowing too frequently.

Basically, the attitude of Federal Reserve personnel is that a bank should operate within the constraint of its own resources. They feel that bankers should not have to rely on central bank resources except in time of need. The legitimate needs to borrow are therefore fairly well defined. First of all, "a bank can borrow for temporary aid in working out portfolio adjustments to meet especially meritorious local demanders."[6] Second, "as long as a bank demonstrates in its overall performance its intention to operate within the limits of its own resources, it can usually arrange temporary accommodation to cover a variety of problems."[7] Third, the Federal Reserve allows borrowing at times when it is tightening up on credit availability. This enables the banking system as a whole to adjust to the new availability of reserves and higher interest rates. Special times may call for a special response; for example, in September 1966, the Federal Reserve allowed for greater borrowing privileges because of the shaky conditions of the financial markets at the time.[8] In 1970, it threw open the discount window to alleviate the pressures on the banks caused by the failure of the Penn Central Railroad and the subsequent crisis in the commercial paper market. The Federal Reserve will also lend to banks in extreme financial difficulty.[9]

Banks are not allowed to borrow to take advantage of the favorable tax treatment of certain securities, to arbitrage interest rate differentials, or to finance speculation in securities, real estate, or commodities.

A bank may borrow from the Federal Reserve by obtaining either a *discount* or an *advance*. A "discount" is actually a "rediscount" of a customer loan meeting closely specified conditions. Instruments meeting these conditions are called "eligible paper" and include commercial, agricultural, and industrial paper; bankers' acceptances and other bills of exchange; construction loans; and factors' paper. An advance is a loan based on the bank's own note secured by eligible paper or government securities.[10] Advances are the most often used form of borrowing.

---

[6] James Parthmos, "The Discount Window," in Timothy Q. Cook, ed., *Instruments of the Money Market,* 4th ed. (Federal Reserve Bank of Richmond, 1977), p. 31.

[7] Ibid., p. 31.

[8] Many bankers, however, interpreted the September 1966 response as a threat that the discount window would be closed.

[9] Two major examples of this are the Federal Reserve's support of the Parsons' chain of banks in the late 1960s and Franklin National Bank in the early to mid-1970s.

[10] These are generally called Section 13 loans, Section 13 being the part of the Federal

Advances may have a maturity of up to 90 days, but most are for a maximum of 15 days. They can be paid off in part or in full before the maturity date, and payment is made by charging the borrowing bank's reserve account. This charge is made automatically if the loan is allowed to go to maturity.

The only personnel authorized to borrow from the Federal Reserve for the bank are individuals chosen and certified by the bank's board of directors. Since the loan application and the note of indebtedness must be received by the Federal Reserve on or before the loan date, it is general practice for banks to leave a supply of signed notes at the Federal Reserve with the date and amount left blank. A telephone call can initiate the loan, and written confirmation will then be sent to provide physical evidence of the request. The collateral used to back the loan must be held either by the Federal Reserve or by another member bank under a custody receipt arrangement. This is generally worked out through correspondent bank agreements. Collateral other than U.S. government securities is often sent to the Federal Reserve in anticipation of borrowing, because officials of the Federal Reserve must determine its eligibility before it will be accepted.

The interest rate charged on these borrowings (the discount rate) is determined by each of the district Federal Reserve Banks, subject to the approval of the Board of Governors of the Federal Reserve System. As originally conceived, a different rate could exist in each of the twelve Federal Reserve districts, to take account of differing conditions among them. This never worked out in practice, seemingly because of the homogeneous nature of U.S. financial markets. Therefore, except in a few isolated cases, the discount rates at the several district banks have all been the same and generally move together, although in theory each district bank has its own rate.

The level of the discount rate is set, in practice, to *follow* market conditions. This is the opposite of the operating procedures in many other developed countries, where the central banks determine the central bank rate and then force market rates to move into line with it. The Federal Reserve tends to move open-market rates by buying or selling U.S. government securities from its portfolio, and then it moves the discount rate

---

Reserve Act in which provision is made for them. A Section 10(b) loan is a loan secured by *any* collateral satisfactory to the lending Reserve Bank. However, 10(b) loans are not as popular as Section 13 loans, because 10(b) loans earn a higher interest rate (½ percent higher than Section 13 loans) and may involve some delay because of the need to obtain approval of the collateral.

into line with market rates. This facilitates commercial bank adjustments because borrowing from the Federal Reserve becomes more favorable as the central bank tightens up on credit and forces interest rates up, and less attractive when monetary policy becomes loose and interest rates are forced down. Rising interest rates encourage the banks to get out of the market and adjust their portfolios with money from the discount window. Since this is considered to be "temporary money," it is assumed that it will be repaid once the transition to the new market position is achieved. When Federal Reserve action allows interest rates to drop, the discount rate lags downward movements in open-market rates, the spread between the two narrows, and open-market rates may even drop below the discount rate. This forces banks out of the discount window and into the open markets. Thus, banks have a relatively cheap backup source of funds when money becomes scarce but reenter the market as funds become more plentiful.

In the absence of these transitional states, the discount rate tends to be a little bit above comparable market rates on federal funds and U.S. Treasury bills. However, since the financial markets are generally in a transitional state, it is hard to tell whether or not this relationship between the discount rate and other rates holds.

Federal Funds

Federal funds are a direct claim to a deposit at the Federal Reserve; that is, they are funds held for member banks in the Federal Reserve System that can be used to satisfy reserve requirements. The ownership of these claims can be sold by one member bank to another, although it is not uncommon now for nonmember banks or securities dealers to participate in this market and "sell" cash or deposits to member banks for their use in satisfying reserve requirements. Thus, small nonmember banks that maintain deposits at correspondent banks can sell their excess balances to the correspondent and the correspondent can then use the funds as reserves. Otherwise, the larger bank will lose the funds as they are withdrawn for sale elsewhere and have to buy other funds as a substitute. In addition, U.S. government securities dealers,[11] as well as other securities dealers, can sell federal funds either to banks or to the Federal Reserve. This is because these dealers have in recent years been paid in federal funds for securities they have sold to banks or to the Federal Reserve. However, the borrowing and lending of federal funds are primarily thought of as trans-

---

[11] U.S. government securities dealers will be discussed more fully later in this chapter.

actions between two member banks in funds on deposit at a Federal Reserve Bank.

Transactions take place between a bank that has excess reserves and a bank that needs funds either to cover reserves lost through adverse clearings or to support asset acquisition. The transactions are usually for very short periods of time—from one to four days—and hence were initially expected to be used only for short-run adjustments to market conditions. However, some banks, primarily the large New York City banks and some big regional banks, have come to rely on federal funds as a permanent source of funds. These banks must be constantly seeking sellers and turning over their portfolio as they deal with many banks at different times. Also, the maturities available in the federal funds market have lengthened, even to the extent that some banks have been known to lend "term" federal funds. The major action in the market, however, is extremely short term.

Trading usually takes place directly between a buyer and a seller, although some transactions are conducted through dealers. Several mechanisms exist for a federal funds transaction. In New York City a transaction takes the form of an exchange of checks drawn on each bank's account at the Federal Reserve. The check of the selling bank is paid immediately, whereas the check of the buying bank is collected through the clearing house and hence not paid until the next day. The interest is included in the clearing house check of the buying bank.

Other transactions follow a somewhat different pattern. Once a deal is reached between two banks, the seller of the funds will notify its Federal Reserve Bank to transfer the sale amount from its account to the buyer's account. If the accounts are in different district banks, the transfer will be made via the Federal Reserve Bank's wire. Written confirmation of the transaction must follow. At the maturity of the transaction the Federal Reserve will reverse the operation.

Federal funds transactions are generally in units of $1 million or more but may be smaller. There is another, "retail" side of the market in which small to medium-sized banks transact with larger correspondents. Amounts traded here have been as small as $20,000 to $25,000.

Four types of banks deal in the federal funds market.[12] First, there are the *sellers*. These are the smaller country or suburban banks that primarily deal with correspondents. When they have excess balances on hand, usually deposits at their correspondent bank, they ask their correspondent to buy them. The correspondents usually do buy the funds as a service to

---

[12] James M. Boughton, *Monetary Policy and the Federal Funds Market* (Durham, N.C.: Duke University Press, 1972), pp. 12–13.

their customers. Because of the passive nature of this purchase, the buying banks are referred to as *intermediaries*. Intermediaries generally carry a deficit balance in their reserve accounts equal to the amount of funds they expect to purchase from their customer banks. If the amount received is greater than expected, the intermediaries will put out the difference to their own correspondent banks, usually in New York.

The *buyers* are primarily those banks that actively search out federal funds as a permanent source of funds and carry large deficit positions in their purchases of funds. These banks are constantly in touch with banks around the country, have the pulse of the market, and basically determine the rate at which funds are traded.

The last group shall be designated *balancers* or *arbitragers*. Although these banks are medium-sized to large, they do not operate in volume in this market or conduct a large enough correspondent business to generate sufficient funds to be considered intermediaries. However, their management is sophisticated enough to tightly control their reserve position daily so that they can play both sides of the funds market (that is, be a buyer or a seller of funds). On some days they may even take advantage of discrepancies in pricing that occur within the market, buying from some in order to sell to others.

The federal funds rate is set by the supply and demand conditions that exist in the markets. However, the largest factor in the market as a whole is the Federal Reserve itself. By the way it conducts its open-market operations, the Federal Reserve can fairly accurately control the excess reserves in the banking system and hence the supply–demand relationship that exists at any one time. In this way it can very closely control the rate on federal funds.

The Federal Reserve wants to control the federal funds rate because the rate plays a very important part in the short-run operating procedures the Federal Reserve follows to achieve its longer-run objectives of monetary control and economic stimulus. Therefore, banks must follow very closely what the Federal Reserve is doing with respect to the federal funds rate and try to anticipate its actions in order to foresee the direction in which the rate can be expected to move in the future.

In conducting open-market operations, the Federal Reserve has generally targeted a range for the federal funds rate instead of choosing a single number. The spread has been as much as ¾ of a percentage point and as small as ¼ of a percentage point. Thus, if the Federal Reserve is aiming for a rate around 7 percent and the target range is ½ of a percentage point, the rate could move between 6¾ percent and 7¼ percent and still be "on target." The spread allows the market some freedom in handling temporary disturbances to the banking system. Because of this, within-week or between-week patterns can develop that can be used in bank planning in the short run.

For example, if everything else is held constant, the federal funds rate seems to be highest on Thursday and Friday and lowest on Tuesday and Wednesday. Many analysts contend that this is a function of the conservative nature of the people who run commercial banks. Being averse to having to borrow from the Federal Reserve System, bankers attempt to avoid being forced into the discount window by unexpected shortfalls in reserves on the last day of the statement week, which runs from Thursday through Wednesday. Thus, they attempt to build up adequate reserve balances at the start of the week. Banks that have excess reserves keep them; those with deficiencies attempt to buy reserves. Later in the week, those with excess reserves and an adequate average balance of reserves accumulated earlier in the week attempt to sell reserves, but demand is lessened because deficient banks have also built up reserve positions. Therefore, with supply lower and demand higher at the beginning of the statement week than at the end, interest rates tend to be higher at the beginning than at the end.

Special daily events may provide opportunities for making a profit. For example, estimations of when the Federal Reserve will enter the market may cause a large bank to accelerate or postpone a federal funds transaction. Fridays are special, because on Fridays banks buy three-day commitments. On a Wednesday, the end of the statement week, banks may observe large movements in the funds rate due to unexpected developments in reserve availability or general efforts of the Federal Reserve. Commercial banks, particularly the larger ones, watch what is going on in the federal funds market very closely, not only for the opportunity to profit, but also for an indication of the direction and intent of monetary policy.

U.S. Treasury Bills

Treasury bills come in a variety of maturities and are issued on a regular basis with maturities of 91 days (three months), 182 days (six months), 270 days (nine months), and 365 days (one year). The three-month and six-month bills are offered to the market each week in an auction conducted by the Federal Reserve. Thus, maturities are generally spaced weekly, at least within six months of the current date. Bidding can be either on a competitive basis, where the investor states the amounts and prices desired, or on a noncompetitive basis, where the investor gets the desired volume at the average price of accepted competitive bids.[13] New issues of nine-month and one-year bills are made only once a month, near the end of the month. Therefore, the end of each month is the maturity date for a number of issues, with other maturities falling within the month.

Treasury bills are sold at a discount from par. On the assumption that the purchase price is 98.46 percent of par, the annual rate of interest for a 91-day bill is determined in the following way:

$$\left(\frac{100 - 98.46}{100}\right)\left(\frac{360}{91}\right) = 6.092 \qquad (12\text{-}1)$$

The bill then pays off at 100 percent of par at maturity. Note that a 360-day year is used in determining the yield. The number of issues available makes it easy for a bank to buy bills for a specified period of time, knowing that it will receive the par value of the bill at the end of that time.

The rate of return on the bill cannot be compared directly with other issues that are coupon-bearing, because the yields to maturity on coupon-bearing issues use a 365-day year and the interest is figured from the purchase price rather than from the discount price as is done on the discount bills. To compare the two, the yield on bills is usually converted to a bond-equivalent basis in the following manner, where the price of the bill is 98.46 percent of par:

$$\left(\frac{100 - 98.46}{98.46}\right)\left(\frac{365}{91}\right) = 6.27 \qquad (12\text{-}2)$$

The quoted yield on the bill is therefore 6.092 percent [from equation (12-1)], but to compare the yield on the bill with a bond, the appropriate yield is 6.27 percent.

In addition to the fact that maturities of U.S. Treasury bills are spaced at relatively short, regular intervals, their major attraction for banks and other financial institutions is the highly organized secondary market for them. This makes the bills easily convertible into cash and makes their yields relatively consistent with the yields on other short-run securities. Thus, should the occasion arise, Treasury bills can generally be expected to reflect the overall opportunities in the market, and a bank can buy or sell them quickly at the going market rate of interest. This is what was described earlier as an elastic supply of securities.

Commercial banks that operate in the Treasury bill market try to space maturities so that funds are always becoming available. If funds are

---

[13] The amount may be prorated if the investor places too large an order.

needed to support loan demand or deposit withdrawals, the bank does not have to sell an excessive amount to obtain the cash. If the funds from maturing bills are not needed, they can always be reinvested in new bill issues. This avoids the expense, called the "turnaround" cost, that comes from selling bills one day and buying them back again after a short time, using them to cover short-run reserve flows. Turnaround costs include not only the administrative and overhead costs of transacting but also the difference between the bid and ask prices on the bills. The longer the time between the sale and the purchase, the more drastically these costs decline as a percentage of purchase price, because the fixed cost is averaged over a longer period of time. Thus, banks that buy and sell continuously are going to have high costs and perhaps would be better off if they either managed their reserves more carefully or found another means of meeting their short-run adjustment problems.

The interest rates on Treasury bills are closely related to other market rates, although there may be periods in which special market factors cause spreads between Treasury bills and other short-run securities to differ markedly. For example, during the oil crisis in 1973–1974, large amounts of money from overseas flowed into the Treasury market with little spillover into other markets. As a result, the yields on Treasury securities stayed remarkably low relative to other open-market rates. The Treasury bill market, except for cases like this, moves closely with other short-term markets.

Treasury bills are used by the Federal Reserve to implement monetary policy. They are the instrument the Federal Reserve most often uses to absorb reserves or add reserves to the banking system[14] in order to maintain its short-run targets for the federal funds rate. Although the Treasury bill market is one of the most efficient markets, commercial banks must be constantly aware of Federal Reserve actions. Federal Reserve decisions to loosen or tighten credit or reverse its policy can affect a bank's need to buy or sell securities and can also affect whether or not a bank may be forced into a capital loss. Of course, Federal Reserve behavior cannot be projected with certainty.

Repurchase Agreements

Whereas federal funds transactions are unsecured loans, repurchase agreements are secured loans. The difference generally lies in the nature of

---

[14] The Federal Reserve does operate in longer-term Treasury issues and in U.S. government agency issues but does this only on a fairly regular basis and generally only on the purchase side.

the participants in the transactions. A federal funds transaction is usually between two commercial banks. The repurchase agreement is generally between a commercial bank or the Federal Reserve and a government securities dealer or other institution in the money market. The latter participants usually work on such a thin capital base that all units dealing with them require that the transactions be secured. From the viewpoint of the bank, a repurchase agreement can be either direct (called a "repo") or a reverse arrangement (called a "reverse repo"), depending on whether the bank is a seller or a buyer, respectively. If a bank sells a Treasury bill to a securities dealer and at the same time agrees to buy back the same security, either on demand or at some specified time in the future at an agreed-upon price, then the transaction is a repurchase agreement. The sale adds some reserves to the bank and at the same time locks in the repurchase price. In other words, it fixes the interest cost of the transaction to the bank. It ensures a given yield to the securities dealer while protecting the bank from adverse movements in bill prices that could make it more expensive to buy back the security.

When the bank lends funds to the securities dealer—that is, buys securities from the dealer under agreement to sell them back at a fixed price sometime in the future—the transaction is a reverse repo. From the dealer's standpoint, this is a repo and is often called a *dealer loan*. Banks can put out funds in this way at guaranteed rates on secured loans.

Maturities run from 1 to 15 days and sometimes longer. Nonfinancial corporations can play a role in this market, usually as a provider of funds, as this is their only outlet for funds with maturities of less than 30 days, the minimum maturity for a negotiable CD. The Federal Reserve frequently uses repos and reverse repos, but these tend to be very short term, never in excess of 15 days.

Interest rates on repurchase agreements must be competitive with other rates in the money markets. Thus, banks will not buy securities (sell funds) unless they can earn at least as much on them as they could by selling the money in the federal funds market. However, rates on other bank collateral loans provide an upper limit to charges, mainly because these other loans are easier to get and do not incur the search costs and fees that are a part of repurchase agreements. In general, evidence seems to indicate that rates on repurchase agreements are around 50 basis points below other collateralized loans at New York banks.[15]

---

[15] Panos Konstas, "Repurchase Agreements: Their Role in Dealer Financing and Monetary Policy," in *Money Market Instruments* (Federal Reserve Bank of Cleveland, 1970), pp. 47–48.

Commercial banks have made increasing use of repurchase agreements in recent years. One example occurred in 1976–1977. Loan demand in this period was relatively low, and large banks had excess funds obtained from maintaining their presence in the CD and Eurodollar markets. As has been pointed out, it is not very profitable for banks to sell CDs and use the funds to buy short-term government securities. Yet this is precisely what the large banks seemed to be doing during the period under review. However, the banks were not totally financing the government securities with the CD money. The term structure of interest rates[16] was such that very short money traded at rates considerably below three-month and six-month money. Thus, the banks were buying the longer-term Treasury bills and then using repurchase agreements to finance their purchase, taking advantage of the spread between the very short rates and the others.[17]

This was perhaps an unusual case; the banks had to buy a large amount of securities because of the liquid nature of the financial markets provided by the Federal Reserve at the time and the slack loan demand. The banks needed something to keep their earnings up. As loan demand picked up, however, and the prospect of rising interest rates became too strong, the banks reduced their portfolio of government securities and stopped using repurchase agreements to fund either securities or loans.

Negotiable Certificates of Deposit

Negotiable certificates of deposit (CDs) are time deposits. They are certificate accounts that some securities dealers have agreed to "make a market" for; that is, the securities dealers have stated their willingness to post rates at which they will buy and sell these instruments. Thus, two markets exist in CDs. There is the primary market, in which banks sell CDs directly to purchasers, and a secondary market, where the instruments are traded. The CD itself is a marketable receipt for funds that are left with a bank for a stated amount of time and at a stated interest rate. The original owner can receive the funds back before maturity, however, by selling the CD in the open market.

Denominations run as low as $25,000, but the majority are written for amounts above $100,000. The maturities run from one month to one year, one month being the shortest allowable by law. Most CDs are for less than

---

[16] See the section "The Term Structure of Interest Rates" later in this chapter.

[17] "From the standpoint of the temporary seller of the securities, an RP represents a source of borrowed funds that can, in effect, be used to finance the same securities or to acquire other types of securities" (P. Konstas, "Repurchase Agreements," p. 43).

six months, and studies have shown that slightly over 70 percent of total CDs outstanding mature within four months.[18]

Interest is calculated on the par value of the certificate and is based on a 360-day year. The interest rate itself is determined by the supply and demand in the marketplace. The market for CDs is highly competitive. The primary source of funds is corporations whose treasurers are concerned with maximizing the return they receive on the money at their disposal; they are highly sophisticated investors and very knowledgeable about market conditions. Others who supply funds to this market are state and political subdivisions, foreign governments, central banks, individuals, and other institutional investors. Because of the size of the usual CD, the general participant is a relatively informed investor who will move around to get the best yields.

Although the market for CDs is competitive, there are times when this market becomes an unreliable source of funds for commercial banks. These are times when the Federal Reserve System forces banks to pay below-market interest rates on CDs, using Regulation Q (the regulation that limits the amount of interest paid on time deposits). Because the usual investor in CDs is very sensitive to interest rate differentials, large runoffs have occurred in maturing CDs. The Federal Reserve has, since the middle of the 1970s, eliminated their use of Regulation Q ceilings for large-denomination CDs. However, the threat is always there that the ceilings could be imposed again.

There are actually two interest rates in existence on CDs. The first is that posted by the banks themselves, and the second is the rate that exists in the secondary market. Although banks will negotiate with large or important customers, most of their transactions are at or slightly above their posted rates. The reason for giving rates slightly better than posted rates is that the banks generally make their "base" rates less than what CDs trade for in the open market. Hence, in order to attract investors they must pay rates comparable to the going market rate. The reason for this slight discrepancy between the primary and secondary markets seems to be that dealers' supplies are limited—they cannot come up with large quantities if an investor wants them; hence, the bank may be able to pay a lower rate for a large quantity of funds. If a bank wants or needs funds, all it has to do is raise its rates slightly or even a bit over the open-market rate,

---

[18] For December 1969, the figure is about 70 percent; see Jane F. Nelson, "Negotiable Certificates of Deposit," in Jimmie R. Monhollon, ed., *Instruments of the Money Market*, 3rd ed. (Federal Reserve Bank of Richmond, 1970), p. 53. For June 1976, the total is 73.6 percent; see Jane F. Nelson, "Negotiable Certificates of Deposit," in Timothy Q. Cook, ed., *Instruments of the Money Market*, 4th ed. (Federal Reserve Bank of Richmond, 1977), p. 59.

and it will get an appreciable increase in deposits. Conversely, it has only to lower its rates slightly if it wants to discourage investors.

Throughout this book the assumption has been made that the supply of money from the CD market to an individual bank that deals in CDs is perfectly elastic. Over a period of several weeks this is perhaps true. However, the assumption does not hold if the time period is reduced to several days. Furthermore, in the 1974–1975 period, some banks that had relied heavily on funds from this market in the early 1970s found that CD money was not available to them because of an overall shortage of funds in the market, or if they were considered "risky" banks they found either that they had to pay more for funds or even, at times, that CD money was not forthcoming at any price.

Even in periods of tight money, the largest banks—those in New York and Chicago and a few in California—usually experience an elastic supply of funds. The time period of concern may have to be increased slightly, but it appears that CD funds are still available even when other banks are having difficulty finding funds. This introduces a distinction between banks that always find these markets available and those that do not, and it raises some interesting policy questions that cannot be elaborated on here.

Eurodollars

Eurodollars are dollar-denominated deposits in European banks and foreign branches of United States banks. These deposits arise through individual, corporate, or government transactions that result in a transfer of dollars to a bank in another country that will accept deposits in U.S. dollars. Eurodollar accounts are usually time deposits with several months' maturity, although overnight or call money deposits are also made. Maturities of two years or more are not infrequent. Interest is paid on all accounts. The recipient bank can then lend these dollars, which transfers ownership of the original dollar claim but allows for credit creation, as with U.S. bank reserves, several times the original dollar amount.

Eurodollars are an important source of funds for American banks, for the market is quite sophisticated. Furthermore, unlike the CD market, the Eurodollar markets are not periodically subject to interest rate ceilings, and hence banks can always bid competitively for funds.

Same-day money is now available to banks, but funds obtained in this fashion have been very expensive. Eurodollars have not, then, been a perfect substitute for federal funds purchases for very short-run adjustments in reserve positions. However, they are commonly used as a permanent source of funds. The only problem in this respect is that banks or their affiliates must be continually active in these markets. They must continually "show their name," or they will not be able to get all the funds they want at the going market rates during periods of reduced domestic supplies of funds. That is, there will be some rationing or price adjustments in this market for those who enter the market infrequently. Thus, a liability-management bank that wants to rely on Eurodollars must invest in the market; it must be in the market continuously whether it needs the funds or not. In order to do this and minimize costs or make some profit at times when loan demand is not sufficient to warrant the purchase of these funds, a bank will play the term structure[19] or use other techniques to look as good as possible in the short run as well as in the long run.

Usually, the foreign branch of a U.S. bank either in London or, more often now, in Nassau will be the organ that deals in this market. Funds are transferred to the domestic bank through a balance sheet entry, although technically they must be transferred through the domestic check-clearing system. In New York these "checks" must pass through the New York Clearing House, and thus credit is not received until the following day when they become deposits in the Federal Reserve account of a member bank.

A popular use of Eurodollar money has been in the financing of weekend or holiday reserve positions. Many banks use overnight deposits on Thursday as a partial substitute for federal funds purchased on Friday. There are two reasons for this. First, in the clearing process, funds purchased on Thursday are not recorded until Friday, and the transaction is not reversed until Monday morning. Second, the amount of reserves the bank has on hand is recorded at the close of business, and a bank's reserves are calculated every day of the calendar week. Thus, if the reserves are on the bank's balance sheet at the close of business on Friday, they will be there for Saturday and Sunday as well.

This accounting procedure does have an effect on bank demand for Eurodollars and hence on interest rate behavior within the week. One Federal Reserve official has observed,

> For a one-day Eurodollar deposit on Thursday, a United States bank in need of funds to meet its reserve requirements will be willing to pay a rate close to three times the anticipated Federal funds rate on Friday;

[19] Since playing the term structure exposes the bank to the risk of mismatching the maturities of assets and liabilities, most banks have "rules" or "constraints" on how much of the foreign portfolio must be in matched maturities. This avoids reckless behavior that may jeopardize the integrity of the bank.

and it will pay a corresponding multiple when the settlement date for these overnight balances precedes any other period when the New York money market is closed for one business day or longer. Thursday-Friday transactions have become so common that the rates have adjusted themselves almost fully to anticipate the federal funds rate on Friday.[20]

In general, the level of rates in the Eurodollar market is consistent with the pressures that exist on money markets throughout the developed world. However, the world nature of these markets may cause the relationship between domestic U.S. and Eurodollar rates to vary over time. Early in their existence, Eurodollars traded at rates no higher than domestic CDs. In recent years, rates on Eurodollar deposits have tended to be above U.S. rates because of the availability and use of these funds in countries with rates considerably higher than those in the United States. This has not prohibited their use by U.S. banks. One reason is that reserve requirements, except for one brief period, have not been assessed against liabilities to foreign branches, hence reducing the cost of these liabilities relative to the cost of CD money. Eurodollar funds are also exempt from certain FDIC fees.

The Eurodollar market has grown to substantial proportions and is relatively broad and deep. Because of these characteristics, individual banks find the supply of funds extremely elastic. To raise a large amount of funds, a bank need only raise its rates slightly relative to the market. It must be careful, however, because if money does become extremely scarce, as it did in 1974, banks that previously were able to obtain funds elastically may no longer be able to or may be faced with suboptimal prices. That is, many participants other than the large New York or Chicago banks found that the market was not always there when they needed it. This has led banks to rely less on the Eurodollar market for their present and potential needs.

NONCONTROLLABLE ASSETS AND LIABILITIES

The markets for the assets and liabilities discussed in the foregoing pages were considered relatively efficient. Because of this, banks can determine the quantities of assets purchased or liabilities sold. Buying or selling more

---

[20] Fred H. Klopstock, "Eurodollars in the Liquidity and Reserve Management of United States Banks," in P. Jessup, ed., *Innovations in Bank Management: Selected Readings* (New York: Holt, Rinehart, and Winston, 1969), p. 498.

or less of an asset or a liability will not alter the interest rate on the instrument or its marginal cost. Optional portfolios will not, therefore, be altered by trading in these markets; purchases or sales of these items are residual decisions. This section deals with those short-term assets and liabilities that are not traded in efficient markets and in which buying or selling more or less can alter optional combinations of assets or liabilities. Therefore, the optimizing bank must set prices at the point where the marginal revenue or marginal cost of the item is equal to the controlling marginal interest cost or return. Quantity will then be determined by the demand or supply and the price set. Banks will not manipulate these instruments to meet balance sheet requirements; these instruments are not residual, in the sense defined earlier.

Included among these items are bankers' acceptances, short-run tax-exempt securities, U.S. government agency issues, and commercial paper.

Bankers' Acceptances

Bankers' acceptances are almost wholly connected with international trade. They represent orders to pay specified amounts of money at specified times by some exporter or importer, which may be an individual or a financial or nonfinancial organization. Specifically, a time draft is written on a bank by an economic unit to obtain funds to pay for goods or foreign exchange. The draft is then "accepted" by the bank, that is, the bank unconditionally guarantees its face value at maturity. The acceptance may then be held by the bank or it may be sold in the secondary market. The less-well-known business firm "buys" from the bank the bank's better-known name, in this way turning a nontradable asset into a tradable one.

The maturities are generally less than six months, with the majority running around three months in duration. Since maturities can be tailored to the firm's trading cycle (the time necessary to receive the goods and sell them), these instruments are virtually riskless. Thus, they trade at interest rates only slightly higher than those on Treasury bills. However, the market is not nearly so perfect and is heavily dependent on the extent of foreign trade. Thus, banks will charge a fee of 1½ percent for prime borrowers and more for others with lower credit ratings for granting the acceptance. Moreover, most firms needing bankers' acceptances have few alternative sources of funds (they cannot get into the commercial paper market). They need the banks' acceptance because they are not well known in the financial markets.

The secondary market consists of only a few dealers. These dealers post the interest rates they will charge, and although some negotiation takes place now, they will do most of their business at these rates. Posted rates tend to lag movements in market rates.

Bankers' acceptances are another type of liquid asset in which commercial banks can invest. However, the market is far from being as efficient as those discussed previously and is quite dependent on the level of foreign trade. Hence, banks cannot rely on it for short-run reserve management or asset/liability management, and they must accept price–quantity relationships that maximize portfolio returns.

Tax-Exempt Obligations

Tax-exempt obligations have played a role in the investment portfolios of commercial banks because they reduce the bank's effective tax rate. More and more short-term tax-exempt securities have come to the money markets in recent years as a result of inflation; the proliferation of government programs has led to more government issues, primarily securities of U.S. government housing agencies; more sophisticated planning has given rise to tax anticipation notes; and financial crises in many cities have brought the need for more municipal bonds. Generally, the markets are quite thin in these issues, and since the alternative sources of funds are limited for some issues, returns can be high for the level of associated risk. However, the banks do have to be extremely careful about the riskiness of individual issues and the fact that these instruments are not nearly as liquid as others.

U.S. Government Agency Issues

Securities are issued by federal government agencies, but the federal government has no legal obligation to back up the credit of these agencies. It is inconceivable, however, that the federal government would not come to the aid of an agency experiencing financial difficulties. Thus, many analysts feel that these instruments are as riskless as fully guaranteed Treasury securities.

Agency issues, however, trade at slightly higher rates than comparable Treasury issues. One reason for this is that the market is somewhat thinner than the Treasury market. Some analysts claim that this is a result of the lack of guarantees; others feel that it is because there are not as many issues available. Through most of the 1970s, the spreads between agency issues and government securities declined, partly because market participants became more familiar with them and partly because the Federal Reserve now can buy and sell agency issues. However, the market still is not as liquid as the Treasury bill market, so although banks can receive a fractionally higher yield than they can earn on a similar Treasury issue, they must realize that they are giving up some liquidity to do so.

Commercial Paper

Commercial paper is nonsecured debt issued on the strength of the issuer's name. Generally, therefore, only corporations with the best credit rating use this market. Although sales finance and personal finance organizations are particularly large users of commercial paper, many other institutions also make use of this market. Commercial banks play a large role, serving as agents for direct and dealer-placed paper. Furthermore, a backup bank line of credit is usually required for market participants.

Commercial banks at one time were the primary purchasers of commercial paper. Since the 1950s, however, demand from other sources has grown considerably, leaving the percentage held by commercial banks relatively small. Thus, on the asset side, banks do not trade in volume enough to consider this market a residual investment. Commercial paper is usually issued directly to customers and can bear maturities from 3 days to 270 days, generally tailored to meet the needs of the customer. Interest rates are very competitive, although lower than the prime rate, and respond quickly to changes in market conditions. Levels of interest rates are comparable to CDs and bankers' acceptances.

Since the late 1960s bank holding companies have issued commercial paper as a device to obtain additional funds to support loans at their subsidiary banks. They can do this either through direct deposit or by the acquisition of loans or other assets originally held by the bank. Banks do not use this source of funds often, relying on it primarily during times of tight money and/or when Regulation Q ceilings are in effect and CD money is available.

GOVERNMENT SECURITIES DEALERS

The foregoing sections of this chapter have described the instruments and markets relevant for an analysis of short-run commercial bank financial management. However, before the actual analysis of this behavior in Chapter 13, two additional factors must be considered: dealers in U.S. government securities and the term structure of interest rates. The first will be dealt with next, and a discussion of the second will conclude the chapter.

United States government securities dealers play a very important role in the money market. To understand the overall efficiency of the money market and the role of the Federal Reserve in that market, one must understand the unique role of these dealers. The fact that many large commercial banks are their own government securities dealers indicates the importance the banks place on the role of the dealer in banking operations.

A dealer is defined as one who "makes a market" in a particular instrument, in this case, U.S. government securities. That is, the dealer must be ready at all times to state the prices at which he or she will buy or sell securities. The dealer makes money from the spread between the bid and ask prices plus any capital gain or loss achieved in taking a position in the market.

Dealers are very important in securing the liquidity of any instrument, because the more dealers a market has, the more efficient it will tend to be. If dealers have ready access to cash or credit, they will be more able to take positions in the market, and this will help to improve the efficiency of the market.

Most business in government securities is done by telephone, with written confirmation following. Millions of dollars can change hands in a very short time, so that the crucial factor for the dealers is the ability to obtain securities or funds quickly in order to carry through a transaction. Securities can be taken out of the dealer's "position," that is, the inventory of securities on hand. Often, however, the ability to transact depends on the dealer having willing sellers and willing buyers on whom to turn a small profit.

These dealers in general work on a very small capital base; they are well leveraged. Thus, to support their positions, they must find short-term financing. This need for money puts them in contact with large segments of the money market and causes the banks or bank dealer departments to go to the money markets to scout up funding for the portfolio. In this way, the specific pressures felt in the U.S. government securities markets because of actual operating conditions, or because of expectations, are transmitted to other areas of the money markets as the dealers draw money from these other areas.

Money market banks have been a large source of dealer loans, including the loans to nonbank dealers. However, in recent years many nonfinancial firms have provided funds, as they started managing their funds more closely and thus wished to place money for very short periods of time. Arrangements can often be tailored to the needs of the lending organization. Dealers, of course, are important in repo and reverse repo financing.

The one major participant in the money market that can upset the market's efficiency is the Federal Reserve System. Since the Federal Reserve needs an effectively functioning money market, it operates in a way that will upset the market as little as possible. In order to maintain market efficiency, the Federal Reserve has been very protective of government securities dealers. The reason is clear and quite valid. If government securities dealers did not exist, then some other form of operation would have to develop to facilitate Federal Reserve open-market operations. In other words, the present market setup seems to be a very efficient way of conducting monetary policy. However, it is based on certain rules, one of which is that the Federal Reserve will not move interest rates too drastically in too short a period of time, particularly if it is attempting to change the direction of interest rates, which might wipe out a dealer who has taken a position long or short.

Why this concern over the U.S. government securities dealers? For one thing, securities dealers work on a relatively small capital base. A substantial capital loss or sustained capital losses could bankrupt them. Second, and perhaps more important, the Federal Reserve relies on these dealers to be available to buy or sell government securities on a moment's notice. This is part of the response the Federal Reserve requires of dealers, if it is to function through them. If the Federal Reserve moves too quickly or reverses itself too quickly, then the risk associated with dealing with it would be very great. There would be more uncertainty than under present operating procedures, and if expectations were not allowed to form with much confidence, the dealers' portfolio behavior would be quite different from what it is now.[21] Dealers would be much less willing to cooperate with the Federal Reserve and absorb its operations. Thus, the market would shrivel and be less efficient, and the Federal Reserve would find that any given amount of reserves it wanted to put in or take out of the banking

---

[21] In the extreme, when the expectations of the market have been greatly disturbed, the market becomes very erratic and possibly even ceases to function. This is because dealers pull out of the market to digest all the new information coming to them in order to build up a new set of expectations. During this time, the number of participants in the market is reduced considerably, and this can give rise to wider than normal fluctuations in interest rates or a complete cessation of trading. This type of condition is what is generally referred to as a "disorderly market."

system would require much greater movements in interest rates. These movements would be required, of course, to entice participants other than dealers to buy or sell the amount of securities needed to achieve the desired change in reserves.

The Federal Reserve also "protects" the government securities dealers during those times when the Treasury is raising funds in the money and capital markets. Government securities dealers absorb a large amount of new issues and, in a sense, serve as investment bankers to the government by facilitating the distribution of these securities to other economic units around the country. Since they must take a large position (buy) in these securities at the time of the financing, they want the money markets to remain relatively stable until the distribution is completed. Otherwise, they would be much less willing to play the investment banker role because of the risk of interest rate movements surrounding the financing.

The Federal Reserve usually contributes to the stability of the money markets at this time by adding reserves to the banking system or taking them out, so as to keep interest rates relatively constant. This is called following a policy of "even keel." Once the financing is over and most of the securities have been distributed, the Federal Reserve returns to the business of attaining its overall economic objectives. All in all, government securities dealers are very important to the money market. And, given the rules that the Federal Reserve observes, the dealers provide an efficient system for the distribution of new issues, an efficient market for holders of existing securities to decrease or increase their holdings of government securities, and an efficient mechanism for the transmission of pressures that exist in the money market. Although one could think of other methods of doing all these things, it seems that, at present, it would be hard to duplicate the practicality of the current framework.

THE TERM STRUCTURE OF INTEREST RATES

The term structure of interest rates is the relationship that exists among the interest rates on different maturities of debt issued by one type of issuer (the federal government, AAA corporation, etc.). Since banks buy or sell assets or liabilities that have different maturities, bank managers must have a firm grasp of the concept of the term structure of interest rates, because a major part of their operation in the shorter run is to constantly make use of the situations created by conditions surrounding the term structure of rates. Three examples point out the significance of this fact. First, commercial banks and other financial intermediaries have assets and liabilities that generally are mismatched; their liabilities have very short-term maturities, and their assets are usually of a much longer term. If short-term instruments generally have a lower rate than the longer-term ones, the bank has a positive spread built into its balance sheet.

A second example was presented earlier, in the section on U.S. Treasury bills, where it was explained that commercial banks purchase U.S. Treasury securities of at least several months' duration and then finance the purchases with daily or weekly repurchase agreements. This is useful only if the very short-term rates are less than the rates on the Treasury securities themselves. A final example of the use of yield curve opportunities is that of a bank "playing the yield curve" in handling its investment portfolio. That is, if short-term rates are lower than long-term rates, a bank can invest in longer-term securities. As the securities mature, they will command a lower interest rate, which (since the coupon rate is fixed) will be realized only if the bonds sell at a higher price in the market. The bank can take a capital gain by selling its bonds and then can invest once again in longer-term issues.[22]

Thus, the theory of the term structure of interest rates attempts to explain the relationship between interest rates on different maturities. The theory begins with a group of securities, homogeneous with respect to default risk and differing only in terms of maturity and coupon. In general, empirical discussions consider only issues of the U.S. government because of all the difficulties associated with holding risk and other terms of the debt constant on other types of securities. The term structure itself is often described with the use of a chart, such as the one presented in Figure 12-1, which plots yield to maturity against time to maturity.

As shown in the chart, the term structure can take many different shapes. For example, it can be flat (line A), rising (line B), falling (line C), or humped (line D). Various reasons are given for the various slopes of the yield curve, but the curves can be best explained by supply and demand conditions.

Assume that there are just two maturities, arbitrarily designated short-term and long-term. If interest rates are expected to remain constant over the life of the securities and if people do not prefer one maturity over the other because of either institutional reasons or risk factors, then it can be argued that the interest rates in both markets will be the same. Invest-

---

[22] It should be noted that although these opportunities may exist, banks have been very careful to put constraints on trading activity because of the risks associated with being wrong in their interest rate forecasts. Commercial banks feel, in general, that their business is to manage loan portfolios and make money on interest rate spreads rather than to take positions with respect to the future and make profits (or losses) or capital gains (or losses).

Yield to Maturity
(%)

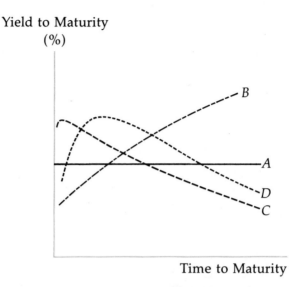

Time to Maturity

FIGURE 12-1   Term Structure of Interest Rates—Possible Curve Shapes

ment opportunities will determine demand considerations, but the important fact is that the suppliers of funds will always put their money in the market with the highest return. Thus, if rates are higher in the long-term market than in the short, funds will move from short-term to long-term instruments, and this movement will drive the rate down in the long-term market and up in the short-term market. Thus, under the assumptions stated above, the two markets would be as shown by the solid lines in Figure 12-2.

Now, assume that the demanders and suppliers of funds expect interest rates to rise. Demanders will reduce their demand for short-term securities and increase their demand for long-term funds. That is, since rates are expected to rise, the demanders of funds (the borrowers) would like to lock in funds at a low interest rate. Suppliers, however, will move in the opposite direction, lending more in the short-term market so that they are not locked into the low rates but have the flexibility to move into the higher, long-term rates at some time in the future. Thus, the supply of funds into the short-term market will increase, whereas the supply into the long-term market will diminish.

The overall effect of this behavior can now be seen in the dashed lines in Figure 12-2. The short-term rates fall because demand for funds in this

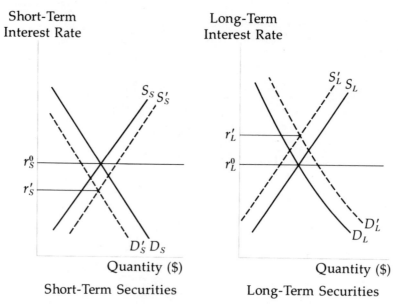

FIGURE 12-2   Market Determination of the Term Structure of
               Interest Rates

market has fallen while supplies have increased; the long-term rates will
rise because the demand has increased while supplies have decreased. The
conclusion is that when market interest rates are expected to rise, the yield
curve will be rising. This is shown by the long-term rate, r'_L, being above
the short-term rate, r'_S. Conversely, when interest rates are expected to fall,
the yield curve will be falling.

Can anything be said about the equilibrium relationships between
short-term and long-term interest rates? Several explanations exist for
equilibrium results, the most universally accepted being the *expectations
theory*. The essence of this theory is that the yield curve is based on investors' expectations of future short-term interest rates. The concept is most
easily transmitted by an example.

Assume an investment horizon of two years. There are two alternatives for the investor: to invest in two one-year Treasury bills or in one
two-year Treasury bond. The decision rule is to choose the alternative that
will maximize the investor's rate of return over the two-year period. The
current one-year bill yields 6 percent. If the investor expects that the one-
year bill that can be bought when the present one matures will yield 6

percent, then how much, in the absence of transactions costs, would the investor have to earn on the two-year bond, compounded annually, to be indifferent between the two alternatives? The answer is that the two-year bond would have to yield 6 percent also. If it yielded less, then the investor would buy the one-year bills; if more, then the two-year bond would be purchased. This would result in a flat yield curve like *A* in Figure 12-1, as implied by the initial conditions in Figure 12-2. If interest rates are expected to remain constant over the investment horizon, the yield curve will be flat.

What rate would be needed on the two-year bond to make the investor indifferent between the alternatives if it was expected that an 8 percent yield on the one-year bill would be available when the current bill matures? The answer is that the two-year bond would need to yield approximately 7 percent. If it yielded less, the investor would favor the two one-year bills; if more, the one two-year issue. This would result in a rising yield curve like *B* in Figure 12-1 and would typify the second set of conditions shown in Figure 12-2. As long as demanders and suppliers expect to benefit more from one alternative than another, they will continue to switch their positions to increase their profits. The expectations theory tells us at what point the market will come into equilibrium; i.e., at what point the market will reach the situation where no investor will expect to increase profits by moving from one alternative to another.

Several assumptions allow such a definite result to be achieved. Because these assumptions abstract from the reality of the marketplace, many analysts have voiced criticism of the *pure* expectations hypothesis. These criticisms generally take one or more of the following forms.

1. *Diverse expectations.* The expectations theory rests on the assumption that all investors have similar or homogeneous expectations about future interest rates. If expectations are not homogeneous, then the expectations hypothesis must depend on the "average" expectations of the market, something that can be defined only by an index. That is, the term structure defines average expectations and cannot be attributed to any one investor.

2. *Transactions costs.* If these costs exist, shifting maturities or issues becomes more expensive, and the returns to the investor must be figured net of these costs.

3. *Liquidity and uncertainty.* Expectations are only expectations and can be held with differing degrees of confidence. Thus, there may be a bias on the part of investors due to the fact that they prefer flexibility in the face of an uncertain future. This bias would lead them to prefer short-term issues to long-term. If this is the case, then even if interest rates were ex-

pected to rise, the yield curve would be rising due to a shift in the supply of funds.[23]

4. *Preferred maturities.* The markets may be segmented because of the institutional preferences of the various participants in the markets. The usual example given is that of life insurance companies. Because they issue long-term liabilities, they prefer to invest in long-term securities to lock in a profit regardless of the movement of interest rates over the length of their contracts.

In general, however, these qualifications do not change the situation much at all. The expectations theory forms the basis for the term structure but is modified to include other factors that help to explain the various positions and shapes of the yield curve.

[23] There could be a shift in demand. If the future is uncertain, demanders may want to lock in "certain" interest rates to avoid financing difficulties in the future. Thus, there would be a relative shift in demand from shorts to longs, accentuating the bias created by the suppliers. Liquidity preference is generally stated in terms of the suppliers of funds. That is why the possible bias created by the demanders is placed in this footnote.

REVIEW QUESTIONS

1. Nonfinancial firms have only one cash management problem; commercial banks have two. Does it seem reasonable that commercial banks should have their cash management divided in this way?
2. How can a bank determine the elasticity of demand or supply of the market assets and liabilities in which it deals? How can the bank tell when conditions change?
3. Why do some bankers feel that borrowing from the Federal Reserve is a sign of bad management?
4. Who supplies funds in the federal funds market, the Treasury bill market, the CD market, and the Eurodollar market? What do many of these participants have in common? Are these characteristics sufficient to make the markets very similar?
5. Many large banks have their own government securities dealer. Why? What does a government securities dealer provide for a bank?

13

Short-Run Reserve Management

Of the time horizons under which bank management functions, that of reserve management is the shortest. Members of the Federal Reserve System operate within a two-week time frame because of the need to meet the reserve requirements set by the Federal Reserve. Nonmembers are usually subject to requirements set by state banking authorities.[1] Thus, the short-run time horizon of many banks is determined by the settlement periods for their reserve accounts, and methods of deriving reserve requirements and techniques for satisfying requirements in optimal fashion are essential ingredients of a bank's operating procedures over the short run.

The chapter begins by describing the manner in which the short-run time horizon for a bank is determined by the mechanics of reserve settlement for member banks in the Federal Reserve System. The philosophy of short-run reserve management followed in this book is then explained. A discussion of how reserves are calculated is illustrated with typical examples and is followed by a review of operating procedures for functioning within this time horizon. After a brief treatment of control procedures, the chapter concludes with some comments on reserve management in major

---

[1] For a recent presentation of state requirements and their enforcement, see R. A. Gilbert and J. M. Lovati, "Bank Reserve Requirements and Their Enforcement: A Comparison Across States," *Review*, Federal Reserve Bank of St. Louis (March 1978), pp. 22–32.

money-center banks and a short section on Federal Reserve operations in the money markets.

THE TIME HORIZON

Whereas the long run is measured in years, the time horizon for short-run reserve management is measured in weeks. For commercial banks that are members of the Federal Reserve System, the horizon is set at two weeks because of the reserve settlement lag allowed by the accounting practices of the Federal Reserve. For banks that are not members of the Federal Reserve System, either the time horizon is determined by the need to meet state reserve requirements or, if this presents no constraint, it should be one that is short enough to allow some forecasting—perhaps a week—but long enough to allow sufficient flexibility in balance sheet adjustment so that the bank will not be forced into unfortunate (unprofitable) operations that result solely from the time period used.

The specific framework adopted here is the one used by the Federal Reserve System. There are three reasons for this.

1. Federal Reserve regulations are the most consistent set of rules applicable to the largest number of banks. They apply to all member banks, whereas any other set of rules would have to be more or less attuned to the specific set of banks in the state to which the rules apply.

2. It is possible that at some time in the future all banks will be members of the Federal Reserve System and thus subject to the same kinds of constraints.

3. The analytical techniques followed in reserve management are the same regardless of the set of rules used, so that whether or not a bank is a member of the Federal Reserve and whether or not it considers itself constrained by reserve requirements, the same general principles apply.

It will, therefore, be assumed that the constraint under which the commercial bank must operate in the short run is that it must maintain a certain amount of funds as its legally required reserves either with the Federal Reserve System or as vault cash. Reserve requirements are "effective" in the sense that they constrain the portfolio decisions of an individual bank. In other words, they force the bank to maintain a portfolio that it would otherwise not have chosen.

A smaller, conservatively managed bank that does not have as much room to maneuver as, say, a larger bank with greater opportunities, might desire to keep excess reserves on hand to protect its reserve position, as well as its profits.[2] An increase in reserve requirements might not cause this bank to reduce excess reserves, because its management may still feel it needs these reserves to protect its ability to meet variations in loan demand or deposit supply. Thus, the reserve requirements are "effective" in that their change necessitates an alteration in the bank's portfolio. Reserve requirements are not "effective" if changes in them do not necessitate portfolio rearrangement.

If reserve requirements are "effective," the time horizon of the bank for meeting these legal requirements is two weeks. The statement week of the Federal Reserve System (the period in which balance sheet information is collected) runs from Thursday through the following Wednesday. Thursday morning begins the new week for the accumulation of reserve balances at the Federal Reserve, with the exception of the amount of reserves the bank is allowed to carry over from the previous week. The carryover provision will be discussed more thoroughly later in this chapter.

The reserve requirements that apply to the current week are computed from the deposits that existed in the week ending one week before the most recent Wednesday. Figure 13-1 illustrates the time relationship. Suppose that the bank is beginning the statement week that starts on December 20, 1979, and ends on December 26. The reserve requirements pertaining to this week are obtained from the deposits of the statement week ending Wednesday, December 12, which is one week earlier than the most recent Wednesday (December 19).

The reason that banks operate within a two-week time horizon is now clear. Not only does the bank know with certainty the reserves it will be required to hold during the current statement week; it also knows with certainty the reserves it will be required to hold during the coming statement week. Thus, the reserve requirements computed during the week ending December 12 apply to the bank's legal reserves for the week beginning December 20. And the reserve requirements computed during the week ending December 19 apply to the reserves required to be on deposit during the week beginning December 27.[3]

THE CARRYOVER PROVISION

Another factor that ties together the two weeks is the carryover provision. Specifically, the reserve carryover provision allows a bank to carry a reserve

---

[2] Remember that "turnaround" costs of adjusting reserve positions quickly through the use of Treasury bills can be quite high.

[3] No time will be spent discussing the reasons for this form of reserve settlement or the forms that preceded it. Each one has its plusses and minuses.

Th	F	Sa	Su	M	Tu	W	Th	F	Sa	Su	M	Tu	W	Th	F	Sa	Su	M	Tu	W	Th	F	Sa	Su	M	Tu	W
		12/12	12/13								12/19	12/20							12/26	12/27							

FIGURE 13-1   The Time Horizon for Reserve Requirements
(Reserves to be held during the week of 12/20 are determined by deposits during the week ending 12/12.)

excess or deficiency in the amount of 2 percent of its reserve requirement into the following week without penalty. Thus, a bank that is keeping its reserves fairly close to its legal requirements can "miss the mark" by 2 percent on either side and be allowed to carry this position into the next week and "meet" its reserve requirement plus or minus the amount carried forward.

This provision creates some flexibility for the banks in that they do not need to be overly concerned about the possibility that events may run against them on the last day or so of the statement week and they will come up short of reserves for the week. If the provision did not exist, banks could protect against this possibility by holding excess reserves. In this sense, the Federal Reserves subsidizes the banking system by allowing the banks to carry over small deficiencies. The return is the social gain of additional credit availability resulting from the reduction in the excess reserve positions of commercial banks.

If banks do not meet their reserve requirements or carry a deficiency in excess of 2 percent, then they are provided the reserves by the Federal Reserve and charged the discount rate plus two additional percentage points as a penalty. If the 2 percent deficiency is not made up the following week, then the Federal Reserve provides the funds for this additional amount and again charges the penalty rate for the deficiency.

Some analysts argue that the penalty rate is not truly a penalty. Particularly if the discount rate is out of line with market rates, as it sometimes is,[4] the penalty rate may be quite cheap. This raises the question of possible abuses in handling reserve positions. It appears, however, that commercial banks have really not abused the carryover privilege. In the first place, banks can borrow more cheaply at the discount rate if they plan their borrowings before a deficiency takes place. There may be some limits on this, but unless a bank has misused its borrowing privilege from the Federal Reserve, this source of short-term money should be available to meet

---

[4] See Chapter 12, p. 352.

the shortage. Second, most banks have other sources of funds; for example, if a particular position looks especially tenuous, the bank can obtain funds from the federal funds market or from a correspondent bank.

If the bank is doing a reasonably good job of managing its reserve position, the 2 percent carryover provides ample leeway in most situations. The only exception appears to be the special case of a smaller bank putting a new person in charge of managing its reserve position. In this case the "new" reserve manager, being unfamiliar with the techniques of managing reserves and lacking knowledge of seasonal and cyclical cash flows, may come up short of required reserves for several weeks running. Since this is a learning problem, it is usually resolved as the manager becomes more familiar with his or her duties.[5]

THE PHILOSOPHY OF SHORT-RUN RESERVE MANAGEMENT

The banking firm's primary operating objective in all other time horizons has been to maximize the economic value of the bank. Within the framework of short-run reserve management, however, it attempts to minimize losses. Readers with experience in microeconomics will note quickly that in theory this is a semantic distinction with no real substance.

This semantic distinction is introduced because of its importance in practical applications. The idea of maximizing the value of the bank carries the connotation of aggressively planning to do as well as possible. This is the correct approach for bankers making their portfolio decisions for the intermediate or long term.

In the short run, bank strategy becomes defensive. Random demands for loans and supplies of funds are of little import in themselves. However, the bank *must* meet its reserve requirements, and these random movements in assets and liabilities may force it either to buy funds at a higher than optimal price because it needs funds quickly or to postpone servicing a loan customer because it may not be able to balance its portfolio within this time span.

Thus, the bank must be defensive in that it must maintain its flexibil-

---

[5] The Federal Reserve is quite helpful in this respect. Since it monitors reserve positions quite closely and since banks almost always meet their requirements, a bank that does not meet its requirement for several weeks in a row is easily identified. The Federal Reserve then checks into the situation, and if it is caused by a new manager (which it almost invariably is), the Federal Reserve will either bring the person to the Federal Reserve or send someone to the bank for a short course in the techniques of reserve management. This usually solves the problem.

ity, its ability to adjust its reserve position within this time horizon, in the face of the random forces impinging on its balance sheet. In short, the bank must sacrifice some income to maintain sufficient flexibility to meet its potential needs, and this sacrifice must be equated, on the margin, with the loss it might incur if it were less flexible or less liquid.

The general philosophy for short-run reserve management will therefore be for the bank to manage its balance sheet within its two-week operating horizon so as to minimize potential losses arising from the vagaries of the loan and deposit markets. The objective is to maintain sufficient liquidity, either in its balance sheet or in what it can borrow, to enable it to be flexible in its response to short-run events unfolding in an unexpected manner.[6]

CALCULATION OF RESERVES

The calculation of required reserves is much the same for all banks. The major differences lie, as would be expected, in the volume, volatility, and number of liabilities with which the bank under review deals. Since the basic principles are the same for all banks, the example developed here will concern a bank that is large enough to be interesting but small enough to avoid the clutter of too many accounts.

Table 13-1 shows an example of the Federal Reserve report of a commercial bank. For ease of presentation, the bank is assumed to have a correspondent relationship with a larger financial center bank and to have no correspondents itself. Furthermore, only passbook savings accounts and nonnegotiable certificates of deposit make up the bank's time and savings accounts.

The bank is predominantly an asset-management bank, although it is capable of buying or selling federal funds at its correspondent if it needs to do so in the very short run. That is, it will alter its reserve position for a week or two by buying or selling Treasury bills outright, but for managing reserves, augmenting or reducing them for a day or two, the bank will adjust reserves via its correspondent bank.[7]

---

[6] In other words, if the bank operates using expected values, it must be prepared for the situation in which actual values are not equal to expected values.

[7] Many smaller banks that do this find that the average of federal funds purchases over, say, the three- to six-month time horizon implied by the model of the banking firm is close to zero. The only exception is if the bank gets itself into trouble. Therefore, it cannot really be considered a liability manager because of its infrequent use of this market.

TABLE 13-1   Report of Deposits, Vault Cash, and Federal Funds Transactions (In thousands of dollars)

Balances for	Demand Deposits Due to Banks	U.S. Govt. Demand Deposits	Other Demand Deposits	Cash Items in Process of Collection	Demand Deposits Due from Banks	Net Demand Deposits	Savings Deposits	Other Time Deposits (31–179 days)	Other Time Deposits (180 days–4 years)	Currency and Coin Deposits	Federal Funds Purchased	Federal Funds Sold
Thurs.		34,554	214,725	28,950	2,650	217,679	112,742	51,415	27,685	4,718		
Fri.		34,602	216,842	27,899	2,897	220,648	113,006	51,418	27,687	4,175		
Sat.		34,612	208,433	27,782	2,918	212,345	113,481	51,419	27,720	3,989		
Sun.		34,612	208,433	27,782	2,918	212,345	113,481	51,419	27,720	3,989		
Mon.		34,612	208,433	27,782	2,918	212,345	113,481	51,419	27,720	3,989		
Tues.		34,618	212,778	27,565	3,422	216,409	113,996	51,423	28,016	4,434		
Wed.		35,107	215,821	27,412	3,106	220,410	114,222	51,431	28,021	4,682		
Totals						1,512,181	794,409	359,944	194,569	29,976		

The bank can therefore adjust its reserve position in the short run in any of three ways. It can (1) buy or sell federal funds at its correspondent bank, (2) buy or sell Treasury bills through its correspondent bank, or (3) borrow at the Federal Reserve's discount window.

Deposits are recorded as of the start of each business day. Therefore, a bank that is open Monday through Friday will record the same amount for deposits on Saturday, Sunday, and Monday of a statement week; if it is also open on Saturday, its Sunday and Monday deposit amounts will be the same. Deposits are recorded on a seven-day basis regardless of the days the banks conduct business.

Second, "cash items in process of collection" and "demand deposits due from banks" are subtracted from the total demand deposits at the bank. In so doing, the Federal Reserve eliminates any double counting that might take place within the banking system. The cash items in the process of collection are checks that have not completed clearing through the Federal Reserve System. Therefore, two deposits pertaining to the same amount of money exist within the banking system. Subtracting the amount from one bank's deposits eliminates the possibility of double counting these funds.

In addition, the demand deposits due *from* banks show up as demand deposits due *to* banks on some other bank's Federal Reserve report. That is, the banking system owes itself something it owns. The bank holding the "demand deposits due to banks" is the present owner of the funds and hence should be responsible for paying the reserve requirement. Therefore, in calculating deposits for an individual bank, the amount of demand deposits due from banks is subtracted from total demand deposits.

As can be seen from Table 13-1, on Thursday morning the bank under review has net demand deposits of $217.7 million, savings accounts totaling $112.7 million, and other time accounts of $79.1 million. Reserve requirements are assessed marginally. The Federal Reserve explains this as follows:

> Required schedules are graduated, and each deposit interval applies to that part of the deposits of each bank.[8]

The reserve requirements and deposit intervals in effect September 30, 1977, are presented in Table 13-2. The requirements for time accounts are also presented in this table.

The reserve requirements for our hypothetical bank can therefore be computed on the basis of the information presented in Tables 13-1 and 13-2.

---

[8] *Bulletin,* Board of Governors of the Federal Reserve System (Washington, D.C.: October 1977), p. A9.

Deposit Type	Deposit Amount ($000)	Required Percent	Required Reserves ($000)
Net demand deposits			
up to $2 million	2,000	7	140
$2–$10 million	8,000	9½	760
$10–$100 million	90,000	11¾	10,575
$100–$400 million	300,000	12¾	38,250
remainder	1,112,181	16¼	180,729
Savings deposits	794,409	3	23,832
Other time deposits, 30–179 days			
up to $5 million	5,000	3	150
remainder	354,944	6	21,297
Other time deposits, 180 days to 4 years			
up to $5 million	5,000	2½	125
remainder	189,569	2½	4,739

Total required reserves	280,597
Less: Vault cash	29,976
Net cumulative amount	250,621
Daily average amount	35,803

The hypothetical bank examined in this case must accumulate $250.621 million in reserve balances at its Federal Reserve Bank during the week beginning the Thursday following the next Wednesday. In other words, the bank's daily balances at the Federal Reserve must average $35.803 million during the week of record.

Vault cash, which satisfies reserve requirements, is subtracted from required reserves during the week in which the reserve requirement is calculated. Although vault cash can be used to satisfy reserve requirements, a bank must keep enough coin and currency on hand to meet transactions needs. However, it is undesirable to keep too many funds in vault cash, because it is hard to transact out of these balances to clear checks, to sell federal funds, or to buy Treasury bills. Thus, the bank will keep the minimum amount of vault cash necessary to avoid embarrassing shortages and keep the rest of its reserves in its account at the Federal Reserve.

Vault cash represents transactions balances that are determined by the level of account activity expected by the bank. The amount will vary with the expected net outflows of deposits; cash on hand will be built up with the approach of a holiday season, when people generally withdraw money from banks, and will be reduced after a holiday, when people generally become net depositors.

TABLE 13-2   Reserve Requirements in Effect
             on September 30, 1977

Deposit	Percent
Net Demand Deposits[a]	
$ 0–2	7
2–10	9½
10–100	11¾
100–400	12¾
over 400	16¼
Time Deposits[b]	
Savings	3
Other	
$0–5 million, maturing in	
30–179 days	3
180 days to 4 years	2½
4 years or more	1
Over $5 million, maturing in	
30–179 days	6
180 days to 4 years	2½
4 years or more	1

Source: *Federal Reserve Bulletin* (October 1977), p. A9.

[a] Net demand deposits are gross demand deposits less cash items in process of collection and demand balances due from domestic banks.

[b] Reserve requirements are also applicable to foreign branches and foreign branch loans to U.S. residents. Negotiable order of withdrawal (NOW) accounts and time deposits have the same requirements as savings deposits.

The Federal Reserve treats vault cash reserves as serving transactions purposes, daily business needs related to the size of the bank, number of transactions, and the opportunity cost of holding cash—quantities that will not be varied to meet reserve requirements. The full adjustment to satisfy reserve constraints, therefore, comes in the bank's account at the Federal Reserve. This makes sense because this is the account the bank uses to adjust its reserve position—for example, to invest excess funds by buying U.S. government securities or selling federal funds, or to add funds by buying federal funds in case of revenue deficiencies.

MANAGING THE RESERVE POSITION

The bank manages its reserve position so that at the close of business each Wednesday it has (1) accumulated a large enough reserve balance at the

Federal Reserve to satisfy its legal obligation for that week, (2) kept actual reserves within 2 percent of the amount required, and (3) accumulated enough reserves to satisfy any deficiency of funds carried over from the previous statement week. The difficulty is that unexpected cash inflows or outflows may occur at such a time and in such a quantity that the bank finds it impossible to meet its reserve plans.

A typical worksheet used by the manager of the reserve position at a commercial bank is presented in Table 13-3. The general need to meet requirements within the balance sheet is similar for all banks. The major differences between banks will usually be in the number of transactions they handle; a greater number of transactions adds to the complexity a money manager faces in satisfactorily achieving the required amount shown in the bottom line of column (1) of this table.

In large money-center banks, the number of transactions is enormous and the reserve position is calculated several times each day. Management of the bank's position is a continuous task. Smaller banks have fewer transactions, and thus the need for constant oversight of the reserve position declines. The reserve balance in some banks is checked only once a day, and adjusting transactions take place infrequently.[9]

The reserve manager now knows exactly what the bank's reserves are for the coming week and the following week. Whereas the manager is interested in the day-by-day reserve position of the current week, next week can be viewed in its entirety. The current week's activity is, and should be, affected by next week's position, but only by the expected surplus or deficit. That is, it is not always best to wait until a given week to conduct reserve operations. If a surplus or deficiency is expected in the future, the reserve manager may want to start doing something about it in the current week, for with the carry-forward provision, present actions can affect future balances at the Federal Reserve.

More time will be spent on this later. For now it will be assumed that the bank expects to meet next week's reserve requirements without any undue pressure placed on operating needs. Thus, the bank will manage this week's reserve position only to meet the legal requirements for the week. Column (1) of Table 13-3 can then be filled in with the known reserves required for the current statement week.

Any surplus or deficit position from the previous week is placed at the head of columns (3) and (8). These amounts are included only in the excess

---

[9] For a more thorough review of reserve management at large money-center banks, see the section on this subject at the end of this chapter. It can be noted for the time being that the larger the bank, the less difficulty there is in conducting short-run reserve management. This, too, is discussed later in the chapter.

TABLE 13-3   A Typical Reserve Position Worksheet
(Amounts in thousands of dollars)

	(1)	(2)	(3)	(4) Federal Funds Transactions	(5)	(6)	(7)	(8)
Reserve Balances at End of:	Required Balances with Federal Reserve Bank	Balances at Federal Reserve Bank Before Adjusting Transactions	Excess or Deficiency (1) − (2) +512^a	Fed. Funds Purchased	Fed. Funds Sold	Other Adjustments	Balances at Federal Reserve After Adjusting Transactions	Final Excess or Deficiency (1) − (7) +512^a
Thurs.	35,803	33,417	− 2,386				33,417	−2,386
Fri.	35,803	32,107	− 3,696	3,000			35,107	− 696
Cum.	71,606	65,524	− 5,570				68,524	−2,570
Sat.	35,803	32,107	− 3,696	3,000			35,107	− 696
Sun.	35,803	32,107	− 3,696	3,000			35,107	− 696
Cum.	143,212	129,738	−12,962				138,738	−3,962
Mon.	35,803	34,860	− 943				34,860	− 943
Cum.	179,015	164,598	−13,905				173,598	−4,905
Tues.	35,803	36,081	+ 278				36,081	+ 278
Cum.	214,818	200,679	−13,627				209,679	−4,627
Wed.	35,803	38,872	+ 3,069	2,000			40,872	+5,069
Cum.	250,621	239,551	−10,558				250,551	
Average	35,803	34,222	− 1,508				35,793	+ 442^b

^{a} Excess carried over from previous statement week.
^{b} Excess to be carried over into the next statement week.

TABLE 13-4   Projected Reserve Balances
for a Hypothetical Week
(In thousands of dollars)

Thurs.	$33,500
Fri.	33,000
Sat.	33,000
Sun.	33,000
Mon.	35,000
Tues.	36,000
Wed.	38,000

or deficiency figures because they do not, of course, affect the actual amounts of deposits on record. If a surplus or deficit position is reached for the week, these starting figures are subtracted out or added to the final balance of the week so that they will not be carried over into the next week.

In addition, reserve positions are computed at the close of each business day at the Federal Reserve Banks. Since the Federal Reserve is open only five days a week, no transactions are recorded over the weekend, and hence the reserve balance that the bank achieves Friday afternoon will also be its deposit balance for Saturday and Sunday.[10]

When holidays occur on Mondays or Fridays, the position is carried a day longer. For example, if a holiday falls on a Monday, the Federal Reserve being closed, the bank's reserve position as of Friday will apply not only to Saturday and Sunday but also to Monday. Hence, locking into a surplus reserve position over a holiday weekend may be a cheap way of meeting reserve requirements for that week.

The game is now to match reserve requirements with actual reserve positions. At the start of the statement week, a bank should forecast its expected reserve position for each day in the coming week. This process will be discussed more thoroughly in the next section. The manager of the reserve position must then plan out the bank's activity during the week, on the basis of the mean forecast of reserve positions and the possible deviations from the mean forecast that might be experienced.

If the projected deposit balances at the Federal Reserve are as shown in Table 13-4, it is likely that the hypothetical bank under review will need to

[10] As is explained in Chapter 12, this makes Eurodollar money on record on Friday extremely valuable, although the transaction may be for only one day. The money involved in the transaction will already be returned to the owner, but the bank will get three days credit for the funds.

buy federal funds sometime during the week in order to meet its reserve requirements. However, if the possible deviations from these expected levels are small, the reserve manager may want to wait until the end of the week, observe how the reserve position is actually developing throughout the week, and then (since the reserve deficiency is not expected to be large) enter the market and buy funds if necessary. Since the distribution of possible outcomes is small and the expected deficit is also small, the manager can wait until more information is available before making a move.

On the other hand, if there is a great deal of uncertainty about the upcoming week, the reserve manager may want to go into the federal funds market early in the week and establish a cushion of reserves so as to avoid the need to go to the market at the last minute for a sizable amount. In this case the bank will sell federal funds toward the end of the week if reserve positions have worked out to be much easier than forecast. The bank will act defensively in this time period, sacrificing returns to be able to satisfy legal reserve requirements.

Thus, the manager of the reserve position vitally needs not only some forecast of the expected values of reserve balances but also some idea of how uncertain the short-run situation is. In a smaller bank it may be the manager's job to obtain this information. In a larger bank the information should be continuously provided to the manager by others within the bank.

FORECASTING RESERVE POSITIONS

The forecasting of reserve positions should be incorporated within the framework of planning asset/liability strategies and long-run growth strategies.[11] However, the forecasts pertaining to longer time horizons should not be redone on a short-term basis. They should be seen as a control mechanism against which the short run can be judged. Thus, there must be continual checking and cross-checking among forecasts of short-run reserve movements, actual short-run movements, intermediate-term forecasts, and the actual achievements of the bank.

One of the lessons of the hectic banking days of the late 1960s and early 1970s was that there must be coordination among the different operations of the bank. All too often banks found themselves supporting loan

---

[11] Again, the reader is cautioned that short-term reserve management is really not a problem for the major money-center banks. The problems discussed here are incorporated into their asset/liability-management programs, and hence reserve requirements should be forecast and controlled within that framework.

portfolios with more purchased funds (federal funds and negotiable CDs) than desirable. This forced the banks into lower earnings and forced some, such as Franklin National and Marine Midland, into embarrassing financial conditions. Care must be taken to incorporate the bank's other activities and plans into its short-term reserve operations.

The main factor influencing the reserve position of the bank is the net clearings of checks at the Federal Reserve. Note that these net clearings include not only clearings of persons and nonfinancial organizations but also correspondent balances of other banks. If a bank has substantial amounts of correspondent balances in due-to accounts, large fluctuations can take place because of interbank transfers and other transactions of the correspondents to meet their own cash needs or possibly because of federal funds transactions.

Thus, projecting these net clearings is very difficult. In many cases the "average" behavior for the time of year can be expected. That is, the bank can use previous experience to monitor the inflow and outflow of funds. But it must also identify any unusual factors that will impinge on reserve balances. Additional costs will be incurred in obtaining this information. One thing that should be checked continuously is the potential activity of large borrowers, or customers with large accounts. The manager of the reserve position should be aware of customers' plans for large deposits or large withdrawals. The withdrawals may not, of course, be connected with existing deposits, because the customer could draw on its line of credit or initiate a new loan and use the funds immediately.

This information should be available at reasonable cost if loan officers and others within the bank are in close enough contact with these customers or are familiar with their operating cycles. Data should also be available on loan contracts and repayments so that the bank is aware of the effects on reserves to be expected from loans maturing or being paid off.

The deferred availability of funds, according to the Federal Reserve's schedule, must be known. The bank must also be aware of the operations of correspondent banks and monitor the problems and needs of these institutions, because the actions of correspondents can cause large flows into or out of the bank's account and have a major impact on the bank's reserve position.

In addition, the reserve manager must know what is happening within his or her own bank; for example, currency and coin orders or deliveries are subtracted from or added to the bank's account at the Federal Reserve. Treasury calls on tax and loan accounts must be made known to the manager. Furthermore, the manager must have information on the maturities of Treasury bills, CDs, and other instruments held by the bank,

TABLE 13-5   Potential Transactions Affecting Reserve Position
(In thousands of dollars)

CREDITS

	Funds Immediately Available	Deferred Items Available	Securities Sales	Currency and Coin Going to Federal Reserve	Maturing Securities, etc.	Other	Total Credits
Thurs.	15,400	5,680	1,900	—	1,300	—	24,280
Fri.							27,500
Sat.							—
Sun.							—
Mon.							24,000
Tues.							24,000
Wed.							26,000

DEBITS

	Charges Against Bank	Securities Purchases	Notes Due	Borrowings from Federal Reserve Due	Coin and Currency Order	Tax and Loan Calls	Maturing Securities and Funds	Other	Total Debits
Thurs.	24,880	—	—	—	1,600	—	—	—	26,480
Fri.									28,000
Sat.									—
Sun.									—
Mon.									22,000
Tues.									23,000
Wed.									24,000

	(1) Reserve Position at Start of Day	(2) Net of Credits Minus Debits	(3) Projected Reserve Balances (1) – (2)
Thurs.	35,700	−2,200	33,500
Fri.	33,500	− 500	33,000
Sat.	33,000		33,000
Sun.	33,000		33,000
Mon.	33,000	+2,000	35,000
Tues.	35,000	+1,000	36,000
Wed.	36,000	+2,000	38,000

because maturing items supply or use funds that may significantly affect the reserve position. Also, if the bank has a securities trading or investment department, reports on planned purchases and sales must be available. Finally, the reserve manager will have information on the maturities of federal funds bought or sold, and on any borrowings the bank may have made from the Federal Reserve.

Once this information has been collected, as shown in Table 13-5 for Thursday, the net position can be calculated. Since the net position represents the change in reserve balances that is expected during the day, it must be added to the reserve position from the previous day. This total will represent the projected reserve balance that is used in Table 13-4 and is the raw material for establishing a plan to meet the required reserves that have been computed and listed in column (1) of Table 13-3.

Some additional information that may be of considerable use to the money manager can be obtained at very little cost. This is information on the uncertainty of the environment in which the manager will be working. It is possible to estimate the distribution of results by calling on the individuals supplying the original data to estimate how correct their forecasts will be. For example, they may be asked what they think the probability is that their forecast is within 5 percent, 10 percent, or 20 percent of the actual future result. Their answers can then be used to construct a distribution table for the aggregate results. Most managers can quantify their feelings well enough for such an exercise to provide useful results at a very low cost to the bank.

TABLE 13-6   Projected Reserve Balances and Dispersion
For Weeks Beginning 12/20 and 12/27

Day	Date	Deviation from Mean Forecast			Mean Forecast ($1000)	Deviation from Mean Forecast		
		−20%	−10%	−5%		+5%	+10%	+20%
Thurs.	12/20		5%	10%	33,500	10%	5%	
Fri.	12/21		10%	20%	33,000	5%		
Sat.	12/22		10%	20%	33,000	5%		
Sun.	12/23		10%	20%	33,000	5%		
Mon.	12/24		5%	10%	35,000	10%	5%	
Tues.	12/25			10%	36,000	20%	10%	
Wed.	12/26			10%	38,000	20%	10%	
Averages for week					34,500			
Next week (beginning 12/27)				15%	37,000	20%		

In Table 13-6 the data supplied in Table 13-4 are augmented with some information of the dispersion of projected reserve balances obtained in the manner just described. In addition, the manager should obtain this type of information for the bank's expected reserve position for the week following the current statement week. The manager now has some idea as to what is to be expected in the coming week. He or she must then try to achieve the quantity of reserves required at the Federal Reserve and yet maintain sufficient flexibility to be able to adjust quickly to the vagaries of the marketplace.

OPERATION

The manager of the bank's reserve position must now decide on a strategy. Given the information derived in Tables 13-1 through 13-5, there are basically five sources the manager can tap to obtain the amount of reserves required by the Federal Reserve:

1. The bank's balances held with its correspondent bank
2. Federal funds
3. Treasury securities
4. Eurodollars
5. Borrowings from the Federal Reserve

For the bank under review it is assumed that balances at the correspondent bank are kept at the minimum necessary to maintain the relationship and that no surpluses or deficits are expected in that account during the coming weeks. Furthermore, this bank cannot get into the Eurodollar market. Thus, only choices 2, 3, and 5 are available to it.

A strategy has been constructed for this particular bank. Management expects little or no difficulty in meeting reserve requirements in the second week, but there is some uncertainty in the current week because of the Christmas holidays. Therefore, the bank will buy some federal funds early in the week, protecting its position and allowing for some flexibility in case outflows are greater than expected. It is desirable to err on the surplus side of its account this week. This will eliminate the chance of ending up with a deficit, and since the surplus can be carried forward into next week, the bank can preserve these funds and even sell federal funds if necessary at that time.

The manager follows this strategy early in the week by purchasing the $3,000,000 in federal funds. If things start out pretty much as expected, there should be a cumulative surplus built up through the weekend. However, the manager must monitor incoming reports daily (or hourly, depending on the bank) to keep informed as to how actual figures are performing relative to expected amounts. If balances are running ahead or behind those expected, if new information becomes available on large customers or securities transactions, or if there are calls on Treasury tax and loan accounts, the manager must be capable of reacting and changing the prescribed plan. That is, it may be necessary to buy or sell federal funds toward the end of the week in order to achieve the desired position. Since much uncertainty had been assumed to surround the occurrences of this week, the reserve manager should be particularly ready to meet unexpected events. Information flow is essential to the operation of short-run reserve management, so that the money manager's actions can be coordinated with events elsewhere in the bank.

CONTROL

The short-term effort for a given week does not end with the completion of the week. The short-term projections were based on certain specific assumptions. The week must be reviewed to see if actual occurrences match expectations and, if not, to discover the underlying reasons for the differences. They could simply arise from random events. However, they could be the result of incorrect assumptions in the original forecast, in which case the bank may have to change these assumptions in future weeks.

For example, the particular week under review may have included a date on which corporate taxes had to be paid. At such times bank loans generally increase as funds are borrowed and then transferred to government accounts. The bank reacts by purchasing federal funds, selling Treasury bills, or borrowing at the Federal Reserve.

Suppose, however, that borrowing is not as great as expected and consequently the reserve manager does not have to buy as large a quantity of federal funds as planned. Upon checking on why firms did not borrow as much as expected, the bank has learned that firms were much more liquid than they had expected to be and were trying to build stronger balance sheets by avoiding short-term borrowing from commercial banks.

Obtaining information of this kind should have two effects on bank behavior, although, as is well known, one week's results cannot be taken to imply a trend. First, this information is well worth recording; the failure of corporations to borrow at this time will affect projected repayments of loans.

Second, this information may contain implications for intermediate-term asset/liability management. If these corporations are shying away from short-term bank loans and are trying to restructure their balance sheets, then overall loan demand may remain weak in the future. If this is the case, banks might find themselves in the position of buying expensive CDs to invest in Treasury securities paying about the same rate of interest. One week does not establish a trend, but the information gathered within the weekly planning activity may be the early warning a bank needs to respond quickly in the intermediate term to a changing economic environment.

Short-term plans must be analyzed for any improvement in short-term operating performance. It is imperative, however, for the long-term health and performance of the bank, that the information from short-term reserve management be incorporated into the planning and control of the planning process over the longer time horizon.

SHORT-TERM RESERVE MANAGEMENT IN MAJOR MONEY-CENTER BANKS

Short-term reserve management, as it has evolved, is not a major problem for large money-center commercial banks. In fact, these banks generally have no single manager or management group assigned to handle reserve management problems. It is usually the senior securities trader who obtains the funds needed to meet reserve requirements or sells the excess funds when these banks are in a surplus position.

The reason for this is relatively simple. An examination of a reserve position worksheet (similar to Table 13-3) prepared by a large bank will reveal entries in both columns (4) and (5). A large bank will usually be both buying and selling federal funds during a statement week and, in fact, may be doing both on the same day. The trader gets information on the bank's reserve position at the beginning of the day and then sets the rates at which the bank should be willing to buy and sell funds. Since large banks are net purchasers of funds, they are generally looking to buy. Transactions start coming in. The bank may sell some funds, or it may buy a large amount. Later in the day, a new report on the bank's reserve position will be received. If funds are coming in too rapidly, the trader may lower the funds rate; if too slowly, the rate may be raised. This continues throughout the day. The bank may be a buyer or a seller of federal funds at different times in the day, although it will usually finish the day as a net purchaser. The result of all this is that the senior trader is balancing the bank's reserve position almost continuously. Reserve requirements can be met by buying or selling some additional funds; satisfying the legal requirement to hold a certain quantity of reserves is not difficult for these institutions.

This is, of course, a simplified description of the actual practice of federal funds trading. The trader is concerned with more than just meeting the reserve requirements of the bank every hour or two. Funds markets are subject to complex, interrelated expectations as to reserve movements within the banking system, loan demand, bank float, daily and weekly cycles in interest rates, possibilities that the Federal Reserve will enter the market, and Treasury financings. The expert trader will attempt to vary the buying and selling of funds so as to obtain the highest possible returns. Thus, the bank will occasionally be short of its reserve requirements if the trader thinks they can be met later at a better price.

In general, however, short-term reserve management is relatively simple for large money-center banks that satisfy their requirements almost continuously. This is not true for smaller banks, because they have neither the information nor the specialists needed to manage their position so closely. The main concern for the large bank, therefore, is the intermediate term, and to manage their positions over this time horizon they have committed large amounts of resources. The intermediate term will be the subject of the next chapter.

A NOTE ON FEDERAL RESERVE OPERATIONS IN THE MONEY MARKETS

There is a whole body of literature on the role of the Federal Reserve in the money markets,[12] so that not much space need be given to the topic here. One important implication of much of the literature is that certain ground rules have been established for Federal Reserve operations in the money markets and that these ground rules are well known and observed. This is

[12] For a thorough understanding of Federal Reserve operations in the money markets and the philosophy behind such procedures, the following articles should be read: J. M. Guttentag, "The Strategy of Open-Market Operations," *The Quarterly Journal of Economics* (February 1966); J. M. Guttentag, "Defensive and Dynamic Open-Market Operations, Discounting and the Federal Reserve System's Crisis Prevention Responsibilities," *The Journal of Finance* (May 1969); R. V. Roosa, *Federal Reserve Operations in the Money and Government Securities Market*, Federal Reserve Bank of New York (July 1956); P. Meek and R. Thunberg, "Monetary Aggregates and Federal Reserve Open-Market Operations," *Monthly Review*, Federal Reserve Bank of New York (April 1971); and A. Holmes, "The Problems of the Open-Market Manager," in *Controlling Monetary Aggregates II: The Implementation* (Federal Reserve Bank of Boston, 1973).

important for commercial banks because banks can be prepared for almost any contingency if they know how the Federal Reserve will react.

The Federal Reserve's present operating procedures seem to provide, in the short run, relatively stable Treasury bill prices and a liquid market. This is achieved by its use of interest rate targets in the short run, even though it uses a monetary aggregate target in the longer run.[13] This means that banks sell securities at going market rates and that the Federal Reserve will be supplying liquidity to the market in times of financial crises.[14] If the central bank continues to conduct its operations in such a fashion, then banks can reduce their excess reserve positions as well as their secondary reserve positions and make more loans.

The Federal Reserve need not act in this way. It could, for example, follow a money supply target in the short run as well as in the longer run. If it did, interest rates would tend to fluctuate more and there would be no guarantee that the Federal Reserve would provide liquidity to the market if market participants needed it.[15] If such were the case, banks would probably hold greater amounts of excess reserves and secondary reserves than they do now, and loan output would be a smaller fraction of their assets.

However, the system could work that way. The important thing is for the banks to know what to expect in the way of Federal Reserve operations and for the Federal Reserve to stick to its rules. Breaking the rules causes uncertainty, which makes banks unwilling to commit themselves. This reduces the efficiency of the financial system.

Current operating methods are very sensible, as the Federal Reserve is concerned about the health of the banking system and the provision of credit to finance economic expansion and development. By providing short-run stability to the money markets and market liquidity during critical times, the central bank is, in a sense, subsidizing the banking industry. Banks can invest in higher-yielding assets than cash or short-term Treasury bills and earn a greater return, and borrowers profit because more money is available for lending. Furthermore, the system is buffered to some extent against financial collapse. What is the cost of this action? Since banks are "guaranteed" liquidity, they are encouraged to take on riskier portfolios.

---

[13] See P. Meek and R. Thunberg, "Monetary Aggregates," or A. Holmes, "The Problems of the Open-Market Manager" (cited in footnote 12). For a fuller explanation of this interpretation, see J. M. Guttentag, "Discussion," in *Controlling Monetary Aggregates II: The Implementation* (Federal Reserve Bank of Boston, 1973).

[14] This has been called by some the "lender of first resort" function.

[15] In fact, they would do just the opposite if they strictly followed a money supply target. See J. M. Guttentag, "The Strategy of Open-Market Operations," *The Quarterly Journal of Economics* (February 1966).

Because banks are riskier than they would otherwise be, it may be that the economy experiences greater swings in economic activity and more inflation than it would under other circumstances.

REVIEW QUESTIONS

1. Should commercial banks be required to meet a reserve requirement? What would happen if they did not need to meet such a requirement? What would be the alternative to required reserves? What would be gained or lost in terms of bank management if no reserves were required?
2. Is the 2 percent carryover provision meaningful? Does it really provide any relief for the small or medium-sized bank it is supposed to help?
3. In practice, is there a difference between accepting a philosophy of minimizing losses and one of maximizing profits?
4. Why does the reserve manager especially need information from the loan department or the deposit function on the activity of large customers? Does the difference in magnitude of customer balances and loans between large and small banks affect your answer?
5. Why are bank clearings continuously the most important factor affecting reserve positions? How easily can they be forecast?
6. Maturing government securities can affect a bank's reserve position at the Federal Reserve. How does the maturing of loans affect reserve positions?
7. If the Federal Reserve operated entirely on a money supply target, what would happen to movements in interest rates and in market liquidity? How would this affect the way commercial banks manage their reserve positions?

14

Asset/Liability Management

As described earlier, asset/liability management is an "intermediate-term" undertaking. Its time horizon is short enough that the bank will not contemplate changing its capital structure or customer base but long enough that the bank does not have to worry about reserve requirements.

A wider range of instruments or markets is available to the bank than for reserve management, and the effort to plan or control events is primary, whereas in the short run, management assumes defensive or reactive positions. Thus, the intermediate term gives the bank an opportunity not only to protect itself against seasonal or cyclical movements of loans and deposits, but also to become more profitable by structuring portfolios in optimal ways.

This chapter begins with a definition of the relevant time horizon for asset/liability management. There follows a discussion of the problems faced by management in the intermediate term and a section on the organization needed for planning the asset/liability structure of the bank. Several techniques used by banks in intermediate-term planning are then presented. The chapter concludes with a short section on control and feedback.

TIME HORIZON

The time horizon relevant for asset/liability management is somewhat longer than that for short-run reserve management and is defined primarily by the makeup of the financial markets in which the bank operates. Moreover, the data the bank works with are more aggregative, in a time sense. Whereas, in managing their reserves, banks concentrate on daily and weekly data, over the intermediate run they work with monthly or quarterly data. At the minimum, then, the bank has a one-month horizon. This is not inconsistent with the availability of funds, since the shortest maturity a bank can offer for a negotiable CD is 30 days.

The maximum length of the time horizon is about six months. Although banks have used longer time periods, some going up to two years, there are two very good reasons for confining asset/liability management to a shorter horizon. First, the markets for instruments traded in this time frame are not as broad and deep when one gets into maturities greater than six months. Treasury bills, negotiable CDs, and commercial paper all have excellent markets up to six-month maturities. Eurodollars have excellent markets up to five or six months. The markets for maturities greater than that are not nearly so good. A bank runs a greater risk of price variation and an inability to get all the funds it needs at going market rates if it deals in this end of the market.[1]

An empirical observation lends some credence to this argument. Large or money-center commercial banks find that the average maturity of their purchased funds portfolio seems to run between 90 and 120 days. They may occasionally go below 90 days or above 120 days, but these banks report that by and large they stay within this maturity range.[2]

The second reason for using a six-month time horizon as the maximum is that sophisticated asset/liability management depends so heavily on interest rate movements. Forecasting interest rates is a hazardous business

---

[1] Recall that a bank needs perfectly elastic supplies of assets or funds to operate either as an asset manager or as a liability manager. Assets and liabilities can be divided into classes on the basis of maturity. Hence, one of the m asset classes may be negotiable CDs with a maturity of less than six months and another may be negotiable CDs with a maturity of more than six months. The argument made here is that while the supply of funds from CDs of less than six-month maturity may be perfectly elastic, so that rate variation is not important, the supply of funds from CDs of greater than six-month maturity may be less than perfectly elastic, so that rate variation does affect the quantity the bank wants to take and the price it is willing to pay. Furthermore, the latter market cannot serve as the residual market.

[2] The information presented in this paragraph was obtained through personal interviews.

at best. Six months may be considered a maximum for reasonable estimates of interest rate movements.

There are several other, lesser reasons for choosing this time horizon. For example, banks' loan portfolios are of relatively short maturity. The average maturity of the vast majority of commercial loans at banks is certainly less than two years, and well over half mature in less than one year. Thus, the commercial loan portfolio, on average, has to turn over or be renewed within a time period that only slightly exceeds the maturities of the market assets and liabilities that are relevant for the intermediate-term management of the bank.

In addition, seasonal factors, a major concern of the intermediate term, rarely last more than six months. Thus, a bank structuring its asset/liability portfolio to meet seasonal outflows or inflows of funds will be dealing in good markets to match their timing requirements.

Reserve requirements, which are the primary cause for short-run reserve management, are no problem at all in the intermediate run. That is, in this time frame every bank becomes more or less like the large money-center banks, buying or selling various assets or liabilities, and to meet their reserve requirements all they have to do is buy or sell more or less of a particular instrument.

The amount of required reserves the bank needs will be ignored, therefore, in the discussions of this chapter. As in the model presented in Chapter 2, required reserves will be subtracted from the liability to which they apply and the argument will be continued in terms of net funds available. The size of excess reserve balances, on the other hand, is an important decision variable for the bank. Even if excess reserves are zero or close to zero, it cannot be concluded that the bank has not made a decision on excess reserves. The correct conclusion is more apt to be that management has decided that the optimal quantity of excess reserves for the bank to hold is very small or zero.

In summary, therefore, the maximum time horizon for asset/liability management is assumed to be no more than six months. Data will be aggregated in terms of months, and reserve requirements will be de-emphasized by netting them out against the liability from which they are computed.

PROBLEMS IN ASSET/LIABILITY MANAGEMENT

Banks face five major problem areas in operating within the intermediate time period. Although banks know who they consider to be their customers, they do not know precisely what amounts of loans and deposits they will be receiving from these customers during any given period of time. Customers, as well as banks, are subject to seasonal influences (peculiar to the individual economic unit, the region, or the nation as a whole), local and national economic activity, the monetary policy of the Federal Reserve System, the performance of the financial markets, and customer relationships. These will be discussed in turn.

Seasonal Loan and Deposit Flows

Banks have been subject to seasonal loan demand and deposit flows almost from their beginnings in history. For example, the most basic kind of bank loan has been the seasonal, self-liquidating loan used to finance the planting–harvest cycle experienced by agricultural customers or the inventory or accounts receivable financing of manufacturing and retail organizations. Deposits have followed such cycles or holiday seasons.

Seasonal flows within a year's time vary among banks, depending on local conditions and the trade cycles of primary customers in the region.[3] The basic management task has been to structure the maturities of assets and liabilities so as to have funds available when they are needed, to earn the highest return possible when the funds are not needed, and to build in sufficient flexibility to meet unusual demands for or withdrawals of funds.

Banks serving a small number of industries in a restricted geographic area generally have found it fairly easy to forecast both the timing and the magnitude of their seasonal flows. Others, serving a greater number of industries or operating in a more open economic environment, find it more difficult to forecast their seasonal flows, and hence they tend to put more effort into projecting these seasonal factors than do smaller banks. Both types of banks aim at the same thing: having sufficient funds available for borrowers and depositors while being as fully invested as possible to earn the best return on their portfolio. Therefore, both attempt to structure the maturity composition of their portfolio to achieve this purpose.

Local and National Economic Activity

Local and national economic activity are also important determinants of the construction of commercial bank asset/liability portfolios. These fac-

---

[3] As banks became larger and grew into regional, national, and international organizations, geographic, as well as industry, diversification became an important consideration in a bank's attempt to meet the seasonal factors in its operations.

tors are imposed on top of the variations that result from seasonal movements. Since banks have not been able to identify these factors as readily as seasonal movements, efforts at judging the impact of economic activity on loan or deposit flows developed at a later stage in bank forecasting than the attempts to project seasonal flows.

It is obvious, however, that the short-run strength of the local or national economy is going to have important ramifications for the bank's portfolio of assets and liabilities. A potentially strong economy with strong loan demand will lead banks to depend more on market liquidity to protect their positions as liquid asset portfolios are reduced to support loan demand and purchased funds become a more important part of portfolio activity. On the other hand, a potentially weak economy with weak loan demand will cause banks to rely less on negotiable CDs and Eurodollars and may even cause a bank that had been primarily a liability manager to switch back to being an asset manager.

Monetary Policy

The future course of monetary policy is a vital element in planning asset/liability portfolios because of the impact the Federal Reserve has on both reserve availability and the level of interest rates. If the Federal Reserve is expected to conduct a tighter monetary policy in coming months, then banks can anticipate a slower rate of growth of nonborrowed reserves relative to loan demands in the future and a rising target level of short-run interest rates. The reverse would be true if the Federal Reserve were expected to conduct an easier monetary policy.

Given these expectations, the bank must structure its assets and liabilities so as to meet the changing availability of funds and the rising cost of short-term funds in a way that will provide flexibility for unexpected loan demands and possibly for disintermediation caused by interest rate ceilings, and yet maximize its returns over the period.

Since the Federal Reserve does not reverse itself in a policy sense within a week's time, the time frame of reference must be the six-month time horizon used by the bank in intermediate-term planning. Bankers have great difficulty, however, in determining when a change in Federal Reserve policy is to take place and when it actually does take place. Under current operating procedures the Federal Reserve does not make public its interest rate or short-run money supply targets. Even if it did, bankers would have some difficulty in interpreting exactly what effect the targets would have on the growth of such important aggregates as nonborrowed reserves and the money supply. Thus, they must always try to decide whether any given Federal Reserve action is a "temporary" change or a "permanent" change in policy. Since banks should react only to "permanent" changes, they must continually monitor Federal Reserve actions and the money market to determine whether or not a new policy change is permanent.[4]

Therefore, banks must always be on the alert for what the Federal Reserve is doing or is planning to do. They must then structure their portfolios (with respect to the maturities of their assets and liabilities) to meet the expected stance of the Federal Reserve. Again, knowledge of the operating rules of the central bank is crucial to deciding how to go about constructing a portfolio.

Financial Markets

In addition to forecasting Federal Reserve action, the bank must forecast the performance of the financial markets. The main contribution this can make to portfolio composition has to do with the term structure of interest rates. The intermediate term is the only period over which the term structure is important to a bank, because in order to maximize profits the bank must use the term structure given it by the market, as well as its own forecast, to construct a portfolio of different maturities of assets and liabilities so as to take full advantage of the opportunities available to it. For example, if bank management feels that interest rates are going to rise, they should lend with as short a maturity as possible and borrow with as long a maturity as possible. This would mean that, if the bank is right in its forecast, lending in the future would be at higher and higher rates but the funds to finance these loans would be locked into at lower rates.[5] Variable-rate loans are desirable in this case, because all loans would then be very short term. If management believes that interest rates are going to fall, the bank would, of course, want to structure these maturities in the opposite fashion. Variable-rate loans work against the bank in the case of falling rates.

These statements about varying the maturity structure of the portfolio make portfolio building sound easy, but this is not the case. In most instances, loan terms such as interest rate, maturity, and fees are fairly well

---

[4] For a more complete examination of this problem, see J. M. Mason, R. J. Rogalski, and J. D. Vinso, "Expectations, Commercial Bank Adjustment, and the Short-Run Performance of Monetary Aggregates" (Working Paper No. 6-77a, Rodney L. White Center for Financial Research, The University of Pennsylvania).

[5] There would be an optimum tradeoff between lending short and borrowing long.

set; they are determined by relative yield considerations, taking into account the bank's customer base and competitive behavior. A large portion of the bank's liabilities have also been determined. The only instruments whose maturities can be managed are the residual or purchased funds instruments: U.S. government securities, negotiable certificates of deposit, federal funds, and Eurodollars. Because the maturities are mixed in these instruments, the bank can alter only slightly the average maturity of its asset or liability portfolio of residual items. Thus, if its portfolio managers can reduce the average maturity of purchased funds from 120 days to 90 days, or vice versa, over several months, they feel they are doing a good job.

The point is that "good" management implies "good" use of available resources. Altering the maturity composition of the portfolio of residual funds may add only a few basis points to the bank's return on equity. However, a few basis points here and a few there add up to a better management record.

A bank might react differently if it assumes that the term structure contains a liquidity premium. Recall that the existence of a liquidity premium implies that short-term interest rates will be below longer-term interest rates, even when the market, on average, expects rates to remain constant. The liquidity premium is a payment for the uncertainty pertaining to the future course of interest rates.

Now, a large proportion of the time, a liquidity premium exists in the very short-term market. That is, in the U.S. government securities market up to one year, longer-term rates generally carry a premium over very short-term rates. Since commercial banks operate predominantly in the short-term end of the maturity spectrum, they can almost always take advantage of a positive yield curve. Two examples will make the point clear.

Example 1   Consider the case where the amount of funds available to invest is fixed and the time period available for investment is known. Funds are needed in three months, and there are two choices available to the bank: It can invest in 91-day bills yielding 8.00 percent, or it can invest in 182-day bills yielding 8.25 percent in the market and sell them at the end of 91 days. This assumes interest rates are expected to remain constant over the three-month time period.

The return to the bank on the two alternative investments can be computed by means of the formula[6]

---

[6] *Securities of the United States Government and Federal Agencies and Related Money Market Instruments*, 27th ed. (New York: First Boston Corporation, 1974), p. 48.

$$D = \frac{A - B}{B} \times C$$

where A = the number of days to maturity of Treasury bills when purchased

B = the number of days the bills are held

C = the difference between the rate at which the bills are purchased and that at which they are sold

D = the alteration in the original cost resulting from the difference between purchase price and sale price over the period held

For the given data,

$$D = \frac{182 - 91}{91} \times .25 = \frac{91}{91} \times .25 = .25$$

Thus, the yield from investing in the 182-day bills and then selling at the end of 91 days is 8.50 percent (8.25 + .25) as compared with the 8.00 percent yield on 91-day bills. Clearly, the 182-day bills are preferable. The only reason they might not be preferable is that rates might not be 8.00 percent in 91 days. If rates rise above 8.50 percent, then the bank would have to sell at a capital loss and its return would be less than 8.50 percent. Therefore, what the bank expects to happen to the 91-day rate is crucial for its behavior. If the uncertainty concerning the future movement in rates is too great, the bank will just stick with the shorter-term investment and accept the smaller yield as a cost of insuring its return.

Example 2   Consider the case of a bank that is not limited in terms of maturity in either its sources or uses of funds. One instance of this is the purchase and financing of Treasury bills. If there is a substantial liquidity premium in the market, particularly for very short-term borrowings such as repurchase agreements, banks may buy six-month or nine-month Treasury bills and finance their portfolio with two-day, three-day, or seven-day repurchase agreements. Their profit is the spread that comes between these very short borrowings and the longer-term securities used as collateral.

This is asset/liability management in the following sense: The six- or nine-month Treasury bills are purchased for reasons other than short-run reserve management. This must be the case, for the bank will not commit itself for that long if it expects the "turnaround" to be very short. It must then be concerned about financing these purchases. Now, if it cannot finance them with low-cost, interest-inelastic liabilities, it must find some other means, because funds obtained by issuing negotiable CDs or buying Eurodollars will be too expensive to make bill purchases worthwhile.

Thus, the bank looks to the very short-term market for financing, and here is where forecasting is again very important. If the bank uses short-term repurchase agreements to finance its Treasury bill portfolio, it must be able at all times to borrow and finance these securities at a positive spread. The liquidity premium must be expected to last for the entire period the bank plans to hold the Treasury bills.

Flexibility is important, for the bank must be able to move out of its bill position if there is much of a threat that the spread will be reduced or even eliminated. This information can be forthcoming from the reserve management aspects of the bank's operations. This is another example of the need for coordination between short-run operations and intermediate-term planning.

Customer Relationships

The importance of customer relationships and the lines of credit that usually go along with them cannot be overstated. It is estimated that borrowers use approximately 30 to 35 percent of their lines during "normal" times, when the financial markets are not pressed for funds. However, during periods of tight money or financial crises, usage may increase to 50 or 60 percent of lines outstanding. Banks must be ready to honor these lines of credit at any time or be prepared to lose some customers.

It is important that asset/liability managers as well as top management know what lines of credit have been extended by loan officers and also what usage may be expected of these lines over the upcoming months. This is also a long-run concern with regard to controlling the portfolio. Here, however, interest is centered on the intermediate term. Unless the people in charge of managing the bank's asset/liability portfolio are aware of loan commitments and their potential usage, they will not be equipped to plan the necessary flexibility in residual commitments for intermediate-term operations.

Commercial banks that have been extremely lax in controlling commitments have been surprised in periods of tight money at how strapped they became for funds because they had so many loan agreements to honor. Appropriate control procedures would have reduced or eliminated the problem.

ASSET/LIABILITY MANAGEMENT—ORGANIZATION AND PLANNING

Asset/Liability Committees

In the past decade, many banks have set up asset/liability management committees. These committees have taken different names, but their purpose has always been the same: to coordinate the management of the sources and uses of funds and to ensure that the pricing structure is correct relative to the market—that the prime rate is set correctly. Committee membership and meeting schedules vary considerably among banks. Thus, no general statement can be made on who should be included on these committees or how often they should meet. It is possible, however, to define loosely who should be involved in decisions relating to asset/liability management and what tools should be used in planning strategy.

Large Banks

The early asset/liability committees of the large money-center banks generally met weekly and included members of top management. Perhaps this was necessary at first as banks searched for a method or concept to follow in managing their portfolios. However, it was soon found that even for the largest banks, weekly meetings were unnecessary. It was also realized that fewer top personnel could be involved. Eventually it became common to assemble five or six people every other week or so. Even these meetings were often more of a review session, tracking developments rather than setting new policy. Intermediate-term markets simply did not change often enough for more frequent sessions. More intensive review meetings, with perhaps a new forecast being developed, were held monthly.

Committee membership usually consists of one person from top management, the president or an executive vice president, the bank economist, the person responsible for the bank's money market operations, and two or three others whose choice varies considerably among banks. Usually someone concerned with long-run operations is included. The bank's foreign operations department may be represented. In many instances, the head of the commercial lending function is a member, and, less often, someone from the retail banking area.

Smaller Banks

At smaller banks, the personnel may not differ much from their counterparts in large banks, but meetings may be much less frequent than in the larger banks. The need to change their asset/liability policy appears less often for these banks, and hence the need for formal meetings declines. Top management should be represented at committee meetings, someone who operates in the market should be there, and someone must represent the commercial lending function. The bank economist must be there, because of all the people in the bank, the economist has perhaps the greatest opportunity to look into the future and perceive evolving trends. The other members of the committee tend to be too involved in daily operations to do this with any regularity.

In most cases, meetings need take place no more frequently than every three or four weeks, with an emergency meeting called if some crisis develops. The reason for this is that asset/liability management, as stated before, is concerned with a six-month time horizon. Changes in market conditions do not generally occur rapidly enough to warrant frequent changes in forecasts and plans. Even so, once it is recognized that the bank's environment has been altered, it takes a while longer to determine what action the bank should take. Changing portfolio strategy and altering price levels are costly, particularly if no other bank follows suit and the decisions have to be reversed within a short time.

The asset/liability committee should review the current plan and discuss a new one at least quarterly, but not much more often. The bank's actual performance should be analyzed in relation to the old plan; assumptions should be checked to see if they are still valid, new assumptions may have to be introduced, and a new forecast and strategy may be developed. The cost of doing this and the management time necessary are not small. The marginal contribution to profit of running through this exercise more frequently would not usually be worth the marginal cost of performing the analysis.

Between meetings, the bank's actual position should be compared with its plan or strategy. This information can be distributed, with a brief analysis, to the members of the asset/liability committee. Informal communication can often keep the participants informed of market developments and the bank's position and make them more aware of evolving situations so that a crisis need not be completely unexpected. Two or three short, informal meetings may take place between major policy meetings.

A small bank needs neither the structure nor the information system of a large bank. It still would be advisable for it to hold quarterly meetings in which developments are reviewed and potentialities are discussed so that new strategies can be devised and written down. Even medium-sized and smaller banks need to put their plans into writing so that they can analyze their progress over time.

More informal meetings are generally sufficient to handle most problems that might arise in these banks. The individual bank must decide for itself just how much communication is needed.

Implementation

As to the actual methods used in asset/liability management, a variety of techniques exist. Some require more time and expertise than others. Again, the individual bank must decide what it can best afford, use, and understand. In the next section several techniques are presented and discussed. Although no conclusion is drawn as to the best technique available, the banking industry seems to be using more and more sophisticated methods of forecasting and profit analysis. The basic benefits of any effort to organize asset/liability management are a complete view of the bank and the process of value maximization, a clearer understanding of the underlying assumptions, and an idea of how sensitive results are to the assumptions. Regardless of the techniques used, these are desirable properties of any planning process. The bank should choose the technique that benefits it the most within its budget and manpower constraints.

TECHNIQUES OF ASSET/LIABILITY MANAGEMENT

Seven techniques of asset/liability management will be presented in this section. Some involve no forecasting at all, while others include highly sophisticated methods of forecasting and balance sheet control. The pros and cons of each will be discussed, although no conclusions are drawn as to the best method available. The best method will depend on the bank and its resources.

Asset Conversion

This is the oldest of the techniques to be presented and is still used, to some extent, by all banks. It evolves out of the nature of banking itself and applies only to the asset side of the balance sheet. If a bank grants only demand loans or short-term, self-liquidating loans, then it could meet all its liquidity needs through maturing loans and interest receipts or by calling in loans. Bank funds would be placed only in seasonal or trade cycle loans needed for financing accounts receivable or inventories or in the shortest-term U.S. government securities.

The problem with this approach is that many loans are continually refinanced, particularly during those times when banks need cash too, so that liquidity is not assured. Second, within the limits of the bank's ability to undertake risk, many profitable opportunities may be missed by keeping only to short maturities. A bank that managed assets in this way would deprive the community in which it operated of longer-term funds, and hence businesses in the area might not be able to take advantage of some of the dynamic opportunities available, and this would restrict the community's economic development. Finally, although this method may work relatively well for the bank if its economic environment is static, if the region is growing the bank may find loan demand growing more rapidly than deposits. It could then be pushed into a tight position much as a successful, growing manufacturing firm encounters working capital shortages when sales outstrip collections.

Asset conversion should be considered in any asset/liability management technique, but it should not be relied on as a bank's sole source of liquidity.

Asset Allocation

There are two types of asset-allocation techniques: the strict asset-allocation approach and the pool-of-funds approach. Both apply to asset-management banks that obtain their money from interest-inelastic sources. The pool approach is actually just a less rigid application of the strict allocation approach.

Strict Asset Allocation In applying the strict asset-allocation technique, the bank divides its liabilities and capital into different categories according to volatility (or velocity). Then it sets guidelines for the percentage of each category that it would like to allocate to each asset class. An example will help provide a clear description of this technique.

As can be seen in Table 14-1, liabilities that have a high degree of volatility require greater allocations of cash and liquid assets to cover them than do less volatile liabilities. Large accounts, which can have a greater

TABLE 14-1   A Hypothetical Example of Asset Allocation in a Bank

	Total Funds	Cash and Due from Banks	U.S. Govt. Securities (under 1 year)	U.S. Govt. Securities (over 1 year)	Other Securities	Commercial and Industrial Loans	Consumer Loans	Real Estate and Mortgage Loans	Fixed Assets
Deposits									
Large accounts	42.4	10.6 (25%)	17.0 (40%)	10.6 (25%)	—	4.2 (10%)	—	—	
Other demand deposits	169.7	25.4 (15%)	17.0 (10%)	8.5 (5%)	8.5 (5%)	67.9 (40%)	42.4 (25%)	—	
Treasury tax and loan	34.6	8.6 (25%)	17.4 (50%)	8.6 (25%)	—	—	—	—	
Savings	115.9	7.0 (6%)	11.6 (10%)	11.6 (10%)	11.6 (10%)	—	—	74.1 (64%)	
Certificates	79.1	4.7 (6%)	4.7 (6%)	4.7 (6%)	—	23.8 (30%)	15.8 (20%)	25.4 (32%)	
Other liabilities	11.2	—	2.2 (20%)	9.0 (80%)	—	—	—	—	
Capital									
Paid-in capital and surplus	39.0	—	—	—	—	—	—	—	39.0 (100%)
Retained earnings and reserves	10.6	—	—	—	—	6.9 (65%)	3.7 (35%)	—	
Desired	502.5	56.3	69.9	53.0	20.1	102.8	61.9	99.5	39.0
Actual	502.5	51.1	71.4	47.8	18.1	126.2	63.3	85.6	39.0
Needed adjustment		−5.2	+1.5	+5.2	−2.0	+23.4	+1.4	−13.9	0

impact on the balance sheet than small ones, are also backed by more liquid assets. Capital, of course, can be applied to the least liquid accounts. The problem comes as the bank requires different levels of liquidity seasonally or at different times in the trade or credit cycle. Unless the makeup of the right-hand side of the balance sheet changes, and in the appropriate direction, the bank's liquidity will remain constant or actually deteriorate as the liquidity needed to support loan demand or deposit outflows increases.

This system provides no way to anticipate needs. Since no forecasting is done, there is an implicit assumption that the future will be exactly like the present. This is a false assumption, for almost every bank experiences some seasonal movements in loan demands and/or deposit flows.

The basic fault with this technique, therefore, is its rigidity. It does not easily allow for a changing economic environment or for the incorporation of other information that may have an important bearing on portfolio decisions. For instance, the technique implies that assets and liabilities are independent of one another when in fact they may not be. Moreover, the emphasis is on providing liquidity for protection against the loss of deposits, whereas one of the major problems of recent years has been unexpected loan demand. Furthermore, nothing is done about maximizing profits or tax planning.

The primary attributes of the system are that it is simple, easy to understand, and inexpensive to operate and that it makes the bank more profitable by carrying fewer liquid assets against the less volatile time and savings accounts than does the pool-of-funds approach. Thus, there are many advocates for this approach, and it will continue to be used, successfully, by many small and medium-sized banks.

Pool-of-Funds Approach   The pool-of-funds approach is more flexible, but in using it a bank sacrifices some income. Basically, in this approach the bank assumes that the right-hand side of the balance sheet is given— this is the pool of funds it has available to use. It then allocates funds to asset classes according to its priorities.

The first priority is to provide for reserves and transactions balances. The assets assigned to this class are usually referred to as *primary reserves* and include such balance sheet items as cash on hand, amounts due from other banks, and legal reserve requirements. Primary reserves, however, cannot be used to satisfy liquidity requirements either for loan demands or for deposit withdrawals. Either the amounts kept in these accounts are legally needed and will disappear if withdrawals are made, or they are in transactions balances, funds needed for day-to-day operations.

Thus, the bank needs other reserves to meet liquidity needs, its second priority. The accounts available to meet these liquidity needs are called *secondary reserves* and include highly liquid, short-term earning assets that can be turned into cash at or near current market quotations in a short period of time. This secondary reserve is generally based on the volatility of loan demand and deposit supply. Therefore, an individual bank must review the composition of its balance sheet and its potential loan demand and determine what level of secondary reserves it needs. This system is more flexible than the previous one, because it is simpler to change the level of secondary reserves needed by the bank as economic conditions change than to alter the allocation makeup of each liability and net worth category. Hence, the bank is more capable of adapting to the future if it uses this form of asset allocation.

The third priority of the bank is its loan portfolio. The pool-of-funds approach determines the size of the portfolio, but not its composition. The bank must make an additional determination of the "legitimate credit needs" of its customers so as to allocate the funds among its borrowers.

Finally, the bank allocates funds to investments. These are generally longer-term, but high-quality, interest-bearing securities that are traded in markets of differing efficiency. Essentially, these are "leftover," or residual, amounts in this technique. Some tax planning may be involved, but in practice it has not been generally done. Since the funds used for investment purposes have been residual, they have more often than not been invested only to earn the highest return possible.

Again, as with the other asset-allocation technique, the essence of this approach is its simplicity and its low administration cost. The major problems associated with this method are its rigidity, its failure to incorporate the future adequately into present portfolio construction, its inability to take into account the complex interactions of both sides of the balance sheet, and its concentration on protection rather than on profitability.

Trend Analysis

Trend analysis is a slightly more sophisticated technique that introduces the future into current portfolio decisions but is still highly dependent on asset allocation. Again, the banks under review are asset-management banks.

Trend analysis allows for the finer distinction of asset and liability classes into permanent and volatile (temporary) subcategories. This is

Demand Deposits

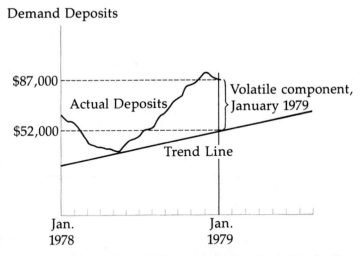

FIGURE 14-1   Trend Analysis Techniques for Determining the Quantity of
Volatile Demand Deposits (Assumed Data)

done, most simply, by determining what proportion of a loan or deposit
class is above the trend for that class at any one time.[7]

Permanent deposits are those funds that are considered to be a relatively stable amount for the bank to invest. They will be affected only by
major factors such as the technological obsolescence or closing of a primary
industry, which would have serious implications for a regional bank. Very
little liquidity need be maintained for these accounts. When the reserve
requirements have been set aside, the remainder may be put into loans or
investments.

Volatile deposits are those within a class that will be withdrawn over
the trade or credit cycle and therefore can be defined as those amounts that
lie above the secular trend of the class of deposits in question.

For example, assume a bank has experienced the month-ending demand deposit totals[8] shown in Figure 14-1. At the end of January 1979 it
had $87,000 in demand deposits, of which $52,000 were considered per-

---

[7] Nonfinancial organizations use trend analysis to identify permanent current assets and
current liabilities; see J. C. Van Horne, *Financial Management and Policy*, 4th ed. (Englewood
Cliffs, N.J.: Prentice-Hall, 1977).

[8] This computation could be done with weekly data, but weekly data are so subject to
random movements that they would tend to hide the movements more relevant for asset/
liability management.

manent and $35,000 volatile. The provision of liquidity against volatile deposits should be the total volatile deposit amount less reserve requirements. The reason for this is that the bank expects to lose these deposits sooner or later, depending on seasonal factors or the length of the credit cycle. In some cases, the time period for loss may be three or four months; in others, it may be nine months to a year. In any event, volatile deposits are funds the bank cannot expect to keep on hand.

This type of study can also be made for other types of liabilities that are not elastically supplied. Liabilities are subject to various influences, and hence their behavior may differ with respect to volatility and timing. Since the bank is an asset manager and is therefore concerned with the provision of liquid assets, it is assumed that no purchased funds are on the balance sheet. If they are, they should not be subject to the analysis performed here, because if they are elastically supplied to the bank, the bank can choose the amount of these funds it will take; variation in quantity will be solely a bank decision and will not depend on market supply.

It is advisable that the bank examine the volatility of total deposits as well as each separate deposit class. Movements in some deposit classes may counter the movements in others. If this happens, the bank could operate safely with less liquidity than otherwise because of the offsetting behavior.

Although its basic liquidity position can be built up in this way, the modern bank must be aware of the need to meet loan demand in excess of expectation as well as unexpected outflows of deposits. Loan demand follows patterns just as deposits do, so that a bank can chart actual movements of loans and determine permanent and volatile loan demand in the same way it determined these components of deposit supply. In this case the bank is concerned with the maximum amount of loans it may find on its books. In Figure 14-2 it can be seen that the loan demand considered to be *permanent* amounts to $41,000; the bank expects to lend this much in bad times as well as in good times. The volatile component of loan demand is the difference between the trend line and perceived permanent amount of loan demand—in this case, $21,000. The bank must be prepared to meet these demands if and when they arise.

The bank can control these amounts to some extent, by changing terms on loans or by rationing. But if it is building up customer relationships and expanding, it may be limited in how much it can rely on these alternatives to choke off loan demand. The best way to meet the situation is to be prepared for the possible increase in demand for loans.

Several other factors must be considered in constructing the bank's balance sheet using this technique. First, there are depositors and borrow-

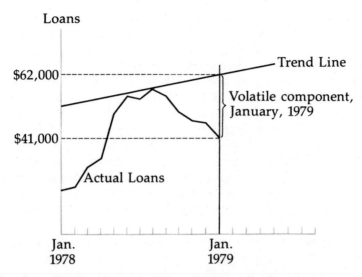

FIGURE 14-2   Trend Analysis Technique for Determining the Volatile
               Component of Loan Demand (Assumed Data)

ers that, because of their size, may affect the bank's liquidity position. The
bank should keep fairly well informed on these customers at all times to
avoid being unprepared for large withdrawals or loans. The size of these
customers in relation to the size of the bank can have a significant effect on
the bank's cash position. However, the bank may sometimes be caught
unawares; for one thing, unexpected events may impinge on their customers. To be prepared for this contingency, the bank allocates some additional funds to liquid assets. Note that this possibility may apply to large
time and savings accounts as well as demand deposit accounts.

Some analysts have recommended that 20 percent of large deposits—
demand, time, and savings—be kept in liquid assets. Furthermore, it has
been suggested that the bank also maintain 20 percent of capital and
surplus in liquid assets, for lending to "good" customers should the demand arise. Very conservative banks will also maintain additional amounts
of liquid assets to protect themselves against uncertain future events, such
as effective Regulation Q ceilings in the face of rising market interest rates.

Trend analysis is more sophisticated than the earlier approaches to
asset/liability management for two reasons. First, it incorporates more than
the current makeup of deposits and loans into bank portfolio construction.
Second, it allows for a distinction between different types of deposits as

well as recognizing that a portion of each deposit and loan class is permanent in the sense that the bank will generally have a base of loans and deposits to work with and must be primarily concerned, for liquidity reasons, with those amounts defined as volatile.

There are still problems with this technique, some of them similar to those of the methods defined earlier. First, the method is still quite rigid. Trend lines can be drawn with little understanding of their underlying causes, and it is very difficult to incorporate changes in trend. For example, a change in the bank's pricing structure or the opening of a new branch will in all likelihood affect the trend line but cannot be easily accommodated in the plan. Second, the bank still has the rigid structure of asset allocation. Once deposits and loans are divided into their permanent and volatile components, the composition of the rest of the balance sheet is relatively fixed.

Furthermore, no effort is made to choose the combination of assets that will maximize before-tax or after-tax returns. The emphasis is on liquidity. Concern is centered on the bank's ability to meet unexpected loan demands or deposit withdrawals, not on higher earnings.

However, cost and ease of understanding and implementation still make trend analysis a desirable and valuable analytical tool for bank use. In addition, it is only slightly less advanced than a more sophisticated planning structure using statistical methods. In turning to these more sophisticated operations, the reader must realize that only the larger banks gain enough additional information with these techniques to make their contributions to profit worth their cost.

Forecasting

The next stage of asset/liability models deals with the bank's actual efforts to accumulate information about the future that can be used in structuring its balance sheet. The banks under consideration here no longer need to be just asset managers; they can also be liability managers. In making its forecasts, a bank must distinguish between the assets and liabilities whose quantities it can control, which can be termed *discretionary* items, and those for which it sets rates but does not control quantities, which can be termed *nondiscretionary* items.

Discretionary and Nondiscretionary Items   Discretionary assets and liabilities are those described earlier as being supplied or demanded elastically. That is, the bank has complete control over the quantities of these assets and liabilities on its balance sheet. Hence the amounts taken are at the discretion of the bank.

Assets and liabilities that are classified as nondiscretionary are those whose amounts are determined by the combination of bank prices, market forces, and long-run bank decisions as to customer base and capital structure. The bank determines the price and nonprice terms it will impose or pay on these items, and then the relative strengths and weaknesses of the market—national, local, regional, or even international—are the primary factor in determining the quantities to be taken by the bank.

The bank may want to include in this category some items that at first glance appear to be discretionary but in actual practice are not. A bank must determine these for itself. For example:

1. The amount of cash necessary for transactions purposes is the amount needed for daily bank operations.

2. Bank management may feel it must maintain a portfolio of municipal issues because of customer ties with state or local governments.

3. Tax and loan accounts of the federal government must be forecast, although no price decisions are involved on these amounts.

4. The bank may have to take a certain amount of federal funds from correspondents (as described earlier) in order to maintain customer relationships.

5. A certain minimum amount of negotiable CDs or Eurodollars must be purchased in order to be assured of the "best" or going market rates at all times.

These requirements have generally been created by the customers or markets the bank decided to serve when it made its decisions relative to the customer base. Most of them mean that some minimum requirement must be satisfied in order for the bank to maintain its base. These are *nondiscretionary* items for intermediate-term planning, although the projected quantities of assets and liabilities result from policy decisions and not from forecasts.

Obtaining Forecasts   There are two ways to obtain inputs for the planning process. The first, which is the more frequently used in actual banking practice, begins with the bank economist, who compiles a forecast of the economy, both national and local, and the interest rates expected to prevail in the period under review. This information is conveyed to the divisional officers, who then assemble their forecasts of the relevant balance sheet items under their charge. Nondiscretionary policy items are also obtained.

Once these projections have been generated, they are collected by a planning or budgeting officer, who, with the help of a planning committee composed of some of the people who devised the data, puts together a picture of the potential balance sheet. Since this balance sheet includes only nondiscretionary items, it obviously will not balance, except by coincidence. The job of the planning committee is to fill in the holes with the discretionary items at the bank's disposal so as to maximize profits over the forecast period.

Once this plan is completed, it is generally taken to a committee of top management personnel, possibly the asset/liability committee, for review and approval. Modifications may be required. Once approved, the plan becomes the working guideline for bank operations until it is revised, either because of a new forecast or because of an emerging situation that calls for a quick response.

This method is much more comprehensive than any technique described earlier. It also costs the bank more in specialized personnel and commitment. There are two specific drawbacks to the method. First, the forecasts are made by many different people, each a specialist in some one area. A given set of economic conditions and interest rates may be interpreted differently by each person. It is the job of the planning committee to iron out discrepancies.[9]

Second, it is difficult or impossible to determine how sensitive the forecasts and results are to the economic climate. It is hard enough to coordinate the information collected for the forecast. To obtain the additional information needed to test the sensitivity of the forecast, several economic scenarios would have to be provided to the officers so that they could develop a distribution of possible outcomes. These distributions would then be combined to obtain a distribution of possible outcomes for the bank as a whole.

In the second technique, the bank uses econometric models to project these nonpolicy, nondiscretionary items. This allows planners to develop thorough, consistent forecasts and to vary their assumptions to test the sensitivity of the forecasts and the overall results of the plan.[10] What is lost,

[9] There is another bias built into this forecasting process. Each department has its own special interest to promote, and it is to be expected that each will take a fairly optimistic view of the potential performance of its own department. Whereas the planning committee must take this reality into consideration, the result is usually a more optimistic forecast for the bank as a whole.

[10] Two references on the use of econometric models in the asset/liability planning of commercial banks are: R. T. Parry and J. C. Howe, "Programming Asset and Liability Management," *The Bankers Magazine* (Autumn 1974), pp. 78–86; and R. H. Cramer and R. B.

however, is the subjective input of people who are very close to the individual markets and have specialized knowledge.

The obvious solution is to develop a planning process in which the bank uses econometric models as well as the inputs that can be obtained from the experts within the bank. The difficulty in practice is that often officers who are expert in, say, lending markets are unfamiliar with econometric techniques and in fact feel threatened by them. As a result, the attempt to communicate and coordinate efforts is usually made reluctantly and with less than full efficiency.

It seems, though, that the use of econometric models in forecasting nondiscretionary balance sheet items does hold some promise for the future. With the improvement of national and regional models that can better predict individual balance sheet items, as well as bank efforts to model their specific markets, the usefulness of the technique increases. Furthermore, as more bankers become familiar with the models and as information on their use and value is more widely disseminated, they will undoubtedly be used increasingly in asset/liability management.

Simulation Models

Simulation or balance sheet models are nothing more than computerized accounting frameworks. They must be used in conjunction with the forecasting techniques suggested in the previous section. These models help the bank in total balance sheet planning—tax planning as well as portfolio construction. They can take into account different sets of economic conditions and allow the bank to test different approaches to balance sheet composition and timing that are usually not handled in a forecasting mode.

Information on the nondiscretionary sources and uses of funds is the basic input for this effort. The planning committee or economics department then tries different mixes of discretionary assets and liabilities in an effort to maximize after-tax earnings. These models are generally quite complex and can be used to examine a multitude of different policy alternatives.[11]

Miller, "Dynamic Modeling of Multivariate Time Series for Use in Bank Analysis," *Journal of Money, Credit and Banking* (February 1976), pp. 85–96.

[11] Perhaps the best known simulation model in the public domain is BANKMOD, developed by the Bank Administration Institute. Information on this system can be obtained from the Bank Administration Institute, 303 South Northwest Highway, Park Ridge, Ill. 60068.

It is also possible to derive the implicit risk-return tradeoff the bank may face. This can be done by varying the forecasts put into the model. By constructing a probability distribution for the occurrence of these events, the bank can estimate the potential variance of earnings in addition to the expected earnings for each possible forecast. In this way the bank can develop several different portfolios, along with the estimated return and variance of each. The asset/liability committee can then examine the results and choose the risk-return tradeoff it desires. Thus, the bank can be more conservative if the economic environment appears uncertain or can choose, if warranted, a riskier portfolio.

Simulation or balance sheet models have been used more by larger banks (primarily the large, money-center banks) than by regional and smaller banks.[12] There seem to be three reasons for this. First, the cost of going through such an exercise once, let alone two or three times, each year is rather high. If the bank has few options available, the potential revenue gain from this type of planning will not warrant the added cost of the modeling effort. Second, larger banks feel that their operations are so complex with so many interrelationships that econometric modeling cannot handle the intricacies of composing their balance sheet. Finally, the personnel needed to conduct this type of operation on an ongoing basis requires a great deal of specialization within the bank. Only the larger banks can afford to specialize to such a degree.

However, the planning of asset/liability composition cannot be handled in a more thorough manner. The major desirable refinements would be a greater use of statistical techniques that could help in achieving consistency in the forecasts and the availability of more current planning data. It could be possible, in the future, to have the program "on-line" (directly accessible) to members of the asset/liability committee, so that the current position of the bank vis-à-vis the plan is always available.

Linear and Dynamic Programming Models[13]

Linear programming and dynamic programming models are mathematical formulations with rules for their solution. Typical input data are

[12] However, the underlying technique can and should be used by many banks. For example, a bank can manually prepare pro forma balance sheets and then run through several different scenarios with a pro forma balance sheet for each. Bank management can then choose the balance sheet plan that is most desirable for its bank.

[13] Descriptions of programming techniques for use in bank portfolio management can be found in: K. J. Cohen and F. S. Hammer, "Linear Programming Models for Optimal Bank

interest rates, legal and policy constraints such as reserve requirements, cash for transactions, pledging requirements, and minimum purchase amounts (e.g., for Eurodollars). Risk information can be entered for various asset and liability classes. The model can then be solved for its optimal solutions—that is, the optimal quantities of all the assets and liabilities in the bank's portfolio.

Since interest rates are the major exogenous variables in these models, the bank can enter various interest rate forecasts to test the sensitivity of the solution. Moreover, policy constraints can be tested to examine how sensitive profits are to the bank's decisions. These models have proven to be fairly sensitive to both; the forecasts and policy decisions dominate the model, so that the results are dependent primarily on them rather than on the factors built into the model. Furthermore, as discussed, the pricing structure in many banks is relatively rigid, particularly in the commercial lending area. This leads to optimal loan portfolios that do not change much with changing economic conditions.

Programming models were more popular when they were first introduced than they are now. Banks found them too sensitive to general interest rate forecasts, more so than the other techniques mentioned here, and not very helpful in structuring bank portfolios because of the banks' unwillingness or inability to alter relative loan rates. Linear programming models called for complete restructuring of balance sheets to achieve optimal portfolios each time the planning exercise was done. The models did not take account of the fact that the interest rate structures on many assets and liabilities were determined by longer-run considerations and thus within the intermediate run were determined by the prevailing demand and supply conditions. That is, all decisions, within policy constraints, were considered to be *discretionary* (management chose the quantities of all assets and liabilities at the start of every planning exercise), whereas the analysis in this chapter has indicated that for some classes the bank has no short-run control over the nondiscretionary items (the classes influenced by long-run decisions that were not variable in the short run).

The models could have been built to include nondiscretionary items, but model builders seemed to feel this detracted from the strength of the technique, namely the determination of optimal portfolios. To put many nondiscretionary items in would have made the programming models

Dynamic Balance Sheet Management," in G. P. Szego and K. Shell, eds., *Mathematical Methods in Investment and Finance* (Amsterdam: North-Holland, 1972); W. F. Beazer, *Optimization of Bank Portfolios* (Lexington, Mass.: Lexington Books, 1975); J. Fried, "Bank Portfolio Selection," *The Journal of Financial and Quantitative Analysis* (June 1970).

Demand Deposits
($)

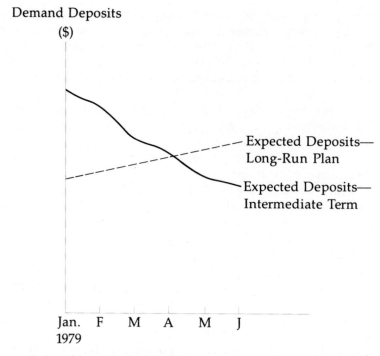

Expected Deposits—
Long-Run Plan

Expected Deposits—
Intermediate Term

Jan.   F   M   A   M   J
1979

FIGURE 14-3   Expected Demand Deposits for the First Six Months of 1979
               (Hypothetical)

more and more like balance sheet models.[14] Hence, few efforts were made
to change them, and as a result they have been used less and less.

PROFIT PLANNING AND CONTROL

The integration of the overall planning processes of the bank, as mentioned
before, is vital for the total growth and development of the bank. Just as the
short-run reserve management strategy should supply control information
to the plan developed for the intermediate term, the intermediate-term
plan should provide control information for the long term.

Basically, the bank has a tracking path similar to that shown for de-

---

[14] To most model builders the insights gained from a model occur during its building or
early use. Thus, interest often wanes after initial construction and operation of a model.

mand deposits in Figure 14-3. The dashed line represents the long-run growth trend devised as a part of the bank's four- to seven-year plan for expansion. The amounts represented by this line do not have to be met within the short-run time frame. The solid line represents the expected growth of demand deposits over the next six months. These forecasts are used in several of the planning strategies that have been described.

Since the intermediate plan is built on the customer base and capital structure underlying the long-run growth path, it should be consistent with that path. Therefore, if the bank tracks its actual accumulation of demand deposits against the projected path, it can gain some information about its ability to meet its longer-term goals. Whether the bank is meeting its goals cannot, of course, be determined in a few weeks or even a few months. If projections are not being met, however, this fact can be flagged at an early time and succeeding developments can be watched closely.

All *nondiscretionary* items should be tracked so that all areas of strength and weakness will be identified. Plans can also be checked for the discretionary assets and liabilities. Specifically, the bank should look for both excessive and unusually small purchases of Treasury bills or acquisitions of funds through the CD market. This will provide information on either the total shortfall or excess needs for funds of the whole bank.

For example, if deposit growth is at least as great as expected, and if loan demand is weak, then either the bank will maintain its scheduled purchases of, say, certificates of deposit and accumulate larger reserve positions than anticipated, or the unexpected surplus of funds will be placed, for the short run, in federal funds or Treasury bills. The bank will have more cash than it anticipated, or more federal funds sold than expected, or a larger quantity of Treasury bills than planned for. In all likelihood, the bank will not be as profitable in this position as it could be with a more appropriate balance sheet structure.

A bank in this situation must review its intermediate-term position, adjust its assumptions if necessary, and possibly plan to buy fewer CDs in the future. If the loan demand continues to be lower than expected, the excessively liquid situation will persist. This may lead the bank to reassess its assumptions about long-term growth. Perhaps the economy is entering a period of slower growth and this was not clearly foreseen in the development of the long-range plan.

As the information on slower growth in loan demand continues to filter into the bank and is checked against projected figures, the bank can begin to analyze the situation and to prepare for a readjustment of other strategies at the earliest reasonable date.

Interrelated and coordinated planning efforts are needed for both operations and control. Communication must exist between all involved in each effort, and willingness to be flexible in the face of unrealized expectations is essential.

REVIEW QUESTIONS

1. Commercial banks in geographically restricted areas may have severe seasonal swings in deposits and loans. These banks may also have limited access to asset/liability markets. What can they do to manage their positions as well as possible?
2. Some analysts feel that the most important impact on the asset/liability management operations of banks is the behavior of the Federal Reserve. Why? What do you think? Can the Federal Reserve create uncertainty?
3. Why is maturity arbitrage more important in the world of asset/liability management than it is in the world of short-run reserve management?
4. What relationship does asset/liability management have to the annual budgeting effort?
5. How can a bank determine the percentages to use for asset allocation? For the pool-of-funds technique? For trend analysis?
6. The most sophisticated methods of asset/liability choice seem the least successful in practice, yet banks and academicians spend a lot of time and money developing new and more sophisticated techniques. Why?
7. Analysts have claimed that the Federal Reserve has a more difficult time controlling the monetary aggregates when banks use liability management than when they use asset management. Using the model developed earlier, determine whether this is true and what the important considerations are.

APPENDIX
The Investment Portfolio

In the chapter just concluded, asset/liability management techniques were discussed on a bankwide level. Several of the methods described are detailed enough to incorporate security type and maturity distribution within the framework of bankwide planning.[1] However, other techniques leave the actual composition of the investment portfolio to be decided by others within the bank. This is consistent with practice. An investment group or department usually exists in the bank and has generally been responsible for formulating and carrying out decisions with regard to the bank's investments in securities, although these decisions must be integrated with the bank's overall asset/liability management. This appendix will examine how an investment portfolio can be put together that will be consistent with the risk-return tradeoff desired by the bank's top management.

The quantity of funds the investment group has to work with is the amount of discretionary funds determined in the planning exercise described within the body of the chapter. These funds, it will be recalled, are the net amount left after the bank determines the *nondiscretionary* sources and uses of bank funds.[2] This amount must be forecast so that the investment department knows what it is expected to work with over the coming period.

It should be noted at this time that the investment portfolio may not always be free for the investment manager to invest. If the bank maintains U.S. Treasury tax and loan accounts or accounts for states and municipalities, some securities must be pledged as collateral for these deposits. Thus, in a liability-management world, such as existed in the early 1970s for many banks, the only securities the investment group has may be those that must be held for pledging. In this case, there is very little the department can do to improve the earnings of the bank except manage the maturity structure of the securities held as collateral.

The investment group, therefore, expects a certain amount of funds to

---

[1] BANKMOD and linear programming models are capable of handling such a detailed analysis.

[2] In other places this net amount is called the "net needs for funds." See S. P. Bradley and D. Crane, *Management of Bank Portfolios* (New York: John Wiley & Sons, 1975), p. 32.

be available to it, and its responsibility is to earn the highest possible return on these funds consistent with the risk the bank can afford on its investment portfolio. The problem is to quantify the risk–return tradeoff available to the bank.

The first factor the bank must consider in setting up its investment program is the planning horizon over which the investment group is expected to operate. This is a crucial consideration, for it determines the entire basis of the risk–return tradeoff of the investment portfolio.[3] The time horizon chosen should be long enough to reflect the turnover of the nondiscretionary portion of the bank's portfolio, but short enough that the markets in which the bank trades securities are efficient.

This is necessary because the bank must be liquid in its investment portfolio (aside from pledging requirements). It may have to take a capital loss if it has to sell securities, but when it wants to get out of its position in a security, it can do so at current market prices. If it operated in less than perfect markets, this would not be the case.[4]

The funds available to the investment group are a residual amount: They are the quantity of funds "left over" after the bank decides on its nondiscretionary sources and uses of funds. Thus, regardless of what the investment people feel about their operations, the main function of commercial banking is commercial banking, and the borrower that deals directly with the bank must be satisfied first. The operations of the investment portfolio must be such that the bank can service unexpected loan demand.

What is the appropriate time horizon? In the body of Chapter 14, a case was made that the time horizon considered for asset/liability management should be somewhere between one month and six months. The same period should be chosen for the management of the investment portfolio, because the investment function must serve the lending function, and not vice versa. In practice, commercial banks have used both extremes and periods in between. There is no *a priori* reason for any specific selection.

The time horizon is crucial because it defines the minimum maturity of a security the bank can buy and not expect to have to sell. That is, if its planning horizon is three months, then the bank could buy a three-month

---

[3] Bradley and Crane (in *Management of Bank Portfolios*, pp. 8 and 210–11) also point out the importance of the bank planning horizon, although their choice of a horizon works out to be different from that presented here.

[4] This statement has nothing to do with the riskiness of securities. A very risky security, one whose price is quite variable, can be traded in a perfect market. The decision not to hold the security on this basis is entirely different from the bank's inability to sell (or buy) the security quickly without having to make some concessions.

Treasury bill and expect to hold it until it matures. The rate of return on the three-month security, the time horizon investment, becomes the focal point of the investment portfolio.

Conceptually, the alternative to the time horizon investment is cash. Thus, if cash has a zero return, then as long as the time horizon investment is expected to have a return greater than zero, the time horizon investment is preferred. That is,

$$(1 - T_m)(r^a_{TH} - b^a_{TH}) > 0 \qquad\qquad \text{(14A-1)}$$

where T_m is the marginal tax rate for the bank, applicable to the return on investment; r^a_{TH} is the yield on the time horizon investment; and b^a_{TH} is the administrative cost of investing in the time horizon investment.

In constructing the total portfolio, all yields can be compared with the yield on the time horizon investment. For investments in securities with maturities shorter than the planning horizon, the return is the geometric mean of expected returns from investing in very short-term securities and then reinvesting in a planned pattern of maturities at *expected* yields. That is, for n periods of investment, the yield is

$$(1 - T_m)[(r^a_x - b^a_x)(r^a_{ye} - b^a_{ye}) \cdots (r^a_{ze} - b^a_z)]^{1/n} \qquad\qquad \text{(14A-2)}$$

where $x, y, \ldots, z$ refer to the various maturities of the plan and the subscript e indicates that the yield is expected.

For taxable securities whose maturity is greater than the time horizon, the holding period yield for the time horizon is computed. If P represents purchase price and S represents sales price, the holding period yield of the ith investment is

$$(1 - T_m)\left(r^a_i - b^a_i + \frac{S_i - P_i}{P_i}\right) \qquad\qquad \text{(14A-3)}$$

where r^a_i and b^a_i are adjusted to the interest yield and average cost for the time horizon. Of course, S_i is the expected sales price of security i.

For nontaxable securities, the yield is reduced to

$$r^a_j - b^a_j + \frac{S_j - P_j}{P_j} \qquad\qquad \text{(14A-4)}$$

for the jth security.

The importance of the use of the marginal tax rate for the bank can now be seen. Since banks have reduced their taxable income in recent years through the use of loan-loss accounts, leasing, and foreign tax credits, it may not be profitable to invest in tax-free securities.[5] Thus, the bank's own expected marginal tax rate should be used to adjust before-tax yields to an after-tax basis to compare the viability of the use of nontaxable issues in the investment portfolio.

Next, it is important to determine the riskiness of each potential investment. The information needed here can be obtained from two sources: the bond table and the historical record of movements in interest rates. These will be discussed in turn.

Mathematically, a bond price, P, is determined[6] by the coupon payment, C, attached to the specific bond and the going market interest rate, r, for the type of security and risk under review. That is, the bond price is the discounted present value of the flow of coupons accruing to the bondholder.

$$P = \frac{C}{(1 + r)} + \frac{C}{(1 + r)^2} + \cdots + \frac{C}{(1 + r)^n} \qquad (14A\text{-}5)$$

It should be emphasized that for consistency the time period of the interest rate used should be the same as the time horizon. This is because the variance measure of interest is the variance that takes place over the time horizon. In determining how interest changes alter bond prices, the interest rate changes must be the same as the time over which the variance was measured.

To determine the elasticity of bond prices with respect to the interest rate, the derivative of (14A-5) is taken with respect to r:

$$\frac{\partial P}{\partial r} = -\frac{C}{(1 + r)^2} - \frac{C}{(1 + r)^3} - \cdots - \frac{nC}{(1 + r)^{n+1}} \qquad (14A\text{-}6)$$

Multiplying through by $-r/P$ results in

$$\epsilon_{P,r} = -\frac{r}{P}\frac{\partial P}{\partial r}$$

$$= \left(\frac{r}{1 + r}\right)\frac{\dfrac{C}{1 + r} + \dfrac{2C}{(1 + r)^2} + \cdots + \dfrac{nC}{(1 + r)^{n+1}}}{\dfrac{C}{(1 + r)} + \dfrac{C}{(1 + r)^2} + \cdots + \dfrac{C}{(1 + r)^n}} \qquad (14A\text{-}7)$$

[5] For more on this, see Bradley and Crane, *Management of Bank Portfolios*, pp. 8–9.
[6] A constant payment is assumed.

$$= \left(\frac{r}{1+r}\right) \frac{\dfrac{1}{(1+r)} + \dfrac{2}{(1+r)^2} + \cdots + \dfrac{n}{(1+r)^n}}{\dfrac{1}{(1+r)} + \dfrac{1}{(1+r)^2} + \cdots + \dfrac{1}{(1+r)^n}}$$

where $\epsilon_{P,r}$ represents the elasticity of the bond price with respect to the interest rate.

Next, the actual interest rate variance over the time horizon of the different maturities must be estimated. Variance is computed by the formula

$$\text{Var}(r) = \frac{\sum_{t=1}^{m} (r_t - \bar{r})^2}{m} \tag{14A-8}$$

where $\bar{r}$ is the mean interest rate of the maturity under review and m is the number of sample points used in estimation. The standard deviation of r, σ_r, is computed by taking the square root of the variance.

Thus, a definition of risk is $\epsilon_{P,r}\sigma_r$. Now for the construction of a portfolio of securities, it is more meaningful to convert these risk measures into units that are comparable. To do this the risk factor of each potential security is divided by the risk factor of the time horizon investment. The time horizon investment is used as the base because, in a world where the only factors that affect the outcome of the bank could be described by the probability distribution of returns, this investment would be the risk-free investment. During the period of the time horizon investment, no additional changes in the investment portfolio are expected to take place; the time horizon investment will be held to maturity. Thus, it serves as a yardstick to measure the relative risk of all other investments.

The risk relative of an investment (the risk of any given maturity relative to the risk of the time horizon investment) can therefore be computed as follows:

$$\frac{\text{Risk factor of security of maturity } m}{\text{Risk factor of time horizon investment}}$$

$$= \frac{\epsilon_{P_m,r_m} \cdot \sigma_{r_m}}{\epsilon_{P_{TH},r_{TH}} \cdot \sigma_{r_{TH}}}$$

$$= \text{Risk relative of investment with maturity } m \tag{14A-9}$$

The riskiness of different combinations of maturities can also be computed, and a risk relative for that portfolio can be computed. To be complete, it can be imagined that a continuous combination of risk relatives

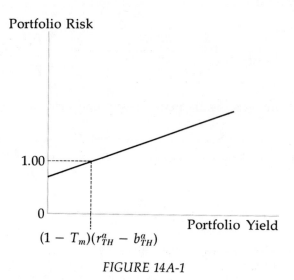

Portfolio Risk

1.00

0

$(1 - T_m)(r^a_{TH} - b^a_{TH})$

Portfolio Yield

FIGURE 14A-1

and returns can be computed from the many combinations of maturities available to the bank.

Once these data are computed, the investment department has an investment tool to help decision makers. The data can be easily presented in a chart, such as the one shown in Figure 14A-1. In this figure the portfolio risk (the risk relative of a given combination of maturities) is presented on the vertical axis and the yield of the portfolio on the horizontal axis. The one point of interest that sets up the diagram is the point determined by the time horizon investment. As can be seen from equation (14A-9), the risk relative of the time horizon investment is 1, and the yield, described in equation (14A-1), is $(1 - T_m)(r^a_{TH} - b^a_{TH})$. All other combinations of maturities are measured relative to this. Investments in securities with an average maturity less than the time horizon investment will generally have a smaller yield and a lower risk relative. Investments with an average maturity greater than the time horizon will yield more but in general carry a higher risk relative.

This information is not sufficient to determine the exact choice of a portfolio. Some additional input is needed. First, the bank needs a forecast of the direction of movement in interest rates. Second, management must make some decision as to how much relative risk it wants to undertake. Third, the bank must consider the cost of shifting out of assets whose maturity exceeds the time horizon. This may require adjustments in the relevant cost factors (the b's) to account for transactions costs.

If interest rates are expected to rise, then it might be expected that portfolio preferences would lie toward the time horizon investment to avoid capital losses in the case of unexpected needs to convert assets to cash. Conversely, if rates are expected to fall, the choice might be pushed further to the right of the time horizon investment. If great uncertainty surrounds any given forecast, then management might temper its position by not moving as far to the right as if the situation seems more certain.[7] A situation about which managers do not feel very confident at all may lead to a choice of a portfolio with an average maturity less than the time horizon.

The important thing is that the investment department must create enough information that management can judge not only the return on the bank's portfolio over the return on cash but also the bank's risk exposure from the uncertainty of receiving this yield. One valuable thing about the method presented here is that the riskiness of the portfolio is independent of the forecast of interest rates. Some of the more sophisticated methods mentioned in Chapter 14 are not. In addition, an explicit decision is determined by an optimization program. This allows management to impose its own (changeable) preferences on the decision making at the time a decision is to be made.

One additional point requires discussion. Two investment techniques used by banks have been a subject of much debate: the *laddered approach*, where maturities in the portfolio are spaced evenly, and the *barbell approach*, where securities held are concentrated at either end of the maturity spectrum. The question is, how does the foregoing analysis relate to structuring an investment portfolio in either of these two ways?

The answer is that if the risk-return tradeoff looks similar to that of Figure 14A-1, then it is more likely that the laddered approach will be taken. What this chart shows is that the risk-return tradeoff is constant throughout the maturity spectrum, so that concentrating maturities provides very little extra in the way of potential return, if a rise or fall in interest rates has been forecast.

However, those who prefer the barbell approach contend that the middle-maturity range, say from 3 to 15 years, does not experience the variance of interest rates or price shown by the short- and long-term issues; the risk-return tradeoff is not constant throughout the maturity spectrum. This is, of course, an empirical matter that can be tested. Hence, the risk-

---

[7] For a recent presentation of how this type of analysis might be pursued, see D. Vickers, *Financial Markets in the Capitalist Process* (Philadelphia: University of Pennsylvania, 1978), Chapters 8 and 9.

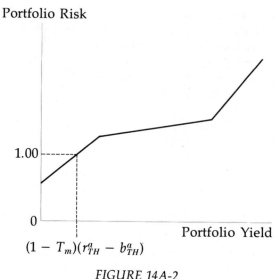

Portfolio Risk

1.00

0

Portfolio Yield

$(1 - T_m)(r_{TH}^a - b_{TH}^a)$

FIGURE 14A-2

return tradeoff curve may not be shaped as in Figure 14A-1, but may be more like that shown in Figure 14A-2. Here we see that throughout the middle-maturity ranges risk rises with yield but not so rapidly as either the short-term or long-term securities.[8] Thus, with a given forecast, the benefits of investing predominantly in short-term securities or in long-term securities outweigh the additional return and only slightly higher risk of the middle-range portfolios. The reason is that if interest rates are expected to rise, the bank will benefit from being very short because it can reinvest quickly at higher and higher rates. Since intermediate-term securities lock the bank in for a longer time, the bank will find it more costly to take advantage of the rising rates, because it will have to sell securities in its portfolio at a loss.

If interest rates are expected to fall, the bank will prefer a combination of the longest and shortest securities because they are the riskiest in terms of risk tradeoffs but are the most likely securities to benefit from a decline in rates. Since interest rates on middle-maturity securities are not as volatile, the potential for gain is not as great. The technique used should depend on an empirical examination of interest rate variance and the risk-return preferences of management.

---

[8] Bradley and Crane, *Management of Bank Portfolios*, p. 7.

Index